GERMANY'S GENOCIDE OF THE HERERO:
KAISER WILHELM II, HIS GENERAL,
HIS SETTLERS, HIS SOLDIERS

GERMANY'S GENOCIDE OF THE HERERO: KAISER WILHELM II, HIS GENERAL, HIS SETTLERS, HIS SOLDIERS

JEREMY SARKIN

UCT PRESS

JAMES CURREY

Germany's Genocide of the Herero:
Kaiser Wilhelm II, His General, His Settlers, His Soldiers

First published 2010 by UCT Press
an imprint of Juta and Company Ltd
First Floor, Sunclare Building
21 Dreyer Street, Claremont, 7708
Cape Town, South Africa

© 2011 UCT Press

ISBN 978-1-91989-547-5

James Currey
is an imprint of Boydell & Brewer Ltd
PO Box 9, Woodbridge, Suffolk IP12 3DF, UK
and of
Boydell & Brewer Inc.
668 Mt Hope Avenue, Rochester, NY 14620, USA

www.boydellandbrewer.com
www.jamescurrey.com

ISBN 978-1-84701-032-2 (James Currey hardback)

All rights reserved. No part of this publication may be reproduced or transmitted in any form or by any means, electronic or mechanical, including photocopying, recording, or any information storage or retrieval system, without prior permission in writing from the publisher. Subject to any applicable licensing terms and conditions in the case of electronically supplied publications, a person may engage in fair dealing with a copy of this publication for his or her personal or private use, or his or her research or private study. See Section 12(1)(a) of the Copyright Act 98 of 1978.

Project Manager: Corina Pelser
Editor: Cindy Taylor
Proofreader: Jennifer Stastny
Typesetter: ANdtp Services
Cover designer: Elsabe Gelderblom, Farm Design
Indexer: Sanet le Roux

Typeset in 10.5 on 13.5 pt Bell MT

This book has been independently peer-reviewed by academics who are experts in the field.

The authors and the publisher have made every effort to obtain permission for and to acknowledge the use of copyright material. Should any infringement of copyright have occurred, please contact the publisher and every effort will be made to rectify omissions or errors in the event of a reprint or new edition.

TABLE OF CONTENTS

FOREWORD BY THE PARAMOUNT CHIEF OF THE HERERO	v
PREFACE	viii
ACKNOWLEDGEMENTS	x
INTRODUCTION	1
What is in this book?	3
Why the genocide was committed	6
German perpetrators and Herero victims	14
The role of Kaiser Wilhelm II	16
The relationship of the Herero genocide to the Holocaust	19
Methodology, terminology and definitions	27
CHAPTER ONE: AETIOLOGY OF A GENOCIDE	35
Introduction	35
The importance of GSWA to Germany	49
Removing obstacles and luring potential settlers	57
Reasons for targeting the Herero and Nama land holdings	62
Strategies to obtain land for settlement and livestock	64
Appropriating Herero land and cattle during and after the war	81
Interracialism, mixed-race German citizens and alcoholism	86
Teaching the 'Natives' a lesson and promoting Germany's image	90
CHAPTER TWO: IMPLEMENTING THE GENOCIDE: ANNIHILATING 'THE AFRICAN TRIBES WITH STREAMS OF BLOOD AND STREAMS OF GOLD':	98
German brutalities before 1904	99
1904 and beyond: the intent, the order and the extermination of the Herero	106
The intended meaning of *vernichten*: a political or military strategy or call for genocide?	121
The number of Herero killed in the genocide	130
When did the genocide begin?	137
Was the killing of women and children specifically sought?	144
Conclusion	148

CHAPTER THREE: DID THE KAISER ORDER THE GENOCIDE? 149

Introduction. 149
The Kaiser's personality 154
The debate about the role of the Kaiser: was he the decision-maker or was he a shadow Emperor? 162
The Kaiser and the military 165
The Kaiser's record of brutality 168
The role of the Kaiser in the colonies. 175
The Kaiser and German South West Africa. 176
Did the Kaiser appoint General von Trotha? 184
Why the Kaiser chose Von Trotha 185
Did the Kaiser give Von Trotha a specific genocide order? 188
Would Von Trotha have kept the genocide order secret? 191
The role of German law in keeping the genocide order secret 196
Military culture 205
Praise and support 217
Conclusion 223

CONCLUSION 226

Introduction. 226
German colonial policies 228
German South West Africa's unique status among Germany's colonies 230
German and international politics at the turn of the twentieth century 231
The aims of the Herero genocide 232
German state action 234
The Herero genocide as a precursor to the Holocaust 237
Conclusion 237

BIBLIOGRAPHY 239

INDEX 266

Foreword by the Paramount Chief of the Herero

Just as the human predicament transcends all boundaries of time and place, the eternal facts of life revolve around problems of living together that every individual, community and nation must face. Perhaps we should be cognizant of the true meaning of life and community and the inevitability of wrong behaviour being a precarious foundation to lay any cornerstone of civilisation on. A century has now passed since scholars began to realise the need of interpreting this particular episode in history and to scientifically analyse the event from an unbiased perspective. It has become critical to expose the insidious social mechanisms and manipulations perpetrated by the foreign occupiers of Namibia and thereafter to apply legal ramifications against the guilty. Allowing the truth to come to the fore and rendering a legal and moral remedy thereupon.

It seems that most of the seven deadly sins were manifest in the collective psyche of the colonialist of that era.

The German body-politic planned these events and formed financial and political alliances to gain access to land and resources. Thereafter an insidious game of monopoly ensued. The cost of human and social devastation was an irrelevant consideration, in the occupier's stratagem. The anthropologists of the time held closely the social Darwinian concept of evolution, permitting the racist seed to germinate the colonialists' views of the natives of the land as sub-human and backward. The anthropologist's role was to scientifically legitimise these cataclysmic events.

From a race-relationship perspective, this event seems to emphasise all the contradictions and moral dilemmas that continue to exist in the Euro-African diplomatic discourse. One might deduce that the examination and application of a remedial process would be of pre-eminent importance in today's global dialect. The negative psychosis that existed in the colonial *force majeure* appears to be the penultimate racial reticulation event in Africa.

The colonialist's primary objective was to pilfer and exterminate if challenged.

When the German colonialists were confronted by effective resistance from the ill-equipped but gallant Herero tribesmen, the result was extreme paranoia from the German high command. News flashes were received in Germany. The Kaiser and his government were forced into a state of embarrassment, their military prowess and reputation were in jeopardy. Loss of face amongst other European nations had to be arrested.

The perceived audacity of the Herero resistance against a self-absorbed German nation resulted in the Kaiser dispatching their most feared General, a man of ruthless resolve, General Lothar von Trotha, who had garnished a reputation for himself in conducting brutal campaigns against Africans in German East Africa. General von Trotha and the military reinforcements were promptly deployed. Thereupon the infamous *Vernichtungsbefehl*, or extermination order to annihilate every man, woman and child of Herero descent, was promulgated.

The Herero genocide in 1904 was the inaugural holocaust, succeeded by the Jewish Holocaust in the 1940s and enacted by the same sovereign power. The latter was implemented as a packaged theory acquired from the first genocidal experience. The Aryan supremacy ideology of Hitler was acquired from the author of eugenics and the incumbent Chancellor of Berlin University during the Second World War. Professor Eugen Fischer's experimentation on the human brain using the Nama and Herero as guinea pigs is an appalling testimony to human arrogance. As to what the findings of the University of Berlin in this regard were, the question still remains unanswered.

Germany paid recompense to the Jewish people for the atrocities exerted on them during the Second World War. It is expected that they do the same for the Herero.

Professor Jeremy Sarkin's treatise is intelligible and lucid in its vocabulary, suggests formidable objectives into healing the callous brutality of the past. The pen that traced these lines belongs to a man whose philosophical background is deeply rooted in the behavioural sciences. The direction and emphasis of this work expresses veneration for a people who encountered gruesome sufferings and have survived. Not only is the author writing from a historical perspective, legal precedent and moral criteria, he is also imbued with political introspection. The author graphically paints the ordeal of the Nama and Herero of Namibia and with ingenuity contextualises the amorphous mess of the extermination order with the socio-economic imbalances of the present and critically shapes the thinking for the future society.

At this juncture in human evolutionary history, the world has become one interconnected matrix and Africa has been co-opted into the global marketplace. She has now evolved and is a target market for the Global Industrial movement.

Social blindness and arrogance is one of the afflictions of our time. Of course, the German-Herero saga is not yet consummated. We have been compromised in growth and influence. Our relatives were set upon by savages with hunting rifles, muskets and war machinery; we were thought of as sub-human and inferior.

The dynamic that was introduced by the European, in yonder years, was incomprehensible to our ancestors. The discernment of the modern moral consciousness is now a science and the world's citizenry is in transition.

Now we are able to elicit the co-operation of dexterous, fine human beings, who are endowed by nature to be masters of truth, who do not suffer from political partisanship. We can therefore scrutinise and apply to law and expose the issue to remedy and recompense.

Professor Jeremy Sarkin is one such man: we view his genius as a gift from Nature herself. We congratulate him and salute his scholarly expertise. We thank him for all his work. In defining the boundaries of human behaviour, in the context of the attempted extermination of our people with the express intent of revealing the truth about this catastrophic event.

Herero Paramount Chief Kuaima Riruako
Windhoek, Namibia
September 2010

Preface

This is the second book that I have written on the Herero genocide that occurred in then German South West Africa, now Namibia. I have also written a number of journal articles. The first book, *Colonial Genocide and Reparations Claims in the 21st Century: The Socio-Legal Context of Claims under International Law by the Herero against Germany for Genocide in Namibia, 1904–1908*, was published by Praeger Security International in 2009. That book illustrated the theoretical and legal viability of the Herero's claims for reparations against Germany as a result of its genocidal behaviour. It also examined the political and legal significance of the Herero claims for reparations from Germany as a result of the genocide. In the process of exploring the historical and legal legitimacy of this claim, several themes emerged. Firstly, it is crucial to appreciate the enduring legacy that the genocide has played upon Herero identity to the present day. The lasting effects of population decimation, land dispossession and political marginalisation continue to haunt the Herero and impede their economic, social, and political progress in modern-day Namibia. Secondly, as the historical legal analysis set forth here has illustrated, Germany's actions at the turn of the last century clearly violated not only present-day prohibitions against genocide, slave labour and crimes against humanity, but existing customary and treaty norms of the time. Thirdly, it is equally clear that international law in the 1900s not only proscribed crimes against humanity and genocide, but also provided reparations to survivors of such atrocities; reparations that form the basis of civil-damages cases today. Fourth and finally, the success or failure of the Herero's claims for reparations as a result of the 1904 genocide will have profound effects upon these historically victimised peoples and individuals and their aggressors.

This present book is a book of history. It deals with what occurred at the turn of the twentieth century and, crucially, why the genocide occurred. It also examines why, and by whom, the genocide was ordered. The historical events are important, as without them is not possible to fully appreciate the political climate of present-day Namibia, Herero claims of reparations and reaction thereto. Land is the common denominator amongst these issues, given that it both motivated German colonial policy toward German South West Africa (GSWA) and continues to unsettle relations among Namibia's ethnic groups today. In this context, the history of the Herero warrants closer examination; not only because they were singled out (along with the Nama and Damara peoples) for extinction by the German colonial powers, but also because that isolated abuse continues to marginalise the Herero in Namibia today. Due to their historical sovereignty over arable land and unwillingness to fully submit to German settler dominance, the Herero were targeted with systematic killing, eviction, deprivation of land and other atrocities. The stagnated economic and political position of the Herero today indicates that the tribe has not recovered from this abuse.

Present-day Namibia remains embroiled in a simmering land conflict that — as in colonial times — is exacerbated by the nation's dry and arid climate, which subjects the little crop-suitable land available to great conflict. However, the economic marginalisation of the Herero and other minorities today stems from more than merely climatic conditions. The colonial and current dispossession of Herero land has continued to affect the tribe's socio-economic status. Germany's colonial occupation of GSWA has had, and continues to have, profound effects on the identity and memory of the Herero and their relations with other groups in modern-day Namibia. German customs have influenced the tribe's dress and religious practices, a vivid reminder of their past. The decimation of a large percentage of the tribe's population has reduced the Herero to a minority in independent Namibia. The dispossession of land and cattle amongst the Herero left them economically disabled, even to this day. Land was, however, not the only factor that lead to the genocide, as this book attests to.

Acknowledgements

The book emerges out of my work in Namibia over the past decade. It is the product of archival and other research, including numerous interviews conducted in Namibia, Botswana, Germany, South Africa and elsewhere. The interviewees included members of the Herero, Damara and Nama communities in Namibia, South Africa and Botswana. I thank many of them who provided me with very important information, photographs and postcards.

Many people over the years have assisted me with the work I have done on these issues. The work has been a passion and done for the cause of social justice. I thank all the people who have provided me with assistance in many ways throughout this period in all parts of the world.

There are many people who have helped in the process to write this book. I have had a close relationship with Herero Paramount Chief Kuaima Riruako. I thank him for the information he has provided and the access he has provided me to the many Namibians who have provided insights and information. Another person who been of great assistance is Malcolm Grant. He was a source of much information because of the role he has played with the Herero for many years. He is a very generous person in many different ways. Others who have assisted me include Ryan Schneeberger (photographs), Johanna Kahatjipara (postcards), Werner Hillebrecht (Namibian National Archives), Ester Muinjangue, Ranongouje Arnold Tjihuiko, Inge Jazepa Neumann, Festus Ueripaka Muundjua, Clement Daniels, Norman Tjombe, Kae Matundu-Tjiparuro, Vitura Kavari and Jatah Kazondu. Many others have been gracious with their time and knowledge.

I also want to thank the NGOs Connectas and SUR-Human Rights who helped to fund this research.

Namibia is a vast, beautiful and wonderful country. The people are hospitable. It is my home away from home. I always look forward to visiting the country and seeing the many friends that I have built up over the years.

This book has taken a number of years to write. I would therefore like to thank my former home institution, the University of the Western Cape, Cape Town, South Africa. I also worked on the book while I was at the Fletcher School of Law and Diplomacy at Tufts University in Medford Massachusetts, USA, where I was Visiting Professor of International Human Rights from September 2006 to June 2008. I would also like to thank the Law School at Washington and Lee University in Lexington, Virginia, who appointed me Scholar-in-Residence from January to April 2006 and Hofstra University School of Law in Hempstead, New York, where I was Distinguished Visiting Professor of Law in 2008 and 2009.

Sandy Shepherd, publisher for the University of Cape Town Press in Cape Town, and Boydell and Brewer Limited in London, have been wonderful to work with and I am indebted to them.

I would like to thank my family, Rosanne, Eryn and Hannah, for their love and support in spite of my long time periods away from home and the many hours of writing when I am.

Jeremy Sarkin
Cape Town
September 2010

Introduction

...there are crimes which men can neither punish nor forgive. When the impossible was made possible it became unpunishable, unforgivable absolute evil which could no longer be understood and explained by the evil motives of self-interest, greed, covetousness, resentment, lust for power and cowardice; and which therefore anger could not revenge, love could not endure, friendship could not forgive.

– Hannah Arendt[1]

Germany's colonisation of Namibia, then German South West Africa (GSWA), encompasses one of the worst atrocities ever: the genocide of between 60 000 and 100 000 indigenous Herero people at the beginning of the twentieth century.[2] Tens of thousands of people — men, women and children — were killed in a very short period of time. Water wells were sealed and poisoned[3] to prevent access to water.[4] Thousands, including women and children were condemned to slavery in the German military and civil institutions, as well as for private companies and on German farms.[5] Surviving Herero women were forced to become 'comfort women' for the

---

1   Arendt, H. quoted in Baehr, P. (ed) (2000) *The Portable Hannah Arendt*. New York: Penguin, 139.
2   On the legal issues and claims under international law see Sarkin, J. (2009) *Colonial Genocide and Reparations Claims in the 21st Century: The Socio-Legal Context of Claims under International Law by the Herero against Germany for Genocide in Namibia, 1904–1908*. Westport: Praeger Security International.
3   The 1899 Hague Convention, to which Germany was a signatory, prohibited the use of poison (article 23(a) of the Regulations contained in the Annex to the Convention).
4   See further Sarkin, J. (2009) *Colonial Genocide and Reparations Claims in the 21st Century: The Socio-Legal Context of Claims under International Law by the Herero against Germany for Genocide in Namibia, 1904–1908*. Westport: Praeger Security International.
5   See further Goldblatt, I. (1971) *History of South West Africa: From the beginning of the nineteenth century*. Cape Town: Juta.

settlers and soldiers.[6] German geneticists came to the country to perform racial studies of alleged Herero inferiority. Herero skulls and skeletons were shipped to Germany, supposedly for further study. Various concentration camps were established[7], in which the mortality rate was more than 45 percent.[8]

Evidence of these Herero killings was seen for several years after 'long lines of white bones lay bleaching in the sun, marking the track the stricken people had tried to follow across the wilderness'.[9]

---

[6] Winifred Hoernle wrote in her diary on 10 October 1912: 'It made me quite miserable, however, to hear of goings on at a German police camp and I really got quite *Aufgeregt* over it. Each man has what he calls his *Bambus*, a young native girl whose duty it is to wash his clothes and to fulfill what they call the *Kleines affaire...*' In Carstens, P., Klinghardt, G. & West, M. (1987) (eds) *Trails in the thirstland: The anthropological field diaries of Winifred Hoernle*. Cape Town: Centre for African Studies, University of Cape Town, 41.

[7] The company *Otavi Minen AG* admitted in their hundredth-year anniversary publication in 2000 that the colonial authorities supplied labour to German businesses during the Herero war, which the businesses used as forced labour. In that publication one paragraph reads: 'Because of the Herero War it was difficult to get enough employees to build the railway. We were happy about every Herero who registered voluntary. The Government sent us also prisoners of war (Hereros): 900 men, 700 women and 620 children.' *Otavi Mines Minerals 100th anniversary commemorative publication (1900–2000)* Thus, there seems to be acceptance that even women and children were used as forced labour. In early 1904 Hereros working in Swakopmund were interned on two Woermann line ships anchored off the coast of the town for use as labour. See Erichsen, C.W. (2004) *The Angel of Death has descended violently among them: A study of Namibia's concentration camps and prisoners-of-war, 1904–08*. MA thesis (History), University of Namibia, chapter 2, 57. Arthur Koppel Company was involved in railway construction and used Herero slave labour for that purpose. Gewald notes that the exodus of people after the concentration camps were closed caused Woermann Lines to be short of labour for loading their ships. Gewald, J-B. (1999) 'The road of the man called Love and the sack of Sero: The Herero-German War and the export of the Herero labour to the South African Rand'. 40(1) *Journal of African History*, 21–40, 29.

[8] Erichsen, C.W. (2003 August/September) 'Namibia's island of death'. *New African*, 46.

[9] Eveleigh, W. (1915) *South-West Africa*. Cape Town: Maskew Miller, 134.

Nama and Herero prisoner-of-war camp, Alte Feste, in background, 1904

What is in this book?

This book examines these colonial atrocities in then GSWA. It explores the events within the context of GSWA as the only German colony considered for settlement and the only colony where settlement was actually attempted. This fact fundamentally coloured the events of the time.

The book deals with Germany's brutal march to achieve its goals in GSWA by any means possible in the relatively short period of Germany's colonial years, which stretched from 1885[10] to 1915[11], although Germany was present in GSWA before 1885. Although the Herero war appears to be

---

10 To stop the annexation of the territory by the Cape of Good Hope, Chancellor von Bismarck announced, in 1884, that it was under the protection of Germany.
11 Germany occupied GSWA until World War I, but lost it when South African and British forces marched into the territory. In terms of the Treaty of Versailles, Germany formally lost its colonies in 1919.

the only 'genocide'[12] Germany conducted within its colonies, it exercised brutality in many. Yet the view that the events in GSWA were somehow an aberration persists. Of course, the Herero genocide and the atrocities committed against the Nama and the Damara are qualitatively different from other German perpetrations at the time in their scale and brutality, but the intent to kill thousands upon thousands of indigenous peoples in different parts of Germany's colonial empire is very apparent. Further, it is problematic to argue that the events in GSWA, while unique in scope, were an aberration. The Germans slaughtered thousands elsewhere, but their intent did not seem to be to wipe out an entire group as such and thus does not meet the definitional criteria of the term 'genocide'. However, given the evidence that hundreds of thousands of people were killed during certain German campaigns in some of its colonies, the Herero genocide is actually no aberration. It is certainly no anomaly in terms of the viciousness with which it was conducted and the extent to which unarmed civilians, including women and children, were executed. The Herero genocide was not an isolated incident, but a pervasive trend.

Germany's actions in the colonies are embedded in the historical context of the Berlin Conference of 1884–1885, in which the colonial powers divided the lands of Africa among them and were determined to benefit from the spoils of their enterprise.[13] In fact '[the] marginal role of Germany in the West's colonial past was tied to a desire to catch up with other colonial powers, which without a doubt led to a discarding of humanitarian principles in countries like Namibia.'[14] The bequest of the 1884–1885 Berlin Conference that carved up Africa, imposing arbitrary borders that exist still today, has had major reverberations. This is especially true in terms of the conflicts that have racked the continent.[15] The colonial legacy of land and other types of dispossession still plays out in very fundamental ways today.

---

[12] See further Sarkin, J. (2009) *Colonial Genocide and Reparations Claims in the 21st Century: The Socio-Legal Context of Claims under International Law by the Herero against Germany for Genocide in Namibia, 1904–1908*. Westport: Praeger Security International.

[13] *Ibid.*

[14] Niekerk, C. (2003) 'Rethinking a problematic constellation: Postcolonialism and its Germanic contexts' 23 (1 & 2) *Comparative Studies of South Asia, Africa and the Middle East*, 58, 62.

[15] See Sarkin, J. (2002) 'Finding a solution for the problems created by the politics of identity in the Democratic Republic of the Congo (DRC): Designing a constitutional framework for peaceful co-operation'. In Konrad Adenauer Foundation (eds) *The Politics of Identity*. Pretoria: Konrad Adenauer Foundation.

This study does not examine German colonialism in general or the reasons behind Germany's late entry into the colonial race, but it is important to note that Germany was the last European power to enter the colonial pursuit.[16] In a very short period it acquired and lost Cameroon, German East Africa, GSWA, Togo, German New Guinea, Bismarck Archipelago, the Solomon Islands, the Marshall Islands, Kiaochow from China (in 1898 and 1899), the Carolines, the Marranas and Palva Islands (purchased from Spain) and Western Samoa (in an exchange with Britain).[17] By the turn of the twentieth century Germany's colonies comprised more than a million square miles, with an indigenous population of about 14 million and a German-settler population of 29 000.[18] However, Germany never amassed as much territory as the other colonisers and this was a blow to the country's prestige. Critically for the Herero, the territories that Germany managed to obtain were not as valuable as those of the other European powers.[19] This is significant as Germany's colonies, and GSWA in particular, must be seen in the context of Germany's desire, at least at the end of the nineteenth century and early twentieth century, to address emigration by developing another Germany in Africa. By the turn of the twentieth century, the notion that Germany was a nation with 'insufficient space' had developed.[20]

GSWA was also regarded as important trade partner, especially in light of an increasing population in Germany that required food and employment. Additionally, creating a settlement colony provided an opportunity to maintain traditional German ways and values, which were declining due to modernisation. Settling Germans in a suitable colony made it possible to preserve 'pre-capitalist forms of life'.[21] The idea was, therefore, to send people to cultivate crops and live a more traditional lifestyle.

Germany's acquisition and management of GSWA took place against the backdrop of the international politics of the time. Germany wanted to build its reputation and prestige as an important political power in Europe and the

---

[16] Zimmerer, J. and Zeller, J. (2008) *Genocide in German South-West Africa: The Colonial War of 1904–1908 and its aftermath.* Monmouth: Merlin Press

[17] Baumgart, W. (1987) 'German imperialism in historical perspective'. In Knoll, A.J. & Gann, L.H. (eds) *Germans in the tropics: Essays in German colonial history.* New York/London: Greenwood Press, 151–164, 155.

[18] Bullock, A.L.C. (1939) *German's colonial demands.* London: Oxford University Press, 2.

[19] Aydelotte, W.O. (1970) *Bismarck and British colonial policy: The problems of South West Africa 1883–1885* (2 ed). New York: Russell & Russell, v.

[20] Ritter-Petersen, H.G. (1991) *The Herrenvolk mentality in German South West Africa 1884–1914.* DLitt (History). Pretoria: University of South Africa, 60.

[21] *Ibid*, 46.

world. Acquiring colonies and developing settler communities, especially in GSWA, was an important part of this plan.[22] Because Germany's international prestige was closely intertwined with its colonial power and wealth, it forcefully repelled any attempts by the local population to oust the settlers. Ironically, this very conduct caused Germany to become the first colonising power to lose it colonies.[23] At the conclusion of World War I, because of the provisions of the Versailles Treaty, Germany lost its colonies.

Apart from international status, acquiring colonies was important for building national prestige and vindicating policies within Germany, but the attempt at achieving a large-scale settlement was 'at odds with reality'.[24] The number of settlers never reached the desired settlement demographics. However, for the current discussion, that is not of primary concern. More important is Germany's desire and attempt to establish a new homeland. The events of 1904 partly unfolded as they did because this dream was not translated into a reality.

This book does not examine the legal and socio-legal issues around these matters; that was the subject of a previous book, *Colonial Genocide and Reparations Claims in the 21st Century: The Socio-Legal Context of Claims under International Law by the Herero against Germany for Genocide in Namibia, 1904–1908*, published by Praeger Security International in 2009. The analysis in that book was that the events then were not only international crimes from a present-day perspective, but were international crimes at the time. Therefore, it was argued, reparations for what occurred are due to the victims today. The study viewed those atrocities in the context of the developing norms of reparations internationally, regionally and domestically and the development of historical claims in general. It appraised the Herero genocide events in light of the current critical legal issues regarding the extent to which international law affects historical claims for reparations. The book also examined the effect of the genocide on Namibia today and what the Herero are doing to attain redress. It explored the state of reparations theory and practice around the world, as well as the role of apologies in coming to terms with the past, referencing the apology Germany gave to the Herero community in 2004.

---

[22] Bley, H. (1967) 'Social discord in South West Africa 1894–1904'. In Gifford, P. & Louis, W.M.R. (eds) *Britain and Germany in Africa; Imperial rivalry and colonial rule.* New Haven: Yale University, 607–630.

[23] Aydelotte, W.O. (1970) *Bismarck and British colonial policy: The problems of South West Africa 1883–1885* (2 ed). New York: Russell & Russell, v.

[24] Ritter-Petersen, H.G. (1991) *The Herrenvolk mentality in German South West Africa 1884–1914.* DLitt (History). Pretoria: University of South Africa, 53.

Why the genocide was committed

One of the major questions addressed in this book is why the Herero were the target of genocide.[25] Why did Germany not commit genocide against other groups too, particularly those who rebelled against its rule in other territories? This study focuses on Germany's short colonial period and specifically its role in then GSWA. Germany's conduct in some of its other colonies is only examined to provide a comparative perspective to the treatment it meted out in GSWA.

The book contextualises the reasons for the genocide. For instance, it argues how the genocide can be understood in terms of the global milieu and the internal climate in Germany of the time and how these played out vis-à-vis Germany's goals in GSWA. The study contends that the genocide was not the work of one general from Germany or the practises of the German military in general, but that it was inexorably propelled by Germany's national goals at the time. The book will argue that the Herero genocide was linked to Germany's late entry into to the colonial race, which led it to frenetically acquire multiple colonies all over the world within a very short time, using any means available, including ruthlessness. This study proposes two main reasons for the genocide and the subsequent ill-treatment of the Herero. The genocide was not perpetrated due to the existing military culture of the time, which generally quelled rebellions in this way. From 1871, due to the ideological evolution of the notion of *Kaiserreich*, a unique institutional structure developed, resulting in Germany's rise as an authoritarian state with a brutal military and ruthless military elite, which considered itself above the law. At the same time, it was a state with an increasingly powerful parliament elected by universal suffrage; a state keen at times on counterbalancing the authoritarian elements of the constitution.

However, the *Reichstag* often allowed the Kaiser and the military to conduct campaigns with little or no oversight. The state espoused 'self-discipline',[26] a system which, combined with a military culture of ruthlessness and brutality, explains the willingness of German troops to carry out the killings, but it should not be mistaken for the motivation behind the genocide.

The genocide was firstly meant to punish the Herero for impudently rebelling against German colonial rule and for supposedly killing Germans during the uprising at the beginning of 1904. This rebellion, and the inability to deal with it

---

25 On the legal claims under international law see further Sarkin, J. (2009) *Colonial Genocide and Reparations Claims in the 21st Century: The Socio-Legal Context of Claims under International Law by the Herero against Germany for Genocide in Namibia, 1904–1908.* Westport: Praeger Security International.
26 Ritter-Petersen, H.G. (1991) *The Herrenvolk mentality in German South West Africa 1884–1914.* DLitt (History). Pretoria: University of South Africa, 79 & 80.

quickly and effectively, dented German prestige at home and abroad. The order for genocide was not only meant to deter any Herero survivors from further insurrection, but also to send a message to all the communities in GSWA and other colonies that rebellion in any form would not be tolerated.

Secondly, the genocide was a means to gain occupancy of Herero land and possession of their livestock. For a long time, Germany had desired more land in its favourite colony, as it wanted to expand the settlement of Germans in GSWA. Much was invested there and various measures were taken to persuade German settlers to go there. The intent was to create a new Germany in Africa, which would add prestige and honour to the Fatherland. GSWA was viewed as the most attractive of Germany's colonies, as it was relatively disease-free and there was much arable land and abundant cattle. The climate and living conditions were favourable and compared well with other parts of the Empire. The primary incentive for potential settlers would be the acquisition of farmland. Germany hoped that the promise of adequate land holdings would stem the continual migration in which settlers were opting for the United States and other countries. Still, Germany realised early on that it would not be able to deliver on this promise without peace and stability in GSWA. Land was needed not only to attract new settlers to the territory, but to appease the existing settler community, which was dissatisfied that its land holdings were too small to be economically productive (data on the sale of land at the time have been cited as evidence). At the time the majority of land in GSWA was not owned by German companies or settlers. It was occupied and owned by the indigenous groups. The settlers believed that the land ought to be emptied of these people so that settlers could establish farms. For the settlers the Herero farmlands became a confiscation target. Benjamin Madley notes that the policy 'of *tabula rasa* or "creating a map scraped smooth", to facilitate dispossession and ethnic cleansing' occurred to permit the removal of the locals and the notion of 'empty' land and unworthiness, allowed genocide and dispossession to be rationalized.[27] From 1895, other types of land clearance or 'forced removals' followed: the land was needed for settler occupation and the authorities did their utmost to drive the Herero off it. The settlers were frustrated by Governor Theodor von Leutwein's[28] more moderate policy

---

[27] Madley, B. (2004, June) 'Patterns of frontier genocide 1803–1910: The aboriginal Tasmanians, the Yuki of California and the Herero of Namibia'. 6 (2) *Journal of Genocide Research*, 167–192, 168.

[28] Theodor Gotthilf von Leutwein was *Landeshauptmann* from 1894 to 1898 and Governor from 1898 to 1905. Bley, H. (1967) 'Social discord in South West Africa 1894–1904'. In Gifford, P. & Louis, W.M.R. (eds) *Britain and Germany in Africa: Imperial rivalry and colonial rule*. New Haven: Yale University, 607–630, 607.

towards the indigenous communities and his protection, to some degree, of the needs and land of these communities. Given that GSWA operated largely as an isolated territory, Governor von Leutwein acted as the German supreme authority[29] and had significant control over policy in the territory. The settlers were angry and resentful because they believed that Governor Leutwein's policies were to their disadvantage. They criticised him and the administration vocally and openly and demanded that extreme measures be taken against the Herero. The settlers wanted the Herero to lose their land and cattle and wished to destroy their tribal system so that they could be used as labour. The settlers consequently embarked on a vociferous campaign both within GSWA and Germany to change the policies in GSWA.

1903 postcard of Governor Leutwein with Herero group

They received support from various quarters and, when the uprising began, Germany had clearly decided to deal with the Herero community in no uncertain terms. The timing of events show that this was no coincidence; from

---

29 Bley, H. (1967) 'Social discord in South West Africa 1894–1904'. In Gifford, P. & Louis, W.M.R. (eds) *Britain and Germany in Africa: Imperial rivalry and colonial rule.* New Haven: Yale University, 607–630, 608.

1903 a concerted effort was made to attract settlers and Germany's Colonial Department established a formal colonisation policy for the territory.[30]

The seminal influence of the German view of race, racial identity and racial superiority on the unfolding events cannot be overlooked. This book shows how the Germans, in their attempts to confirm their belief that their race was superior, were preoccupied with race identification and the origins of races. In addition to regarding the Herero as inferior and consequently being indifferent to their status and position, a colonial propaganda campaign in GSWA and Germany depicted the Herero as the initiators of a 'race war' during which they apparently indiscriminately killed many German settlers and mutilated their bodies. This was clearly designed to gain support in Germany for the policy that would soon be carried out by General von Trotha. He insisted all along that Germany was fighting a 'race war'.[31] However, the truth and extent of the alleged Herero atrocities on settlers and German troops are questionable. It seems that the Herero avoided killing women and children.[32] The alleged widespread mutilation of German corpses seems to have been mere propaganda. The Rhenish Missionary, August Kuhlman, investigated the majority of such reports and found them to be false. Even Hauptman Francke, in a 1920 lecture, stated the allegations had no basis. While it is possible that there were such cases, it seems that the allegations were predominantly racist propaganda.[33] It is likely that such cases were publicised to promote a racial dimension to the events in GSWA and so ensure support for the intended actions of the German troops. It does seem, though, that the abuse and mutilation came mostly from the German forces. Bringing back severed hands and other body parts was a method approved by the field commanders, sanctioned by German officials and uniformly carried out by soldiers under German control as a way of proving to their commanders that they had killed

---

[30] Erichsen, C.W. citing to Voeltz, R.A. (1988) 'German colonialism and the South West Africa Company, 1894–1914'. 50 *Monographs in International Studies. Africa Series*, Athens OH: Ohio University Center for International Studies, 86.

[31] Schrank, G.I. (1974) *German South West Africa: Social and economic aspects of its history 1884–1915*. PhD thesis (History). New York University, 162.

[32] The reality of civilian deaths was very different. On the plaque at the memorial outside the *Alte Feste* in Windhoek to fallen Germans between 1903 and 1908, civilian casualties are listed as 119 men, four women and one child. Sole notes that Maherero specifically forbade the killing of women and children. Sole, T.E. (1968, December). 'The Südwestafrika Denkmunze and the South West African campaigns of 1903–1908'. 1(3) *Military History Journal*, 19–23. The fact that so few women and children were killed seems to verify the policy of not killing them.

[33] Ritter-Petersen, H.G. (1991) *The Herrenvolk mentality in German South West Africa 1884–1914*. DLitt (History). Pretoria: University of South Africa, 200.

who they said they had.³⁴ In an unpublished manuscript titled 'The Germans in Africa',³⁵ Raphael Lemkin, thought by many to be the author of the word genocide and the impetus behind the Genocide Convention, notes that before the events in GSWA in 1904, mutilations practiced by soldiers against the indigenous population were sanctioned by the German officials, who ordered the soldiers to bring back the ears of those they killed to prove the number killed. Lemkin writes that because the ears of women were used to increase the numbers, German commander Dominik ordered that the heads of those killed be brought back instead. The difficulty of accomplishing this led to the severing of the genitals of those killed instead. This practice so horrified the British government that it complained to the German Ambassador in London in 1902. The Imperial Chancellor wrote to the Governor of the Cameroons asking for an end to this practice and 'to abstain in all instances from illegal acts and cruelties towards the natives and during any necessary punitive expeditions to abstain from all habits incompatible with the civilised state, such as the mutilation of corpses'.³⁶

The facts indicate that it was the Germans who killed women and children in large numbers during this time in GSWA. When August Bebel, a member of the German Parliament, was told 'unsatisfactorily' that women and children were being killed because the combatants were using them as shields,³⁷ this was met with scepticism. There was no denial that women and children were being killed. In fact, when these atrocities became known in Germany, Chancellor von Bülow demanded an explanation. Not denying the occurrences, the Chief of the General Staff, Alfred Graf von Schlieffen, replied that women had taken part in the fighting and 'were the chief instigators of the cruel and awful tortures'.³⁸ Chancellor von Bülow, at the time recognising that problematic conduct was occurring, argued that such activity 'will demolish Germany's reputation among the civilized nations and feed foreign agitation against us'.³⁹ When Chancellor von Bülow attempted at the end of 1904 to revoke

---

34 'Africanus' (1917) *The Prussian lash in Africa*. London: Hodder and Stoughton, 21.
35 The manuscript is 52 pages long and deals with a number of rebellions and the manner in which they were dealt with in German-occupied territories in Africa. It is to be found at the Jacob Rader Marcus Center of the American Jewish Archives, Cincinnati, the Raphael Lemkin papers, Box 6, Folder 9.
36 Lemkin, R. (undated) 'The Germans in Africa', found at the Jacob Rader Marcus Center of the American Jewish Archives, Cincinnati, the Raphael Lemkin papers, Box 6, Folder 9, 46.
37 Bridgman, J. (1981) *The revolt of the Hereros*. Los Angeles: University of California Press, 46.
38 *Ibid*, 127.
39 Hull, I.V. (2005) *Absolute destruction: Military culture and practices of war in Imperial Germany*. Ithaca: Cornell University Press, 64.

General von Trotha's order, he called the methods used 'inconsistent with the principles of Christianity and humanity'.[40] A 1907 report by Paul Rohrbach, a former senior German colonial official in GSWA, recognised the violations that occurred. He stated that there was a 'strong inner resistance of our officers and men against literal obedience to this blood order (*blutbefehls*)'.[41] Similarly, Goldblatt reports that there 'were many German soldiers who did not strictly carry out Von Trotha's orders',[42] while Wellington notes that it was common knowledge that some soldiers refused to obey the order and were consequently sent to Togoland and Cameroon by Von Trotha.[43]

German troops at a water hole prevent the Herero from accessing the water

[40] Helmut Bley translates the words as 'contradictory to all Christian and humane principles'. Bley, H. (1971) *South West Africa under German rule 1894–1914*. London: Heinemann, 163. See also Helbig, H. (1983) *Mythos-Deutsch-Südwest: Namibia und die Deutschen*. Weinheim/Basel: Beltz Verlag, 158.
[41] Wellington, J.H. (1967) *South West Africa and its human issues*. Oxford: Clarendon Press, 208.
[42] Goldblatt, I. (1971) *History of South West Africa: From the beginning of the nineteenth century*. Cape Town: Juta, 148.
[43] Wellington, J.H. (1967) *South West Africa and its human issues*. Oxford: Clarendon Press, 208.

General von Trotha admitted to the killing of women, although indirectly, by admitting to denying them access to water. He wrote an article in the *Deutsche Zeitung*, stating that:

> It is obvious that the war in Africa does not adhere to the Geneva Convention. It was painful for me to drive back the women from the waterholes in the Kalahari. But my troops were faced with a catastrophe. Had I made the smaller waterholes available to the women, then I would have been faced with an Africa Beresina.[44]

These issues will be dealt with again later, when dealing with the importance of the British Blue Book, as the reports contained in it include eyewitness accounts of the violence committed on the Herero.

A propaganda campaign was launched in Germany at the time justifying what was occurring. This may have been, at least in part, to inspire German volunteers to sign up for the military and travel to GSWA to fight the Herero. Placards were posted in Berlin and throughout Germany asking for reservists to volunteer to serve in GSWA at the special colonial rate of pay.[45] The fact that this occurred is further recognition that atrocities were being committed.

Prior to 1903, Germany had some success in gaining more land for the would-be and existing settlers without jeopardising peace and stability. Various strategies such as friendship treaties, credit schemes and purchases were employed to obtain land, the bulk of which belonged to the Herero. However, by 1903, further land acquisition was impeded by the refusal of existing inhabitants, which badly sabotaged Germany's plans to provide land for its settlers. The most arable and fertile land was not yet in its possession. To exacerbate matters, Berlin received reports of conflict in its favourite colony: blacks were being favoured over whites and interracial relationships and marriages were creating a mixed-race group entitled to German citizenship. At the same time the Herero were under increasing pressure, as the rinderpest (a viral plague affecting cattle) epidemic and harsh climatic conditions forced them to sell their land to the settlers. They were sufficiently aware of the settlers' discontent and, considering the history of German occupation elsewhere, they must have realised that it would only be a matter of time

---

[44] Rahn, W. (1997) 'Sanitätsdienst der Schutztruppe für Südwestafrika während der Aufstände 1904–1907 und der Kalahari-Expedition 1908'. *Beiträge zur deutschen Kolonialgeschichte*, 83. Quoted in Nordbruch, C. (2004) 'Atrocities committed on the Herero people during the suppression of their uprising in German South West Africa 1904–1907? An analysis of the latest accusations against Germany and an investigation on the credibility and justification of the demands for reparation'. Paper delivered to the European American Culture Council, Sacramento, 25 April 2004. Available at: http://www.nordbruch.org/artikel/sacramento.pdf.

[45] *The Times* (London) 9 May 1904, 9.

before they would be subjected to similar inhumane treatment and lose more, if not all, of their land.

These circumstances and mutual tensions provided fertile ground for conflict. In GSWA the pressure on the Herero was such that it would only take a spark to trigger a revolt. Of importance is the fact that reserves for the Herero were discussed and legislated. Being aware of these developments, the Herero realised that their land was shrinking and fears of future land losses were justified. For the Germans, the rebellion provided the perfect excuse and opportunity to acquire the land and rid the area of the Herero, whom they had struggled to control during the previous 15 years. The path towards an order of genocide was further paved when German troops had difficulty quelling the 1904 Herero rebellion.[46] That the well-trained and well-equipped European troops struggled against the natives, who supposedly had few and old weapons and little ammunition, seriously damaged German reputation, not to mention its pride. Thus, if a strategy of genocide was not yet in place by then, it was certainly put in place by mid-1904 to achieve all the goals set out above, especially land clearance.[47] As Katjavivi observed, this strategy was so successful that by 1911 the best land in south and central GSWA was in the hands of white settlers.[48]

German perpetrators and Herero victims

Although Don Foster has argued that '[w]hen considering evil deeds, there are at least three perspectives, three points of view: those of perpetrators, of victims and of onlookers'[49] sometimes called bystanders, this book limits itself largely to the perpetrators. The role of onlookers is problematic, because it is difficult to distinguish between onlookers and perpetrators in this context.[50] As far as the perpetrators are concerned, the questions of what guilt is and for what conduct there ought to be guilt, have been extensively debated. Karl Jaspers has noted that there are different levels of guilt, including criminal, moral, political and metaphysical guilt.[51] Criminal and civil liability normally focus on those who

---

[46] Zimmerer, J. and Zeller, J. (2008) *Genocide in German South-West Africa: The Colonial War of 1904–1908 and its aftermath*. Monmouth: Merlin Press

[47] Stratton, J. (2003) 'It almost needn't have been the Germans: The state, colonial violence and the Holocaust'. 6 (4) *European Journal of Cultural Studies*, 507–527, 515.

[48] Katjavivi, P. (1989) *A history of resistance in Namibia*. Paris/London/Addis Ababa: UNESCO, 11.

[49] Foster, D. (2000, March) 'Entitlement as explanation for perpetrators' actions'. 30 (1) *South African Journal of Psychology*, 10.

[50] Vetlesen, A.J. (2000, July) 'Genocide. A case for the responsibility of the bystander'. 37 (4) *Journal of Peace Research*, 519–532.

[51] Jaspers, K. (2001) *The question of German guilt*. New York: Fordham University Press, 25.

gave the orders or carried out the acts in question. Mark Drumbl has noted that the morally guilty are those who 'conveniently closed their eyes to events or permitted themselves to be intoxicated, seduced or bought with personal advantages or who obeyed from fear'.[52] Certainly, the settlers in GSWA were not onlookers or bystanders but direct participants. They provided a major impetus for the genocide, because they complained vociferously to Germany and to the Kaiser about the lenient policy towards Africans, the Herero in particular. They wanted the Herero land and wanted it for free and did not care by what means they were to get it. When the conflict occurred, Germany clearly accepted the settlers' assessment and demands and decided that it was time to deal with the matter once and for all. The Kaiser's view must have been that the killing of settlers and the reputed mutilations of their corpses had to be avenged and that the remaining settlers had to be rescued from their long-lamented predicament. Some settlers wanted more than the subjugation of the Herero and espoused their extermination. Although some may have supported General von Trotha's genocidal approach initially, they clearly changed their minds when they realised the long-term negative impact on their labour needs. Settlers benefited significantly from the use of Herero slave labour. In this regard men and women were made to work for both military and civil authorities. Herero slave labour was given to private enterprise, as well as to the settler community. The role of the settler community is addressed later.

It is, however, also clear that, beyond their vocal demands for severe treatment of the Herero, at least some of the settlers participated in the genocide itself, taking part in the shootings, beatings, hangings, starvation and rapes inflicted on Herero men, women and children,[53] although to what extent is unclear. Schrank has suggested that more than 500 settlers acted as reservists and participated in the war alongside regular troops.[54] Swan suggests that Governor Leutwein maintained a trained reserve, many of whom were former soldiers, in the settler community. He postulates that this reserve was comprised of 34 officers, 730 men and about another 400 men who could use a rifle and ride a horse.[55] It must be remembered that many of

---

[52] Drumbl, M. (2005) 'Collective Violence and Individual Punishment: The Criminality of Mass Atrocity'. 99 *Northwestern University Law Review*, 539, 572.

[53] Gewald, J-B. (2003) 'The Herero genocide: German unity, settlers, soldiers and ideas'. In Bechhaus-Gerst, M. & Klein-Arendt, R. *Die (koloniale) begegnung: AfrikanerInnen in Deutschland 1880–1945, Deutsche in Afrika 1880–1918*. Frankfurt am Main: Peter Lang, 109–127, 110.

[54] Schrank, G.I. (1974) *German South West Africa: Social and economic aspects of its history, 1884–1915*. PhD (History). New York University, 158.

[55] Swan, J. (1991) 'The Final solution in South West Africa'. 3(4) *Military History Quarterly*, 36–55, 45.

the settlers were former soldiers who had remained behind in the territory after completing their military service.

Other indigenous communities also periodically participated, by either supporting the Germans or joining those who attempted to oust the colonisers from the territory.

The role of the church is relevant and frequently more biased than is widely portrayed.[56] The presence of the missionaries in the Herero reserves and their attempt to prevent further Herero land losses has been extensively debated. It has been argued that the missionaries attempted to prevent the Herero from moving away from their missionary stations, as they wanted to protect their own sphere of influence. Their protective role was thus motivated by their desire to keep more Hereros in areas where they could fall under the influence of the church.[57] Be that as it may, the church and the missionaries promoted self-interests that were incongruent, if not antithetical, to the positions of the local communities.[58]

The role of Kaiser Wilhelm II

Writings on genocidal events generally proffer two models: the 'intentionalist' perspective, which holds that leaders intend to carry out such killings, and a 'functionalist' or 'interactive' approach, which does not disregard the role of the leaders, but gives precedence to the reality of the occurrence on the ground.[59] As Isabel Hull has noted, while there are many vexing questions about what occurred in GSWA, 'the most vexing is the question of intentionality. Was the extermination of the Herero planned and if so by whom? Was it policy from the Berlin, from the Kaiser or from the General Staff? Was it intended from the beginning by the commander, General Lothar von Trotha, a natural product of his racism?'[60]

---

[56] On the role of the Catholic Church see Beris, A.P.J. (1996) *From mission to local church: One hundred years of mission by the Catholic Church in Namibia*. Windhoek: Roman Catholic Church.

[57] See generally Gewald, J-B. (2002, June) 'Flags, funerals and fanfares: Herero and missionary contestations of the acceptable, 1900–1940'. 15 (1) *Journal of African Cultural Studies*, 105.

[58] See further Voeltz, R.A. (2000) 'Review of mission, church and state relations in South West Africa under German rule (1884–1915)'. 33 (1) *The International Journal of African Historical Studies*, 153–155.

[59] Gellately, R. & Kiernan, B. (2003) 'The study of mass murder and genocide'. In Gellately, R. & Kiernan, B. (eds) *The specter of genocide: Mass murder in historical perspective*. Cambridge: Cambridge University Press, 11.

[60] Hull, I.V. (2005) *Absolute destruction: Military culture and practices of war in Imperial Germany*. Ithaca: Cornell University Press, 5.

General Lothar von Trotha in full ceremonial uniform

This book will attempt to answer to these questions. The examination of the Kaiser's role will not include an overall assessment of his years on the throne, but will be limited mainly to the period around 1904 and his conduct in respect to the genocide in GSWA. Until now, some accounts have presented the genocide as the product of a rogue German general, denying the German government's responsibility. This in itself is problematic, because both Schlieffen, the chief of the General Staff, and the Kaiser had some say in, and to some extent supported, what was being done.

This study recounts the reasons why the Kaiser likely issued the order and why proof of this has not emerged. This was not the first or the only time that the Kaiser ordered ruthless and brutal conduct. On dispatching soldiers to the Boxer Rebellion[61] at the end of July 1900, Wilhelm told his troops in an impassioned speech:

---

61   Tan, C.C. (1967) *The Boxer Catastrophe*. New York: Octagon Books.

You must know, my men, that you are about to meet a crafty well-armed foe! Meet him and beat him. Give no quarter! Take no prisoners! Kill him when he falls into your hands![62]

Clearly the Kaiser's words implied that no survivors should be left after an attack. Although it had long been held that any order of 'no quarter' was inhumane and unacceptable, for it was not a permissible method of warfare,[63] the Kaiser gave this command. Regarding the specific order to exterminate the Herero, proposals contained in a secret report to the Kaiser about what to do with the Herero were implemented almost exactly. At the very least, this suggests that the General and the Kaiser discussed the report and its contents; otherwise the recommendations could not have been taken up. The language used by General von Trotha and others in reports clearly shows that Von Trotha had met the Kaiser. It is also clear that Von Trotha regularly gave and received communications from the Kaiser, which either directly ordered the extermination or, at the minimum, gave the General very wide latitude, including the use of illegal means to achieve Germany's goals.

Even after warfare had come to an end, Germany was committed to dealing with the Herero finally and ruthlessly. After the initial battles in 1904, warfare died down and by June 1904 there were few encounters between the German troops and the Herero. Specifically, the battle at Oviumbo on 13 April 1904 was followed by a long period of relative calm. The Herero had congregated far from the Germans at the Waterberg.[64]

Ostensibly the combat was over, the Herero had withdrawn and the Kaiser had forbidden any negotiations with them, but the façade of a state of war was maintained so that the Herero could be attacked again.[65] The events of 11 August 1904 at the Waterberg confirm that Germany clearly wished to continue the war and that its goal was not to defeat the Herero in the military sense, but to annihilate them. Germany's intention was to make the Herero disappear from the territory, either by killing them or allowing them to flee through the open end of the cordon, which would lead them into the waterless desert of what is today known as Botswana.

---

[62] O'Connor, R. (1973) *The Boxer Rebellion*. London: Robert Hale, 182. See further Balfour, M. (1964) *The Kaiser and his times*. Boston: Houghton Mifflin, 226.
[63] Detter Delupis, I. (1987) *The law of war*. New York: Cambridge University Press, 252.
[64] Pool, G. (1991) *Samuel Maherero*. Windhoek: Gamsberg MacMillan, 240.
[65] Gewald, J-B. (1996) *Towards Redemption: A socio-political history of the Herero of Namibia between 1890 and 1923*. Leiden: CNWS Publications, 205.

German *Schutztruppe* at the Waterberg 11 August 1904

Chapter three, which deals with the role of the Kaiser, reveals his history of violence and his ordering of brutal actions, even against his own citizens. Von Trotha's language reveals that he received orders from the Kaiser and that he would not amend these orders without direct instruction to do so. The chapter also illuminates the personality of the Kaiser and his penchant for inflicting pain and suffering. The Kaiser's anti-Semitism is examined in the context of his attitude towards the Herero, as are his writings, which reveal his desire for the extermination of Jews. Thus, a pattern in his propensity for genocidal events comes to light.

The chapter also demonstrates how over the years various people, including those present in the *Reichstag*, have theorised that the Kaiser was behind the order. Von Trotha's silence is not surprising; he knew that he was not supposed to have been aware of what happened when the Kaiser made the infamous 'Hun' speech in which he, in very intemperate language, demanded that no quarter be given. Von Trotha must have known that the Chancellor was against such statements and orders by the Kaiser. He also knew that, had he revealed the Kaiser's role, the law would have come down heavily on him. A civilian who questioned the German army's tactics had been convicted and sentenced to five years in prison. Given this context and the order that soldiers were not to reveal what had occurred or publish their diaries, Von Trotha, a general of long standing who had for years followed direct and very specific orders with brutal effect, would not likely have implicated the Kaiser. Would he have jeopardised his pension and standing so close to retirement?

It is unsurprising that no direct evidence has been found linking the Kaiser personally and directly to the genocide, as great efforts were made to sanitise and edit the Kaiser's words and actions while he ruled. Even after 1918, when he went into exile, care was taken to limit revelations about the role of the Kaiser, a process that continued long after he died in 1941. However, his letters calling for the extermination of the Jews have been since found. These, along with the evidence amassed in chapter three, would suggest that the Kaiser played a far greater role in the genocide than has previously been acknowledged.

The relationship of the Herero genocide to the Holocaust

The links between the Holocaust and the Herero genocide have been the subject of some research, especially in recent years. Some have drawn parallels. The similarities between the two in methodology, philosophy, ideology and personality suggest that the link may not be as complex as had been thought. The connection is not necessarily about the convoluted notions of totalitarianism or fascism, but simply about emulating and refining a race-based ideology of eliminating those perceived to be inferior and impure, improving and augmenting the use of ethnic identification labelling, ethnic branding, slave labour, concentration camps and exterminations.

The following extract regarding the Holocaust also pertains to the Herero genocide and elucidates further parallels:

> To understand a criminal event like the Holocaust it is crucial to distinguish between the intentions, including the ideology and world-view of the human beings who did the killing and the structural conditions under which the murders were perpetuated. Both are crucial to an understanding of the Holocaust or any other genocide. Though the intentions of one group of killers may have been different from another, the possibility, nevertheless, remains that the structural conditions that allowed murderous intentions to be actualized in genocidal behavior were comparable and institutive. Besides the motives of the perpetrators, an etiology of genocide must address those factors that helped the killers to seize power and those that facilitated the implementation of their murderous policies.[66]

Regarding the Herero extermination order, Soggot has noted that it 'was delivered in an aura of Gothic megalomania which decades later found its

---

[66] Melson. R. (1992) *Revolution and genocide: On the origins of the Armenian Genocide and the Holocaust.* Chicago Illinois: Chicago University Press, 37.

resonance in the frenzied declamations of a different Führer'.[67] Certainly the role of the Kaiser and Führer are key to understanding why the genocides happened in the different periods. The State gave two leaders the space to achieve the goals they wished to accomplish, including genocide. Neither State nor government attempted to rein either in as they carried out these brutal objectives. The role of the Kaiser is therefore a key theme explored here.

While the concept of genocide has generally been linked to the Holocaust and the prosecution of those responsible at Nuremberg,[68] many scholars have intrinsically linked the origins of German genocide in the 1930s and 1940s to what transpired in the German colonies. The most recognised of these scholars is probably Hannah Arendt.[69] This link does not equate the Herero genocide and the Holocaust,[70] given that the magnitude of the latter sets them apart.

Evidently, the 'techniques and concepts' used in the Holocaust were originally designed during colonial times to exterminate the Herero during the occupation of GSWA.[71] Stratton argues that the construction of Jews as an inferior race, which was also employed with the Herero, is what allowed the Holocaust to occur.[72] He further shows how the practices of the colonial times were refined and applied during the Nazi era.[73] So many violations undertaken during the Nazi period were first accomplished in GSWA against the Herero. Practices such as prohibiting marriages between Germans and locals,[74] genetic experimentation,

---

67 Soggot, D. (1986) *Namibia: The violent heritage*. London: Rex Collings, x.
68 Ratner, S.R. & Abrams, J.S. (1997) *Accountability for human rights atrocities in international law*. New York: Oxford University Press, 24. The Charter did not, however, use the term 'genocide'.
69 According to Arendt, H. (1975) *The origins of totalitarianism*. New York: Harcourt Brace, 'African colonial possessions became the most fertile soil for the flowering of what later was to become the Nazi elite. Here they had seen with their own eyes how peoples could be converted into races and how, simply by taking the initiative in this process, one might push one's own people into the position of the master race. Here they were cured of the illusion that the historical process is necessarily "progressive".' Arendt, H. (1951) *The origins of totalitarianism*. New York: Harcourt Brace & Jovanovitch, 206–07.
70 On the question of the parallels to the Holocaust and claims for restitution, see Barkan, E. (2000) *The guilt of nations: Restitution and negotiating historical injustices*. Baltimore: Johns Hopkins University Press, 304.
71 Meister. R. (2005 January) 'Never again: The ethics of the neighbor and the logic of genocide'. 15 (2) *Postmodern Culture*, fn 32.
72 Stratton, J. (2003) 'It almost needn't have been the Germans: The state, colonial violence and the Holocaust'. 6 (4) *European Journal of Cultural Studies*, 507–527, 507.
73 *Ibid*, 507–527.
74 Mixed marriages were retrospectively banned in GSWA in 1907. Gambari, I.A. (1971, October) 'Review of H Bley *South-West Africa under German Rule, 1894–1914*; South-West Africa (Namibia): Proposals for action'. 9 (3) *The Journal of Modern African Studies*, 484–486, 484.

the wearing of ethnic identity symbols, concentration camps and exterminations all first existed in GSWA and were adopted in Nazi-controlled Europe in the 1930s and 1940s. During the Holocaust the skin and other body parts of those exterminated were collected and used. Similarly, Herero women were forced to clean Herero skulls of their skin and flesh with glass. These were then sent to the Pathological Institute in Berlin.[75] The collection of Herero skulls seems to have taken place from 1905 when Lieutenant Ralf Zürn, the same person who has been blamed for starting the war, was contracted to provide a Herero skull. He was subsequently requested to provide more skulls and there were rumours that thousands more were shipped to Germany.[76] It is also rumoured that Zürn kept a Herero skeleton as a trophy and took it back to Germany upon his return.[77] Other German officials and troops also kept body parts obtained in GSWA.[78] Certainly skulls and corpses harvested from the concentration camps were supplied.[79] Doctors employed by the German forces (Dansauer, Jungels, Mayer and Zollner) also collected Herero body parts and sent them to Germany (see the front cover of this book).[80] Heynen notes that:

> *The eugenicist depictions of racial types emerged simultaneously with the development of a significant colonial postcard industry, in particular in the then German colony of what is now Namibia. The popularity in Germany of these postcards grew significantly after the 1905 genocide of the Nama and Herero by the occupying German military and the so-called 'Hottentot election' in 1907 which pushed the issue of imperialism even more into the public eye. Not surprisingly given these contexts, images of colonial control, in particular beatings of Africans by the military and pornographic images of African women, were the most popular representations.*[81]

---

[75] Dedering, T. (1999) 'A certain rigorous treatment of all parts of the nation: The annihilation of the Herero in German South West Africa, 1904'. In Levine, M. & Roberts, P. (eds) *The massacre in history*. New York: Oxford: Berghahn Books.

[76] Zimmerman, A. (2001) *Anthropology and antihumanism in imperial Germany*. Chicago: University of Chicago Press, 245.

[77] Zimmerman, A. (2003) 'Adventures in the skin trade: German anthropology and colonial corporeality'. In Penny, H.G. & Bunzl, M. (eds) *Worldly provincialism: German anthropology in the Age of Empire*. Ann Arbour: University of Michigan Press, 156, 177.

[78] *Ibid*, 156–178.

[79] *Ibid*, 157, 175.

[80] In 2008 a number of the skulls were found at Charite University of Berlin and the University of Freiburg in Freiburg. It was reported in April 2010 that the German government is to repatriate them to Namibia.

[81] Heynen, R. 'Urban space and the spectacle of progress: Kracauer, Benjamin and marginality in Weimar visual culture'. Paper presented at *Culturepoles*, Canadian Association of Cultural Studies. Available at: http://www.culturalstudies.ca/proceedings04/pdfs/heynen.pdf [accessed on: 13 April 2005].

Postcard of Herero and Nama people

Thus Judy Scales-Trent has noted that:

> *The Nazis saw links between Jews and 'Negroes' everywhere. In their view, Afro-Germans, like Jews, had a 'hybrid character,' one which led to a host of 'racial maladies,' as well as mental defects. Hitler often commented on the relationship between the two groups. He thought that it was the Jews who had brought African soldiers into the Rhine region of Germany. When Hitler said that it was important to protect 'not only against Jewish, but also against any and every racial infection,' he was thinking also about Africans and descendants of Africans. When he described the 'racial chaos and confusion' that would ultimately allow the 'Hebrew' to 'slowly rise to world domination,' he meant 'a bastardization and Negrification of cultural mankind and thereby ultimately... a lowering of its racial value.' He not only saw Jews everywhere, he also saw Negroes everywhere.*[82]

Underscoring the link between GSWA and the Holocaust, Zimmerman states that '[t]he Holocaust brought to Europe practises developed in colonial Africa, as the genocidal war against the Herero and the role of anthropologists in that

---

[82] Scales-Trent, J. (2001) 'Racial purity laws in the United States and Nazi Germany: The targeting process'. 23 (2) *Human Rights Quarterly*, 260–307.

war make all too clear'.[83] Some 30 years later, in 1936, the Kaiser Wilhelm Institute of Anthropology in Berlin-Dahlem noted that some of its research consisted of collecting and classifying human skulls from Africa, training Waffen-SS doctors and conducting studies in race-crossing.[84] Which specific skulls are referred to is unclear, but the skulls of Africans, including those of the Herero, were still under examination during Nazi times. The collecting of skulls and body parts seems to have been part of exploring the theory that Jews and black people were related and that the Jews' racial impurity was attributed to them being hybrids of the 'Negro' and the 'Oriental'.[85]

Bley supported Arendt's views regarding the link between Nazi policy and what occurred in the colonies, especially GSWA.[86] Jonassohn[87] addresses the same issues, clarifying in the process that many have misquoted Arendt, while others have linked the two periods through the use of notions such as fascism. Jonassohn endorses the direct links between the two eras, citing the human experimentations, the philosophy, the racism and the denials. Racism was clearly a prominent feature of both times. In the years of German colonial rule, locals in all German colonies in Africa endured 'genocide, incarceration in concentration camps, starvation, forced labour, deportations, expropriation of property, torture and a mixed marriage law sanctioned by the *Reichstag*, which prevented the marriages of whites and blacks. Despite the protest of liberals in the *Reichstag*, overt racism continued until Germany was forced to surrender its colonies'.[88]

The Germans referred to the locals in racist terms, calling them 'baboons' or 'vermin'.[89] The pervasive dehumanisation of the victims through language, specifically images of infectivity and contamination, is a typical feature of genocide and related abuse. Calling people 'lice', 'rats', 'cockroaches' and 'weeds' not only dehumanises them, but also serves to mobilise people to take action, to

[83] Zimmerman, A. (2001) *Anthropology and antihumanism in Imperial Germany*. Chicago: University of Chicago Press, 245.
[84] Kesting, R.W. (1998, Winter) 'Blacks under the swastika: A research note'. 83 (1) *The Journal of Negro History*, 84–99, 92.
[85] Procter, R. (1988) *Racial hygiene medicine under the Nazis*. Cambridge, Massachusetts: Harvard University Press, 114.
[86] Bley, H. (1971) *South-West Africa under German rule 1894–1914*. London: Heinemann. See a review of Bley's book addressing this matter: Gann, L.H. (1973) 'South-West Africa under German rule, 1894–1914'. 6 (1) *The International Journal of African Historical Studies*, 121–126, 121.
[87] Jonassohn, K. (1996, Jan–Feb) 'Before the Holocaust deniers'. 33 (2) *Society*, 31–39.
[88] Kesting, R.W. (1998, Winter) 'Blacks under the swastika: A research note'. 83 (1) *The Journal of Negro History*. 84–99, 85.
[89] Stoecker, H. (ed) (1986) *German imperialism in Africa: From the beginnings until the Second World War*. London: C Hurst & Co, 52.

'clean up'.[90] Victims of genocide are often not perceived as individuals, but only as part of a group,[91] a perception enhanced by these debasing metaphors.

Regarding racism in GSWA it has been noted: 'The Germans regarded Africans as equal to animals, with no independent rights to existence except as servants...Sexual relationships between the races were strongly forbidden, so that white supremacy might not be weakened nor the purity of German lood and race be polluted.'[92] These words apply equally to racial attitudes during the Nazi era.

This view of the indigenous population is exemplified by the words of Von Trotha on his arrival in GSWA that 'no war may be conducted humanely against non humans'.[93] Both Kesting[94] and Jonassohn[95] identify these views as specific links between GSWA and Nazi Germany, citing examples by individuals such as Eugen Fischer and Paul Rohrbach. Jonassohn points out how the writings of Paul Rohrbach, advocating the extermination or expulsion of the indigenous population to provide space for white settlers, later became part of the Nazi ethos. To confirm the link between the two eras Jonassohn also refers to Eugen Fischer, who conducted human experiments in GSWA and later in Nazi Germany. In 1913 Fischer published a book dealing with race and GSWA entitled *The Bastards of Rehoboth and the Problem of Miscegenation in Man*. From 1927 to 1942 Fischer was director of the Kaiser Wilhelm Institute of Anthropology in Berlin-Dahlem. He also served as a judge on the Superior Genetic Health Court.[96] He identified the need for a practical eugenics (race hygiene) and asserted: 'I do not categorize every Jew as inferior as Negroes and I do not underestimate the greatest enemy [Jews] with whom we have to

90   Bauman, Z. (1989) *Modernity and the holocaust*. Cambridge: Polity.
91   Smith, R.W. (1999) 'State power and genocidal intent: On the uses of genocide in the twentieth century'. In Chorbajian, L. & Chirinian, G. (eds) *Studies in Comparative Genocide*. New York: St Martin's Press 3–14, 4.
92   Gambari, I.A. (1971, October) 'Review of H Bley *South-West Africa under German Rule, 1894–1914*; South-West Africa (Namibia): Proposals for Action'. 9 (3) *The Journal of Modern African Studies*, 484–486, 484 & 485.
93   Hull, I.V. (2003) 'Military culture and the production of final solutions in the colonies: The example of Wilhelminian Germany'. In Gellately, R. & Kiernan, B. (eds) *The specter of genocide mass murder in historical perspective*. Cambridge: Cambridge University Press, 154.
94   Kesting, R.W. (1998, Winter) 'Blacks under the swastika: A research note.'. 83 (1) *The Journal of Negro History*, 84–99, 85.
95   Jonassohn, K. (1996, Jan–Feb) 'Before the Holocaust deniers'. 33 (2) *Society*, 31–39.
96   Kesting, R.W. (1998, Winter) 'Blacks under the swastika: A research note'. 83 (1) *The Journal of Negro History*. 84–99, 92.

fight.'[97] His position strongly influenced Nazi philosophy and presented an important motivation for the Holocaust.[98]

In a similar vein, Paul Gilroy draws attention to the connection between those who served in the colonies and those who participated in the Nazi atrocities.[99] He asks: 'How many of the ordinary men and women who became Hitler's willing executioners had previously served in the German colonial forces or had other experiences of Germany's blood-soaked Imperial adventurers?'[100] Beyond ideology, Hull believes that the military acted as a crucial link between imperialism and the final solution.[101] However, the military was neither the sole nor the predominant connection, as will be further discussed.

Gann and Duigan differ from the abovementioned discourse on the link between the colonial history and the Holocaust, claiming that the argument has 'numerous weaknesses' and overemphasises the importance of colonialism for Germany.[102] They maintain that the colonies did not play a significant role in the German economy and, in the years after World War I, the 'colonial idea did not become popular'.[103] According to them, very few individuals were employed in the colonial administration. However, Gann and Duigan acknowledge the extent to which the colonies were prized and the benefits that were sought. That these benefits were not necessarily attained does not diminish the efforts put forth to achieve them. Ultimately, not many individuals were placed in the colonies in order to save resources, but certainly considerably more resources were invested in GSWA, the favoured colony, than in any of the other German colonies.

According to Gann and Duigan, the interpretation that links colonialism and totalitarianism also overlooks divergences in ideology and sociology that existed at the time, arguing that many people were not anti-liberal, against democracy or against industrial civilisation.[104] Even so, it is indisputable that

---

[97] Ibid, 84–99, 87.
[98] Jonassohn, K. (1996, Jan–Feb) 'Before the Holocaust deniers'. 33 (2) Society, 31–39.
[99] Gilroy, P. (1998) 'Afterword: Not being inhuman'. In Cheyette, B. & Marcus, L. (eds) Modernity, culture and the Jew. Cambridge: Polity Press, 288.
[100] Ibid, 297, 288.
[101] Hull, I.V. (2003) 'Military culture and the production of final solutions in the colonies: The example of Wilhelminian Germany'. In Gellately, R. & Kiernan, B. (eds) The specter of genocide mass murder in historical perspective. Cambridge: Cambridge University Press, 141, 143.
[102] Gann, L.H. Duigan, P (1977) The rulers of German Africa 1884–1914. Stanford: Stanford University Press, 228.
[103] Ibid, 228.
[104] Ibid, 229.

many of the practices of the Nazi era, such as concentration camps[105] and experimentations,[106] originated in the colonies. Gann and Duigan disagree, arguing that the mechanisms and institutions of totalitarianism were produced by World War I rather than by colonial practices. In their view there is no proof that the relocations of people during Nazi times were inspired by what happened during colonialism and that not even the

> *terror tactics of the kind used by Von Trotha in South-West Africa suffice on their own to create a totalitarian state. The Germans in South-West Africa, for all their ruthlessness, were no more brutal against the Herero than the Australians had been in their treatment of the Tasmanians, than the Americans were in their conduct toward the Indians or than the Hausa were to be in their dealings with the Ibo in northern Nigeria. Yet none of these atrocities led to the creation of totalitarian states.*[107]

Still, the fact remains that many of the atrocious deeds that occurred during the colonial period were replicated some 40 years later. Gann and Duigan's theory patently misses the point: it is about the type of conduct that occurred, not whether it resulted in the creation of totalitarian states.

Mamdani captures the key issue by arguing that the connection between Herero genocide and the Holocaust was race branding.[108] The way that these Africans were treated was the same treatment that was 'later applied to Jews and other enemies of the Nazi regime in Germany, by the same units of troops that had practiced their deadly craft on Africa'.[109] In fact, Zirkel notes that the brutality amongst German soldiers was apparent long before World War II and that the troops on the ground often committed major atrocities without being ordered to do so. She points out one of the differences between the

---

105 Concentration camps were not uniquely German. The British, for example, used them during the Anglo-Boer War some three or four years prior to the Germans using them in GSWA.
106 Similarly, human experimentation was not uniquely German either. Again the British provide an example — they did likewise with Indian political prisoners at the Andaman Islands penal colony. Colijn, G.J. (2003, December) 'Carnage before our time: Nineteenth century colonial genocide'. 5 (4) *Journal of Genocide Research*, 617–625.
107 Gann, L.H. & Duigan, P. (1977) *The rulers of German Africa 1884–1914*. Stanford: Stanford University Press, 237.
108 Mamdani, M. (2002, December) 'Making sense of political violence in postcolonial Africa'. 3 (2) *Identity, Culture and Politics*, 4. See also Mamdani, M. (1996) *Citizen and subject: Contemporary Africa and the legacy of late colonialism*. Princeton: Princeton University Press.
109 Quoted in Nordbruch, C. 'Atrocities committed on the Herero people during the suppression of their uprising in German South West Africa 1904–1907. An analysis of the latest accusations against Germany and an investigation on the credibility and justification of the demands for reparation'. Available at: http://www.nordbruch.org/artikel/sacramento.pdf

East African and GSWA campaigns: in GSWA a military commander gave a military order to commit abuses, while in East Africa local troop leaders simply carried out the violence on their own.[110] Ostensibly, Berlin did not order either of these acts; were this not true, Zirkel would be correct.

A further link between the activities in GSWA and Nazi Germany is the support the German population afforded both regimes.[111] The Germans in GSWA and Germany knew about and generally supported the brutal treatment of the indigenous population, paralleling the attitudes of the German citizens toward Jewish people during World War II, as documented in the Goldhagen thesis.[112] Similarly, Soggot notes that the 'all embracing authoritarian regime thus imposed upon the Hereros enjoyed the approval of most Germans'.[113] The evidence above therefore undermines Hull's notion that military culture or military practices were the predominant link between the two eras.

Methodology, terminology and definitions

While the literature on the Herero genocide has grown in recent years, much work remains to be done, especially by those directly affected. The Herero themselves ought to be doing more writing on what happened to them and the legacy of that violence. The oral history exists. In this regard it has been noted by Erichsen in 2008 that, unlike

> any other groups that took part in this research, the Herero/Mbanderu respondents were able to track the direct impact of the war on their own families, providing both the names of people who had died and the places where they died.[114]

---

[110] Zirkel, K. (1999) 'Military power in German colonial policy: The Schutztruppen and their leaders in the East and South West Africa, 1888–1918'. In Killingray, D. & Omissi, D. (eds) *Guardians of Empire: The armed forces of the colonial powers, 1700–1964*. Manchester: Manchester University Press, 102.

[111] Soggot, D. (1986) *Namibia: The violent heritage*. London: Rex Collings, x.

[112] The most well-known account of the German citizenry's attitude to the Holocaust is by Daniel Goldhagen. Goldhagen, D. (1996) *Hitler's willing executioners: Ordinary Germans and the Holocaust*. New York: Vintage Books. See also Mann, M. (2000) 'Were the perpetrators of genocide "ordinary men" or "real Nazis"? Results from fifteen hundred biographies'. 14 (3) *Holocaust and Genocide Studies*, 331–366; Maier, C.S. (1988) *The unmasterable past: History, Holocaust and German national identity*. Cambridge, Massachusetts: Harvard University Press; and Shandley, R.R. (ed) (1998) *Unwilling Germans? The Goldhagen debate*. Minneapolis: University of Minnesota Press.

[113] Soggot, D. (1986) *Namibia: The violent heritage*. London: Rex Collings, x.

[114] Erichsen, C. (2008) *'What the elders used to say' Namibian perspectives on the last decade of German colonial rule*. Windhoek: Namibia Institute for Democracy and the Namibian-German Foundation, 48.

Generally speaking, because there are often few survivors of genocides, victims and their perspectives are generally neglected in genocide studies. They are hardly ever primary subjects in these studies and rarely share equal subject status with perpetrators. Referring to the lack of writing on the Herero genocide, Cornevin asserted in 1969 that

> *studies published before World War I were almost all by German authors and have essentially a documentary and didactic character. They aim at instructing the metropolitan country about the economic importance of these colonies, so rapidly acquired during the course of 1884 and 1885. Those published after 1918 are written by Germans, English, French, Americans and Belgians who are all more or less biased and pass moral judgements on German colonization of Africa. From 1945 onward the communist writers of East Germany come to confirm, in works written from the archives in Potsdam, the charges against German colonialism published between the two wars by English and French authors and to utter a cry of alarm against the neo-colonialism of West Germany.*[115]

Equally relevant to the Herero genocide is the recognition, made in reference to the Holocaust, that neglect to study atrocities is extremely harmful:

> *In some ways, the effect of this academic neglect may be comparable to the damage done by those who deny the Holocaust. While I am by no means suggesting a moral equivalency between those who, for various reasons, omit reference to genocide and those who actively work to mislead and repress truth, I am asserting that both behaviours have somewhat similar results. That is, the failure of social scientists to adequately address the study of genocide contributes to perceptions and attitudes that, through exclusion, minimize the importance and significance of genocide. That is essentially what Holocaust denial is all about.*[116]

Until recently, the historiography on GSWA has relied almost exclusively on German sources. Even authors with a more expansionist and critical view have often relied on these sources. Bley, for example, noted that the sources for his 1971 book were 'almost entirely derived from the European side'.[117] Since then, there has been a growth in research on colonialism and specifically on the Herero genocide. A more balanced picture is now emerging, drawing from

---

115 Cornevin, R. (1969) 'The Germans in Africa before 1918'. In Gann, L.H. & Duigan, P. *Colonialism in Africa 1870–1960*. Cambridge: Cambridge University Press, 223. Also cited in Jonassohn, K. & Bjornson, S.K. (1998) *Genocide and gross human rights violations*. New Brunswick: Transaction, 73. Gann also observes the biases of the various stages. Gann, L.H. (1973) 'South West Africa under German Rule 1894–1914'. 6 (1) *The International Journal of African Historical Studies*, 121–126, 121.
116 Alvarez, A. (2001) *Governments, citizens and genocide: A comparative and interdisciplinary approach*. Bloomington: Indiana University Press, 3.
117 Bley, H. (1971) *South-West Africa under German rule 1894–1914*. London: Heinemann, Introduction no page number.

a wider array of sources. A number of eyewitness accounts do exist and some victim accounts are found in the Blue Book, which recorded accounts of the atrocities committed during the Herero war.[118] Since the British produced the Blue Book during World War I reservations about its objectivity remain. However, the sentiments contained in the 1918 Report were already present in a British report of 1909, which stated:

> The great aim of German policy in German South West Africa, as regards the native, is to reduce him to a state of serfdom, and, where he resists, to destroy him altogether. The native, to the German, is a baboon and nothing more. The war against the Hereros, conducted by General Von Trotha, was one of extermination; hundreds — men, women and children — were driven into desert country, where death from thirst was their end; whose [sic] left over are now in great locations near Windhuk [sic], where they eke out a miserable existence; labour is forced upon them and naturally is unwillingly performed.[119]

Herero women being forced to wash German uniforms

118 Administrator's Office Windhuk [sic] (9 ed) (1918) *Report on the natives of South-West Africa and their treatment by Germany*. London: His Majesty's Stationery Office.
119 Report by Captain H. S. P. Simon, 'Report on German South West Africa', 6 April 1909, FO 367/136 quoted in Louis, W.M.R. (1967) 'Great Britain and German expansion in Africa 1884–1919'. In Gifford, P. & Louis, W.M.R. (eds) *Britain and Germany in Africa: Imperial rivalry and colonial rule*. New Haven: Yale University, 3–46, 33–34.

In August 1912, another British foreign office official commented:

> In view of the cruelty, treachery [and] commercialism by which the German colonial authorities have gradually reduced their natives to the status of cattle (without so much of a flutter being caused among English peace loving philanthropists) the [Portuguese] S. Thome agitation in its later phases against a weak [and] silly nation without resources is the more sickening. These Hereros were butchered by thousands during the war & have been ruthlessly flogged into subservience since.[120]

Given that many British government reports predating World War I mention these same issues, the contents of the Blue Book cannot solely be regarded as the propaganda of a nation at war. Certainly, the timing of the report directly relates to the war. If the war had not taken place, the reports of the atrocities might not have been collected and chronicled in this way, but the war context per se does not reduce the veracity of its findings.

However as this book shows, there was acceptance even in Germany at the time that such conduct was occurring. There are many accounts at the time of the type of crimes that were occurring which support the findings of the Blue Book. As noted earlier in this chapter, there is much evidence about what was taking place. In addition, various newspapers in the Cape Colony, for example, published a number of eyewitness accounts of what was occurring. At the time some British humanitarians did protest, but 'the notorious campaign against the Hereros...did not arouse British opinion of the time'.[121] However, Kenneth Mackenzie has noted that there was a

> long, coherent and inflexible opposition to German methods. British and colonial officials and commentators well qualified to remark on German colonial activity did so in definite and generally uncomplimentary terms long before 1914. Overwhelming evidence of the widespread dislike and hostility of what occurred is contained not only in unpublished private papers, but also in a steady stream of articles and comments in the published journals and newspapers of the time.[122]

In 1905 O Eltzbacher did launch an especially virulent attack on Germany, saying that the Germans' 'ill-treatment of the South West Africa natives undoubtedly constitutes, not a private injury, but a public wrong [and] an

---

120 Quoted in Louis, W.M.R (1967) 'Great Britain and German expansion in Africa 1884–1919'. In Gifford, P. & Louis, W.M.R. (eds) *Britain and Germany in Africa: Imperial rivalry and colonial rule.* New Haven: Yale University, 3–46, 38.
121 Bargar, B.D. (1968) 'Review'. XL *Journal of Modern History*, 597.
122 Mackenzie, K. (1974, March) 'Some British reactions to German colonial methods 1885–1907'. 17(1) *The Historical Journal*, 165–75, 166.

offence against justice and humanity'.[123] Articles in various publications reflect the widespread criticism that was evoked by Germany's conduct towards the Herero.[124] On 9 May 1904, before the genocide order was specifically given, Colonial Director Stubel reported in the *Reichstag* that Chancellor von Bülow wrote to Governor Leutwein on 28 March 1904:

> Press reports of letters from the protectorate cause me to point out that steps are to be taken to prevent violations against humanity, against enemies incapable of fighting and against woman and children. Orders in the sense are to be issued.[125]

In the German Parliament the founders of the German Social Democrats, Wilhelm Liebknecht and August Bebel, accused the colonial troops of crimes against the locals in the colonies and the 'handful of Hottentots'[126] in their South West colony. Their objections contributed to the awareness of the German populace and people around the world about what was happening in the colonies.[127]

This book is the product of extensive research, including numerous interviews conducted by the author in Namibia, Botswana, Germany, South Africa and elsewhere.[128] The interviewees include members of the Herero, Damara and Nama communities in Namibia, South Africa and Botswana. In terms of published sources, the book also draws on various primary sources,

---

[123] Eltzbacher, O. (1905, October) 'The German danger to South Africa'. 58 *The nineteenth century and after.* 524–38, 538. Quoted in Mackenzie, K. (1974, March) 'Some British reactions to German colonial methods 1885–1907'. 17 (1) *The Historical Journal,* 165–75, 174.

[124] Mackenzie, K. (1974, March) 'Some British reactions to German colonial methods 1885–1907'. 17(1) *The Historical Journal,* 165–75, 173.

[125] Quoted in Hull, I.V. (2005) *Absolute destruction: Military culture and practices of war in Imperial Germany.* Ithaca: Cornell University Press, 17.

[126] Dedering, T. (1999) 'The prophet's "War against Whites": Shepherd Stuurman in Namibia and South Africa 1904–1907'. 40(1) *Journal of African History,* 1–19, 4.

[127] Babing, A. (2004, October) 'The role of the German Democratic Republic (GDR) in the international struggle against racism, apartheid and colonialism'. Paper presented at *A decade of freedom* Conference, Durban, South Africa, 10–13 October 2004.

[128] Further output of this research is contained in Sarkin, J. (2009) *Colonial Genocide and Reparations Claims in the 21st Century: The Socio-Legal Context of Claims under International Law by the Herero against Germany for Genocide in Namibia, 1904–1908.* Westport: Praeger Security International, as well as a number of journal articles.

translations of the originals and an extensive body of secondary materials and documents.[129]

The use of terminology requires some clarification: the country was called German South West Africa (GSWA) before South Africa took control of it. Then it was called South West Africa (SWA) until independence in 1990. On independence it became Namibia. The name Namibia derives from the desert on its western coastal plain — the Namib.[130] While the name Namibia was in use before the 1960s, it was only in 1968 that the United Nations accepted that name for the country.[131]

Namibia today recognises various ethnic groups: (Rehoboth) Baster, Caprivi, Coloured, Damara, Herero, Kavango, Nama, Owambo, San, Tswana and White.[132] The size of each group is approximately (indicated as a percentage of the total population): Owambo (50 percent), Kavango (10 percent), Damara (7,5 percent), Herero (7,5 percent), Whites (6,5 percent), Nama (5 percent), Coloured (4 percent), Caprivians (3,5 percent), San (3 percent), Rehoboth Basters (2,5 percent), Tswana (0,5 percent) and 'others' (1 percent). As the Owambo constitute half the population (with no other minority group exceeding 10 percent), they dominate the political landscape.

The word 'Herero' is a short form of Ovaherero which means 'people of yesterday'.[133] For the purposes of the book the term 'Herero' is used to denote all Otjiherero-speaking people.[134] A hundred years ago the Herero were a 'disjointed' political group 'laced together by a unique double-clan

---

[129] A useful publication is Wilcox, S.S. (2004) 'The South West Africa People's Organisation 1961–1991: A guide to archival resources and special collections in the Western Cape, South Africa'. 1 *Occasional e-publications series*. Cape Town: University of Cape Town.

[130] Different sources give different explanations of the meaning of 'Namib': some say it is a Nama word meaning 'vast', others explain that it is a Nama/Damara word meaning 'shield' or 'enclosure', as it protects the interior from access by sea and has shielded the indigenous people from colonial settlement until well into the 19th century.

[131] General Assembly Resolution 2372 (XXII) 12 June 1968. See Dale, R. (1976, October) 'Colonial rulers and ruled in South West Africa and the Bechuanaland Protectorate 1884–1966: A framework for comparative study'. 1 *Journal of Southern African Affairs*, 95–110, 95.

[132] Gretschel, H-V. (2001) 'Education in Namibia'. In Diener, I. & Graefe, O. (eds) *Contemporary Namibia: The first landmarks of a post-apartheid society*. Windhoek: Gamsberg MacMillan, 111–128, 111.

[133] Vedder, H. (1966) *South West Africa in early times*. New York: Barnes & Noble, 153.

[134] Gewald, J-B. (1999) *Herero heroes: A socio-political history of the Herero of Namibia 1890–1923*. Oxford: James Currey, 13.

socio-religious system'.[135] The divisions between the Herero were based on economic status as well as historical migration patterns and location within Hereroland. The largest and wealthiest Herero group, the Ovaherero (Herero), came from the Kaokoveld in the north and resided in western Hereroland. The poorest group, the Ovatjimba (Tjimba), remained in the Kaokoveld. The third group had entered the area from Botswana and resided in eastern Hereroland. They were known as the Ovambanderu (Mbanderu) or Eastern Hereros. In turn, each of the three groups consisted of clans (called Otjikutu) that saw each person being bound by about eight different ties of matrilineal descent and twenty separate ties of patrilineal descent. Matrilineal ties governed inheritance of property, while the patrilineal lines governed the religious aspects. These matrilineal clans of the Herero-Mbanderu formed a 'loose kind of confederation'.[136]

Today, the Herero community consists of different groupings: the Herero who live in the central region of the country and the east; the Mbanderu, also in the east; and the Himba and Tjimba in the north-west. In the past, areas were named after the ethnic group living there, but in 1992, the new democratic government of Namibia created new regions to delink the colonial association of ethnicity and area.[137] The Herero reserves of Aminuis, Epukiro, Eastern, Waterberg East, Otjohorongo and Ovitoto created by the German colonial authorities were later reconstituted into Hereroland East and Hereroland West.[138] Today Hereroland East forms part of the Omaheke region and Hereroland West is the Otjozondjupa region.[139] Owamboland's name also changed in 1992 and it was divided into four regions, namely Oshikoto, Ohangwena, Omusati and Oshana.

The most familiar symbol of Herero identity today is their clothing. At their functions the men wear turn-of-the-century German soldier uniforms and Herero women dress in their long brightly coloured Victorian dresses and a headdress that looks like cow horns. Green and black Victorian dresses are

---

[135] Ngavirue, Z. (1972) *Political parties and interest groups in South West Africa: A study of a plural society*. PhD thesis. Oxford University, 7.
[136] *Ibid*, 8–10.
[137] Pankhurst, D. (1995) 'Towards Reconciliation of the land issue in Namibia: Identifying the possible, assessing the probable'. 26 *Development and Change*, 551–585, 552 fn 1.
[138] Harring, S.L. (2002, Winter) 'German reparations to the Herero nation: An assertion of Herero nationhood in the path of Namibian development?'. 104 *West Virginia Law Review*, 393.
[139] Malan, J.S. (1995) *Peoples of Namibia*. Pretoria: Rhino Publishers, 67.

worn by the Ovambanderu, red and black by the Ovaherero women and white dresses by those from Objimbingwe.[140] Ruth First noted that Herero women

> *dominate their surroundings in Victorian dress of carefully studied fashion detail: sweeping, ankle-length skirts, with many underskirts, short bodiced waistcoat, mutton-chop sleeves, long strings of necklaces, braid, pearly buttons and draped shawls, all a faithful replica of the dress worn by the wives of the Rhenish missionaries in the nineteenth century; on their heads high padded turbans replace the three-pronged leather tribal head-dress of earlier days.*[141]

As far as the Nama are concerned, a century ago they consisted of eight tribes including the Rooinasie, or Red Nation, the Franzmanns (after the name of the chief), the Swartboois (after their chief), the Topnaars and the Bondelswartz.

The Damara at the turn of the twentieth century were similarly fragmented and resided in eleven regional groupings.[142]

---

[140] Hendrickson, H. (1994) 'The long dress and the construction of Herero identities in southern Africa'. 53 (2) *African Studies*, 25–54.
[141] First, R. (1967) *South West Africa*. Baltimore: Penguin Books, 27.
[142] Ngavirue, Z. (1972) *Political parties and interest groups in South West Africa: A study of a plural society*. PhD thesis. Oxford University, 13.

CHAPTER ONE

AETIOLOGY OF A GENOCIDE

Genocide 'is never a sudden or unplanned act... It is a deliberate, pre-meditated and carefully orchestrated orgy of mass murder for political purposes... a well organised campaign of carnage...'[1]

Introduction

The historiography of the events around the Herero genocide is subject to a great deal of controversy. The reasons why there was a war (or a rebellion) between the Herero and Germany in 1904 are extensively debated. Even the linguistics are not accepted without argument. Thus, Melber has termed the events between the Germans and the Herero the 'German-Namibian War'.[2] Acknowledging that the use of the word 'Namibia' only emerged in the 1960s, his preference is motivated by political reasons.[3] Neville Alexander has called it 'the first war of anti-colonial resistance'.[4] It was undeniably a resistance conflict, but given the size of the force that was eventually pitted against the Herero and the type of arms and methods used against them, one can hardly classify such a one-sided affair as a war. Other terms, such as 'massacre', 'slaughter' and 'annihilation' seem more apt, as would the term 'genocide'. Although the first few months of the conflict might fit the description of a war, thereafter the conflict involved a superior force hunting down its opponents and wiping them out by all means possible.

Another subject matter that remains unsettled is when the war or rebellion started and finished. According to Du Pisani the war occurred between 1902

---

[1] Johnson, S. (2003) *Peace without justice: Hegemonic instability or international criminal law*? London: Ashgate Publishing, 200.
[2] Melber, H. (1985) 'Namibia's the German roots of Apartheid'. 27 (1) *Race and Class*, 63–77, 73.
[3] See Sarkin, J. (2009) *Colonial Genocide and Reparations Claims in the 21st Century: The Socio-Legal Context of Claims under International Law by the Herero against Germany for Genocide in Namibia, 1904–1908*. Westport: Praeger Security International.
[4] Alexander, N. (1983) *The Namibian war of anti-colonial resistance 1904–1907*. Windhoek: Namibian Review Publications, fn 1.

and 1907. However, he groups the Nama[5] and Herero rebellions together.[6] Other tribes also rebelled, including the Bondelswartz in 1903.[7] In 1904, in addition to the rebellions by the Herero, Nama and Bondelswartz, the Franzmanns, the Red Nation and the Veldschoendragers also rebelled. The Bethanie chief initially refused to participate, but his tribe defied him and joined in. The Rehoboths, however, decided it was more advantageous for them to support the Germans.[8] Therefore, the Herero uprising or war, if seen without the involvement of others, began in 1904.

The end date of the war is also subject to debate. While some claim 1906, others state 1907, while others, such as Sole, claim that the war ended in 1908.[9] While some groups like the Bondelswartz ended their fight in 1906, other groups like the Franzmanns continued. From the German perspective in February 1907, the troop commander stated that he was not against the 'lifting of the state of war in South West Africa until the end of March'.[10] Thus, even though combat continued, the state of warfare was publicly rescinded on 31 March 1907. In fact, the battle waged by resistance leader Jakob Morenga continued until he was killed on 20 September 1907. Masson notes this date and the death of Jakob Morenga, arguing that this was 'to the Germans the final act in the suppression of the great Herero-Nama insurrection of 1904–7'.[11] It is argued by some that 1908 is the end of the war because it

---

[5] The rebellion of the Nama was recognised as an anti-colonial resistance movement. In this regard Tecklenburg, then deputy governor of GSWA, reported to the Colonial Department in January 1905 that '[t]he one and only reason for the rebellion is the desire to end German colonial rule'. Stoecker, H. (ed) (1986) *German imperialism in Africa: From the beginnings until the Second World War.* London: C Hurst & Co, 59. This continued resistance to German rule was provoked by their losses of land and cattle. Had the local population not been treated unfairly and had German rule not been as brutal, the rebellion might not have occurred.

[6] Du Pisani, A. (1986) *South West African/Namibia: The politics of continuity and change.* Johannesburg: Jonathan Ball, 23.

[7] The Mbanjeru was a Herero tribe, the Bondelswartz a Nama tribe. More about these tribes in the next chapter. However there are three different spellings of Bondelswartz that are used — Bondelswarts/Bondelzwarts/Bondelswartz. Bondelswartz seems to be the correct spelling and will be used throughout.

[8] Stoecker, H. (ed) (1986) *German imperialism in Africa: From the beginnings until the Second World War.* London: C Hurst & Co, 47–60.

[9] Sole, T.E. (1968, December) 'The Südwestafrika Denkmünze and the South West African campaigns of 1903–1908'. 1(3) *Military History Journal* 19–23.

[10] Stoecker, H. (ed) (1986) *German imperialism in Africa: From the beginnings until the Second World War.* London: C Hurst & Co, 61.

[11] Masson, J.R. (1995, June) 'A fragment of colonial history: The killing of Jakob Marengo'. 21 (2) *Journal of South African Studies,* 247–256, 255.

marked the last activity against resistance leader Simon Kooper[12] and the closure of the concentration camps.[13] On 22 December 1908, Deputy Governor Oskar Hintrager noted that there was a 'current state of constant insecurity'.[14] Simon Kooper only agreed to enter into a peace agreement brokered by the British Bechuanaland police in February 1909. Furthermore, there is even evidence of German patrols against the Herero in the Omaheke desert until 1911.[15] Germany's position today is reflected in the 2005 announcement, in which Germany agreed to give Namibia €25 million for development and reconciliation 'in order to heal the wounds left by the brutal colonial wars of 1904 to 1908'.[16]

On the question as to whether it was a rebellion or war, one view is that the Herero rose up in revolt in January 1904. Gewald identifies the specific trigger for the events of 12 January 1904, onwards as a misunderstanding by German Lieutenant Zürn, who panicked and so started the war. Thus, it has been argued that the conflict was the result of misunderstandings prompted by the panic of a colonial official and 'the self-fulfilling prophecy of Herero war that existed within the mind of settler paranoia'.[17] According to this view, the Herero did not initiate the war, but took up arms in response to actions taken against them. Melber concurs that the 'uprising' was an act of self-defence.[18] Lundtofte has stated that 'it may be advanced

[12] Various texts give different spellings of his name as Kooper, Kopper, Koper.
[13] Gewald, J-B. (1999) *Herero heroes: A socio-political history of the Herero of Namibia 1890–1923*. Oxford: James Currey, 141. See also Gewald, J-B. & Silvester, J. (2003) *Words cannot be found. German colonial rule in Namibia: An annotated reprint of the 1918 Blue Book*. Leiden: Brill, 162 fn 146.
[14] Stoecker, H. (ed) (1986) *German imperialism in Africa: From the beginnings until the Second World War*. London: C Hurst & Co, 140–1.
[15] Gewald, J-B. (1999) *Herero heroes: A socio-political history of the Herero of Namibia 1890–1923*. Oxford: James Currey, 141 fn 1.
[16] Hintze, H (2005) 'Germany To Pay N$160 Million For Reconciliation' *The Namibian* Friday, 27 May 2005. On the plaque at the memorial outside the *Alte Feste* in Windhoek to fallen Germans during the warfare casualties are listed for the period 1903–1908. The deaths of 100 officers, 254 non-commissioned officers and 1 180 other ranks from the Schutztruppe are listed as well as seven officers, 13 non-commissioned officers and 72 sailors from the German navy. In addition, the memorial contains the civilian deaths that occurred at the time — 119 men, four women and one child. Thus, the period 1903 to 1908 is recognised although again this is for all events against all groups.
[17] Gewald, J-B. (1999) *Herero heroes: A socio-political history of the Herero of Namibia 1890–1923*. Oxford: James Currey, 141.
[18] Melber, H. (1985) 'Namibia: The German roots of Apartheid'. 27 (1) *Race and Class*, 63–77, 73.

that it was not the Herero, but the Germans themselves who conjured up the conflict'.[19] It has been further argued that the Germans not only instigated the 'war' without provocation or cause, but also prolonged it after the conflict had essentially spent itself.[20] The uprising was concluded by April 1904, but negotiations between the parties were barred because Von Trotha and German troop reinforcements had yet to arrive. In effect, the war restarted after Von Trotha arrived in June 1904. If these views have any validity, then the indigenous population did not rise up or capriciously prolong the war.

Schutztruppe marching from Windhoek Railway Station

19 Lundtofte, H. (2003) 'Radicalization of the German suppression of the Herero rizing in 1904'. In Jensen, S.L.B. (ed) *Genocide: Cases, comparisons and contemporary debates*. Copenhagen: Danish Center for Holocaust and Genocide Studies, 27.
20 Gewald, J-B. (1999) *Herero heroes: A socio-political history of the Herero of Namibia 1890–1923*. Oxford: James Currey.

Herero Chief Kambahahiza Nikodemus Kavikunua being executed on 11 June 1896 for treason for his role in an uprising

Regardless, it must be remembered that this revolt, uprising or war was not without provocation and certainly not an isolated event.[21] Throughout the German colonies, there existed a pattern of forcing local communities into intolerable conditions, which inevitably led to the rebellion of these communities against the colonial masters. Generally, in the late nineteenth and early twentieth centuries, Africans did not simply accept the yoke of colonialism and many fervently resisted the occupation of their countries. As Lundtofte has observed, '[t]he European hunger for power and attempt to

---

21 See further Sarkin, J. (2009) *Colonial Genocide and Reparations Claims in the 21st Century: The Socio-Legal Context of Claims under International Law by the Herero against Germany for Genocide in Namibia, 1904–1908.* Westport: Praeger Security International.

exploit resources in Africa in the 1890s assumed various forms but in most cases provoked Africans to rise in rebellion. Examples of atrocities committed by Europeans in their attempts to pacify these rebellions are innumerable.'[22] However, while the Germans attempted to put all rebellions down, often with extreme force, they treated the Herero differently. In their case, genocide took place, which had not and would not occur elsewhere in the German colonies. Why did the Germans treat the Herero so much more harshly, almost wiping them out completely? This chapter addresses the question through an examination of what happened.

While the Herero uprising in 1904 supposedly took the Germans by complete surprise,[23] they should have expected it. This was not the first time an indigenous group in a German territory had rebelled; in fact, it was a regular occurrence in most of them. Neither was it the first time that a group within GSWA had rebelled.

The Bondelswartz (Nama) rioted only a few months before the Herero uprising in January 1904. Given the enormous tensions between the colonists and the Herero, who had lost land and cattle to the settlers, Germany should have anticipated the rebellion. Already in the 1890s the settlers believed that war was 'imminent'.[24] In addition, the German authorities had ample warnings that their conduct was generating conflict. Interestingly, Governor Leutwein knew that in 1902 and 1903 the Herero were buying rifles and ammunition from the Portuguese[25] and the Cape of Good Hope, even though an 1897 ordinance forbade them to acquire guns (this ordinance caused much resentment).[26]

In 1903, rumours abounded about a looming uprising, to the extent that some settlers prodded their servants to reveal the details of the plan.[27]

---

[22] Lundtofte, H. (2003) 'Radicalization of the German suppression of the Herero rising in 1904'. In Jensen, S.L.B. (ed) *Genocide: Cases, comparisons and contemporary debates*. Copenhagen: Danish Center for Holocaust and Genocide Studies, 15, 15. Lundtofte does go on to differentiate the Herero and other cases by noting that '[i]n most cases the military aims of the colonial powers were directed not to exterminating rebellious native populations but towards imposing total defeat and thereby submission. Thus the suppression of these risings cannot be termed genocide...'

[23] Hellberg, C-J. (1997) *Mission, colonialism and liberation: The Lutheran Church in Namibia 1840–1966*. Windhoek: New Namibia Books, 109.

[24] Gewald J-B. (1999) *Herero heroes: A socio-political history of the Herero of Namibia 1890–1923*. Oxford: James Currey, 106.

[25] Wallenkampf, A.V. (1969) *The Herero rebellion in South West Africa: A study in German colonialism*. PhD thesis. Los Angeles: UCLA, 60.

[26] Ibid, 49.

[27] Gewald, J-B. (1999) *Herero heroes: A socio-political history of the Herero of Namibia 1890–1923*. Oxford: James Currey, 148.

In August 1903, Leutwein reported that a rebellion was imminent and, in a report dated 21 August 1903, noted that it was a danger 'the Schutztruppe was not strong enough to combat'.[28] Furthermore, many armed Herero had gathered at Okahandja in 1903,[29] making it evident that something was in the works. Gewald reports that by January 1904 'German officers and settlers showered one another with rumours and reports on the envisaged Herero insurrection'.[30] Kerina notes that on 5 January 1904, the local German-language newspaper reported: 'Further mobilisation seems to have become necessary. Last night about 200–300 armed Herero moved in a suspicious way in Okakhandja. There are about 300 armed Herero is [sic] Osona. All captains have left their posts. During the past week one noticed certain goings-on, secret meetings, etc., among the captains and others.'[31] The Germans had obviously not taken the signs seriously or, if they had, they had not taken sufficient steps to guard against the possibility of a revolt. Thus, when the uprising broke out there were only 770 soldiers[32] in GSWA,[33] of whom 280 were on police duty.

The war was predictable not only because the Herero were clearly disgruntled and indigenous uprisings were commonplace.[34] Precisely because warfare continued throughout the years of German occupation, the Germans became increasingly despondent that their existing strategies failed to maintain peace, while the settlers became more dissatisfied and demanding. In 1896, Governor Leutwein told Berlin that keeping the peace in GSWA would be unlikely.[35]

[28] Ritter-Petersen, H.G. (1991) *The Herrenvolk mentality in German South West Africa 1884–1914*. DLitt (History). Pretoria: University of South Africa, 170–71.

[29] Hellberg, C-J. (1997) *Mission, colonialism and liberation: The Lutheran Church in Namibia 1840–1966*. Windhoek: New Namibia Books, 109.

[30] Gewald, J-B. (1999) *Herero heroes: A socio-political history of the Herero of Namibia 1890–1923*. Oxford: James Currey, 144.

[31] Kerina, M. (1981) *Namibia: the making of a nation*. New York: Books in Focus, 16.

[32] Hellberg, C-J. (1997) *Mission, colonialism and liberation: The Lutheran Church in Namibia 1840–1966*. Windhoek: New Namibia Books, 110.

[33] Lewin notes that in 1903 there were 34 officers and 785 soldiers in GSWA. Lewin, E. (1915) *The Germans and Africa. Their aims on the dark continent and how they acquired their African colonies*. London: Cassell, 115.

[34] See further Sarkin, J. (2009) *Colonial Genocide and Reparations Claims in the 21st Century: The Socio-Legal Context of Claims under International Law by the Herero against Germany for Genocide in Namibia, 1904–1908*. Westport: Praeger Security International.

[35] Gewald J-B. (1999) *Herero heroes: A socio-political history of the Herero of Namibia 1890–1923*. Oxford: James Currey, 102.

Governor Leutwein with Herero leadership

Settler complaints were innumerable regarding the bad treatment the German colonial rule afforded them. John J Cleverly, a British magistrate, noted in 1890 that 'Europeans complain that they get no redress from the German officials against the natives, no matter what insult or injury they may suffer and that the law for the protection of the white people does not exist'.[36] From as early as the 1896 war with the Eastern Herero, the settlers attacked Governor Leutwein's lenient policies. Leutwein used a policy of diplomacy throughout his 11 years as governor.

He avoided the use of military means unless he thought it absolute necessary and even then he did not use it to subjugate or to achieve control. Leutwein did not want to follow the wishes of the settlers because he doubted that he would be able to defeat the Herero militarily; neither did he want to transgress the various protection treaties that had been entered into by Germany. This

---

[36] In correspondence between Sir H Loch to Lord Knutsford, 24 September 1890, cited in Voeltz, R.A. (1988) 'German colonialism and the South West Africa Company, 1894–1914'. 50 *Monographs in International Studies. Africa Series.* Athens OH: Ohio University Center for International Studies, 7.

he admitted directly.[37] The settlers wanted the complete subjugation of the Herero, including military action against them, but Leutwein refused. He wanted the Herero to gradually adjust to the new structure and systems.[38] Goldblatt succinctly describes the difference between Governor Leutwein and General von Trotha, who was

> a man who believed that the bowl containing the fish should be smashed by heavy hammer blows, rather than by the quiet withdrawal of the water, which was Leutwein's policy.[39]

Of course, Leutwein did not adopt a completely benevolent attitude towards the indigenous people. While the general perception was that Leutwein was favourably inclined toward the local population, his favour simply consisted of different methods and a longer time frame to achieve the same end; that is, a German colony where Africans would *eventually* be subjugated. There were times when Leutwein acted harshly. In fact, Leutwein was initially sent to GSWA in 1894 to end a war raging there. An example of his cruel conduct is evident in the Bondelswartz rebellion, which occurred in October 1903. Leutwein issued a ruthless decree that read:

> *Decree of the Imperial Governor*
> The peace which ruled this land has been broken in an outrageous manner by the Captain of the Bondelswarts in Warmbad and his tribe, through the wicked murder of the District Chief, Lieutenant Jobst, Sergeant Snay, as well as the murder and wounding of more settlers. In this District a condition of war is therefore declared. The laws of war are brought into force…A reward of 500 marks will be granted for the head of each Bondelswart who partook in the murder of my people. A 2000 mark reward is assured for anyone who brings in the head of the new chief.[40]

An expert on the territory in the Colonial Section of the Foreign Office objected to the callousness of the decree and to the use of terms such as 'wicked murder' as well as the placing of bounties.[41] While Leutwein received support for these measures from the settlers, they demanded even sterner measures. One settler group wrote to the government in Berlin on 1 November 1903 and demanded

---

[37] Ritter-Petersen, H.G. (1991) *The Herrenvolk mentality in German South West Africa 1884–1914*. DLitt (History). Pretoria: University of South Africa, 157.
[38] *Ibid*, 156 citing Governor Leutwein's book, *Elf Jahre Gouverneur in Deutsch-Südwestafrika*. Berlin: Mittler, 242, 542, 546.
[39] Goldblatt, I. (1971) *History of South West Africa, from the beginning of the nineteenth century*. Cape Town: Juta & Co, 131.
[40] Schrank, G.I. (1974) *German South West Africa: Social and economic aspects of its history, 1884–1915*. PhD (History). New York University, 143.
[41] *Ibid*, 143–4.

the total extermination of the Bondelswartz and the use of the troops without restriction. The settlers complained that

> the natives are valued above all else by the Governeur and by the Bezirkshauptmann. These cannot do enough in keeping distinctions on the native riffraff. Hendrik Witboy [sic] and his staff, Samuel Maherero, Kajata (a special favourite) are invited and showered lavishly with gifts...[42]

Even before 1903 the settlers' views were endorsed by the military in Germany. The highest military body, the *Grosser Generalstab*, noted: 'He who wishes to colonize the territory must first take the sword and wage war — not with limited and puny means, but with strong measures which command respect and must persevere until the total subjugation of the natives has been accomplished.'[43] As a result of Leutwein's perceived leniency, the settlers held 'stormy meetings' and demanded his replacement.[44] In 1902, the *Deutsche Kolonialgesellschaft*, a publication from Germany thought to represent the voice of the settlers, noted:

> There is certainly no other government in Africa or in the whole world, which spoils the natives more than ours does. Even the English...who have already done enough damage with their eternal slogan 'never shall they be slaves', treat the natives more harshly. The government, ie Leutwein, has an attitude towards the natives similar to that of a Rhenish missionary. It is the professional duty of the missionaries or so they believe, to protect the native from being taken advantage of by the white race and they therefore act in the interests of their black and brown wards. A colonial government which only marginally realizes what it is there for...must have the aim to expropriate the natives of part of their land in order to create farm land for farmers: it must also curtail the freedom of the natives to a large extent in order to ensure sufficient native labour, without which the white farmer and settler will be lost.[45]

The Herero were so concerned about these strident criticisms of the Governor's 'leniency' that Samuel Maherero[46] sent five Herero dignitaries, including his son Fredrich, to Berlin in 1896 to attend the colonial exhibition and to meet with the Kaiser and indicate their support for Germany and the

---

42 Quoted in Ritter-Petersen, H.G. (1991) *The Herrenvolk mentality in German South West Africa 1884–1914*. DLitt (History). Pretoria: University of South Africa, 154.
43 *Ibid*, 155.
44 Gewald J-B. (1999) *Herero heroes: A socio-political history of the Herero of Namibia 1890–1923*. Oxford: James Currey, 106.
45 Quoted in Ritter-Petersen, H.G. (1991) *The Herrenvolk mentality in German South West Africa 1884–1914*. DLitt (History). Pretoria: University of South Africa, 156–57.
46 The Herero had a number of chiefs including Kambazembi, Muretti, Tjetjoo and Zacharias. Some argue that Maherero was the supreme leader, although many dispute this.

Governor.[47] As early as 1896, the Herero were anxious about which reports reached the Kaiser and the consequences these would have for them. At that time, the Herero did not think of Governor Leutwein as particularly sympathetic towards them, although this changed some years later.

In 1903, the settlers' attitude towards the Governor and the GSWA authorities hardened when Leutwein issued a proclamation prohibiting debts repaid with tribal or communal land.[48] The settlers interpreted this as a strategy to protect the Herero and a blow to them, as they had previously benefited from Herero indebtedness brought about by natural disasters and a system of credit. Some attributed the settlers' ill-treatment of the African population to Leutwein's lenient policies. The chief civil servant in the Foreign Office responsible for GSWA wrote on Leutwein's report of 21 August 1903: 'According to reliable communications which I have received it appears that the natives are handled somewhat with kid-gloves. The whites are outraged by this and take the law into their own hands.'[49]

Already by November 1903, following the Bondelswartz uprising, the settlers blamed Leutwein and demanded his replacement by a general from the General Staff. They expected the military to solve the problem, which according to them Leutwein had created. The *Allgemeine Zeitung* published an article to this effect on 12 November 1903.[50] The settlers were hoping to gain control over the entire territory using military force. However, beyond complaining, which they did incessantly and ubiquitously, there was little they could do. As Leutwein was both Governor and commander of the military forces in GSWA, he controlled both the civilian and military decisions there. He did not answer to the military or the Kaiser. Leutwein ignored the settlers' 'indignant yelps and ensured their undying opposition when his actions effectively cut them off from cheap land and their envisaged dream of living as a colonial landed gentry'.[51] As a result, in 1902 and 1903, the authorities in Germany and the Kaiser were constantly bombarded with the settlers' complaints. One settler group wrote to the Berlin government demanding the extermination of the Bondelswartz and the use of the troops without limitation. Paul Leutwein, the son of the Governor, noted that on 31 December 1903, less than two weeks before the supposed uprising, the settlers held a

[47] Zimmerman, A. (2001) *Anthropology and antihumanism in imperial Germany.* Chicago: University of Chicago Press, 244–45.
[48] Ritter-Petersen, H.G. (1991) *The Herrenvolk mentality in German South West Africa 1884–1914.* DLitt (History). Pretoria: University of South Africa, 159.
[49] *Ibid*, 171.
[50] *Ibid*, 190.
[51] Gewald J-B. (1999) *Herero heroes: A socio-political history of the Herero of Namibia 1890–1923.* Oxford: James Currey, 144.

meeting where, in his words, 'in a fiery speech one of the oldest Afrikaners, the Hauptmann v. Francois, called for a general *razzia* against the Herero'.[52]

Given this scenario, the pressure from the white settler community and the pro-settlement lobby in Berlin undeniably contributed to the Herero war.[53] At the time, many calls for the extermination of the Herero were made both in GSWA and Germany; in meetings, in various journals, books and newspapers. One newspaper called for the deportation of all Herero to Samoa, another called for 2 000 Herero to be sent to German East Africa.[54] The *Deutsche Südwestafrikanische Zeitung* of Luderitz wrote in 1904: 'The country must be inhabited by white colonists. Therefore, *the natives must disappear* or rather put themselves at the disposal of the whites.'[55] Just two days after the Herero purportedly rose up, the German Colonial League's Executive Committee in Berlin issued a pamphlet noting that the 'swifter and harsher the reprisals taken against rebels, the better the chances of restoring authority.'[56]

The extent to which the settlers sought the blood of the Herero and retribution was evidenced in the public execution of rebels in Windhoek, which were 'carried out slowly to satisfy the Germans thirst for revenge' and to the glee of settler onlookers who were 'extremely delighted'.[57]

Despite the pressure of the settlers to deal harshly with the Herero and the demands for Leutwein's replacement, the Herero neither conceded to German claims of supremacy, nor were they prepared to accept a second-class or servant role.[58] Consequently, the settlers became more disgruntled, if not downright furious, about Leutwein's approach, which, in their eyes, granted security and freedom to the African population. In March 1904, Missionary August Elger remarked on Leutwein's relationship with the Herero: 'The Governor is very popular with the Herero and the other Natives, he feels sympathetic towards

---

52 *Ibid*, 145.
53 Schmokel, W.W. (1985) 'The myth of the white farmer: Commercial agriculture in Namibia 1900–1983'. 18 (1) *International Journal of African Historical Studies* 93–108, 96.
54 Schrank, G.I. (1974) *German South West Africa: Social and economic aspects of its history, 1884–1915*. PhD (History). New York University, 150.
55 Middleton, L. (1936) *The Rape of Africa*. New York: Harrison Smith and Roman Haas, 276–7.
56 Drechsler, H. (1966) *Let us die fighting: The struggle of the Herero and Nama against the German imperialism (1894–1915)* (Bernd Zöllner, transl). London: Zed Press, 142.
57 Oermann, N.O. (1999) *Mission, church and state relations in South West Africa under German rule (1884–1915)*. Stuttgart: Franz Steiner Verlag, 104.
58 Ritter-Petersen, H.G. (1991) *The Herrenvolk mentality in German South West Africa 1884–1914*. DLitt (History). Pretoria: University of South Africa, 139.

them and is just towards them.'⁵⁹ Leutwein's contention that 'colonial policy should not be conducted in the manner of a Tartar Khan, with blood and iron, but with understanding for the historic customs of local inhabitants' was incomprehensible to the settlers.⁶⁰ They 'demanded from Leutwein that he should use not only persuasion in dealing with the African tribes, but that he should implement a policy that would truly make the settlers the masters over the Africans'.⁶¹

Postcard of Chief Samuel Maherero

Undoubtedly, Berlin was aware of the economic rivalries between the settlers and the local communities for land and livestock. Due to the territory's sparse population, Leutwein did not regard the settlers' urgent drive to improve their economic position as an immediate or acute threat to the local communities. When he did step forward to protect the local communities against the settlers' efforts to take more land and livestock it caused even more resentment and they sent petitions to Berlin, calling for a tougher stance against the Herero.

59 Ibid, 149.
60 Ibid, 156.
61 Ibid, 44.

In a memorandum to the authorities in Germany, in which the settlers demanded compensation for the losses accrued during the war, they argued that Governor Leutwein was responsible for the 'rebellion'. They claimed that assistance given to Samuel Maherero contributed to the inevitability of the insurrection.

In reality, the settlers simply wanted more land quickly and cheaply and therefore searched for ways to force the Herero off their land.

Thus, access to prime agricultural land was the critical determinant in the genocide, assisted to a lesser extent by demands for other riches. It was no coincidence that a German company, founded in 1903, obtained a concession to look for diamonds.[62] There was clearly the belief that diamonds existed on the land, although the first discoveries were only made in 1907–08.

The evidence above shows that, although Berlin most likely made the ultimate decision, the settlers clearly bore some responsibility for the eventual issuing of an extermination order.[63] Their complaints, demands and petitions pressurised Berlin, most likely directly shaping the type of action Berlin found ultimately necessary in response to the rebellion. Their complaints also likely forced Berlin to reconsider Leutwein's suitability for his post.

By 1904, many had lost patience with Leutwein's 'lenient' policies and attempts to bring peace and stability to GSWA. The uprising was probably the last straw. The deaths of German citizens and the inability of the German troops to put down the 'rebellion' in the first few months were an embarrassment to Germany. This prompted the Kaiser to change course radically and use force, rather than persuasion, to deal with the local population. Accordingly, the fist was brought to bear and General von Trotha, who had a history of ruthlessly dealing with uprisings, was sent to GSWA to deal with the problem.

It is important to note that the Kaiser took a major interest in GSWA and played a critical role long before 1904. (Chapter three will review his dominant role in the genocide.) He supported the demands and endeavours of the settlers but had little room to manoeuvre. In March 1903, a correspondence between Leutwein and Maherero was leaked to the press and Gewald notes that 'in the jingoistic attitude that had developed, the settlers found themselves supported by none other than the Kaiser himself'.[64] The Kaiser wrote a note

---

[62] Calvert, A.F. (1969) *South-West Africa during the German occupation 1884–1914*. New York: Negro University Press, 67.

[63] The contribution of the settler community to the uprising and the way the war was conducted still require further research.

[64] Gewald J-B. (1999) *Herero heroes: A socio-political history of the Herero of Namibia 1890–1923*. Oxford: James Currey, 168.

directly, on a report that he received from Chancellor Bulow in 1903, that the general staff of the army ought to be given the right and freedom to conduct operations without being hampered by considerations of the foreign office or the Chancellor.[65] Only after the war broke out in 1904 could Leutwein be relieved of his command, because during wartime the responsibility for the territory fell under the Kaiser and the military.[66] Ultimately, the settler and military stance prevailed, sanctioned by Berlin and the Kaiser.

The Germans' violent action and killings directed at the Herero began months before General von Trotha's arrival and seemed to be the policy of the German government. Even before Von Trotha arrived, a policy of killing all Herero men was apparently in place. At some point, this policy changed to include women and children. Hence, killing the Herero indiscriminately was not the action of a sole rogue general or simply the military culture of the time.[67] Were it the military culture, then genocide would have been perpetrated in all German colonies. Despite the prevalence of violent conduct in many colonies and other occasions of mass murders, only GSWA was subjected to intentional genocide. The policy, if not specifically directed by the authorities, was tolerated by the military, the government and the *Reichstag*.

This chapter evaluates the reasons why the Germans used genocide to quell the Herero rebellion. It shows that the Herero uprising stemmed from a reaction to what was happening in the territory and was common to resistance movements elsewhere where the colonialists attempted to expel natural habitants from their land. In these instances the colonial response, while often similarly ruthless, was *not* primarily aimed at clearing land for settler inhabitation and did *not* evidence the intent to eradicate entire groups.

This chapter explores the motives of the perpetrators, particularly their desire to establish a 'new Germany' in the most attractive of its colonies. It

---

65 Schrank, G.I. (1974) *German South West Africa: Social and economic aspects of its history, 1884–1915*. PhD (History). New York University, 144.
66 See further Sarkin, J. (2009) *Colonial Genocide and Reparations Claims in the 21st Century: The Socio-Legal Context of Claims under International Law by the Herero against Germany for Genocide in Namibia, 1904–1908*. Westport: Praeger Security International.
67 Pfister notes that 'imperialism and militarism permeated everyday life in Germany, reflected in boys' war games and girls' sailor dresses and in every boy's dream of becoming an officer and every girl's dream of marrying one'. Pfister, G. (2005) 'Sport, colonialism and the enactment of German identity — *Turnen* in South West Africa', 4. Paper delivered at the 20th International Congress for the Historical Sciences 3–9 July 2005, Sydney Australia. Available at: www.cishsydney2005.org/images/GertrundPfisterST25.doc
   While true generally, it is also true that there were others on the left that did not subscribe to this culture.

examines the extent to which Germany adopted various strategies to attract more settlers to the territory, to make it more peaceful and give or sell land cheaply to these would-be pioneers.

The importance of GSWA to Germany

Any analysis of genocidal conduct has to take careful account of the context.[68] As with any crime, the motive is important. Melson explains that, to understand the importance of these issues from a criminal point of view, one must examine the intentions of those who did the killing and the structural conditions within which the killings occurred.[69] In this case, a motivation for genocide would assist in explaining the intent of the perpetrators and determining whether the events indeed constituted genocide.

The Herero-German war occurred because the Herero, for a number of reasons, rose up to stop the dispossession of their land. Equally, the German response, genocide, occurred for a number of reasons, the most important of which was the desire to gain more land for their settlers. Land was thus a prime factor in the uprising, but also the principal reason why the rebellion had to be quelled through genocide.

Creating a 'new Germany' in Africa

During Germany's colonial era, the country wished to create a 'new Germany' in one of their colonies, where emigrating settlers could establish new homes and Germany would have the space to expand.[70] At the end of the nineteenth century, the German population was increasing rapidly. Between 1890 and 1913 it grew from 49 million to 65 million, despite emigration.[71] Furthermore, between 1881 and 1890, emigration averaged 145 000 persons per year. In

---

[68] See further Sarkin, J. (2009) *Colonial Genocide and Reparations Claims in the 21st Century: The Socio-Legal Context of Claims under International Law by the Herero against Germany for Genocide in Namibia, 1904–1908*. Westport: Praeger Security International.

[69] Melson, R. (1992) *Revolution and genocide: On the origins of the Armenian genocide and the Holocaust*. Chicago: University of Chicago Press, 37.

[70] See further Sarkin, J. (2009) *Colonial Genocide and Reparations Claims in the 21st Century: The Socio-Legal Context of Claims under International Law by the Herero against Germany for Genocide in Namibia, 1904–1908*. Westport: Praeger Security International.

[71] Kennedy, P. (1982) 'The Kaiser and German *Weltpolitik*: Reflections on Wilhelm II's place in the making of German foreign policy'. In Röhl, J.C.G. & Sombart, N. (eds) *Kaiser Wilhelm II, new interpretations: The Corfu papers*. Cambridge/New York: Cambridge University Press, 143–168, 144.

1882, it reached 250 000.[72] It has been estimated that in the century before World War I, six million Germans emigrated from their homeland.[73] Between 1887 and 1907 over a million Germans left Germany, mainly for the USA. Although the emigration numbers began to fall after 1900,[74] it is estimated that the year 1903 alone saw 25 million Germans settling in the USA.[75] Berlin fervently sought ways of redirecting this outflow. They wanted Germans to stay within the home territories and, since GSWA was regarded as one of its most attractive colonies, the German government considered it a prime destination for emigrants.[76] A 'new Germany' would hopefully address both the rapid population growth and the problem of emigration. Despite Germany's eagerness, few were interested in settling in GSWA.[77] They were reluctant to move to an unstable region with little infrastructure. Consequently, Germany actively had to find ways to make this prospect more appealing.

One of the driving factors behind German colonialism was the notion that it provided a 'safety valve for the state'; alternative markets that could absorb overproduction would limit the possibility of revolution.[78] Therefore, economics and the need for new markets were strategic reasons to acquire colonies; the plan for a new German settlement was an ever-stronger rationale. The colonies provided a venue and the opportunity 'to save the worthy aspects of the old system'.[79] Walther notes that a second Germany would serve as a place 'away from the anxieties and dislocations resulting from industrialization and the dissatisfaction over the "incompleteness" of German unification'.[80] Furthermore, the notion of a new *Heimat*, a second Germany and the economic benefits of German settlement in the colonies complemented each other.[81] Thus, from early on the idea of settlement motivated Germany to join the

---

72 Lewin, E. (1915) *The Germans and Africa. Their aims on the Dark Continent and how they acquired their African colonies.* London: Cassell, 45.
73 Haarhoff, D. (1991) *The wild South-West: Frontier myths and metaphors in literature set in Namibia, 1760–1988.* Johannesburg: Witwatersrand University Press, 64.
74 Hendersen, W.O. (1938, November) 'Germany's trade with her colonies, 1884–1914'. 9 (1) *Economic History Review*, 1–19, 2.
75 Lewin, E. (1915) *The Germans and Africa. Their aims on the Dark Continent and how they acquired their African Colonies.* London: Cassell, 46.
76 *Ibid*, 1, 37.
77 Haarhoff, D. (1991) *The wild South-West: Frontier myths and metaphors in literature set in Namibia, 1760–1988.* Johannesburg: Witwatersrand University Press, 66.
78 Stoecker, H. (ed) (1986) *German imperialism in Africa: From the beginnings until the Second World War.* London: C Hurst & Co, 22.
79 Walther, D.J. (2002) *Creating Germans abroad: Cultural policies and national indemnity in Namibia.* Athens, Ohio: Ohio University Press, 10.
80 *Ibid*, 12.
81 Stoecker, H. (ed) (1986) *German imperialism in Africa: From the beginnings until the Second World War.* London: C Hurst & Co, 22.

race for the colonies. By April 1890 a Colonial Office had been established in Germany to pursue this goal.

This alone does not mean that there was a specific intent to start a war against the Herero, but it is plausible that over the course of the war German leaders saw the 'rebellion' as a welcome opportunity to create a 'clean slate'.

GSWA as an attractive place for settlement

Germany developed two distinctive models for its colonies: one model centred around trade, while the other centred on settlement.[82] The model in GSWA was the latter. In general, Germany focused more intently on its rule in GSWA than on its other colonies. However, Gann and Duigan point out that, before 1904, Germany saw East Africa as its prized possession.[83] At that time, GSWA was thought to be a very harsh environment with meagre economic prospects. This perception gradually changed and eventually GSWA became the more appealing and suitable for settlement of the colonies.[84] Eventually, more Germans settled in GSWA[85] than in any other German colony in Africa. According to Gann and Duigan the 'Germans were determined to turn the country into a white man's country',[86] mainly because of its good climate for Europeans[87] and minimal disease.[88] (Of course, the settlers did not manage to escape disease; apparently more Germans were killed by disease during the war than by the Herero.[89]) Even as early as 1882, Adolf Lüderitz, a Bremen merchant, commented on GSWA as a place where settlers could find a permanent home.[90] In 1879, the *Berlin Geographische Nachrichten* published

---

82 Gann, L.H. & Duigan, P. (1977) *The rulers of German Africa 1884–1914*. Stanford: Stanford University Press, 149.
83 *Ibid*, 173.
84 Balfour, M. (1964) *The Kaiser and his times*. Boston: Houghton Mifflin, 55. See also Hendersen, W.O. (1938, November) 'Germany's trade with her colonies, 1884–1914'. 9 (1) *Economic History Review*, 1–19, 2.
85 Palmer, A. (2000) *Colonial genocide*. Adelaide: Crawford House.
86 Gann, L.H. & Duigan, P. (1977) *The rulers of German Africa 1884–1914*. Stanford: Stanford University Press, 122.
87 *Ibid*.
88 Diebold, E., Engelhardt, S. & Iskenius, D. (2004, December) 'Facing the past to liberate the future: Colonial Africa in the German mind'. 6 *Humanity in Action. Reports of the 2004 Fellows in Denmark, Germany and the Netherlands*. New York, 53–57, 53. See Gründer, H. (2004) *Geschichte der deutschen Kolonien*. Paderborn: Ferdinand Schöningh Verlag.
89 See Madley, B. (2004, June) 'Patterns of frontier genocide 1803–1910: The aboriginal Tasmanians, the Yuki of California and the Herero of Namibia'. 6 (2) *Journal of Genocide Research*, 167–192, 186.
90 Wallenkampf, A.V. (1969) *The Herero rebellion in South West Africa: A study in German colonialism*. PhD thesis. Los Angeles: UCLA, 183.

an article by Ernst von Weber, calling for a German colony in South West Africa.[91] Reports commissioned by the Imperial Government confirmed that it was an ideal place for settlers.[92]

In the mid-1880s Germany undertook investigations into the potential of GSWA as a place for settlement. In 1886, *Reichskommissar* Heinrich Ernst Göring explored the possibilities for agriculture. He wrote a very positive and optimistic report, considered one of the most influential, recommending that dams be built to assist such endeavours. In his report, Göring extolled the virtues of Hereroland over other parts of GSWA. Critically, Kienetz notes that he somewhat exaggerated the agricultural potential of the area and especially that of Hereroland.[93]

In 1887, the Colonial Society also investigated the possibility of agricultural settlement. Their report was positive as well, citing that the climate was healthy for Europeans and would 'allow a European to do strenuous work, even if it would seldom be necessary to work as hard as in Europe'.[94] The *Reichstag* supported this, stating in 1893 that the territory was of great value for settlement purposes.[95]

The overriding distinction between GSWA and Germany's other colonies was that the German Government viewed the former as the ideal site for creating a new United German Nation because of its favourable conditions and climate. As the territory became more attractive, the number of settlers increased, as did the need for land.[96]

So important was the land issue that the German South West Africa Company was formed on 30 April 1885,[97] about two months after the Berlin Conference had ended. Already at that time Germany's goals were 'land for settlement, cattle for export, gold and diamonds for mining and Africans to work for long hours for little or no money'.[98] Hence, the phase of industrial

---

[91] Eveleigh, W. (1915) *South-West Africa*. Cape Town: Maskew Miller, 117.
[92] Walther, D.J. (2002) *Creating Germans abroad: Cultural policies and national indemnity in Namibia*. Athens, Ohio: Ohio University Press, 2.
[93] Kienetz, A. (1975, December) *Nineteenth-century South West Africa as a German settlement colony*. PhD thesis. University of Minnesota, 431.
[94] Ritter-Petersen, H.G. (1991) *The Herrenvolk mentality in German South West Africa 1884–1914*. DLitt (History). Pretoria: University of South Africa, 48.
[95] Wallenkampf, A.V. (1969) *The Herero rebellion in South West Africa: A study in German colonialism*. PhD thesis. Los Angeles: UCLA, 184, 211 fn 4.
[96] *Ibid*, 183.
[97] Stoecker, H. (ed) (1986) *German imperialism in Africa: From the beginnings until the Second World War*. London: C. Hurst & Co, 4.
[98] Packenham, T. (1992) *The scramble for Africa: White man's conquest of the Dark Continent from 1875–1912*. New York: Avon Books, 606.

activity in GSWA began, which quickly dominated trade in the territory and resulted in the GSWA Company taking over the land acquired by Lüderitz.

Despite the fervour with which Germany expounded upon the benefits of GSWA, it did not always see the colony in a positive light. The hardships of drought and famine, the inability to find diamonds and gold, the poor grade of cattle and the unwillingness of the Herero to trade even these cattle[99] all conspired to tarnish the promise GSWA once seemed to hold. At times, Germany was undecided whether to keep the colony[100] and its policy in and towards GSWA vacillated.[101] Given Bismarck's policy on colonies and the financial problems of the GSWA Company, it was anticipated that Germany might withdraw. In the early 1890s, the Kaiser was prepared 'to give up South West Africa if necessary so that all our energies may be focussed on East Africa'.[102] The refusal of many indigenous groups, including the Witboois, Bondelswartz, the Veldschoendragers, the Franzmanns and the Khoi, to sign protection treaties exacerbated matters.[103] So uncertain was Germany that, in 1891, Chancellor Caprivi announced that one more year of trial should determine whether GSWA should be kept or not.

However, at the time the German Colonial Company already regarded GSWA very favourably. A resolution was passed that stated:

> *[t]hat this meeting regards the Colony of South West Africa as one of the most valuable German dependencies. Owing to its situation that colony is destined to secure to German influence its decisive position in South Africa. The favourable climate and the available uninhabited areas make settlement by German farmers and agriculturists possible on a large scale. In order to promote the development of the colony in the right direction and to utilise for the benefit of the Mother-country all the advantages there to be derived, the Imperial Colonial Administration should come to the help of the spirit of German enterprise by securing peace there and the establishment of an organised administration. This meeting gives utterances to the conviction that the costs of an established Government on the lines followed by the English in Bechuanaland will very soon be covered by the revenues of the colony.*[104]

---

99 *Ibid*, 606.
100 Stoecker, H. (ed) (1986) *German imperialism in Africa: From the beginnings until the Second World War.* London: C. Hurst & Co, 42.
101 Haarhoff, D. (1991) *The wild South-West: Frontier myths and metaphors in literature set in Namibia, 1760–1988.* Johannesburg: Witwatersrand University Press, 66.
102 Quoted in Stoecker, H. (ed) (1986) *German imperialism in Africa: From the beginnings until the Second World War.* London: C Hurst & Co, 43.
103 Stoecker, H. (ed) (1986) *German imperialism in Africa: From the beginnings until the Second World War.* London: C. Hurst & Co, 41.
104 Quoted in Gewald, J-B. & Silvester, J. (2003) *Words cannot be found. German colonial rule in Namibia: An annotated reprint of the 1918 Blue Book.* Leiden: Brill, 41.

In 1893, it was noted in the *Deutsche Kolonialzeitung* that

> German South West Africa is the only one among our colonies that appears suitable to satisfy one of the main demands of the creators of Germany's colonial movement, namely to possess our own overseas territories that are partially capable of absorbing the current of German emigration.[105]

At the same time, German interests, especially from the business sector, grew sufficiently so that, by 1892, pressure on the Chancellor to remain in the territory and enhance its military forces was growing.[106] In 1893, he claimed, in the *Reichstag*, with respect to GSWA: 'Now it is ours, German territory and it must remain so.'[107]

However, all was not yet plain sailing. Due to the financial difficulties of the GSWA Company, it entered into an arrangement with British merchants to sell its land and mining ventures for three million marks. However, the deal required the German Chancellor's consent, and, after a long period of indecision, he did not give it.[108] Despite all the problems and the lack of interest at the time in GSWA, the Chancellor's lengthy pondering and refusal to grant consent for the GSWA Company sale suggests that Germany was not yet willing to relinquish the colony. Germany permitted some British capital to be invested in the colony and granted a concession in Damaraland, which was later taken over by Cecil John Rhodes. This and other British investments resulted in the dominance of British monopoly capital by the mid-1890s.[109] However, things changed rapidly after the 1896 failure of the Jameson Raid into today's Zimbabwe, which put an end to Rhodes' designs on GSWA.[110]

Only from 1898 did the economy of the colony shift fundamentally towards domination by German finances. German capital, mainly from the *Deutsche Bank* (one of the defendants in the Herero court cases that have been brought by the Herero against various multinational corporations in the USA for reparations for the genocide over the last few years)[111] and the

---

[105] *Deutsche Kolonialzeitung*, 19 August 1893, quoted in Walther, D.J. (2002) *Creating Germans abroad: Cultural policies and national indemnity in Namibia*. Athens, Ohio: Ohio University Press, 9.

[106] Stoecker, H. (ed) (1986) *German imperialism in Africa: From the beginnings until the Second World War*. London: C. Hurst & Co, 43.

[107] *Ibid*, 43.

[108] *Ibid*, 42.

[109] *Ibid*, 43.

[110] *Ibid*, 43.

[111] Sarkin, J. (2009) *Colonial Genocide and Reparations Claims in the 21st Century: The Socio-Legal Context of Claims under International Law by the Herero against Germany for Genocide in Namibia, 1904–1908*. Westport: Praeger Security International.

Disconto-Gesellschaft came to GSWA.[112] At this point, the need to achieve control and force the local inhabitants to accept German rule became apparent.[113] In 1899, Major von François wrote: 'The fact that the Africans possess the bulk of the land, to use and dispose of at their will, is not to be discussed but to be disputed with a rifle.'[114] German geographer Friedrich Ratzell echoed this sentiment in 1900, remarking: 'Thousands of natives less, hundreds of thousands of square kilometres of free land more for the whites. More space for culture, more people who contribute to culture, more people who enjoy its blessings.'[115] This remark corresponded to a statement by the *Kolonialzeitung* (DKZ) in 1895, which read: 'Regarding the German Colonial policy of today, one should not forget that the white colonial movement is a continuation of the strivings of patriotic men to acquire suitable emigration areas.'[116] These three comments support the hypothesis that the war against the Herero was an intentional strategy to appropriate their land.[117] The *Deutsch Südwestafrikanische Zeitung* of 22 January 1901 was also unambiguous:

> *[T]he land, of course must be transferred from the hands of the natives to those of the whites, [this] is the object of colonization in the territory. The land shall be settled by whites. So the natives must give way and either become servants of the whites or withdraw...*[118]

Protecting their investments

The importance of GSWA to Germany is evidenced by the huge sums of money it invested in the territory by way of subsidies and administrative expenses.[119] The

---

[112] Stoecker, H. (ed) (1986) *German imperialism in Africa: From the beginnings until the Second World War.* London: C. Hurst & Co, 44.

[113] *Ibid.*

[114] Ritter-Petersen, H.G. (1991) *The Herrenvolk mentality in German South West Africa 1884–1914.* DLitt (History). Pretoria: University of South Africa, 32–33.

[115] Quoted in Smith, H.W. (1999) 'The logic of colonial violence: Germany in South West Africa (1904–1907), the United States in the Philippines (1899–1902)'. In Lehmann, H. & Wellenreuther, H. (eds) *German and African nationalism: A comparative perspective.* Oxford: Berg, 205–31, 213.

[116] Haarhoff, D. (1991) *The wild South-West: Frontier myths and metaphors in literature set in Namibia, 1760–1988.* Johannesburg: Witwatersrand University Press, 64.

[117] See for example Harring, S.L. (2002, Winter) 'German reparations to the Herero nation: An assertion of Herero nationhood in the path of Namibian development?' 104 *West Virginia Law Review,* 393, 401.

[118] In Madley, B. (2004, June) 'Patterns of frontier genocide 1803–1910: The aboriginal Tasmanians, the Yuki of California and the Herero of Namibia'. 6 (2) *Journal of Genocide Research,* 167–92, 182. Citing Wellington, J.H. (1967) *South West Africa and its human issues.* Oxford: Clarendon Press, 194

[119] Eveleigh, W. (1915) *South-West Africa.* Cape Town: Maskew Miller, 146.

subsidies Germany gave to GSWA far exceeded those given to its other African colonies.[120] Between 1884 and 1914 the German Reich gave 278 million marks to the colony, while German East Africa was given 122 million, Cameroon 48 million and Togo 3.5 million marks.[121] German companies mirrored this same spread of resources and investments over the same period: they invested 141 million marks in GSWA, 166 million in East Africa, one million in Cameroon and four million in Togo.[122] German expenditure on GSWA multiplied sixfold between 1903 and 1904 and then multiplied threefold again over the 1904–05 period.[123] However, while expenditure was 11.17 million in 1903, 66.45 million in 1904 and 163.7 million in 1905; it dropped to only 62.67 million in 1906 and 35.08 million in 1908; it fell again to 34.08 million in 1909.[124] Revenue remained negligible throughout, in the range of 390 000 marks in 1898 and rose to a maximum of 1.76 million marks by 1911.[125]

The high number of armed forces Germany sent to the territory further evidences the extra attention it gave to the protection of GSWA as a national asset. In 1901, there were 772 German troops in GSWA for a population of about 200 000, whereas East Africa, with a population of 6 million, only received 1 400 troops and Cameroon, with a population of 3.5 million, only received 900 troops.[126] Clearly, this high ratio of troop numbers per capita demonstrates a bias towards GSWA. Even in 1914, the greatest numbers of troops in Africa were found in GSWA; of the total 6 461 troops, 2 760 were stationed in GSWA.[127] When the racial breakdown of troops is considered, the discrepancy is even more apparent: in 1914, 1 954 of the 2 411 white troops

---

[120] Later the generous subsidies became problematic in the context of the profits made by various companies there. From 1907, the German Colonial Society for South West Africa held 32 percent of the land, comprising virtually all the arable land as well as most of the mining rights. However, GSWA still needed subsidies and it had cost a lot to quell the Herero rebellion — which had, at least in part, been caused by the practices of this and other companies. Epstein, K. (1959, October) 'Erzberger and the German colonial scandals, 1905–1910'. 74 (293) *English Historical Review*, 637–63, 645.

[121] Stoecker, H. (ed) (1986) *German imperialism in Africa: From the beginnings until the Second World War*. London: C. Hurst & Co, 191. Stoecker also includes the figures for two non-African colonies: Kiaochow got 174 million marks and Samoa 1.5 million.

[122] Gann, L.H. & Duigan, P. (1977) *The rulers of German Africa 1884–1914*. Stanford: Stanford University Press, Appendix E.

[123] *Ibid*, 258.

[124] *Ibid*, 258.

[125] *Ibid*, 258.

[126] *Ibid*, 71.

[127] *Ibid*, 106.

in all German colonies were stationed in GSWA.[128] The Germans did not want African troops in GSWA,[129] as they 'were convinced that only white soldiers could effectively defend the white presence'.[130] Furthermore, soldiers regarded GSWA as a prime posting and as a result troops stationed there were forced to sign up for longer periods. A soldier's term in GSWA was three and a half years, as compared to two years in West Africa.[131]

Removing obstacles and luring potential settlers

The need for peace and stability

The ongoing conflict that permeated the territory worked against emigration from Germany. Conflict had racked the area for as long as the Germans had been there and Stoecker corroborated that the continuing wars inhibited German settlement in the colony.[132] As a result, from early on Germany consistently tried to achieve peace and stability. In 1890, an attempt was made to halt hostilities between the Witboois and the Herero.[133] However, when the war between these groups ended in 1892, it was met with ambivalence as the Germans realised the value of intergroup hostilities: while fighting each other, the groups were not focused on the German invasion and attempts to take land holdings. Yet, the ongoing conflict made the territory less appealing to settlers. By 1904, the German government was set on attracting more settlers and they knew that without peace their efforts would be thwarted.[134] Von Trotha stated that 'SWA is or should be just that colony where the European himself can work to support his family, free from interference…with a fair amount of security'.[135] Thus, the colonialists saw the battle for the new nation as one of wrestling control from and gaining control over the Africans, while

---

[128] *Ibid.*
[129] *Ibid.*
[130] *Ibid*, 122.
[131] *Ibid*, 117.
[132] Stoecker, H. (ed) (1986) *German imperialism in Africa: From the beginnings until the Second World War.* London: C. Hurst & Co, 52–54.
[133] *Ibid*, 44.
[134] Walther, D.J. (2002) *Creating Germans abroad: Cultural policies and national indemnity in Namibia.* Athens, Ohio: Ohio University Press, 13.
[135] Erichsen, C.W. (2004) *The Angel of Death has descended violently among them: A study of Namibia's concentration camps and prisoners-of-war, 1904–08.* MA thesis (History). University of Namibia, 274. Citing Poole, G. (1990) *Samuel Maherero.* Windhoek: Gamsberg MacMillan, 248.

at the same time increasing white settler numbers.[136] Professor Moritz Bonn, Director of the German Colonial School, also recognised this and, in a 1914 address to the Royal Colonial Institute on German Colonial Policy, he stated:

> *We wanted to concentrate on Africa the emigrants we were losing at the beginning of the colonial enterprise. We wanted to build up on African soil a new Germany and create daughter states as you have done in Australia and in Canada. We carried this idea to its bitter end. We tried it in South-West Africa and produced a huge native rising, causing the loss of much treasure and many lives. We tried to assume to ourselves the functions of Providence and we tried to exterminate a native race whom our lack of wisdom had goaded into rebellion. We succeeded in breaking up the native tribes, but we have not yet succeeded in creating a new Germany.*[137]

While Leutwein had achieved a good measure of stability in the years preceding the war, the period immediately prior to the war saw greater turmoil. Zirkel attributes the end of the pre-war stability not to the government, but rather to the settlers.[138]

Attracting German settlers to GSWA

Developing GSWA as an attractive colony for German settler immigration required various enticement strategies. Potential immigrants were lured with appealing portrayals of the territory. Hence, a civil servant, Clara Blockmann,[139] went to GSWA to write travel books to persuade Germans to settle there.[140] Germany also had to ensure that there would be German women to cohabit and marry white male settlers and so it introduced a programme

---

[136] Wildenthal, L. (1996) 'She is the victor: Bourgeois women, nationalist identities and the ideal of the independent women farmers in German South West Africa'. In Eley, G. (ed) *Society, culture and the state in Germany 1870–1930*. Ann Arbour: University of Michigan, 371–95, 374.

[137] Eveleigh, W. (1915) *South-West Africa*. Cape Town: Maskew Miller, 140.

[138] Zirkel, K. (1999) 'Military power in German colonial policy: The Schutztruppen and their leaders in the East and South West Africa, 1888–1918'. In Killingray, D. & Omissi, D. (eds) *Guardians of Empire: The armed forces of the colonial powers, 1700–1964*. Manchester: Manchester University Press, 91–113, 94.

[139] Blockmann's books included *German woman in South West Africa* (1910) and *Letters from a German girl in South West* (1912). In the former, she wrote that GSWA was to become the 'New Germany on African soil'. Blockmann, C. (1910) *German woman in South West Africa*, iv. Quoted in Wildenthal, L (1996) 'She is the victor: Bourgeois women, nationalist identities and the ideal of the independent women farmers in German South West Africa'. In Eley, G. (ed) *Society, culture and the state in Germany 1870–1930*. Ann Arbour: University of Michigan, 371–95, 374.

[140] Wildenthal, L. (1996) 'She is the victor: Bourgeois women, nationalist identities and the ideal of the independent women farmers in German South West Africa'. In Eley, G. (ed) *Society, culture and the state in Germany 1870–1930*. Ann Arbour: University of Michigan, 371–95, 371.

to lure more German women to GSWA.[141] From 1878, the German Colonial Society (DKG) began to recruit women for the colonies.[142] The GSWA programme was initiated in 1897 and the first sponsored women arrived in 1898.[143] In 1899, Prince Franz von Arenberg remarked on the importance of the programme, stating that 'the point of the whole matter is not to send servant girls to South West Africa, but rather to found German families there and this whole contractual relationship is just a transitional stage'.[144]

Other measures to boost recruitment included the issuing of numerous ordinances from 1892. It was essential to enhance agriculture production and make GSWA agriculturally self-sufficient, hence there were ordinances 'demanding the establishment of gardens and plantations and the growing of certain crops and fruits'.[145] Seeds, plants and fish to stock dams were brought to GSWA. The colonial authorities in Windhoek also established a fund in 1901 to grant loans to those who wished to settle there.[146] In 1901, an amount of 100 000 marks was allocated for settlement and, in 1903, a further 300 000 marks was added. In 1903, a Commissioner for Settlement, Paul Rohrbach, was appointed, an indication of the premium placed on the task of attracting and supporting settlers. Another major objective was the construction of colonial infrastructure.[147] Given these strategies, Stoecker commented that 'it was clear that the Africans were to be expelled from all their lands in a

[141] Ibid, 371–95, 382. See also Lora Wildenthal, L. (2001) *German woman for Empire, 1885–1945*. London: Duke University Press.

[142] Stoecker, H. (ed) (1986) *German imperialism in Africa: From the beginnings until the Second World War*. London: C. Hurst & Co, 211. Drechsler, H. (1980) *Let us die fighting: The struggle of the Herero and Nama against the German imperialism (1894–1915)*, (Bernd Zöllner, transl). London: Zed Press, 114.

[143] See generally O'Donnell, K. (1999) 'Poisonous women: Sexual danger, illicit violence and domestic work in German Southern Africa 1904–1915'. 11 (3) *Journal of Woman's History*, 32–54.

[144] Wildenthal, L (1996) 'She is the victor: Bourgeois women, nationalist identities and the ideal of the independent women farmers in German South West Africa'. In Eley, G. (ed) *Society, culture and the state in Germany 1870–1930*. Ann Arbour: University of Michigan, 371–95, 382–83.

[145] Lau, B. & Renier, P. (1993) *100 years of agricultural development in colonial Namibia: A historical overview of visions and experimenting*. Windhoek: The National Archive of Namibia, 5.

[146] Drechsler, H. (1980) *Let us die fighting: The struggle of the Herero and Nama against the German imperialism (1894–1915)* (Bernd Zöllner, transl). London: Zed Press, 114.

[147] Lau, B. & Renier, P. (1993) *100 years of agricultural development in colonial Namibia: A historical overview of visions and experimenting*. Windhoek: The National Archive of Namibia, 6.

matter of years'.[148] This was clear to many and even the Rhenish Missionary society realised what was to occur and demanded the establishment of Herero reserves that would be 'inviolable'.[149]

To some extent, Germany's strategies were successful. More Germans settled in GSWA than in any other German colony, even the Pacific.[150] Although German territory in South West and East Africa was approximately the same size, the GSWA settler population was more than double that of East Africa, tenfold more than that of Cameroon and a hundredfold more than that of Togo.[151] In 1891, there were only 310 Germans in GSWA, but by 1903 there were 2 998 Germans and a white population of 4 640.[152] Between 1897 and 1903, the number of white farmers trebled. This huge increase in settlement from the mid 1890s, compounded by the fact that no more land was available along the railway, resulted in a great deal of pressure for more land.[153]

Germany feared that Afrikaners and Cape colonialists might move to the area and in the process subsume valuable resources and land. In 1890, Chancellor Otto von Bismarck, who had initially been opposed to the idea of colonies,[154] argued that the best way to stop this was to get Germans to settle there:

> *The question of the settlement of the protectorate through immigrants...is of the greatest importance for [GSWA's] future. A speedy settlement of the areas suitable for farming would contribute to a faster development of the country...On the other hand, one cannot overlook that also here exists the danger of the prevalence of non-German interests in the protectorate. This danger is all the more so present, as the regions suitable for agriculture...are relatively limited and consequently the immigration of Boers and Cape colonists in large numbers would present serious impediments to a future German settlement.*[155]

To affect this 'speedy settlement' the colonial authorities introduced policies allowing soldiers to acquire farms in GSWA. It is not surprising that these

---

[148] Stoecker, H. (ed) (1986) *German imperialism in Africa: From the beginnings until the Second World War.* London: C. Hurst & Co, 49–50.

[149] *Ibid*, 50.

[150] Gann, L.H. (1987) 'Marginal colonialism: The German case', 1–17. In Knoll, A.J. & Gann, L.H. (eds) *Germans in the tropics: Essays in German colonial history.* New York/London: Greenwood Press, 1–17, 2.

[151] *Ibid*.

[152] Other whites included English and Afrikaners.

[153] Stoecker, H. (ed) (1986) *German imperialism in Africa: From the beginnings until the Second World War.* London: C. Hurst & Co, 49.

[154] Kaulich, U. (2003) *Die Geschichte der ehemaligen Kolonie Deutsch-Südwestafrika (1884–1914) Eine Gesamtdarstellung* (2 ed). Frankfurt am Main: Peter Lang.

[155] Quoted in Walther, D.J. (2002) *Creating Germans abroad: Cultural policies and national indemnity in Namibia.* Athens, Ohio: Ohio University Press, 10.

individuals constituted the majority of settlers.[156] Inevitably, their military background must have contributed to the culture and ethos of the settlers and must have influenced the eventual choice of a military solution to the land problem.

To make land acquisition more attractive, the price set for sales of land to settlers was reduced in 1898 and former colonial soldiers were not required to pay anything on condition that they started working the land within six months of acquiring it and did not sell it for ten years. If they did not meet these conditions, the land would revert back to the government. This would help ensure a stable settler community, preventing people from coming for a short period and making a quick profit. However, as mentioned before, the settlers not only wanted free land, they wanted large tracts of land, arguing that small plots were not economically viable. The initial allotment of smaller plots was later discontinued, as many in the homestead settlement programmes went bankrupt.[157] At this time, some argued that productive and lucrative farming would only be possible if the settlers were given at least 5 000 hectares each.[158] Thus, the settlers continued to exert pressure for greater allotments. It was clear that larger areas of land were necessary to retain the farmers.

Attempts to entice German settlers intensified in the early 1890s. The allocation in 1906 of 500 000 marks for this purpose indicates the increased emphasis on developing settlement during and after the war.[159] Captain von Francois also sought to attract settlers to the territory to engage in crop cultivation. In his 1899 book he wrote: 'When our colony is fully settled it will be able to offer a home to 10 000 farmers and just as many merchants and tradesmen'.[160] It soon became clear that purchase would not yield enough large farms, but conquest would.

At the same time, the settlers vociferously complained about other issues. One source of discontent was their indebtedness and their inability to farm on the allocated holdings they had to pay for. Certainly, one of their primary aspirations was to get free land, without having to raise loans. Public meetings were held in Windhoek and Swakopmund in which settlers directly pressurised the authorities in Berlin and GSWA to take action. Attempting to alleviate their plight, the settlers tried to restrict the arrival of new settlers,

---

156 *Ibid*, 14.
157 Ritter-Petersen, H.G. (1991) *The Herrenvolk mentality in German South West Africa 1884–1914*. DLitt (History). Pretoria: University of South Africa, 50.
158 *Ibid*, 49.
159 *Ibid*, 50–53.
160 Von Francois, C. (1899) *Deutsch-Südwest-Afrika*. Berlin: Dietrich Reimer, 133. Quoted in Kienetz, A. (1975, December) *Nineteenth-century South West Africa as a German settlement colony*. PhD thesis. University of Minnesota, 818.

arguing that newcomers would not be able to cope with the challenges that would face them. The authorities in Berlin likely saw this as a deterrent to potential settlers and must, therefore, have felt pressure to pacify the local settler community. In 1897, the Colonial Society noted in a report that the way to get settlers to GSWA was to provide free land.[161] The solution to the problem, both for the settlers and the authorities, lay in the taking of Herero land. These realities confirmed the pressure on the Herero and that they were not unjustified in their growing sense of insecurity.

Simultaneously, the settlement commission addressed the broader issues of attracting and assisting more German settlers. The commission's overall recommendation was that more work was needed to create an appealing environment for those considering settling in the territory. Friedrich von Lindequist, the Governor of the colony from 1905 to 1907, wrote: '[I]t is at the moment one of the most important tasks of the colonial and protectorate administration to make German South West Africa an object of attraction for German emigration'.[162] In 1909, Wilhelm Kulz, architect of self-government in GSWA, wrote:

> *Whoever has seen the country knows that a German new land can be created here, with an active population…and knows that the way is open to give a form to German life that would make it a joy to live in this country. In the not too distant future, may German South Africa blossom into such a land that is a blessing to itself and the Motherland.*[163]

Reasons for targeting the Herero and Nama land holdings

Part of the vision of GSWA as the new German home outside Europe entailed the development of it as an agricultural site.[164] The Germans were mainly interested in the southern and central parts of Namibia, occupied by the Herero and the Nama. This land was suitable for agriculture and the Germans thought the Herero had the best and cheapest land for grazing.[165] The northern parts, occupied by the Owambo, were less attractive because of the low rainfall.[166]

---

[161] Ritter-Petersen, H.G. (1991) *The Herrenvolk mentality in German South West Africa 1884–1914*. DLitt (History). Pretoria: University of South Africa, 93.

[162] Walther, D.J. (2002) *Creating Germans abroad: Cultural policies and national indemnity in Namibia*. Athens, Ohio: Ohio University Press, 16–19.

[163] Ibid, 28.

[164] Gann, L.H. & Duigan, P. (1977) *The rulers of German Africa 1884–1914*. Stanford: Stanford University Press, 149.

[165] Stoecker, H. (ed) (1986) *German imperialism in Africa: From the beginnings until the Second World War*. London: C. Hurst & Co, 48–49.

[166] The Himba, Kavango and Owambo escaped land seizures. Suzman, J. (2002) *Minorities in imperial Namibia*. London: Minority Rights Group International, 7.

In addition, the Germans thought the northern land contained no minerals and thus did not regard the region as suitable for white settlement.[167] Besides, because the Owambo territory was densely populated the Germans thought it would be too difficult to conquer militarily.

Having ruled out conquering the Owambo, the Germans targeted the Herero and Nama, not only because their land was most suitable but also because they controlled the largest areas. Initially, the Herero held about 13 million hectares. Due to natural disasters (discussed below) they had lost more than three million hectares by 1903. The table below gives a breakdown of the more than 30 million hectares under indigenous control in 1903:[168]

Table 1.1: Land ownership by indigenous peoples in GSWA in 1903

GROUP	HECTARES (PER MILLION)
Herero	10
Owambo	10
Bondelswartz (Nama)	4
Rehoboth Basters	2.2
Bethanie (Nama)	2
Witboois (Nama)	2
Veldschoendragers (Nama)	1.5
Berseba Hottentots (Nama)	0.6
Simon Kooper (Nama)	0.6
Red Nation (Nama)	0.5
Zwartboois (Nama)	0.2

As can be seen, with the exception of the Owambo, the Herero and the Nama groups held most of the land. The Germans were not equally interested in or threatened by the Nama: they were relatively few in number, their land was in the south and they had fewer cattle. Yet, they did use the Bondelswartz/Nama uprising in 1904 as a pretext to occupy and take possession of Namaland.[169] Although the Nama were brutally punished and their numbers drastically reduced by the killings, they were not systematically exterminated like the Herero.

---

167 Werner, W. (1993, March) 'A brief history of land dispossession in Namibia'. 19(1) *Journal of Southern African Studies*, 29–39.
168 Figures from Du Pisani, A. (1986) *South West African/Namibia: The politics of continuity and change*. Johannesburg: Jonathan Ball, 26.
169 Stoecker, H. (ed) (1986) *German imperialism in Africa: From the beginnings until the Second World War*. London: C. Hurst & Co, 59.

Nama soldiers being executed at Gibeon in 1905 with women and children spectators

The difference in the treatment meted out to the two groups relates primarily to the comparative desirability of their land. It is also hypothesised that the Nama were spared because they apparently did not mutilate the bodies of dead German soldiers, as the Herero were alleged to have done.[170]

Strategies to obtain land for settlement and livestock

From the 1890s onward, discussions brewed in Germany on how to transfer the land in GSWA to the settlers.[171] In 1890, Paul Rohrbach, previously referred to apropos the link between the Herero genocide and the Holocaust, emphasised this desire for the land and the philosophy prevalent at the time:

> *The decision to colonise in South-West Africa could after all mean nothing else but this, namely, that the native tribes would have to give up their lands on which they*

---

[170] Hull, I.V. (2005) *Absolute destruction: Military culture and practices of war in Imperial Germany*. Ithaca: Cornell University Press, 67.

[171] Stoecker, H. (ed) (1986) *German imperialism in Africa: From the beginnings until the Second World War*. London: C. Hurst & Co, 48.

had previously grazed their stock in order that the white man might have the land for the grazing of stock.... By no arguments whatsoever can it be shown that the preservation of any degree of national independence, national property and political organisation by the races of South-west Africa, would be of greater or of an equal advantage for the development of mankind in general or of the German people in particular, than the making of such races serviceable in the enjoyment of their former possessions by the white race.[172]

Rohrbach's views were neither isolated nor extreme. In fact, he was held in such high regard that he was appointed a member of the commission established to determine compensation for those whites who had suffered damage during the war. Formal policy reflected this desire to get the land.

Acquiring settler land from the locals

The colonial authorities employed many methods to acquire land and control in GSWA. Broadly, there were three processes, categorised by time period:

- between 1884 and 1894 protection treaties and purchases were used;
- from 1894 to 1904 increasing military and bureaucratic control were employed; and
- from 1905 to 1915 resistance was obliterated and land was forcibly taken.[173]

Sometimes, devious means were used to get landowners to part with more land than they intended. In 1883, land was bought from a local chief; he calculated the area for the sale in miles, assuming the dimensions were measured using the English mile or 1.5 kilometres. Afterwards, the Germans insisted they had agreed to the German mile, which measures 7.4 kilometres.[174] Another allegation concerns huge amounts of land obtained from Samuel Maherero in the early 1890s in exchange for a salary. The Germans knew the land he traded was not under his control, but under the control of other chiefs whom they did not consult.[175] Alcohol was often used to induce 'sales' of land. In fact,

---

[172] Quoted in Scott, M. (1958, July) 'The international status of South West Africa'. 34 (3) *International Affairs*, 318–29, 321.

[173] Du Pisani, A. (1987) 'Namibia: The historical legacy'. In Totemeyer, G., Kandetu, V. & Werner, W. (eds) *Namibia in perspective*. Windhoek: Council of Churches, 16.

[174] Drechsler, H. (1980) *Let us die fighting: The struggle of the Herero and Nama against the German imperialism (1894–1915)* (Bernd Zöllner, transl). London: Zed Press, 23.

[175] Gewald, J-B. & Silvester, J. (2003) *Words cannot be found. German colonial rule in Namibia: An annotated reprint of the 1918 Blue Book*. Leiden: Brill, 79.

there are allegations that Maherero was plied with alcohol before signing land sale documents.[176] A friend of Maherero testified to this:

> I knew Samuel well...he was very fond of liquor and the Germans kept him well supplied. He used to get cases of rum and brandy...Samuel was afraid of his life...He told me that the Germans made him drunk and got him to sign papers he knew nothing of and for which he was sorry afterwards...Samuel, in his better moments, bitterly complained of how the Germans had taken advantage of his weakness...[177]

Other times, local leaders did not realise that land was being sold and not merely lent. Samuel Kutako's statement below confirms this:

> Under the Herero law the ground belonged to the tribe in common and not even the chief could sell or dispose of it. He could give people permission to live on the land, but no sales were valid and no chief ever attempted to sell his people's land. Even the missionaries who settled amongst us, only got permission to live there. Land was never sold to Germans or anyone else. We did not have any idea of such a thing.[178]

In the initial stage, between 1884 and 1894, land acquisition involved purchases and the offering of protection to the inhabitants in exchange for land.[179] The Germans were not militarily strong enough at the time to attain the land they wanted and had, therefore, to rely on a system of friendship treaties and sales. However, during the first decade of German advancement, the Herero technically did not sell any land to them,[180] as their land was communal and the chiefs were merely the custodians of the land and not authorised to sell it.

---

[176] Apparently alcohol was also used to coax Nama chiefs. See Melber, H. (1984) 'Ein Bremer Kaufmann und die Folgen. Die Landgeschäfte des Adolf Lüderitz und die Proklamation "Deutsch-Südwestafrikas". Eine ideologiekritische Dokumentation'. *Informationsdienst Südliches Afrika*, 6. Also noted in Schuring, E. (2004) *History obliges: The real motivations behind German aid flows in the case of Namibia*. MA thesis (Law & Diplomacy). Fletcher School of Law and Diplomacy, Tufts University, 28 fn 92. See also Heywood, A., Lau, B. & Ohly R. (eds) (1992) *Warriors, leaders, sages and outcasts in the Namibian past*. Windhoek: Michael Scott Oral Records Project (MSORP).

[177] Gewald, J-B. & Silvester, J. (2003) *Words cannot be found. German colonial rule in Namibia: An annotated reprint of the 1918 Blue Book*. Leiden: Brill, 92.

[178] Contained in the Blue Book and found in Gewald, J-B. & Silvester, J. (2003) *Words cannot be found. German colonial rule in Namibia: An annotated reprint of the 1918 Blue Book*. Leiden: Brill, 91.

[179] Katjavivi, P. (1989) *A history of resistance in Namibia*. Paris/London/Addis Ababa: UNESCO, 7–8.

[180] Drechsler, H. (1980) *Let us die fighting: The struggle of the Herero and Nama against the German imperialism (1894–1915)* (Bernd Zöllner, transl). London: Zed Press, 111.

The Germans formed a land-settlement syndicate and in 1892 the syndicate made a request for large stretches of land. The German authorities did not agree to it then, as they believed they would be unable to defend such a grant to indigenous groups who also claimed that land. When Captain von François realised that agents of the syndicate were taking land anyway and 'acting recklessly', he requested Berlin suspend the work of the syndicate. The request was refused, but Berlin told the syndicate to confine its land acquisition to the areas around Windhoek (at least for the time being).[181]

Natural disasters: hurting the Herero and helping the Germans

The years before the Herero-German war were a time of extensive competition between the Herero and the settlers for land and cattle.[182] Unfortunately, a series of natural disasters between 1896 and 1899 ultimately defeated the Herero's ability to resist German dominance. The rinderpest, malaria, typhoid and locust plagues 'smoothed the path of German colonial development',[183] as it assisted the colonisers in subjugating the local population.[184] During the rinderpest epidemic, the German colonial administration enforced culling and implemented a programme of vaccination in which cattle were killed to produce the vaccine.[185] This engendered further resentment among the Herero towards the Germans. A simultaneous drought exacerbated matters.[186] Although approximately 10 000 Herero died during that period from malaria, it was the rinderpest epidemic and the destruction of their cattle that proved most devastating.

---

[181] Gewald, J-B. & Silvester, J. (2003) *Words cannot be found. German colonial rule in Namibia: An annotated reprint of the 1918 Blue Book.* Leiden: Brill, 77.

[182] Zimmerman, A. (2003) 'Adventures in the skin trade: German anthropology and colonial corporeality'. In Penny, H.G. & Bunzl, M. (eds) *Worldly provincialism: German anthropology in the Age of Empire.* Ann Arbour: University of Michigan Press, 173.

[183] Packenham, T. (1992) *The scramble for Africa: White man's conquest of the Dark Continent from 1875–1912.* New York: Avon Books, 607.

[184] Ofcansky, T.P (1981) 'The 1889–97 rinderpest epidemic and the rise of British and German colonialism in Eastern and Southern Africa'. 8 (1) *Journal of African Studies,* 31–38, 31.

[185] Bollig, M. & Gewald, J-B. (2000) 'People, cattle and land — An introduction'. In Bollig, M. & Gewald, J-B. (eds) *People, cattle and land: Transformations of a pastoral society in southwestern Africa.* Köln: Rüdiger Koppe Verlag, 19.

[186] Werner, W. (1998) *No-one will become rich: Economy and society in the Herero reserves in Namibia 1913–1946.* Basel: P. Schlettwein, 43.

Prior to the epidemic, the Herero were largely able to resist German expansion, but these disasters irrevocably changed the economic balance.[187] The rinderpest decimated many of the Herero's livestock, while the settlers only lost about half their herds, as they had been inoculated.[188] The export figures illustrate the value of cattle to the economy: in 1901 they yielded 120 225 marks; in 1902, 1 023 637 marks and in 1903, 2 337 682 marks.[189] Even better revenues were expected as the Anglo-Boer War resulted in cattle losses in the Cape, Transvaal and Orange Free State.

Herero cattle being confiscated

[187] Drechsler, H. (1980) *Let us die fighting: The struggle of the Herero and Nama against the German imperialism (1894–1915)* (Bernd Zöllner, transl). London: Zed Press, 69.
[188] Werner, W. (1998) *No-one will become rich: Economy and society in the Herero reserves in Namibia 1913–1946*. Basel: P. Schlettwein, 42–43.
[189] Wallenkampf, A.V. (1969) *The Herero rebellion in South West Africa: A study in German colonialism*. PhD thesis. Los Angeles: UCLA, 52.

According to Werner, the rinderpest epidemic acutely affected Maherero, which made him more disposed to sell the land.[190] Although Werner notes that colonial officials reported in 1897 that Maherero will 'sell farm land', it is uncertain whether he intended to sell or simply loan the land for usage. After the rinderpest epidemic Leutwein and his administration introduced legislation to limit the sales of more Herero land.[191] Like Werner, Gewald claimed that the Herero were willing to sell their land but were prohibited from doing so. These restrictions on land sales curbed the settlers' access to land and they 'felt cheated of their rightful prize'.[192] They resented Leutwein, as they saw him and his policies as obstacles to obtaining more land. Sidelining him meant a probable change in policy and, therefore, pressure from the settlers in all likelihood influenced the decision to marginalise Leutwein in 1904.

Getting the Herero livestock

Having acquired land, the settlers desperately needed animals for breeding and transport. Paul Rohrbach pointed out that

> The chief necessity in the establishment of the new settlers was the supply of the stock and the difficulties in this direction increased in every proportion with the growth of the newly opened up farming positions. Every newly founded farming venture required, above all things, a supply of breeding stock. The White ranchers and farmers who had breeding stock, held onto them as far as possible and only sold in cases of extreme necessity; moreover no farm had at the time been so far developed that the number of stock acquired by breeding was in excess of the available grazing ground. So for the newly arrived farmer no other course remained but, before starting business as a farmer, to enter into trading work with the Hereros and there to acquire the cows he needed by barter...
> In addition to breeding stock the future farmer required transport oxen. The Hereros were also the chief producers of these...the trade with the Hereros constituted for the commencing farmer the normal channel through which in the first instance he could get possession of the required breeding stock...it is, therefore an error to take it for granted that before the rebellion (1904) the farmer and trader were distinct and separate occupations. In any case, there were very few persons who had not found it necessary to be traders first of all before they could become farmers. When public opinion in Germany, on the outbreak of the 1904 rebellion, sharply criticised the excess

---

[190] Werner, W. (1998) *No-one will become rich: Economy and society in the Herero reserves in Namibia 1913–1946*. Basel: P. Schlettwein, 43.

[191] Gewald, J-B. (2000) 'Colonization, genocide and resurgence: The Herero of Namibia, 1890–1933'. In Bollig, M. & Gewald, J-B. (eds) *People, cattle and land: Transformations of a pastoral society in southwestern Africa*. Köln: Rüdiger Koppe Verlag, 202.

[192] *Ibid.*

of the traders, no one in the country wanted to admit ever having been a trader and everyone had always been a farmer only.[193]

Initially, the settlers attempted to get access to the locals' sheep and cattle through purchases and trades. Later, other strategies were used to put pressure on the Herero and the other tribes to trade or sell. One such manoeuvre was introducing a law that fined people if their cattle trespassed on land belonging to a German farmer. If the fine was not paid, which often happened as the indigenous population did not have access to currency, the cattle would be confiscated.[194] Eyewitness Samuel Kutako noted:

> *The next reason for our rebellion was the appropriation of Herero lands by the traders, who took the ground for their farms and claimed it as their private property. They used to shoot our dogs if they trespassed on these lands and they confiscated any of our cattle which might stray there. If holy cattle trespassed we were allowed to get them back, if we paid three to four ordinary cattle in exchange for only one.*[195]

This statement speaks for itself. However, Kutako's assertion that land was a reason for the Herero revolt is supported by the slogans of the Herero women during the war: to encourage their warriors, they chanted, 'Whose land is Hereroland? Hereroland is our land!'[196]

Another appropriation strategy was the system of credit. The local population was given access to credit to buy animals and other products, but repayment was often demanded on short notice and involved high interest rates. If they could not pay, their cattle and land were confiscated. On the one hand, Leutwein tried to treat the indigenous population fairly, but on the other he knew he had to facilitate the transfer of land and cattle into the hands of the settlers.[197] He describes Herero 'war fever' resulting from a misunderstood agreement that involved the confiscation of their cattle:

> *[A]dvantage was taken in the beginning of 1896, when a force under Major Mueller took away several thousands of cattle belonging to Hereros at Heusis and Aris. Only then did the significance of the agreement become clear to the Hereros. Excitement and war fever extended throughout the entire Protectorate. The white traders in the interior were threatened and had to take hurried flight. As characteristic...I*

---

193 Quoted in Gewald, J-B. & Silvester, J. (2003) *Words cannot be found. German colonial rule in Namibia: An annotated reprint of the 1918 Blue Book.* Leiden: Brill, 83.
194 Fraenkel, P. & Murry, R. (1985) *The Namibian Report, No 19.* London: Minority Rights Group International, 6.
195 Gewald, J-B. & Silvester, J. (2003) *Words cannot be found. German colonial rule in Namibia: An annotated reprint of the 1918 Blue Book.* Leiden: Brill, 91.
196 Stoecker, H. (ed) (1986) *German imperialism in Africa: From the beginnings until the Second World War.* London: C. Hurst & Co, 56.
197 Ibid, 48.

here wish to mention that the son and nephew of the paramount chief, who, at the time were doing voluntary service with the troops at Windhuk[sic], burst into tears on hearing of the confiscation of these cattle and begged for immediate release from military duty. The war fever slacked down at Okahandja, when, some days later, the half share of the proceeds of sale, in terms of the agreement, was paid to the chief as indication that the German Government merely acted in the exercise of its rights under the agreement. Outside Okahandja however the desire for war increased and eventually even the Europeans were infected, not only private persons, but also members of the Government. Especially among a section of the Officers, the war fever, combined with under-estimation of their opponents was very noticeable.[198]

By 1902, Herero cattle stocks stood at just under 46 000, down from about 100 000 at the beginning of the 1890s.[199] German stocks stood at about 45 000 — most of which they bought or confiscated from the Herero.[200] The loss of their cattle had a pronounced and profound effect on the Herero, both economically and otherwise. Madley points out that the 'Herero language contains over a thousand words for cattle, the animals figure prominently in Herero religion and soured cow's milk is the staple of the traditional diet. Cattle also conferred wealth, prestige and political power on Herero men. In his 1906 book, *Die Herero*, the Reverend Irle observed that the Herero's "whole object in life was the increase and preservation of his herds". As the Herero sold cattle for European goods, they helped undermine their own society'.[201] Charles van Onselen concurs: the loss of cattle 'should be measured not simply in terms of numbers, for amongst cattle-keeping people this was far more than simply an economic blow. For African peasants, cattle formed not only a source of wealth but the pivotal point of a complex and interwoven social, political and economic system'.[202] The sales forced many Herero to take jobs.[203] According to Gann and Duigan, 'the ravages of rinderpest, brutalities

[198] Gewald, J-B. & Silvester, J. (2003) *Words cannot be found. German colonial rule in Namibia: An annotated reprint of the 1918 Blue Book*. Leiden: Brill, 79.
[199] Werner, W. (1998) *No-one will become rich: Economy and society in the Herero reserves in Namibia 1913–1946*. Basel: P. Schlettwein, 44. Madley, B. (2004, June) 'Patterns of frontier genocide 1803–1910: The aboriginal Tasmanians, the Yuki of California and the Herero of Namibia'. 6 (2) *Journal of Genocide Research*, 167–92, 182–3.
[200] Madley, B. (2004, June) 'Patterns of frontier genocide 1803–1910: The aboriginal Tasmanians, the Yuki of California and the Herero of Namibia'. 6 (2) *Journal of Genocide Research*, 167–92, 182–3.
[201] *Ibid.*
[202] Van Onselen, C. (1973) 'Reaction to rinderpest in Southern Africa 1896–97'. 13 (3) *Journal of African History*. Quoted in Werner, W. (1998) *No-one will become rich: Economy and society in the Herero reserves in Namibia 1913–1946*. Basel: P. Schlettwein, 47.
[203] Gann, L.H. & Duigan, P. (1977) *The rulers of German Africa 1884–1914*. Stanford: Stanford University Press, 174.

inflicted on Africans by individual Germans, a pervasive sense of insecurity, the forfeiture of land and the fear of future deprivations — all combined to produce an explosion'.[204]

Exploiting war to gain land

The formulation of a formal policy for the colonisation of the territory by the Colonial Department in Berlin in 1903[205] signifies that the primary interest of Germany in that period was the future settlement of the area. However, the process of acquiring land for the new settlers was hampered by the general reluctance of the indigenous people, as well as existing companies, to sell their land.

By the 1890s, various concession companies held huge parcels of land, which they were hesitant to let go of.[206] These companies managed the process of selling the available farms and they were loath to sell these farms at prices that the potential settlers were able to afford.[207] According to Goldblatt, these companies 'held back sales of land for speculative purposes'.[208] The 1903 Annual Report of the Otavi Mine Company noted that no land had been sold for two years, as it was hoped that prices would improve.[209] When companies did sell land, they charged the settlers very high prices. Both the reluctance to sell and the high prices intensified the pressure for land. Only after the war, in 1907, when the Herero land became available,[210] was an agreement reached with these companies on prices.[211]

Further protections to assist German settlers included the introduction of a land-control system by the German colonial administration, which ensured

---

[204] *Ibid.* See also Ofcansky, T.P (1981) 'The 1889–97 rinderpest epidemic and the rise of British and German colonialism in Eastern and Southern Africa'. 8 (1) *Journal of African Studies*, 31–38.

[205] Voeltz, R.A. (1988) *German colonialism and the South West Africa Company, 1884–1914; Allies in Apartheid — Western capitalism in occupied Namibia*. Monographs in International Studies, Africa Series No. 50. Athens, Ohio: Ohio University Center for International Studies, 86.

[206] Adams, F., Werner, W. & Vale, P. (1990) *The land issue in Namibia: An inquiry.* Windhoek: Namibian Institute for Social and Economic Research, University of Namibia, 11.

[207] Botha, C. (2000, May) 'The politics of land settlement in Namibia, 1890–1960'. 42 *South African Historical Journal*, 232–76, 233.

[208] Goldblatt, I. (1971) *History of South West Africa: From the beginning of the nineteenth century.* Cape Town: Juta, 156.

[209] Schrank, G.I. (1974) *German South West Africa: Social and economic aspects of its history, 1884–1915.* PhD (History). New York University, 128.

[210] *Ibid*, 94–99.

[211] Botha, C. (2000, May) 'The politics of land settlement in Namibia, 1890–1960'. 42 *South African Historical Journal*, 232–76, 233.

greater access to land by German settlers than by anyone else; non-Germans had to pay higher prices for land. This kept the price of land for German settlers even lower than the market price and in fact depressed the market price. This land policy acted as a major deterrent to the immigration of settlers from other countries, including South Africa.[212]

By this time, the Germans realised the expediency of war. Intergroup conflicts diverted the attention of the indigenous people away from the Germans' arrogation attempts and they could actively use the animosities between the tribes to strengthen their position. War had also previously proved a useful strategy to gain land and cattle from the Mbanderu (the Eastern Herero). During 1896 and 1897, the Germans were able to seize about 12 000 cattle from them as a result of war. Other rebellions had the same consequences and each time more cattle were seized.[213] Hence Governor Leutwein noted, in 1895, that war had proved useful in achieving German goals and this war against the Herero would thus be a profitable endeavour.[214] German cabinet minister Von Tattenbach also proclaimed the benefits of the war to a Portuguese counterpart, stating that 'however regrettable the Herero uprising may be, it will lead to that vast territory being taken into possession and German South West Africa becoming a well-ordered and promising colony rather than a so-called sphere of interest'.[215]

War not only had the potential to achieve an enduring peace, but it would also properly subjugate the local population, who had access to the best land. Around the time of the battle of the Waterberg, 11 August 1904, the Kaiser announced a new settlement initiative for GSWA. The timing of this initiative would indicate that the 1904 attempt to exterminate the Herero was no coincidence, nor was it an impulsive strategy chosen by the German troops in the field. In fact, Germany had contemplated the annihilation of the Herero as early as 1895. Lundtofte notes that 'Leutwein underlined in 1895 that should the Herero refuse to conform to these demands then there were only two alternatives: that Germany withdrew from Herero territory or that the Herero be annihilated by military force — Leutwein regarded the use

---

212 Silvester, J. (1998) 'Beasts, boundaries and buildings: The survival and creation of pastoral economics in Southern Namibia 1915–35'. In Hayes, P., Silvester, J., Wallace, M. & Hartman, W. *Namibia under South African rule: Mobility and containment 1915–1946*. Oxford: James Currey, 95–116, 103.
213 Stoecker, H. (ed) (1986) *German imperialism in Africa: From the beginnings until the Second World War*. London: C. Hurst & Co, 51.
214 *Ibid.*
215 *Ibid*, 52–54.

of military force as the most likely outcome'.[216] Although annihilation does not necessarily mean extermination (and this will be dealt with later), can an alternative interpretation really hold water given that the ultimate goal was to remove a largely civilian population from their land? Can one militarily annihilate women and children?

Richard Voeltz reinforces the argument that the acquisition of Herero land was the prime motivation for the genocide by emphasising the needs of both the settlers and British companies. He argues that Germany based the economic growth of the territory on British concession companies and white settlement and therefore had no option but to support the policies of these corporations towards the Herero.[217]

Schutztruppe at Waterberg in 1904, on foot with horses

[216] Lundtofte, H. (2003) 'Radicalization of the German suppression of the Herero rising in 1904'. In Jensen, S.L.B. (ed) *Genocide: Cases, comparisons and contemporary debates*. Copenhagen: Danish Center for Holocaust and Genocide, 15, 24–25.

[217] Voeltz, R.A. (1988) *German colonialism and the South West Africa Company, 1884–1914; Allies in Apartheid — Western capitalism in occupied Namibia*. Monographs in International Studies, Africa Series No. 50. Athens, Ohio: Ohio University Center for International Studies, 54.

General von Trotha's own words confirm that the land was a primary motivation for exterminating the Herero. In his letter to Chief of the General Staff Schlieffen on 4 October 1904, in which he states that he is unable to rescind the extermination order without instruction from the Kaiser, he also wrote that it remained to be seen 'if they will try to regain possession of their old pastureland by force or by complete submission'.[218] In other words, Von Trotha was concerned that the Herero might attempt and/or succeed in regaining some of their land — through force or negotiation. This shows that his aim was not merely achieving a military victory: he was executing a strategic plan to get the land.

The Herero rebellion 'afforded a long-sought pretext for a military conquest of the territory'.[219] The colonisers appear to have goaded the Herero into rebellion for this purpose. Cattle seizures provoked anxiety and agitation, as cattle were basic to the Herero economy and pastoralist culture.[220] The Nama received similar treatment and it is likely that other groups would have too, had the Herero not taken the bait. Masson formulates it as follows: 'It is more than probable that, had the Herero War not broken out at the beginning of 1904, the Germans would have found some pretext to exterminate a potential military challenge from the Witboois.'[221] Already in 1905 a British observer, noting that the Herero and Nama had been decimated, commented:

> There can be no doubt, I think, that the war has been of an almost unmixed benefit to the German colony. Two warlike races have been exterminated, wells have been sunk, new waterholes discovered, the country mapped and covered with telegraph lines and an enormous amount of capital has been laid out.[222]

Creating Herero reserves

The authorities had long contemplated the creation of reserves for the protection of the Herero, despite their initial opposition. Already in April 1898, the authorities decreed that tribal reserves would be created in certain

---

218 Hull, I.V. (2005) *Absolute destruction: Military culture and practices of war in Imperial Germany*. Ithaca: Cornell University, 59.
219 Stoecker, H. (ed) (1986) *German imperialism in Africa: From the beginnings until the Second World War*. London: C. Hurst & Co, 52–54.
220 Katjavivi, P. (1989) *A history of resistance in Namibia*. Paris/London/Addis Ababa: UNESCO, 1.
221 Masson, J. (2001) *Jakob Marengo: An early resistance hero of Namibia*. Windhoek: Out of Africa, 23.
222 Contained in Dedering, T. (1999) 'A certain rigorous treatment of all parts of the nation: The annihilation of the Herero in German South West Africa, 1904'. In Levine, M. & Roberts, P. (eds) *The massacre in history*. Vol.1 War and Genocide Series. New York/Oxford: Berghahn Books, 217.

regions[223] and from that time on public deliberations and debates took place about the location of these reserves. While the Herero had not lost that much land by 1898 and 1899, natural disasters had forced them to sell more their land and, by 1903, they had lost about 3.5 million of their 13 million hectares. In 1901, the Rhenish Mission Society shared the Herero's concern about further losses and recommended the establishment of reserves to protect some land for the Herero.[224] The settlers rejected the request.[225] Leutwein likely agreed with the missionaries and was unwilling to accede to the wishes of the settlers, which resulted in complaints to Berlin about his stance.

Postcard of Chief Henrik Witbooi of the Nama (left), with Governor Leutwein (centre) and Chief Samuel Maherero (right)

[223] Ritter-Petersen, H.G. (1991) *The Herrenvolk mentality in German South West Africa 1884–1914*. DLitt (History). Pretoria: University of South Africa, 161.
[224] Werner, W. (1998) *No-one will become rich: Economy and society in the Herero reserves in Namibia 1913–1946*. Basel: P. Schlettwein, 45.
[225] Gewald J-B. (1999) *Herero heroes: A socio-political history of the Herero of Namibia 1890–1923*. Oxford: James Currey, 144.

Despite Leutwein's apparent intentions, the Herero accurately interpreted the missionaries' request for reserves as a forewarning that they were going to lose even more land. The acceptance by the authorities of legislation for the creation of the reserves presumably reinforced their fears. Given the initial hesitation of the German authorities, the intention behind the establishment of these reserves is debatable. Ostensibly, it provided protection for the Herero, but it could easily have been a convenient solution regarding where to relocate the soon-to-be-landless Herero.

During 1903, the authorities held discussions with the Herero on the establishment of reserves.[226] In December 1903, weeks before the war, the colonial authorities determined the reserve boundaries. The Herero objected to some boundaries, because the reserves were small, in an unfamiliar part of the country and the land was not particularly good for grazing.[227] Most Herero leaders contested the size of the reserves, with the exception of Maherero, who appeared to favour small reserves because they meant more land could be sold. The German officials responsible not only rejected nearly all the Herero's suggestions for revising the borders, but also treated them with contempt. A few reserve boundaries were revised in negotiation with the relevant Herero communities and some chiefs signed agreements to that effect. Yet other borders were unilaterally declared and imposed and the signatures of the relevant leaders were simply forged.[228] These boundary lines were then simply announced as definitive and unalterable, which, naturally, caused intense acrimony.

Not only were the Herero disgruntled about the establishment of the reserves and the way it was handled, but they must have been further aggravated that the settlers rejected the reserve policy.[229] The settlers wanted all the Herero land and felt that the protection offered by the reserves still amounted to overly kind treatment. Furthermore, the settlers' opposition was due to the fact that Africans would be allowed various rights on those reserves and would only be subject to the authority of their tribal chiefs.

The announcement of the reserve boundaries on 8 December 1903, a month before the uprising, was hardly coincidental. The whole process — the selective discussions regarding the reserves, the settlers' opposition to them,

---

226 *Ibid.*
227 *Ibid*, 145–47.
228 *Ibid*, 147.
229 Ritter-Petersen, H.G. (1991) *The Herrenvolk mentality in German South West Africa 1884–1914*. DLitt (History). Pretoria: University of South Africa, 167.

the lack of adequate consultation[230] and the unilateral determination of the boundaries — appreciably exacerbated the Herero's exasperation, anger and anxiety. They duly recognised that the 'benevolent' process constituted yet another example of their disregarded rights.[231]

Increasing pressure on the Herero

Many theories have been advanced about the reasons for the Herero uprising, but this chapter does not address them in depth. Rather, it evaluates the precipitants in the context of the German goals of the time and how this resulted in genocide. Broadly, the rationale for the uprising and the reasons for using genocide to put it down intersect: the Herero wanted to protect their land and livestock, while the Germans wanted to acquire their land and livestock. As the Germans took over possession of their land and cattle, it provoked the anxiety and agitation of the Herero, who realised that increasingly more of their resources were going to be lost to the Germans.[232] The uprising 'enabled' Germany to respond with genocide and this response allowed for quicker and cheaper procurement of the Herero's resources.

As noted earlier, the Herero resistance was neither gratuitous nor isolated.[233] It had precedents in both other German colonies and in GSWA. As discussed above, shortly before the Herero War, the Bondelswartz revolted against the colonial enterprise.[234] In fact, Governor Leutwein was away, attempting to deal with the uprising of the Bondelswartz in the south of the territory when the Herero rose up in January 1904. The Herero allegedly consciously used this opportunity as defences were weaker, with many German troops in the south. It is also possible that the Herero rebelled because they had heard rumour that Leutwein had been killed during the Bondelswartz revolt, leaving them in fear of what any less 'lenient' leader succeeding him would

---

[230] Werner, W. (1998) *No-one will become rich: Economy and society in the Herero reserves in Namibia 1913–1946*. Basel: P. Schlettwein, 45

[231] Gewald J-B. (1999) *Herero heroes: A socio-political history of the Herero of Namibia 1890–1923*. Oxford: James Currey, 148.

[232] Katjavivi, P. (1989) *A history of resistance in Namibia*. Paris/London/Addis Ababa: UNESCO, 1.

[233] Robinson has argued that the success or failure of policies introduced in various colonies has much to do with the way in which the local inhabitants responded to them. See Robinson, R. (1986) 'The eccentric idea of imperialism, with or without Empire'. In Mommsen, W.J. & Osterhammel, J. (eds) *Imperialism and after: Continuities and discontinuities*. London: Allen & Unwin, 267–89.
Even at the time some blamed colonial policies for uprisings.

[234] Eveleigh, W. (1915) *South-West Africa*. Cape Town: Maskew Miller, 134.

do to them. In a subsequent letter to Leutwein, dated 13 June 1904, Samuel Maherero confirmed that they had believed he had been killed. In this letter Maherero listed the reasons for rising up, including that ten of his men had been killed by German troops under Lieutenant Zürn, that the same official plotted to assassinate him and, crucially, that he had heard that Leutwein had been killed in the Bondelswartz rebellion.[235] The Herero viewed Leutwein as the bulwark between them and the land-hungry settlers and the threat of the military, so his alleged death must have alarmed them.

The overriding determinant of the rebellion was the Herero increasing disempowerment as they lost more land and cattle. Alexander maintains that 'the land question [rather than the problem of wages or political rights] was the central question'[236] in the Herero uprising and therefore the war must be anti-colonial. At that time, the Settlement Commissioner, Paul Rohrbach, also held this view. Rohrbach argued that the Herero saw increasing numbers of German settlers arriving to take more land and realised that even the protection treaties could not stem the tide of settler land-claims over the whole territory. According to him, the rebellion was 'a struggle for national independence from the Germans. The Herero feared the expropriation of their land by the whites'.[237] In addition, Alexander, Werner and others correctly cite other contributing factors, such as the general maltreatment meted out to the Herero, the bias in the dispensing of justice, the system of trade and credit that indebted them and the establishment of reserves.[238]

Both Bley and Gewald raise the issue of the Herero's 'perceptions' of the situation. Gewald's observation that the Herero acted on their perceptions implies that their fears were unfounded or exaggerated. Bley suggests that the 'actual losses of land were less significant than the Herero head-men felt' but that they *believed* that 'German expansion would never stop and that the German government would not honour its protection treaties'.[239]

---

[235] Oermann, N.O. (1999) *Mission, church and state relations in South West Africa under German rule (1884–1915)*. Stuttgart: Franz Steiner Verlag, 95.

[236] Alexander, N. (1983) *The Namibian war of anti-colonial resistance 1904–1907*. Windhoek: Namibian Review Publications, 26.

[237] Rohrbach, P. (1907) *Deutsche Kolonialwirtschaft, vol. I: Südwestafrika*. Berlin/Schoneberg: Buchverlag der Hilfe, 353. Cited in Ritter-Petersen, H.G. (1991) *The Herrenvolk mentality in German South West Africa 1884–1914*. DLitt (History). Pretoria: University of South Africa, 193.

[238] Alexander, N. (1983) *The Namibian war of anti-colonial resistance 1904–1907*. Windhoek: Namibian Review Publications, 26.

[239] Bley, H. (1971) *South-West Africa under German rule 1894–1914*. London: Heinemann, 143.

While it is true that land sales by the chiefs were not continuing at the same rate as they were in the five or so years preceding 1903, the Herero had lost huge sections of land in that period and the process persisted. Herero territory was shrinking rapidly. Their 'perceptions' that they were about to lose even more land were accurate, as they soon lost almost all their land and animals.

The establishment of reserves must have contributed to their concern and resentment. In his book, *Elf Jahre*, Leutwein primarily attributed the Herero rebellion to the creation of reserves, saying the Herero believed it to be a ploy to get control of their land.[240] In a 1904 report, Rhenish missionary Kuhlman concurred with Leutwein's view.[241]

Gewald maintains that it was not the Herero chiefs, but the missionaries who were opposed to the sale of land. Admittedly, many chiefs were amenable to selling their land or at least susceptible to influence, because they were under pressure from the colonial authorities and the settlers. Debt forced some to sell. The natural disasters had reduced their cattle holdings and made them dependent on other sources of income to feed their communities. Despite all this, the Herero people were generally opposed to the sales and believed the chiefs had no right to trade their land.

The planned Otavi railroad exacerbated the land issue, as it would cut through Hereroland, dividing the land into strips and leaving less land suitable for farming[242] (in 2001 the Herero sued the company in question[243]). According to some scholars the railway route prompted the Herero to rebel.[244] Bridgman notes that by 1900 very little Herero land had been alienated, but as the railroad construction reached Windhoek, the pace of the land loss

---

[240] Leutwein, T.G. (1906) *Elf Jahre Gouverneur in Deutsch-Südwestafrika*, Berlin: Mittler, 276. Cited in Ritter-Petersen, H.G. (1991) *The Herrenvolk mentality in German South West Africa 1884–1914*. DLitt (History). Pretoria: University of South Africa, 192.

[241] Ritter-Petersen, H.G. (1991) *The Herrenvolk mentality in German South West Africa 1884–1914*. DLitt (History). Pretoria: University of South Africa, 193.

[242] Drechsler, H. (1980) *Let us die fighting: The struggle of the Herero and Nama against the German imperialism (1894–1915)* (Bernd Zöllner, transl). London: Zed Press, 132.

[243] The company being sued is *Deutsche Bank*. It was a member of the Otavi Mines and Railway Company's board from 1900 to 1938. *Disconto-Gesellschaft*, a principal investor in the Otavi Mines and Railway Company, later merged with *Deutsche Bank* — hence the suit against the bank.

[244] See Madley, B. (2004, June) 'Patterns of frontier genocide 1803–1910: The aboriginal Tasmanians, the Yuki of California and the Herero of Namibia'. 6 (2) *Journal of Genocide Research*, 167–92, 182, relying on Wood, B. (ed) (1988) *Namibia 1884–1984: Readings on Namibia's history and society*. London: Namibia Support Committee, 195.

dramatically increased.[245] From 1897, land settlement changed rapidly and the number of white settlers rose from 1 774 in 1895 to 4 640 by 1903.[246] By 1910, as a result of the war and the consequent increased access to land, settler numbers had grown to 10 664 whites, including 7 935 Germans.[247]

The promulgation of the Credit Ordinance in 1903 also increased pressure on the Herero. This ordinance provided that the Herero's outstanding debts to Germans would be written off if not collected within a year.[248] This sparked a ruthless campaign by the settlers to collect Herero debt. About 106 000 claims were filed against the Herero in the newly created civil courts.[249] This resulted in huge resentment towards the traders.[250] Even the leader of the Social Democrats in Germany, August Bebel, stated in the *Reichstag* that he believed the Germans and traders had caused the Herero to rebel.[251]

The comprehensive and unremitting way in which the arrival of the Germans impinged on the Herero provided sufficient provocation for rebellion. Bridgman notes that in 1903 'the day when the Hereros would not have enough to continue their traditional ways of life was fast approaching'.[252] He also pointed out that by 1904 'the Hereros had so many reasons for rebelling that it might be more profitable to ask why they had not acted sooner'.[253] They were generally being treated poorly and disrespectfully, trade and credit agreements often involved premeditation if not deception, they were systematically being deprived of their land and livestock, they were soon to be confined to small reserves to which they had not agreed and they believed the only official who treated them justly had been killed. There seems to be ample evidence to suggest that such comprehensive exertion of pressure on the Herero was designed to force them into actions that could justify reprisals.

---

[245] Bridgman, J. (1981) *The revolt of the Hereros*. Los Angeles: University of California Press, 57.

[246] Werner, W. (1998) *No-one will become rich: Economy and society in the Herero reserves in Namibia 1913–1946*. Basel: P. Schlettwein, 43.

[247] Botha, C. (2000, May). 'The politics of land settlement in Namibia, 1890–1960'. 42 *South African Historical Journal*, 232–76, 273.

[248] Bridgman, J. (1981) *The revolt of the Hereros*. Los Angeles: University of California Press, 57.

[249] Schrank, G.I. (1974) *German South West Africa: Social and economic aspects of its history, 1884–1915*. PhD (History). New York University, 134.

[250] Bridgman, J. (1981) *The revolt of the Hereros*. Los Angeles: University of California Press, 57.

[251] *Ibid*, 70.

[252] *Ibid*, 57.

[253] *Ibid*.

Appropriating Herero land and cattle during and after the war

In 1903, before the war, Germany had acquired substantial land assets: they owned more than 19 million hectares, the concession companies owned more than 29 million hectares and the settlers just less than four million hectares. More than 31 million of the approximately 83 million hectares in GSWA were still in the hands of the indigenous population.[254] Put another way, in 1904, of the total of 500 000 square kilometres deemed suitable for settlement, whites only owned 28 000 (5.6 percent). At this time, more than a quarter of Herero land[255] was in the hands of settlers and, according to Bridgman, the pace at which Herero land was being taken predicted that complete dispossession was imminent.[256] Yet the settlers were still unsatisfied. They felt the process of acquiring more fertile land was too slow and more than 31 million hectares remained under the control of the indigenous population.[257]

During the war, the German authorities acted very quickly to confiscate land and cattle. In May 1905, while the war was still ongoing, the colonial administration announced that all tribal land would be expropriated. This was formalised in December 1905.[258] On 23 March 1906 it was announced that all property of the Herero, north of the Tropic of Capricorn, had been forfeited to the state. This became 'legal' on 7 August 1906 because, supposedly, 'no complaints were received'.[259] The Germans exerted control over the Herero in many ways at this time: from 1907 all locals over eight years of age had to carry identification and only with the consent of the Governor could they get land. So while the war continued (it 'officially' ended on 31 March 1907), German settlers increased in number, the number

---

[254] Werner, W. (1998) *No-one will become rich: Economy and society in the Herero reserves in Namibia 1913–1946*. Basel: P. Schlettwein, 44.

[255] On the land issue see further Richardson, H.J. (1984) 'Constitutive questions in the negotiations for Namibian independence'. 78 *American Journal of International Law*, 76.

[256] Bridgman, J. (1981) *The revolt of the Hereros*. Los Angeles: University of California Press, 52. See also Madley, B. (2004, June) 'Patterns of frontier genocide 1803–1910: The aboriginal Tasmanians, the Yuki of California and the Herero of Namibia'. 6 (2) *Journal of Genocide Research*, 167–92, 182.

[257] De Villiers, B. (2003, April) *Land reform: Issues and challenges. A comparative overview of experiences in Zimbabwe, Namibia, South Africa and Australia*. Johannesburg: Konrad Adenauer Foundation Occasional Papers, 30.

[258] The 1899 Hague Convention, to which Germany was a signatory, prohibited the seizure of the property of an enemy in article 23(g) of the Regulations contained in the Annex to the Convention.

[259] Werner, W. (1998) *No-one will become rich: Economy and society in the Herero reserves in Namibia 1913–1946*. Basel: P. Schlettwein, 47.

of German farms grew and German commercial agriculture output grew. It is not surprising, therefore, that the settlers supported the various decrees issued that affected the rights and resources of the Herero and others during these years.[260] They were no bystanders; they were directly involved in the further dispossession of the Herero because ultimately they benefited most. Today, many of the descendants of these settlers are still in possession of the land acquired then.

After the war, land holdings changed dramatically in favour of the white settlers — their land holdings rose from under four million hectares to 13.5 million hectares. By 1914 whites owned five times more land, at 140 000 square kilometres (28 percent).[261] The converse applies to the indigenous people — by 1915, black ownership of the land had fallen from the pre-war 31 million hectares to 13 million hectares. Yet land dispossession did not happen equally across the country; it was far more prevalent in the central and southern areas that the Nama and Herero previously occupied.

For Germany to realise its colonial dream, it was imperative to quash the Herero rebellion. Officials of the Colonial Office propounded the value of the territory on two occasions. On 30 January 1905, Dr Stuebel, the Director of the Colonial Office, stated that Germany had always seen GSWA as a settlement colony. On 23 March 1906, Hohenlohe Langenburg, the Deputy Director of the Colonial Office, repeated that GSWA was an area for settlement and rejected the view that it was worthless. He claimed that 700 of the soldiers who came to fight the Herero wanted to remain in GSWA, a demonstration of their appreciation of the value of GSWA.[262]

The extermination order announced by Von Trotha in Otjiherero stated that all the Herero were to vacate the land, as it now belonged to the Germans. The inclusion of the stipulation about land in the extermination order unambiguously shows that the intention was to drive the Herero out in order to take over the land. If they did not comply, they would have to deal with German guns. Soggot suggests that establishing a purely white society may have been part of the reason for the genocide.[263] Palmer argues, on the other hand, that the

---

[260] Bley, H. (1967) 'German South West Africa after the conquest 1904–1914'. In Segal, R. and First, R. *South West Africa: Travesty of trust.* London: Andre Deutsch, 35–53, 37.

[261] Ritter-Petersen, H.G. (1991) *The Herrenvolk mentality in German South West Africa 1884–1914.* DLitt (History). Pretoria: University of South Africa, 251.

[262] Wallenkampf, A.V. (1969) *The Herero rebellion in South West Africa: A study in German colonialism.* PhD thesis. Los Angeles: UCLA, 184–85.

[263] Soggot, D. (1986) *Namibia: The violent heritage.* London: Rex Collings, 4.

genocide was meant to 'prevent the reoccupation of the land by the Herero'.[264] She seems to suggest that the Herero rebellion of 1904 was aimed at reclaiming Herero land lost through sales and that it, therefore, had to be put down to prevent repossession. It is likely that Von Trotha had similar thoughts. Once the rebellion began, the Herero initially grouped together at Waterberg (partly for its defensive position) and thus were off their land (the land they still owned).

The immediacy with which steps were taken to acquire more land highlights the centrality of land acquisition as a motive for the genocide. In September 1904 even Governor Leutwein, probably in recognition of both the direction events were taking and his inability to change it, wrote in a report to the Colonial Office that 'the main objective of our colonial policy... must finally be white settlement'.[265] The *Denkschrift* of 29 November 1904, noted:

> *The solution of the land question always remained an exceedingly difficult problem. Land was the most important possession of the Natives while on the other hand it was the foundation for European settlement. Here lies from the beginning a difficult conflict of interests.* [266]

The genocide also targeted cattle in addition to land and with it the Herero identity. Herero cattle ownership was seen as a threat to German settlements.[267] In August 1907, colonial authorities issued new directives that further destroyed the Herero and their identity. They could no longer own cattle, a fundamental aspect of Herero culture. The breeding of livestock required special permission, which was not granted until 1912.[268] A ban was placed on traditional forms of organisation[269] and a number of chiefs and headman were executed as ringleaders of the uprising.[270] Even after 1908, when the concentration camps for the Herero were dismantled, all Africans over the age of eight had to wear

---

[264] Palmer, A. (1998, January) '*Colonial and modern genocide: explanations and categories*'. 21 (1) *Ethnic and Racial Studies*, 89–115, 94.
[265] Wallenkampf, A.V. (1969) *The Herero rebellion in South West Africa: A study in German colonialism*. PhD thesis. Los Angeles: UCLA, 207.
[266] *Ibid*.
[267] Bley, H. (1971) *South-West Africa under German rule 1894–1914*. London: Heinemann, 253.
[268] Werner, W. (1998) *No-one will become rich: Economy and society in the Herero reserves in Namibia 1913–1946*. Basel: P. Schlettwein, 47.
[269] Drechsler, H. (1980) *Let us die fighting: The struggle of the Herero and Nama against the German imperialism (1894–1915)* (Bernd Zöllner, transl). London: Zed Press, 231; Ritter-Petersen, H.G. (1991) *The Herrenvolk mentality in German South West Africa 1884–1914*. DLitt (History). Pretoria: University of South Africa, 240–243; Soggot, D. (1986) *Namibia: The violent heritage*. London: Rex Collings, 11.
[270] Katjavivi, P. (1989) *A history of resistance in Namibia*. Paris/London/Addis Ababa: UNESCO, 11.

metal passes which had the imperial insignia, magisterial district and labour number.[271] By then the Herero had forcibly become wage seekers as their own wealth had been stripped away.[272] So successful was this push the Herero into the labour force that by 1912, 90 percent of all Africans males in the Police Zone[273] were employed and only 200 Herero and Nama were not unemployed.[274]

Clearly, one problem with exterminating the Herero is that they would be lost as a labour force. Gann and Duigan attribute this lack of adequate consideration for the labour needs of the colony to Von Trotha, stating that he was a 'narrow-minded military specialist quite incapable of foreseeing the social or economic consequences of the strategy of annihilation'.[275] Stoecker, who calls Von Trotha a 'butcher in uniform', agrees that he was only interested in military victory and not in the future of the colony.[276] According to Stoecker, Von Trotha had one ambition only and that was to be able to report to the Kaiser that he had dealt with the rebellion.[277] The perception of some settlers and bureaucrats that the Herero did not make particularly good workers (the Bergdamara were thought to be the best)[278] probably contributed to the priority for security and peace over the need for labour. However, Epstein has pointed out that 'the policy of exterminating natives was not only a crime, it was also a blunder. The German colonies could never become large-scale areas of white settlements. Their economic development depended upon the existence of a native population'.[279]

---

271 Gewald, J-B. (2003) 'Imperial Germany and the Herero of Southern Africa: Genocide and the quest for recompense'. In Jones, A. (ed) *Genocide, war crimes and the West: Ending the culture of impunity.* London: Zed Press, 59–77, 63.

272 Drechsler, H. (1980) *Let us die fighting: The struggle of the Herero and Nama against the German imperialism (1894–1915)* (Bernd Zöllner, transl). London: Zed Press, 231.

273 GSWA was divided by the Red Line — a fence established in 1896 which separated the north from the southern and central parts to try and control the rinderpest epidemic. The southern and central parts were known as the Police Zone, as that is where control and settlement took place.

274 Bley, H. (1971) *South-West Africa under German rule 1894–1914.* London: Heinemann, 250.

275 Gann, L.H. & Duigan, P. (1977) *The rulers of German Africa 1884–1914.* Stanford: Stanford University Press, 110.

276 Stoecker, H. (ed) (1986) *German imperialism in Africa: From the beginnings until the Second World War.* London: C. Hurst & Co, 55.

277 *Ibid*, 57.

278 See Erichsen, C.W. (2004) *The Angel of Death has descended violently among them: A study of Namibia's concentration camps and prisoners-of-war, 1904–08.* MA thesis (History). University of Namibia, 283.

279 Epstein, K. (1959, October) 'Erzberger and the German colonial scandals, 1905–1910'. 74 (293) *English Historical Review,* 637–63, 648.

The genocidal intent of the war remained apparent even after the war ended; the Germans were not satisfied with having killed most of the Herero and having taken their land and cattle, they also implemented various measures to destroy the ethnic loyalty and identity among the remaining Herero. In 1907, 'foremen' appointed by the colonial administration replaced the system of chiefs.[280] The following statement by the Commissioner for Settlement counters the notion that the genocide was primarily the work and policy of a 'rogue' general, Von Trotha. Regarding the surviving Herero, he declared that 'our job is to strip the Herero of his heritage and national characteristics and gradually to submerge him, along with other natives into a single colored working class'.[281] The 'physical' genocide was not enough — the nationhood of the Herero needed to be obliterated.

The centrality of the land issue is illustrated by the fact that commercial farming in GSWA only really began after 1907.[282] Botha notes that settlement in GSWA truly took off after the war in 1908, partly because larger loans were given to the settlers.[283] In the 20 years between 1887 and 1907, only 480 farms were sold, but the war brought such change to GSWA that many German settlers were willing to focus on farming. In 1907 alone, 202 farms were sold and in 1908 another 147 were sold.[284] In 1904, whites owned 338 farms.[285] By 1913, there were 1331 white-owned farms and the white population had risen to 14 480.[286] Half the agricultural land in the Police Zone (the southern and central parts below the Red Line) was taken up by white farms. Whites, of whom 914 were German and the rest mainly Afrikaners, owned 1 042 of these farms. These white farmers owned 183 167 large livestock or ninety percent of the total of 205 643. Blacks owned only 22 476 cattle in the whole territory.[287] However, blacks owned about

---

[280] Stoecker, H. (ed) (1986) *German imperialism in Africa: From the beginnings until the Second World War.* London: C. Hurst & Co, 128. See also Bley, H. (1971) *South-West Africa under German rule 1894–1914.* London: Heinemann, 211.

[281] Sautman, B. (2001, Fall). 'Is Tibet China's colony? The claim of demographic catastrophe'. 15 *Columbia Journal of Asian Law,* 81, 86.

[282] Werner, W. (1998) *No-one will become rich: Economy and society in the Herero reserves in Namibia 1913–1946.* Basel: P. Schlettwein, 61.

[283] Botha, C. (2000, May). 'The politics of land settlement in Namibia, 1890–1960'. 42 *South African Historical Journal,* 232–76, 233.

[284] Stoecker, H. (ed) (1986) *German imperialism in Africa: From the beginnings until the Second World War.* London: C. Hurst & Co, 144.

[285] Suzman, J. (2002) *Minorities in imperial Namibia.* London: Minority Rights Group International, 7.

[286] Stoecker, H. (ed) (1986) *German imperialism in Africa: From the beginnings until the Second World War.* London: C. Hurst & Co, 144.

[287] Adams, F., Werner, W. & Vale, P. (1990) *The land issue in Namibia: An inquiry.* Windhoek: Namibian Institute for Social and Economic Research, University of Namibia, 15.

one third of all the small livestock.[288] A colonial memorandum on land holdings gives the following breakdown of farm sizes in 1913:
- seven land owners owned more than 100 000 hectares — that included the Rhenish missionary society and the Catholic Mission;
- 11 owned between 50 000 and 100 000 hectares;
- 88 farms comprised between 20 000 and 50 000 hectares;
- 275 farms consisted of between 10 000 and 20 000 hectares;
- 481 farms were between 5 000 and 10 000 hectares; and
- 275 farms were smaller than 5 000 hectares.[289]

Interracialism, mixed-race German citizens and alcoholism

Other developments in GSWA at the time added pressure on the Kaiser and the Germans to take action in their prize colony. Generally, there was concern that the settler community consisted only of working-class people and social outcasts.[290] This concern was exacerbated by the many interracial liaisons, which must have been anathema to those in Germany. Colonial Director Bernhard Durnberg stated that

> *the white race, being vastly inferior in numbers to the indigenous population, should maintain a superiority in life style and occupation, in order not to lose its reputation and sink down into the raw mass of natives and half casts. Thus, they should not work next to or in competition with Africa labourers.*[291]

Pfister notes that the 'efforts to make German South West Africa an exact copy of Germany and a breeding ground for German culture were accompanied by two fears: the fear of the "other" (ie that contacts with Africans would distort their own identity) and the fear of their own group, (ie that national and racial identity among the migrants might be all too fragile)'.[292]

German men fraternised with black women partly because there were only 19 white women for every 100 white male settlers.

---

[288] Werner, W. (1998) *No-one will become rich: Economy and society in the Herero reserves in Namibia 1913–1946*. Basel: P. Schlettwein, 48.

[289] Stoecker, H. (ed) (1986) *German imperialism in Africa: From the beginnings until the Second World War*. London: C. Hurst & Co, 144–45.

[290] Ritter-Petersen, H.G. (1991) *The Herrenvolk mentality in German South West Africa 1884–1914*. DLitt (History). Pretoria: University of South Africa, 97.

[291] *Ibid*, 86.

[292] Pfister, G. (2005) 'Sport, colonialism and the enactment of German identity — *Turnen* in South West Africa', 24. Paper delivered at the 20th International Congress for the Historical Sciences 3–9 July 2005, Sydney. Available at www.cishsydney2005.org/images/GertrundPfisterST25.doc

Süd-West-Afrika: „Ein Sonntag-Nachmittag im Herero-Dorf".

Postcard from GSWA showing mixed-race relationships between the settlers, soldiers and the Herero

The settlement commissioner Paul Rohrbach noted: 'That unmarried settlers have black bed and table fellows is as natural here as eating and drinking; the white traders do it likewise, the soldiers on the small and large posts, no less. Only, it is prohibited to take the native women into the men's quarters there.'[293] Those back home must have been appalled that the settler men not only had sexual and other liaisons with black women, but wanted to.[294] The number of mixed-race children in GSWA is subject to debate, but it seems that by World War I there were between 3 200 and 4 300.[295] The authorities were gravely concerned that the white race would degenerate into an inferior mixed race group.[296]

---

[293] Ritter-Petersen, H.G. (1991) *The Herrenvolk mentality in German South West Africa 1884–1914.* DLitt (History). Pretoria: University of South Africa, 105.
[294] *Ibid*, 104.
[295] *Ibid*, 108.
[296] See generally Wildenthal, L. (2001) *German woman for Empire, 1885–1945.* London: Duke University Press.

While these concerns increased from 1904 onwards, they had existed before and Leutwein himself considered this a serious problem in the mid-1890s.[297] He contended that in 50 years the colony would no longer be German but a 'bastard colony'.[298] In fact, the issue had been of concern since the 1880s when some Rhenish missionaries suggested the incidence of mixed marriages. Commissioner Heinrich Ernst Göring rejected this, but it continued to remain a problem and was raised with the Colonial Department by Governor Leutwein on a number of occasions in the late 1890s. Leutwein attempted to find ways to limit the affects of interracial marriages during this period but was told that the constitutional provisions as far as the children from such unions having German citizenship applied to GSWA. He was also told that nothing could be done about these unions and their effects.[299]

Leutwein's concerns were that the children from interracial liaisons received their father's citizenship and the authorities feared that they would, therefore, be equal to whites in the territory. The concern was not always about the actual number of mixed-race children, but the perception it created.[300] While the numbers of intermarriages were low, the fact that they occurred at all caused a panic and by 1890 colonial marriage registrars refused to officiate or sanction such unions.[301] There were only 24 legally recognised interracial unions by 1905. It seems that the number of sexual relationships was also low before that time, but this changed with the arrival of the German troops.[302]

[297] Krautwurst, U.R. (1997) *Tales of the 'land of stories': Settlers and anti-modernity in German colonial discourses on German South West Africa, 1884–1914*. PhD (History). Connecticut: University of Connecticut, 129.

[298] Pierard, R. (1971) 'The transportation of white women to German South West Africa, 1898–1914'. 12(3) *Race*, 317–322, 317.

[299] Krautwurst, U.R. (1997) *Tales of the 'land of stories': Settlers and anti-modernity in German colonial discourses on German South West Africa, 1884–1914*. PhD (History). Connecticut: University of Connecticut, 582–6.

[300] Ritter-Petersen, H.G. (1991) *The Herrenvolk mentality in German South West Africa 1884–1914*. DLitt (History). Pretoria: University of South Africa, 109–10.

[301] Lusane, C. (2003) *Hitler's Black Victims: The Historical Experiences of Afro-Germans, European Blacks and African Americans in the Nazi Era*. New York: Routledge 46–7.

[302] Oermann, N.O. (2003) 'The law and the colonial state: Legal codification versus practise in a German colony'. In Eley, G. and Retallack, J. (eds) *Wilhelminism and its legacies: German modernities, imperialism and the meanings of reform, 1890–1930*. New York: Berghahn, 176.

Mixed marriages were considered such a serious problem that a decree was issued in 1905 prohibiting magistrates from marrying mixed couples.[303] Church marriages were also prohibited.[304] A 1905 report spelled out the rationale for this measure:

> Male half-caste offspring would otherwise become subject to military duty, would be able to hold public offices, would have the right to vote when this was eventually instituted and would generally enjoy all political rights associated with the German nationality, which they would automatically gain legally by descent. These consequences were considered to be very dangerous, not only for the purity of the German race and the German social norms, but in particular as they undermined the power status of white people as a whole... It was considered that the prohibition of mixed marriages would not prevent sexual contacts between whites and Africans and the ensuing creation of half-caste children. These liaisons should, however, not be sanctioned legally and the offspring should not be legitimate or be allowed to participate in the political process of the country. The proclamation was also considered to have beneficial effects on the frequently very immature social attitudes of the settlers.[305]

Further steps were taken in 1907 and 1908 to dissolve those marriages that had taken place and to deprive white spouses of interracial unions of their civil rights, including the right to vote. In 1912, these marriages gained some degree of acceptance, as long as the couple obtained a certificate claiming that the lifestyle and the way the children were raised met the requirements of morals and decency.[306]

It is not surprising that, in this context, a concerted effort was undertaken to encourage white women to go to GSWA to keep the settler population pure. In a public lecture the mayor of Bückeburg, a Mr Kültz, implored white German women to go to GSWA by appealing to their patriotism, stating that 'it would be sad for German women if they could not muster enough from their midst who would regard it as a great noble cause to bring victory to German family life, to German culture, to German heritage in the new German territory'.[307] The system developed to attract German women included incentives, such as subsidised transport costs. The first women were sent to GSWA in 1896

---

[303] See further and on the issue of mixed relationships Zimmerer, J. In Zimmerer, J. & Zeller, J. (2008) *Genocide in German South-West Africa: The Colonial War of 1904–1908 and its aftermath.* Monmouth: Merlin Press, 19–37.

[304] Bley, H. (1967) 'German South West Africa after the conquest 1904–1914'. In Segal, R. and First, R. *South West Africa: Travesty of trust.* London: Andre Deutsch, 35–53, 37.

[305] Ritter-Petersen, H.G. (1991) *The Herrenvolk mentality in German South West Africa 1884–1914.* DLitt (History). Pretoria: University of South Africa, 122–23.

[306] *Ibid*, 123–27.

[307] *Ibid*, 116.

and, by 1902, 57 women had arrived there.[308] So concerned was the Colonial Society with miscegenation, which they deemed a 'cancer', that they alone, by 1907, had sent 501 potential brides to the colony and in 1905 began collecting funds to build a maternity home.[309]

Alcoholism was also a problem amongst the settler community. Colonial Director Durnburg noted that the average daily consumption of beer by white men in GSWA was 1.4 litres.[310] Berlin must have been alarmed by the deterioration of character in the very colony that was supposed to be the second *Heimat*, where they planned to preserve the traditions of pre-industrial Germany. The onslaught of issues in the colony; including alcoholism, interracial liaisons, mixed-race children entitled to German citizenship, the settlers' vociferous complaints about the 'protection' of the indigenous people and their lack of land, all must have led the Kaiser and others to act decisively. Genocide provided the answer: it would free up large tracts of land, it would punish those who challenged the *Reich* and it would conclusively settle the sovereignty issue and ensure German control. Thus, when the rebellion occurred and German citizens were killed, Germany plotted revenge and eradicating the Herero community undoubtedly must have seemed an attractive option to the decision-makers in Berlin.

Teaching the 'Natives' a lesson and promoting Germany's image

There are other hypotheses as to why the Germans dealt so ruthlessly with the Herero.[311] An event like genocide typically has a multifactorial aetiology.[312] Although the overarching motive was acquisition of land and livestock, a multiplicity of factors — including ideologies, intentions, the historical milieu, power relationships, cultural and religious beliefs and practices, precipitants, structural facilitating conditions, et cetera intersected and accrued to result in the eventual execution of genocide.

---

[308] *Ibid*, 111.
[309] Pierard, R. (1971) 'The transportation of white women to German South West Africa, 1898–1914'. 12(3) *Race*, 317–322, 318–319.
[310] Ritter-Petersen, H.G. (1991) *The Herrenvolk mentality in German South West Africa 1884–1914*. DLitt (History). Pretoria: University of South Africa, 98 fn 49.
[311] Frank Chalk and Kurt Jonassohn argue that the Herero blocked German access to wealth by not allowing them to attain their economic goals in the region. See Chalk, F. & Jonassohn, K. (1990) *The history and sociology of genocide: Analyses and case studies*. New Haven: Yale University Press, 23.
[312] See further Sarkin, J. (2009) *Colonial Genocide and Reparations Claims in the 21st Century: The Socio-Legal Context of Claims under International Law by the Herero against Germany for Genocide in Namibia, 1904–1908*. Westport: Praeger Security International.

The Germans likely saw the cost of quelling the Herero uprising, which was about 400 million marks[313] at that time,[314] simply as the cost of doing business in the colony, specifically to obtaining access to the land. So critical to the colonial enterprise was the subjugation of the Herero that thousands of German troops were sent to GSWA.[315] If Germany allowed the Herero to stand up for themselves, it would inevitably lead the way for other groups in GSWA and other colonies to follow suit. For Germany, this was not an option. The Herero and the other tribes had to be taught a lesson and the dire consequences were meant to deter others from contemplating rebellion. Many colonising nations utilised this strategy and Germany had employed it before 1904 in GSWA, specifically in 1896 against the Mbanderu.[316] Academic Trutz von Trotha has stressed that massacres were the best strategies for the colonialists to achieve the highest degree of intimidation with the least amount of resources.[317] In a review of Trutz von Trotha's work, Andreas Eckert notes that this 'tactic enables the invaders to demonstrate their absolute domination and establish their own monopoly of power'.[318] The Deputy Governor of the time, Hans Tecklenburg, underscored the idea that the Herero had to be subjugated in such a way that it would deter them (and anyone who may consider rebelling): 'The more the Herero tribe feels the consequences of the uprising, the less they will strive for repeating another one.'[319]

As noted before, Gewald attributed the outbreak of the war to settler paranoia, a series of misunderstandings and German colonial official Zürn, who

---

[313] Hull believes the cost of putting the rebellion down was 600 million marks. She notes that of the 14 000 soldiers deployed, 1 500 died. Hull, I.V. (2003) 'Military culture and the production of final solutions in the colonies: The example of Wilhelminian Germany'. In Gellately, R. & Kiernan, B. (eds) *The specter of genocide mass murder in historical perspective.* Cambridge: Cambridge University Press, 144.

[314] Stoecker, H. & Sebald, P. (1987) 'Enemies of the colonial idea'. In Knoll, A.J. & Gann, L.H. (eds) *Germans in the tropics: Essays in German colonial history* (2ed). New York/London: Greenwood Press, 59–72, 63.

[315] Eveleigh, W. (1915) *South-West Africa.* Cape Town: Maskew Miller, 137.

[316] Stoecker, H. (ed) (1986) *German imperialism in Africa: From the beginnings until the Second World War.* London: C. Hurst & Co, 47.

[317] Von Trotha, T. (1994) *Koloniale Herrschaft: Zur soziologischen Theorie der Staatsentstehung am Beispiel des' Schutzgebietes Togo'.* Tübingen: J.C.B. Mohr.

[318] Eckert, A. (1997) 'Theories of colonial rule'. 38 (2) *Journal of African History,* 325–26, 325.

[319] Quoted in Schuring, E. (2004) *History obliges: The real motivations behind German aid flows in the case of Namibia.* MA thesis (Law & Diplomacy). Fletcher School of Law and Diplomacy, Tufts University, 33.

supposedly panicked.[320] Yet, Oermann dismisses this hypothesis in favour of Horst Drechsler's view that the Herero rebellion was planned and intended to drive the Germans out of GSWA.[321] Oermann agrees that Lieutenant Zürn played a role in precipitating the rebellion, but not to the extent Gewald alleges. Regardless of whether German officials set the war in motion or the Herero rose up in a planned event, the rebellion acted as a catalyst for the Germans to get what they wanted: arable, fertile land[322] with greater security for existing and potential settlers. However, it seems clear that Gewald is correct in assuming that Herero action was merely reactionary, not causative.

Postcard of Herero patrol dated 1906

[320] Gewald J-B. (1999) *Herero heroes: A socio-political history of the Herero of Namibia 1890–1923*. Oxford: James Currey, 142. See also Bley, H. (1971) *South-West Africa under German rule 1894–1914*. London: Heinemann, 133–43.

[321] Oermann, N.O. (1999) *Mission, church and state relations in South West Africa under German rule (1884–1915)*. Stuttgart: Franz Steiner Verlag, 95.

[322] Bullock, A.L.C. (1939) *Germany's colonial demands*. London: Oxford University Press.

The genocide was also committed 'as a reprisal for having the gall to rebel against *Herrenvolk* colonial rule'.[323] Bridgman notes in this regard that the 'various victories by the Hereros in the months of March and April, glorious as they were at the time, sealed the fate of the tribe for they convinced the military authorities in Berlin that nothing short of total annihilation would be acceptable'.[324]

In August and November 1904, colonial authorities refused Governor Leutwein permission to negotiate with the Herero and turned down the Rhenish Missionary Society offer to use missionaries as peacekeepers.[325] Neither did Berlin seek negotiation. These actions demonstrated that the intention was not to find a peaceful or political solution, but a military one, which would expedite the seizure of land and cattle. If the Germans were to negotiate successfully and make peace with the Herero, it would have undermined their attempts to acquire the Herero land. Newly arriving German settlers continued the push for the most arable land,[326] and thus supported violent action against the Herero and other indigenous groups.[327] Gewald argues that due 'to German short-sightedness and conflicts within the German military and administration, opportunities to come to a negotiated settlement with the Herero were constantly ignored in favour of a needlessly protracted genocidal war'.[328] This was not the result of short-sightedness nor ignoring opportunities; the intention was to exterminate the Herero. Germany wanted a long-term result that precluded the possibility that the Herero might rise up again to take back their land. Thus it was not a 'needlessly protracted genocidal war'. Both the Berlin authorities and the settlers wanted the war.

The war would have ended by 1905, if the initial *Vernichtungsbefehl* was not rescinded by the Kaiser in an attempt to limit damage to Germany's international reputation. Instead, the war became protracted and the genocide now had to be achieved more surreptitiously than was initially intended. This led to the use of new tactics, such as maintaining the cordon that pushed the Herero into the desert to die and working and starving them to death in the concentration camps.

---

[323] Nagan, W.P. & Rodin, V. F. (2003–2004) 'Racism, genocide and mass murder: Toward a legal theory about group deprivations'. *National Black Law Journal*, 133, 176.

[324] Bridgman, J. (1981) *The revolt of the Hereros*. Los Angeles: University of California Press, 92.

[325] Oermann, N.O. (1999) *Mission, church and state relations in South West Africa under German rule (1884–1915)*. Stuttgart: Franz Steiner Verlag, 100.

[326] See Böhlke-Itzen, J. (2004) *Kolonialschuld und Entschädigung: Der deutsche Völkermord an den Herero (1904–1907)*. Frankfurt am Main: Brandes & Apsel, 37.

[327] Gambari, I.A. (1971, October). 'Review of H Bley *South West Africa under German Rule, 1894–1914*; South-West Africa (Namibia): Proposals for action'. 9 (3) *Journal of Modern African Studies*, 484–86, 484.

[328] Gewald J-B. (1999) *Herero heroes: A socio-political history of the Herero of Namibia 1890–1923*. Oxford: James Currey, 141.

Living conditions on the Shark Island concentration camp

The need for punishment and the consequent decision to exterminate the Herero also stem from Von Trotha's exasperation at failing to subjugate them.[329] Obtaining undisputed sovereignty in GSWA was important because Germany 'still suffered from social, regional and professional cleavages' despite their unification in the 1870's — hence 'colonialism became a vehicle to unite the Nation'.[330] In fact, the Kaiser had a vision of German expansion and sought to improve its status in world affairs.[331] Colonies helped reinforce central power in Germany[332] and German prestige and pride were now intricately tied to

---

[329] Eveleigh, W. (1915) *South-West Africa*. Cape Town: Maskew Miller, 134.
[330] Walther, D.J. (2002) *Creating Germans abroad: Cultural policies and national indemnity in Namibia*. Athens, Ohio: Ohio University Press, 2.
[331] Kennedy, P. (1982) 'The Kaiser and German *Weltpolitik*: Reflections on Wilhelm II's place in the making of German foreign policy'. In Röhl, J.C.G. & Sombart, N. (eds) *Kaiser Wilhelm II, new interpretations: The Corfu papers*. Cambridge/New York: Cambridge University Press, 143–68, 158.
[332] Schnieder, T. (1967) 'Political and social development in Europe'. In *The new Cambridge modern history, XI: Material progress and worldwide problems, 1870–1898*. Cambridge: Cambridge University Press, 243–73, 252.

its colonies.[333] Because Germany was the last European country to build a colonial empire, it undertook the process rapidly and ruthlessly. Furthermore, German colonies were less extensive than those of other colonial powers and it was seen that 'Germany had not done well in the scramble for Africa'.[334] The Herero rebellion challenged 'German state authority and prestige',[335] hence the rush to put it down quickly before it caused too much damage to Germany's reputation and before it could significantly undermine Germany's ability to serve as an influential colonial power.[336]

Simmons's analysis of British colonialist grandiosity and rage[337] also applies to the Germans. She cites Elleke Boehmer's observation that 'the final decades of the 19th century were a time also of growing self doubt and cultural panic... as expressions of anxiety about social regression and national decline were widespread'.[338] The British, like the Germans, were plagued by national and international insecurity and were resentful that their empire was not 'as fabulous as advertised'.[339] According to her, the vulnerable grandiosity of the imperialist had to be shored up by the imperial subjects; the identity of the imperial power was boosted by 'subjugating the native'.[340] If these imperial subjects, in this case the Herero, dared to thwart the ambitions of the empire,

---

[333] The Kaiser believed that achieving a colonial empire was a way to increase Germany's national prestige. Bullock, A.L.C. (1939) *Germany's colonial demands*. London: Oxford University Press, 90.
[334] Gann, L.H. & Duigan, P. (1977) *The rulers of German Africa 1884–1914*. Stanford: Stanford University Press, 45.
[335] Hull, I.V. (2003) 'Military culture and the production of final solutions in the colonies: The example of Wilhelminian Germany'. In Gellately, R. & Kiernan, B. (eds) *The specter of genocide mass murder in historical perspective*. Cambridge: Cambridge University Press, 146.
[336] *Ibid.*
[337] Simmons, D. (2003) 'Chivalry, "mutiny" and Sherlock Holmes: Three aspects of imperial grandiosity and rage'. *Psychology of the Self Online*. Available at: www.psychologyoftheself.com/papers/simmons.htm
[338] Boehmer, E. (1995) *Colonial and postcolonial literature: Migrant metaphors*. Oxford: Oxford University Press, 33. Cited in Simmons, D. (2003) 'Chivalry, "mutiny" and Sherlock Holmes: Three aspects of imperial grandiosity and rage'. *Psychology of the Self Online*. Available at: www.psychologyoftheself.com/papers/simmons.htm
[339] Simmons, D. (2003) 'Chivalry, "mutiny" and Sherlock Holmes: Three aspects of imperial grandiosity and rage'. *Psychology of the Self Online*. Available at: www.psychologyoftheself.com/papers/simmons.htm
[340] Jan Mohamed, A.R. (1986) 'The economy of Manichean allegory: The function of racial difference in colonialist literature'. In Gates, H.L. (ed) *Race, Writing and Difference*. Chicago: University of Illinois Press, 85. Cited in Simmons, D. (2003) 'Chivalry, "mutiny" and Sherlock Holmes: Three aspects of imperial grandiosity and rage'. *Psychology of the Self Online*. Available at: www.psychologyoftheself.com/papers/simmons.htm

it typically reacted with excessive rage and revenge. The Germans, like the British in India, experienced challenge to their authority as an 'assault on their grandiosity' and the 'hysteria' of their response shows what a severe threat it was to their self-image. The Herero uprising, like the Indian Mutiny of 1857, was therefore not treated 'simply as a physical challenge to be put down, but as a terrifying assault' upon their identity and their fantasies of power.[341]

In addition, Germany saw the Herero's attack on the white settlers, which resulted in the deaths of approximately 150 settlers, as an unprovoked, motiveless assault on the entire German nation. These deaths came only weeks after the Bondelswartz also killed several German farmers during their uprising.[342] Getting revenge and sending a firm message to the locals was all the more vital.

Calls to punish the Herero came from various parts, including the Commandant of Swakopmund. He sent a telegram to the German Foreign Office on 19 January 1904 stating that 'the Hereros must be disarmed, mercilessly punished and rounded up to perform forced labor for the railway'. The chief engineer of the Otavi railway wrote to the head of German South West Africa affairs in the Colonial Office, also on 19 January 1904: 'All here in the colony agree that this rebellion must be put down with severity and that all those responsible must receive their just desserts.' The commander of the ship *HMS Habicht*, which was diverted to GSWA, wrote on 4 February 1904, to the Imperial Naval Office, that 'the most severe punishment needs to be inflicted on the enemy…The only way to restore calm and confidence among the whites is to disarm the rebels completely and to confiscate all their land and cattle'.[343] All these statements occurred at the beginning of the war. When the 'rebellion' could not readily be put down sentiments towards the Herero, especially in Berlin, hardened even further.

The settlers reflected these same attitudes, as noted above. A missionary observed that the settlers were 'consumed with inexpiable hatred and a terrible thirst for revenge, one might even say they are thirsting for the blood of the Herero. All you hear these days is "make a clean sweep, hang them, shoot them to the last man, give no quarter". I shudder to think what may happen in the months ahead. The Germans will doubtless exact a grim vengeance'.[344]

---

[341] Simmons, D. (2003) 'Chivalry, "mutiny" and Sherlock Holmes: Three aspects of imperial grandiosity and rage'. *Psychology of the Self Online.* Available at: www.psychologyoftheself.com/papers/simmons.htm
[342] Oermann, N.O. (1999) *Mission, church and state relations in South West Africa under German rule (1884–1915).* Stuttgart: Franz Steiner Verlag, 93.
[343] Drechsler, H (1986) *Let us die fighting.* Berlin: Akademie-Verlag, 145.
[344] *Ibid.*

Jacob Morenga (seated) with some of his guerrilla fighters

GSWA soon gained the image of 'the problem child of its colonies'.[345] This blow to German prestige was exacerbated by the inability of the German troops to quickly and efficiently put down the rebellion with all the resources at their disposal. A newsletter of 18 November 1904, *The Owl*, from to Cape Town, South Africa, noted:

> *Summed up in a few words, it may be said that for sheer incompetence to deal with native enemies, for gross inability to cope with a situation beyond prescribed parading and for utter inability in handling troops against a heavily hampered enemy, the campaign against the Hereros stands out blackly in the history of South African warfare.*[346]

---

[345] Hull, I.V. (2005) *Absolute destruction: Military culture and practices of war in Imperial Germany.* Ithaca: Cornell University Press, 8.

[346] *The Owl* (Cape Town) 18 November 1904.

In spite of this, Dr W Kluz, in his book *Deutsch Süd-Afrika in 25 Jahre* (1909), wrote:

> The greater part of the work done in the first twenty-five years of German rule in South Africa has been accomplished by German troops. The colony in its present form and in its possible future development as a German country, would be an impossibility without the fights and the successes of the German soldier. In the past as well as in the future, there are other factors in the forefront of German dominion in addition to the soldier; but for the first twenty-five years he holds first place.[347]

Critically, even the German political parties normally opposed to military expropriation supported sending troops to quell the rebellion in GSWA. They knew what was being done. If the German state gave no direct order, at the very least it condoned the actions taken and directly supported them by the granting the necessary resources to carry out the genocide.

---

[347] Calvert, A.F. (1915) *South West Africa: During the German occupation 1884–1914*. London: T. Werner Laurie, 30.

CHAPTER TWO

IMPLEMENTING THE GENOCIDE: ANNIHILATING 'THE AFRICAN TRIBES WITH STREAMS OF BLOOD AND STREAMS OF GOLD'[1]

I am sending a word to you Hereros, you who are Hereros are no longer under the Germans... You Hereros must now leave this land it belongs to the Germans. If you do not do this I shall remove you with the big gun. A person in German land shall be killed by the gun. I shall not catch women and the sick but I will chase them after their chiefs or I will kill them with the gun. These are my words to the Herero nation.
— The Great General of the Kaiser, Trotha[2]

In order to secure the peaceful White settlement against the bad, culturally inept and predatory native tribe, it is possible that its actual eradication may become necessary under certain conditions.
— Settlement Commissioner Dr Paul Rohrbach[3]

1   Von Trotha, cited in many sources including Bridgman, J. (1981) *The revolt of the Hereros*. Los Angeles: University of California Press, 111–12; Gewald J-B. (1999) *Herero heroes: A socio-political history of the Herero of Namibia 1890–1923*. Oxford: James Currey, 174.
2   General von Trotha's order as translated from the Otjiherero version that he issued in October 1904. Quoted in Gewald, J-B. & Silvester, J. (2003) *Words cannot be found. German colonial rule in Namibia: An annotated reprint of the 1918 Blue Book*. Leiden: Brill, 108 fn 110. Steinmetz cites the same decree and the differences in translation are interesting:
    'I, the great General of the German soldiers, send this letter to the Herero people. The Herero are no longer German subjects... The Herero nation must leave the country. If they do not leave, I will force them out with the *Groot Rohr* [cannon]. Every Herero, armed or unarmed... will be shot dead within the German borders. I will no longer accept women and children, but will force them back to their people or shoot at them. These are my words to the Herero people. The great General of the powerful German Emperor.' *Bundesarchiv, Reichskolonialamt (RKA, R1001), Vol. 2089*, Berlin, 7. In Steinmetz, G. (2005) 'From 'Native Policy' to exterminationism: German Southwest Africa, 1904'. In *Comparative Perspective, Theory and Research in Comparative Social Analysis, Paper 30*. Los Angeles: Department of Sociology, UCLA, 1. Available at: http://repositories.cdlib.org/cgi/viewcontent.cgi?article=1036&context=uclasoc
3   Settlement Commissioner Dr Paul Rohrbach quoted in Lusane, C. (2003) *Hitler's Black Victims: The Historical Experiences of Afro-Germans, European Blacks and African Americans in the Nazi Era*. New York: Routledge, 43.

German brutalities before 1904

Many have debated whether German cruelty in the colonies exceeded that of other colonial powers. According to Cooper, what the Germans did to the Herero was 'among the most inhumane actions of the colonial era'.[4] On the other hand, Howard notes the matching brutality of the British: 'The British were often quite ruthless in their suppression of resistance. For example, every person in the market of the village of Muruka (Kenya) was slaughtered to revenge the killing of one British soldier in 1902.'[5] Yet others have argued that despite their abhorrent treatment of the Herero and Nama, 'the Germans treated the Herero more carefully than the British had treated Aboriginal Tasmanians or white Californians the Yuki'.[6] Similarly, Stratton argues that Germany's colonial history was 'no more bloodthirsty than that of the other European nation states'.[7] Some at the time even saw the results of the genocide as positive.

While German conduct towards the Herero was unique in that it constituted genocide, brutal violence against and mass killings of colonial subjects were ubiquitous and date back to the earliest times of German settlement. Even if the general violent conduct was not specifically ordered, it was habitually condoned; more often it was exalted and rewarded by those in authority, both in and outside the military. Kesting reports that from 1885 to 1918 'blacks residing in German South West Africa, Togo, the Cameroons and German East Africa experienced genocide, incarceration in concentration camps, starvation [and] forced labour deportations...'[8] The Germans committed such atrocities before and after they inflicted them on the Herero, not only in Africa, but also in colonies such as Samoa[9] and New Guinea. Although

---

[4] Cooper, A.D. (2001) *Ovambo politics in the twentieth century.* Lanham: University Press of America, 9.

[5] See Howard, R.E. (1986) *Human rights in Commonwealth Africa.* Totowa, New Jersey: Rowman & Littlefield, 9.

[6] See Madley, B. (2004, June) 'Patterns of frontier genocide 1803–1910: The Aboriginal Tasmanians, the Yuki of California and the Herero of Namibia'. 6 (2) *Journal of Genocide Research,* 167–92, 183.

[7] Stratton, J. (2003) 'It almost needn't have been the Germans: The state, colonial violence and the Holocaust'. 6 (4) *European Journal of Cultural Studies,* 507–27, 516.

[8] Kesting, R.W. (1998, Winter) 'Blacks under the swastika: A research note'. 83 (1) *Journal of Negro History,* 84–99, 85. See also Blackshire-Belay, C.A. (1992, December) 'German imperialism in Africa: The distorted images of Cameroon, Namibia, Tanzania and Togo'. 23 (2) *Journal of Black Studies,* 235–46.

[9] See Kennedy, P.M. (1974) *The Samoan tangle: A study in Anglo-German-American Relations 1878–1900.* Dublin: Irish University Press. See also Hempenstall, P.J. (1978) *Pacific islanders under German rule. A study in the meaning of colonial resistance.* Canberra: Australian National University Press.

reports indicate that the German 'scorched earth policy in suppressing the 1905–1907 Maji Rebellion'[10] in Tanzania left between 80 000 and 300 000 Africans dead,[11] some sources put this figure as high as half a million.[12] Two governmental commissions of enquiry investigating the Maji-Maji rebellion reported that the outbreak of the conflict is primarily attributable to the draconian policies of the Government and their ruthless implementation by its people in the area.

Brutality was thus common not only in relation to the Herero. Nor did it cease when the 1904 order was withdrawn — neither in GSWA nor in other parts of the world. According to Lundtofte, 'the threshold between total war and genocide in the colonies is…very low and easily crossed. Even the dividing line between the arbitrary destruction of the means of subsistence of African tribes in French and British colonies and the encirclement and forced containment on the barren plains is not great'.[13] Yet, the Herero genocide was not merely an escalation of violence that crossed a threshold; 'in the Herero case German conduct not only departed in character from the conduct of others but also from the German conduct in quelling other African rebellions'.[14] The genocide was not the independent action of a rogue general, nor was it an arbitrary military strategy decided upon by the soldiers in the field. The Herero were treated differently because of what they had done, because they had contested the process of colonisation. The reprisals were meant to send a message to the Herero and to other groups about the consequences of insubordination. However, most importantly, German authorities undertook the genocide because they wanted the Herero land and cattle.

---

10 Sautman, B. (2001, Fall) 'Is Tibet China's colony?. The claim of demographic catastrophe'. 15 *Columbia Journal of Asian Law*, 81, 86. See also Zirkel, K. (1999) 'Military power in German colonial policy: The Schutztruppen and their leaders in the East and South West Africa, 1888–1918'. In Killingray, D. & Omissi, D. (eds) *Guardians of Empire: The armed forces of the colonial powers, 1700–1964*. Manchester: Manchester University Press, 91–113, 102.

11 See further Diebold, E., Engelhardt, S. & Iskenius, D. (2004, December) 'Facing the past to liberate the future: Colonial Africa in the German mind'. 6 *Humanity in Action. Reports of the 2004 Fellows in Denmark, Germany and the Netherlands*. New York, 53–58.

12 Zirkel, K. (1999) 'Military power in German colonial policy: The Schutztruppen and their leaders in the East and South West Africa, 1888–1918'. In Killingray, D. & Omissi, D. (eds) *Guardians of Empire: The armed forces of the colonial powers, 1700–1964*. Manchester: Manchester University Press, 91–113,102.

13 Lundtofte, H. (2003) 'Radicalization of the German suppression of the Herero rising in 1904'. In Jensen, S.L.B. (ed) *Genocide: Cases, comparisons and contemporary debates*. Copenhagen: Danish Center for Holocaust and Genocide Studies, 15, 52.

14 Ibid, 15, 19.

Corporal punishment was prevalent in German colonies as a way to deal with local populations.[15] In Cameroon even women were flogged and flogging was so common it became known as the '25 country' (referring to the standard sentence of 25 lashes).[16] In East Africa, too, corporal punishment was extensively used[17] and 50 lashes could be imposed on one occasion.[18] In Togo the local inhabitants were disciplined with 15 strokes for 'offences' such as 'perpetual laziness'.[19] According to Stoecker, flogging in German colonies was rivalled by no other colonial master except in the Belgian Congo.[20] Yet it was widely criticised in Germany and in the *Reichstag*. Socialist and democratically inclined political parties claimed it was inhuman, brutal and unworthy of a state that had abolished flogging as a punishment in many parts in 1848 and completely removed it from its penal code in 1871.[21] The parties generally accused the colonial troops of crimes against the locals in the colonies and the 'handful of Hottentots'[22] in the South West colony. They specifically objected not only to the suppression of the Herero but also to the cruel action taken in East Africa (today Tanzania,[23] Rwanda and Burundi).[24]

In GSWA corporal punishment by the settlers was common despite the fact that 'the colonial right to discipline of employers in South West Africa had

---

[15] Knoll, A.J. (1939) *Togo under imperial Germany 1884–1914*. Stanford: Hoover Institution Press.

[16] Stoecker, H. (1987) 'The position of Africans in the German colonies'. In Knoll, A.J. & Gann, L.H. (eds) *Germans in the tropics: Essays in German colonial history* (2 ed). New York/London: Greenwood Press, 119–29, 123.

[17] Read, J.S. (1969) 'Kenya, Tanzania and Uganda'. In Milner, A. (ed) *African penal systems*. London: Routledge & Kegan Paul, 91–164.

[18] Stoecker, H. (1987) 'The position of Africans in the German colonies'. In Knoll, A.J. & Gann, L.H. (eds) *Germans in the tropics: Essays in German colonial history* (2 ed). New York/London: Greenwood Press, 119–29, 123.

[19] Knoll, A.J. (1939) *Togo under imperial Germany 1884–1914*. Stanford: Hoover Institution Press, 71.

[20] Stoecker, H. (1987) 'The position of Africans in the German colonies'. In Knoll, A.J. & Gann, L.H. (eds) *Germans in the tropics: Essays in German colonial history* (2 ed). New York/London: Greenwood Press, 119–29, 123.

[21] *Ibid*.

[22] Dedering, T. (1999) 'The prophet's "War against Whites": Shepherd Stuurman in Namibia and South Africa 1904–1907'. 40 (1) *Journal of African History*, 1–19, 4.

[23] See further Illife, J. (1969) *Tanganyika under German rule, 1905–1912*. Cambridge: Cambridge University Press.

[24] See generally Knoll, A.J. & Gann, L.H. (eds) (1987) *Germans in the tropics: Essays in German colonial history*. New York/London: Greenwood Press.

no clear basis in positive law'.[25] The courts in GSWA also applied corporal punishment in sentencing and, during 1903 and 1904, 340 such sentences were imposed.[26] The number of such punishments continued to rise thereafter, so that by 1911 and 1912, 1 655 floggings were imposed. Yet the practice was even more prevalent in other parts of the colonial empire — between 1912 and 1913, 8 057 such sentences were imposed in German East Africa and 4 800 in Cameroon.[27] The arbitrary, harsh and brutal nature of the judicial system in the German colonies has been widely criticised[28] and John Iliffe argues that 'no study of German administration can have any reality without stressing the horrors of the almost unrestricted flogging'.[29]

In addition to the corporal punishments meted out by the courts, common assaults were also routine, so much so that the colonial secretary in Dar es Salaam noted in 1907 that 'nearly every white man walks around with a whip…and almost every white man indulges in striking any black man he chooses to'.[30] In GSWA, employers regularly assaulted or killed their Herero labourers. In a letter to the Nama chief, Witbooi, Samuel Maherero complained that the Germans regularly and arbitrarily killed Herero and Nama people.[31] The courts did not offer any protection either. Under-Chief Daniel Kariko of the Omaruru stated: 'Our people were being robbed and deceived right and left by German traders, their cattle were taken by force; they were flogged and ill-treated and got no redress. In fact the German police assisted the traders instead of protecting us.'[32] Governor Leutwein's comments support this contention. He noted that 'racial hatred has become rooted in the very

---

25 Schwirck, H. (2002) 'Law's violence and the boundary between corporal discipline and physical abuse in German South West Africa'. 36 *Akron Law Review*, 81, 89 & 105.
26 Stoecker, H. (1987) 'The position of Africans in the German colonies'. In Knoll, A.J. & Gann, L.H. (eds) *Germans in the tropics: Essays in German colonial history* (2 ed). New York/London: Greenwood Press, 119–29, 124.
27 *Ibid.*
28 *Ibid.*
29 *Ibid.*
30 *Ibid,* 119–29, 125.
31 Katjavivi, P. (1989) *A history of resistance in Namibia.* Paris/London/Addis Ababa: UNESCO, 9; Madley, B. (2004, June). 'Patterns of frontier genocide 1803–1910: The aboriginal Tasmanians, the Yuki of California and the Herero of Namibia'. 6 (2) *Journal of Genocide Research*, 167–92, 184; Drechsler, H. (1980) *Let us die fighting: The struggle of the Herero and Nama against the German imperialism (1894–1915)* (Bernd Zöllner, transl). London: Zed Press, 143.
32 Gewald, J-B. & Silvester, J. (2003) *Words cannot be found. German colonial rule in Namibia: An annotated reprint of the 1918 Blue Book.* Leiden: Brill, 84.

framework of justice'.[33] The severe bias of the justice system is evident in the edict issued by the *Deutsche Kolonialbund*, which stated that in court only the evidence of seven Coloured persons could outweigh the evidence of one white man.

The treatment accorded to Herero women was specifically abusive.[34] Even before the war, rape was so common in GSWA that the German settlers gave it names like '*Verkafferung* or going native and *Schmutzwirtschaft* or dirty trade'.[35] When a Swiss newspaper ran a story about the gang rape of a Herero woman, colonial officials noted that such incidents were not unusual: 'The wholesale rape of Herero women by German soldiers' continued long after 1908.[36] If the practice was so widespread before and after the war, there is reason to believe that among captive Herero women during the war the incidents of rape increased. Yet there do not seem to have been any prosecutions for these rapes.[37] One incident in particular infuriated the Herero: a settler killed the daughter-in-law of a Herero chief because she refused his sexual advances. The Herero's anger intensified when a German court acquitted the settler. Even though the killer was convicted on appeal, his three-year sentence was interpreted as an indication that Herero life was of little worth to the Germans.[38]

Schwirck describes how the Germans treated the indigenous population similarly to 'enemies of the *Reich*', with 'exceptional laws' applying to them. Specifically, the 'genocidal military treatment' accorded to the Herero 'markedly contrasted with that of women and children or of servants for that

---

[33] Bley, H. (1971) *South-West Africa under German rule 1894–1914*. London: Heinemann, 140. Quoted in Madley, B. (2004, June) 'Patterns of frontier genocide 1803–1910: The aboriginal Tasmanians, the Yuki of California and the Herero of Namibia'. 6 (2) *Journal of Genocide Research*, 167–92, 181.

[34] See various chapters in Zimmerer, J. and Zeller, J. (2008) *Genocide in German South-West Africa: The Colonial War of 1904–1908 and its aftermath*. Monmouth: Merlin Press.

[35] See Madley, B. (2004, June) 'Patterns of frontier genocide 1803–1910: The aboriginal Tasmanians, the Yuki of California and the Herero of Namibia'. 6 (2) *Journal of Genocide Research*, 167–92, 183, relying on Rohrbach, P. (1907) *Deutsche Kolonialwirtschaft, vol. I: Südwestafrika*. Berlin/Schoneberg: Buchverlag der Hilfe, 243.

[36] Gewald, J-B. (1999) 'The road of the man called Love and the sack of Sero: The Herero-German War and the export of the Herero labour to the South African Rand'. 40(1) *Journal of African History*, 21–40, 28–9.

[37] Drechsler, H. (1980) *Let us die fighting: The struggle of the Herero and Nama against the German imperialism (1894–1915)* (Bernd Zöllner, transl). London: Zed Press, 130–33.

[38] See Madley, B. (2004, June) 'Patterns of frontier genocide 1803–1910: The aboriginal Tasmanians, the Yuki of California and the Herero of Namibia'. 6 (2) *Journal of Genocide Research*, 167–92, 181.

matter'. Unlike the latter groups who 'played undeniably crucial roles in social reproduction', 'natives' were seen as 'apart from rather than a part of German society and at times even as socially expendable. Legal discrimination against natives...represented, then, an amalgam of the types of discrimination present in contemporary German law'.[39]

Before the uprising, the Herero leader, Samuel Maherero, stressed this brutality in his attempt to elicit support from other groups. But complaints about German viciousness were nothing new. As early as 1893, Nama Chief Hendrik Witbooi complained to the Cape Undersecretary for Native Affairs. The response to that letter, below, indicates the reluctance of those at the Cape to get involved:

> *Complaint of treatment received at hands of Germans*
> Good Friend,
> The Honourable the Secretary for Native Affairs has instructed me to reply to your letter of the — to inform you that your communication of the 4*th* August last, addressed to the Magistrate Walvis Bay complaining of the treatment which you have received at the hands of the Germans, having been referred to Her Majesty's Government, a reply has been received by His Excellency the High Commissioner from the Secretary of State to the following effect: That the British Government has promised that of Germany not to interfere in certain parts of West Africa among which is your District and that it is impossible to take back that promise. That the British Government has no knowledge of and is in no way responsible for anything that may be done in those countries over which German protection is exercised and would advise you, if you have any complaints to make to lay them before the German Imperial Commissioner at Windhoek.
> The Colonial Government therefore, you will see, cannot interfere in any matters occurring within the area of the German Protectorate.
> I remain your Friend
> J Rose-Innes
> Under Secretary for Native Affairs[40]

In a letter to Hendrik Witbooi of the Nama dated 11 January 1904, just as the war began, Maherero wrote:

> *All our obedience and patience with the Germans is of little avail, for each day they shoot someone dead for no reason at all...Let us die fighting rather than die as a*

---

[39] Schwirck, H. (2002) 'Law's violence and the boundary between corporal discipline and physical abuse in German South West Africa'. 36 *Akron Law Review*, 81, 104.

[40] Contained in Gewald, J-B. & Silvester, J. (2003) *Words cannot be found. German colonial rule in Namibia: An annotated reprint of the 1918 Blue Book*. Leiden: Brill, 203.

result of maltreatment, imprisonment or some other calamity. Tell all the kapteins [captains] down there to rise and do battle.[41]

Maherero's letter shows that the behaviour of the Germans had been legally problematic for a long time; murder of the Herero was commonplace long before the arrival of Von Trotha and the extermination order. It also shows that the uprising was neither unprovoked nor without motive; it was in direct response to the Germans' actions. It was also retaliation for the many years of steady encroachment on Herero land[42] and the rapid removal of the Herero's cattle. Lundtofte remarks that the 'long term objective of expropriating the Herero's land and cattle, happening at greater speed than Leutwein had wished, was nearing accomplishment'.[43] He does, however, acknowledge that 'cruel punishments, rape and murder, were... the main provoking factors to be found in the very limited source material on the Herero's decision to rise in rebellion'. Madley[44] also notes that the Herero's political frustration centreed on German treatment of Herero women, general physical abuse and legal inequality under colonial law:[45] 'Furthermore legal usage institutionalized the inferior position of the Herero; whites received short prison terms or were acquitted for the murder of blacks, while blacks were put to death for the murder of whites.'[46]

---

41 Drechsler, H. (1980) *Let us die fighting: The struggle of the Herero and Nama against the German imperialism (1894–1915)* (Bernd Zöllner, transl). London: Zed Press, 143; Katjavivi, P. (1989) *A history of resistance in Namibia*. Paris/London/Addis Ababa: UNESCO, 9; Madley, B. (2004, June) 'Patterns of frontier genocide 1803–1910: The aboriginal Tasmanians, the Yuki of California and the Herero of Namibia'. 6 (2) *Journal of Genocide Research*, 167–92, 184.

42 See further Werner, W. (1993, March) 'A brief history of land dispossession in Namibia'. 19 (1) *Journal of Southern African Studies*, 135.

43 Lundtofte, H. (2003) 'Radicalization of the German suppression of the Herero rising in 1904'. In Jensen, S.L.B. (ed) *Genocide: Cases, comparisons and contemporary debates*. Copenhagen: Danish Center for Holocaust and Genocide, 15, 26.

44 See Madley, B. (2004, June) 'Patterns of frontier genocide 1803–1910: The aboriginal Tasmanians, the Yuki of California and the Herero of Namibia'. 6 (2) *Journal of Genocide Research*, 167–92, 181.

45 See further Gewald, J-B. (1996) *Towards Redemption: A socio-political history of the Herero of Namibia between 1890 and 1923*. Leiden: CNWS Publications, 205. Gewald examines the start of the war, which ultimately led to the ensuing genocide and counters the contention that the letters which Maherero allegedly wrote to his followers and Nama-leader Hendrik Witbooi to 'instigate a Herero insurrection' were not a call to war.

46 Lundtofte, H. (2003) 'Radicalization of the German suppression of the Herero rising in 1904'. In Jensen, S.L.B. (ed) *Genocide: Cases, comparisons and contemporary debates*. Copenhagen: Danish Center for Holocaust and Genocide, 15, 27. Footnotes omitted.

German troops carrying out mass hangings in GSWA

1904 and beyond: the intent, the order and the extermination of the Herero

In 1904, thousands of Herero — men, women and children, young and old — were killed. The methods employed demonstrate intent to commit genocide. No distinction was made between between killing combatants and non-combatants. The most specific indication of the order for genocide was the proclamation issued by General Lothar von Trotha on 2 October 1904. In that document he decreed:

> The Herero people will have to leave the country. Otherwise I shall force them to do so by means of guns. Within the German boundaries, every Herero, whether found armed or unarmed, with or without cattle, will be shot. I shall not accept any more women or children. I shall drive them back to their people otherwise I shall order them to be shot.
> Signed: the Great General of the Mighty Kaiser, von Trotha[47]

---

[47] Von Trotha's order as translated from the Otjiherero version. Quoted in Gewald, J-B. & Silvester, J. (2003) *Words cannot be found. German colonial rule in Namibia: An annotated reprint of the 1918 Blue Book.* Leiden: Brill, 108 fn 110.

Some scholars, such as Brigitte Lau, have denied the existence of the order itself. In 1989, she noted that no original copy of the order in German existed.[48] However, Berat argues correctly that subsequent references to the order in German colonial documents confirms the veracity of it.[49] Besides, the original order *has* been located and now resides in the Botswana National Archives.[50]

The refutation of the existence of the extermination order (maintained until a copy was found) demonstrates the extent of the denialist efforts. This is mirrored by the repudiation of the contents of the Blue Book in which the British recorded the genocide after Germany lost control of South West Africa at the close of World War I. As noted in the Introduction, the Blue Book is a valuable resource as it is one of the only documents recording African voices on the war. Besides affidavits taken from black eyewitnesses at the time,[51] much of the Blue Book, as Wellington points out, consists of translations of German sources. The veracity of these records has not been questioned, neither have the translations been criticised as inaccurate.[52]

The Blue Book was the first investigation into the genocide. As Rhoda Howard-Hassmann points out, 'Germany committed genocide in South-West Africa with an impunity broken only by a British inquiry after the former country's defeat in World War I.'[53] So keen were the German settlers to suppress evidence of the genocide that they attempted to have the Blue Book banned as post-war British propaganda. The all-white legislative assembly adopted a motion to destroy all copies of it. Its distribution was prohibited and

---

48   See Lau, B. (1989, April) 'Uncertain certainties: The Herero-German war of 1904'. *Mibagus*, 2, Windhoek.
49   Berat, L. (1993) 'Genocide: The Namibian case against Germany'. 5 *Pace International Law Review*, 5 fn 75.
50   Gewald, J-B. (1994) 'The great general of the Kaiser'. 26 *Botswana Notes and Records*, 67–76, 67.
51   Steinmetz does, however, recommend some caution: 'It is advisable to work with the original version of the "Blue Book" given the large number of typographical errors in the re-edited volume. And while the latter contains many useful annotations, its editors are too credulous vis-à-vis the testimony contained in the document. Historians do not need to rely too heavily on a book with obvious legitimatory motives when enough damning evidence is available from the German archives themselves.' Steinmetz, G. (2005) 'From "Native Policy" to exterminationism: German Southwest Africa, 1904'. In *Comparative Perspective, Theory and Research in Comparative Social Analysis, Paper 30*. Los Angeles: Department of Sociology, UCLA, 3 fn 4. Available at: http://repositories.cdlib.org/cgi/viewcontent.cgi?article=1036&context=uclasoc
52   Wellington, J.H. (1967) *South West Africa and its human issues*. Oxford: Clarendon Press. Cited in Jonassohn, K. (1996, Jan–Feb) 'Before the Holocaust deniers'. 33 (2) *Society*, 31–39.
53   Howard-Hassmann, R.E. (2005) 'The second great transformation: Human rights leapfrogging in the era of globalization'. 27 (1) *Human Rights Quarterly*, 1–40, 33.

library copies were removed and destroyed. In the rest of the British Empire, the Blue Book was also removed from libraries and sent to the Foreign Office.[54]

As for evidence of the order on paper or in German, the existence of such an order is confirmed by various sources, including General von Trotha himself. He wrote the following about the order on the day of issuing it:

> *I believe that the nation as such should be annihilated... I find it most appropriate that the nation perishes instead of infecting our soldiers and diminishing their supplies of water and food... They have to perish in the Sandveld[55] or try to cross the Bechuanaland border.*[56]

While these words are not equivalent to an extermination order, this document certainly spells out Von Trotha's intent, particularly as it was written on the same day as the order. Despite this, people such as Lau have denied that the Germans intended to commit genocide or even that they carried it out at all. They dismiss cited statements by German commanders that show genocidal intent as mere psychological warfare tactics.[57]

A recent example of such right-wing revisionist writing is a 2004 paper by Claus Nordbruch. According to him, the debate about past genocides is stifled by the 'extremists', and 'lots of exterminationist publications are saturated with overused and worn out shut-up words such as genocide, brutality, fascism, German tyranny, extermination politics and of course Holocaust'.[58] He dismisses writings that describe the events as genocide as prejudiced:

---

[54] See Gewald, J-B. (2003) 'Herero genocide in the twentieth century: Politics and memory'. In Abbink, J., De Bruijn, M. & Van Walraven, K. *Rethinking resistance: Revolt and violence in African history.* Leiden: Brill, 279–304, 288–89.

[55] The Sandveld, also called the Omaheke desert, is the barren, infertile area in the central part of the country, near the Waterberg plateau, bordering Botswana.

[56] General von Trotha in a note he wrote. Quoted in Gewald J-B. (1999) *Herero heroes: A socio-political history of the Herero of Namibia 1890–1923.* Oxford: James Currey, 173; and Bridgman, J. (1981) *The revolt of the Hereros.* Los Angeles: University of California Press, 128–129. Gewald notes the policy was clearly to ensure the 'extermination of a whole tribe, nothing living was to be spared...the orders were an extermination...with no turning back'. Gewald J-B. (1999) *Herero heroes: A socio-political history of the Herero of Namibia 1890–1923.* Oxford: James Currey, 174.

[57] See Lau, B. (1989, April) 'Uncertain certainties: The Herero-German war of 1904'. *Mibagus,* 2, Windhoek, 4, 8.

[58] Nordbruch, C. (2004) 'Atrocities committed on the Herero people during the suppression of their uprising in German South West Africa 1904–1907? An analysis of the latest accusations against Germany and an investigation on the credibility and justification of the demands for reparation'. Paper delivered to the European American Culture Council, Sacramento, 25 April 2004. Available at: http://www.nordbruch.org/artikel/sacramento.pdf

> *Nowadays, these accusations dominate mainstream historiography, which uncritically conforms to Zeitgeist, as well as the politically correct journalism. It does so, mainly, because non-Marxist historians conveniently adapted their East German colleagues' publications without checking the facts thoroughly. In this way, it was possible for Marxist views to flow into school and text books worldwide. If you prefer, call them 'progressive views' who, characteristically, often turn out to be nothing more than genuinely anti-German.*[59]

Surprisingly, he states that 'there is, however, no doubt about the fact that the Herero had suffered a dreadful fate. While surmounting the Sandveld and the long thirst periods they lost the far biggest part of their cattle and many people too'. Yet he maintains that the Herero's forced march into the desert was a planned migration and the real tragedy was the poor rainfall that year.

Despite these sorts of refutations, there can be no doubt that Von Trotha intended to wipe out the Herero. He declared to the Governor:

> *I know the tribes of Africa... They are all alike. They only respond to force. It was and is my policy to use force with terrorism and even brutality (gruesomeness). I shall annihilate the African tribes with streams of blood and streams of gold.*[60]

This statement indicates the roots of the *Übermenschen* notion, through its blatant racial prejudice and hatred. It also shows the superciliousness afforded by the power imbalance — an industrialised European nation was waging war against a much smaller African population that did not have even a fraction of the resources at their disposal. Von Trotha also wrote:

> *That nation must vanish from the face of the earth. Having failed to destroy them with guns, I will have to achieve my end in that way [the extermination order]...*[61]

There is both direct and indirect evidence of the intent to destroy the Herero entirely as a tribe. Indirect evidence is varied and overwhelming and includes the organised, systematic, selective and efficient killings by the German detachments, the burning down of Herero houses and kraals, the confiscation

---

59 Ibid.
60 Cited in many sources, including Bridgman, J. (1981) *The revolt of the Hereros.* Los Angeles: University of California Press, 111–12; Gewald, J-B. (1999) *Herero heroes: A socio-political history of the Herero of Namibia 1890–1923.* Oxford: James Currey, 174. See also Helbig, H. & L. (1983) *Mythos-Deutsch-Südwest: Namibia und die Deutschen.* Weinheim/Basel: Beltz Verlag, 153.
61 Drechsler, H. (1980) *Let us die fighting: The struggle of the Herero and Nama against the German imperialism (1894–1915)* (Bernd Zöllner, transl). London: Zed Press, 161.

of their cattle and the poisoning of waterholes and wells. To cite a specific example: in a 1916 report published in the *Journal of the African Society*, Lieutenant-Colonel Stanley Archibold Markham Pritchard gives an account of his visit to the area and what he found. He states that, having investigated the allegations against the Germans about their treatment of the Herero, he found that it 'was true' that they had been subjected to 'barbarous treatment' and that thousands had been 'murdered' and others driven out to 'die of hunger and thirst'.[62]

Von Trotha ordered the area where the Herero were to be sealed off by a 250–kilometre cordon to the west and southwest, making it virtually impossible for anyone to escape the desert.

Poſten mit Maſchinengewehr.

Propaganda postcard with *Schutztruppe* at a machine-gun post in 1904

[62] (1916, October) 'Experiences in German South West Africa'. XVI (LXI) *Journal of the African Society*, 1–6, 1–2.

Thus, the Herero were forced into the desert, which had too few water holes for the thousands of fugitives. When the pursuit stopped and the Herero went to the water holes, they were shot.[63] Von Trotha himself wrote to the Chancellor on 1 October that some of the Herero wanted to surrender 'but fear being shot to death and punished'.[64] To prevent the survival of the Herero forces, Von Trotha sealed most of the water wells and poisoned the small number of remaining wells. As a result, thousands died. The use of food and water as weapons of war was not new — over the centuries, many a conqueror has used deprivation of food and water to control populations. For example, in the U.S. in the late nineteenth century, bison were deliberately hunted to extinction to deprive the natives of a vital food source. This policy was so effective that by the turn of the century no bison remained and the indigenous population could be subjugated through diet control.[65]

Schutztruppe defending a water hole

[63] Hull, I.V. (2005) *Absolute destruction: Military culture and practices of war in Imperial Germany*. Ithaca: Cornell University Press, 53.
[64] *Ibid*, 54.
[65] Peter Duigan also comments on the similarities between the Herero and the American Indians. Duigan, P. (1969, April) 'Review of John Wellington's *South West Africa and its human issues*'. 74 (4) *American Historical Review*, 1333–334, 1333.

In the GSWA scenario, the strategy involved sealing and poisoning the water wells to strip the Herero of this lifeblood. According to Richard Herz, the act of poisoning the wells alone constitutes genocide.[66] The German General Staff itself agreed that the desert had inflicted a worse fate on the Herero than 'German arms could ever have done'.[67] The intent was clear from a report that stated: 'If, however, the Herero were to break through, such an outcome of the battle could only be even more desirable in the eyes of the German Command because the enemy would then seal his own fate, being doomed to die of thirst in the arid Sandveld.'[68] The deprivation of water would qualify under the legal definition of genocide, which incorporates a category identifying measures like denying members of the group food, water, shelter, health care and other necessities of life.[69] By driving the Herero into the Sandveld, a waterless desert, poisoning the few waterholes left and sealing off the area with a guarded cordon to make it impossible for anyone to escape, their actions met the criteria for the legal definition of genocide. Thus, this alone is enough evidence to prove the presence of genocidal intent. (This will be dealt with in more detail later in the text.)

Nonetheless, several revisionist authors have attempted to downplay the extent and severity of German violations. Nordbruch, for example, tries to minimise what occurred by stating:

> The basic humane attitude of the German soldiers towards their hungry, thirsty and exhausted prisoners is depicted by private Paul Harrland, for instance, who in 1905 accompanied such a transport from Otjimbinde to Okahandja: 'The German soldier's good nature comes through as he shares everything with these poor chaps [...] hunger and more hunger! We pitied the poor children, who couldn't be blamed for anything [...] In particular there was an emaciated young woman

---

66 Herz, R.L. (2000 Winter). 'Litigating environmental abuses under the Alien Tort Claims Act: A practical assessment'. 40 *Virginia Journal of International Law*, 545, 609.
67 In Drechsler, H. (1980) *Let us die fighting: The struggle of the Herero and Nama against the German imperialism (1894–1915)* (Bernd Zöllner, transl). London: Zed Press, 156.
68 *Ibid*, 155.
69 Nsereko, D. (2000) 'Genocide: A crime against mankind'. In McDonald, G.K. & Swaak-Goldman, O. (eds) *Substantive and procedural aspects of international criminal law — The experience of international and national courts, vol. 1*. The Hague: Kluwer Law International, 129.

who gained all our sympathy. With child-like love she led her blind mother on a leather strap.[70]

Even if the Harrland account is true — and it is one of a few documented instances of humane treatment — it neither negates the reality that other incidents occurred, nor does it neutralise the brutality documented in other accounts. A few exceptions do not disprove the ample evidence to the contrary. Moreover, the relevant episode quoted by Nordbruch occurred in 1905, not in 1904, when the extermination order was in force, most of the violence took place and when the cruelty was most intense. Besides, accounts emanating from German soldiers would obviously reflect a self-complimentary bias; one would hardly expect them to volunteer accounts of their own viciousness. Nordbruch's scant evidence is hardly convincing that this example was one of many, as he contends, especially given the huge amount of evidence testifying to German brutality on the contrary. A German soldier, Stuhlmar, has noted: 'We had been explicitly told beforehand that this dealt with the extermination of a whole tribe, nothing living was to be spared.'[71] This account proves that the authorities had communicated the intent even before the order was given. Bridgman cites an eyewitness, one Bergdamara, who testified under oath that 'the Germans spared no one. They killed thousands and thousands. I saw the slaughter for day after day'.[72]

The Kaiser ordered Von Trotha to rescind the extermination order in late 1904. Yet, in 1905, Von Trotha still applied his policy of extermination and no surrender to certain groups of the Herero and the Nama. Although the Kaiser publicly instructed him to rescind the order as a diplomatic initiative, it would appear that he permitted Von Trotha to continue covertly with his ruthless plans. Von Trotha's continued pursuit of similar tactics is evident from his own words. In April 1905 he issued a proclamation stating:

70 Harrland, P. 'Zwei Wochen aus dem Tagebuche eines Gefreiten bei der Kolonne', in *Deutsche Reiter*, 288. Quoted in Nordbruch, C. (2004) 'Atrocities committed on the Herero people during the suppression of their uprising in German South West Africa 1904–1907? An analysis of the latest accusations against Germany and an investigation on the credibility and justification of the demands for reparation'. Paper delivered to the European American Culture Council, Sacramento, 25 April 2004. Available at: http://www.nordbruch.org/artikel/sacramento.pdf
See also Nordbruch, C. (2002) *Der Hereroaufstand von 1904*. Stegen am Ammersee: Kurt Vowinckel Verlag; (2004) *Völkermord an den Herero in Deutsch-Südwestafrika? Widerlegung einer Lüge*. Tübingen: Grabert Verlag.
71 Quoted in Gewald, J-B. (1996) *Towards Redemption: A socio-political history of the Herero of Namibia between 1890 and 1923*. Leiden: CNWS Publications, 209.
72 Bridgman, J. (1981) *The revolt of the Hereros*. Los Angeles: University of California Press, 126.

> *The great and mighty German Emperor is prepared to pardon the Hottentot people and has ordered that all those who surrender voluntarily shall be spared. Only those who killed Whites at the outbreak of the rebellion or ordered Whites to be killed, have forfeited their lives under the law. I announce this to you and add that those few refusing to surrender will suffer the same fate as that suffered by the Herero people who, in their blindness, believed that they could successfully wage war against the mighty German Emperor and great German People. I ask you: Where are the Herero people today? Where are their chiefs today?... You shall come with your entire clans, carrying a white cloth or a stick and no ill shall befall you; you will find work and be given food until the great Emperor has announced new arrangements for the peace after the war; Whosoever believes after this that the pardon cannot extend to him would do best to leave the country; for wherever he is seen on German soil, he will be shot at, until the last one has been exterminated...*[73]

Although these words ostensibly offer pardon, protection and reward, the last paragraph is as unambiguous as the original order: the Germans intended to expel, exterminate and not permit surrender. Raphael Lemkin notes that even steps taken by Von Trotha's successor were not really an amnesty and he uses the word amnesty in quotation marks.[74]

At that time, numerous reports and eyewitness testimonies of ruthless conduct were obtained. Reports of what was happening in GSWA appeared in the Cape Town newspapers.[75] An eyewitness account reported by the *Cape Argus* in 1905 quoted Percival Griffiths, who stated:

> *When they fall they are sjamboked by the soldier in charge of the gang, with his full force, until they get up. Across the face was the favourite place for the sjamboking and I have often seen the blood flowing down the faces of the women and children from their bodies, from the cuts of the weapon. I have never actually seen one die under this treatment but I have seen one woman who in spite of all the soldiers sjamboking could not get to her feet, being at last carried away and I feel sure, although I cannot say so positively that she must have been dying. Their funerals took place daily. They*

---

[73] Proclamation issued 'To the Rebelling Hottentots' at Gibeon on 22 April 1905. Quoted in Heywood, A. & Maasdorp, E. (transl) (1989) *The Hendrik Witbooi papers.* Windhoek: National Archives of Namibia, 220.

[74] Lemkin, R. (undated) untitled and unpublished manuscript dealing with the Herero, found at the Jacob Rader Marcus Center of the American Jewish archives Cincinnati, the Raphael Lemkin Papers, Box 6, Folder 12, 13.

[75] A 1903 newspaper report alleged that major atrocities were being committed and that the Germans had annihilated the Orlams. 'German rule in South-West Africa: Some interesting facts'. *Cape Times*, 18 November 1903. Extract found in Gewald, J-B. & Silvester, J. (2003) *Words cannot be found. German colonial rule in Namibia: An annotated reprint of the 1918 Blue Book.* Leiden: Brill, 157 fn 143.

averaged while I was there from 9 to a dozen daily, with many children and babies among them.[76]

Merciless treatment already occurred in 1903, as evident in a November 1903 report in the *Cape Times*:

> *[T]he whole tribe was practically annihilated. As an instance of the way in which the Germans treated rebellion, there were at the close of the war*[77] *twenty odd prisoners in the hands of the Germans. These were marched to Keetmanshoep [sic] for trial. On the way any falling out, unable to walk, were shot on the spot and the remainder on arrival at Keetmanshoop were tried and shot...It was noted not a single native of the district attended the execution.*[78]

Two years later, the *Cape Argus* ran a number of stories on the GSWA atrocities. By then, the extermination order had been lifted, but killings and other major human-rights violations continued. The edition of 25 September 1905 contained extracts from interviews the newspaper conducted with six or seven eyewitnesses who were visiting the area at the time. Three days later the newspaper again ran a story covering four more eyewitness statements. One of the articles in the *Cape Argus* of 25 September 1905 was titled 'The German operations: British subjects as combatants: Further evidence: Women and children hanged and shot: Sensational allegations'.[79] The article contained the testimony of a 'young Transvaal Dutchman', one F Wepener, who described how he had seen eight women and six children executed. He noted:

> *They were all strung up to the trees by the neck and then shot. But why were they killed? The Germans said they were spies, but they were captured with the natives*

---

[76] 'In German SW Africa: Further startling allegations: Horrible cruelty: British subjects as combatants'. 28 September 1905. *Cape Argus*. Reproduced in Gewald, J-B. & Silvester, J. (2003) *Words cannot be found. German colonial rule in Namibia: An annotated reprint of the 1918 Blue Book*. Leiden: Brill, 347.

[77] Although the Herero-German war started earlier than its official date, the war referred to here probably signifies the Bondelswartz rebellion.

[78] 'German rule in South-West Africa. Some interesting facts'. *Cape Times*, 18 November 1903. Also reproduced in Gewald, J-B. & Silvester, J. (2003) *Words cannot be found. German colonial rule in Namibia: An annotated reprint of the 1918 Blue Book*. Leiden: Brill, 157 fn 143.

[79] Others included 'In German SW Africa: Further startling allegations: Horrible cruelty: British subjects as combatants'. *Cape Argus*, 28 September 1905. A similar letter also appeared in the same edition of the *Cape Argus*. Reproduced in Gewald, J-B. & Silvester, J. (2003) *Words cannot be found. German colonial rule in Namibia: An annotated reprint of the 1918 Blue Book*. Leiden: Brill, 341 onwards.

with whom we had been fighting and some of the children could not have been older than five. A lieutenant gave the order. Five soldiers would take each woman or child in turn, put a rope round their neck, string them up over a branch and then shoot them. No, the women did not shriek for mercy. They never said a word. They were glad to be released from their suffering, for they had been very cruelly treated. The children were quiet, too, as a rule. Like the women they had had a bayonet into them time after time, as well as being badly treated in other ways. All the women and children we captured while I was on the march were treated the same way. I have seen at least twenty-five of them with my own eyes hanged and shot.

According to Ronald Dreyer, reports of the events in GSWA were so disturbing that the Government of the Cape Colony was concerned, mainly because of its proximity to the Cape.[80] The British wanted to address the situation by means of cooperation, not confrontation. Already in 1897 the then British Foreign Minister, Lord Rosebery, stated that 'it won't be easy to tell a great military power that its troops wage war like Barbarians'.[81] Sir Charles Eliot, Royal Commissioner for British East Africa from 1901 to 1904, wrote in his 1905 book: 'The Germans are said to deal with natives more severely than we do and to be less popular with them.'[82] Another observer at the time noted that 'the German [Von Trotha] forbade the killing of women and children but all armed men who were captured soon met their fate'.[83]

The Rhenish Missionary Kuhlman noted in a report dated 18 May 1904 that German soldiers had told him they had orders not to take prisoners.[84] Thus it is clear that, from early on, German forces took no prisoners and executed the captured.

---

[80] Dreyer, R. F. (1987) *The mind of official imperialism: British and Cape government perceptions of German rule in Namibia from the Heligoland-Zanzibar Treaty to the Kruger telegram, 1890–1896.* Essen: Reimar Hobbing. In Gewald, J-B. & Silvester, J. (2003) *Words cannot be found. German colonial rule in Namibia: An annotated reprint of the 1918 Blue Book.* Leiden: Brill, xxvi.

[81] Letter from Lord Rosebery, 7 June 1897, quoted in Gewald, J-B. & Silvester, J. (2003) *Words cannot be found. German colonial rule in Namibia: An annotated reprint of the 1918 Blue Book.* Leiden: Brill, xxvi.

[82] Quoted in Schnee, H. (1926) *German colonization past and future: The truth about the German colonies.* London: George Allen & Unwin, 63.

[83] Bridgman, J. (1981) *The revolt of the Hereros.* Los Angeles: University of California Press, 125.

[84] Ritter-Petersen, H.G. (1991) *The Herrenvolk mentality in German South West Africa 1884–1914.* DLitt (History). Pretoria: University of South Africa, 202.

Schutztruppe patrol with Herero prisoners of war 1904

Some, such as Poewe, have argued that the phrase 'no male prisoners will be taken' could be subject to various interpretations. She argues: 'If the readers assume it is psychological warfare, then it means that Herero, already scattered in little guerrilla bands, would be so afraid as to stay away from German troops, making the taking of prisoners unnecessary.'[85] However, this practice was not new to the German troops, even in GSWA, where, as early as the 1890s, Von Francois had issued an order that 'the troops have the task of annihilating

---

85 Poewe, K. (1985) *The Namibian Herero: A history of their psychosocial disintegration and survival.* Lewiston, NY: Edwin Mellen, 64–65. In his review of Poewe's book Mokopakgosi noted that 'while specialists will find the book disappointing, the Namibian people, for whom it is said to have been written, are more likely to find some parts of it somewhat offensive'. Mokopakgosi, B. (1988, July) 'Review: *The Namibian Herero: A history of their psychological disintegration and survival*'. 87 (348) *African Affairs*, 480–81. Another reviewer considered the book 'a bold effort of imagination, but as history or social science it is seriously flawed'. Alnaes, K. (1989) 'History of trauma'. 30 (1) *Journal of African History*, 179–80.

the Witbooi tribe'.[86] A groom of Von Trotha, Manuel Timbu, asserted: 'I was for nearly two years with the German troops and always with General von Trotha. I know of no instance in which prisoners were spared...the soldiers shot all natives we came across.'[87] Jan Kubas, a Griqua man from Grootfontein who served with the German troops, testified under oath to the compilers of the Blue Book confirming this practice. He noted that:

> The Germans took no prisoners. They killed thousands and thousands of women and children along the roadsides. They bayoneted them and hit them to death with the butt ends of their guns. Words cannot be found to relate what happened; it was too terrible. They were lying exhausted and harmless along the roads and as the soldiers passed they simply slaughtered them in cold blood. Mothers holding babies at their breasts, little boys and little girls; old people too old to fight and old grandmothers, none received mercy; they were killed, all of them and left to lie and rot in the veld for the vultures and wild animals to eat. They slaughtered until there were no more Hereros left to kill. I saw this every day; I was with them. A few Hereros managed to escape in the bush and wandered about, living on roots and wild fruits. Von Trotha was the German General in charge.[88]

General von Trotha rationalised the killing of Herero prisoners, maintaining that they carried infectious diseases and that the German soldiers were unable to look after them.[89]

The accounts of killings during the extermination-order period (1904) are supplemented by accounts of the Herero being sexually abused (which Helmut Bley states reached 'catastrophic proportions')[90], tortured, starved and killed in the concentration camps.[91] They were used as slave labour on military and

---

86 Bridgman, J. (1981) *The revolt of the Hereros*. Los Angeles: University of California Press, 45, citing to Drechsler, H. (1966) *Südwestafrika unter deutscher Kolonialherrschaft — Der Kampf der Herero und Nama gegen den deutschen Imperialismus (1884–1915)*. Berlin: Akademie-Verlag, 79.
87 See Madley, B. (2004, June) 'Patterns of frontier genocide 1803–1910: The aboriginal Tasmanians, the Yuki of California and the Herero of Namibia'. 6 (2) *Journal of Genocide Research*, 167–92, 186–7.
88 Cited in Gewald, J-B. & Silvester, J. (2003) *Words cannot be found. German colonial rule in Namibia: An annotated reprint of the 1918 Blue Book*. Leiden: Brill, 117.
89 See Madley, B. (2004, June) 'Patterns of frontier genocide 1803–1910: The aboriginal Tasmanians, the Yuki of California and the Herero of Namibia'. 6 (2) *Journal of Genocide Research*, 167–92, 186, relying on Poole, G. (1990) *Samuel Maherero*. Windhoek: Gamsberg MacMillan, 270.
90 Bley, H. (1967) 'German South West Africa after the conquest 1904–1914'. In Segal, R. and First, R. *South West Africa: Travesty of trust*. London: Andre Deutsch, 35–53, 36.
91 Schneider-Waterberg, H.R. (2003) 'Konzentrationslager als Einrichtungen kolonialer Kriegsführung in Südlichen Afrika. Zum Bedeutungswandel eines Begriffes'. 6 *Befunde und Berichte zur Deutschen kolonialgeschichte*, 11–19.

civilian projects such as the building of railway lines. Between 27 December 1905 and 1 November 1906, 900 prisoners were used to build the 94-mile (151 kilometre) railway line between Lüderitz and Aus.[92]

Some Herero were deported to Cameroon as slaves, where they were forced to perform hard labour. As a result of the back-breaking work and difficult climatic conditions, many died.[93] The following is but one account from a non-German source, one Hendrik Fraser:

> *On my arrival in Swakopmund I saw many imprisoned Herero prisoners of war... There must have been about 600 men, women and children prisoners. They were in an enclosure fenced in with barbed wire. The women were made to do hard labour just like the men... Those who did not work well were brutally flogged with sjamboks... I was there six months and the Hereros died daily in large numbers as a result of exhaustion, ill-treatment and exposure. They were poorly fed and often begged... for a little food... The soldiers used the young Herero girls to satisfy their passions.*[94]

Similarly, Missionary[95] Elger described what he observed:

> *And then the scattered Herero returned from the Sandfeld. Everywhere they popped up — not in their original areas — to submit themselves as prisoners. What did the wretched people look like?! Some of them had been starved to skeletons with hollow eyes, powerless and hopeless, afflicted by serious diseases, particularly with dysentery. In the settlements they were placed in big kraals and there they lay, without blankets and some without clothing, in the tropical rain on the marshlike ground. Here death reaped a harvest! Those who had some semblance of energy naturally had to work. [...] It was a terrible misery with the people; they died in droves. Once 24 came together, some of them carried. In the next hour one died, in the evening the second, in the first week a total of ten — all to dysentery — the people had lost all their energy and all their will to live [...] Hardly cheering cases were those where people were handed in to be healed from the effects of extreme mistreatment (schwerer Misshandlungen): there were bad cases amongst these.*[96]

---

[92] Gewald, J-B. & Silvester, J. (2003) *Words cannot be found. German colonial rule in Namibia: An annotated reprint of the 1918 Blue Book.* Leiden: Brill, 171 fn 155.

[93] *Ibid*, 173.

[94] Fraser quoted in Gewald, J-B. & Silvester, J. (2003) *Words cannot be found. German colonial rule in Namibia: An annotated reprint of the 1918 Blue Book.* Leiden: Brill, 174–75.

[95] On the role of missionaries see Gewald, J-B. (2002) 'Missionaries, Hereros and motorcars: Mobility and the impact of motor vehicles in Namibia before 1940'. 35 (2–3) *International Journal of African Historical Studies*, 257–85. See also Gewald, J-B. (2002, June) 'Flags, funerals and fanfares: Herero and missionary contestations of the acceptable, 1900–1940'. 15 (1) *Journal of African Cultural Studies*, 105–18.

[96] Elger, cited in Gewald, J-B. (2003) 'Herero genocide in the twentieth century: Politics and memory'. In Abbink, J., De Bruijn, M. & Van Walraven, K. *Rethinking resistance: Revolt and violence in African history.* Leiden: Brill, 279–304, 285 (brackets in original).

Construction of the Lüderitz railway line using Herero slave labour

Dr Heinrich Vedder, a famous historian later appointed to represent Namibian Africans in the South African Senate, attested to the dire conditions in the concentration camps:

> Shortly thereafter vast transports of prisoners of war arrived. They were placed behind double rows of barbed wire fencing, which surrounded all the buildings of the harbour department quarters [Hafenamtswerft] and housed in pathetic [jämmerlichen] structures constructed out of simple sacking and planks, in such a manner that in one structure 30–50 people were forced to stay without distinction as to age and sex. From early morning until late at night, on weekdays as well as on Sundays and holidays, they had to work under the clubs of raw overseers [Knütteln roher Aufseher], until they broke down [zusammenbrechen]. Added to this the food was extremely scarce: Rice without any necessary additions was not enough to support their bodies, already weakened by life in the field [as refugees] and used to the hot sun of the interior, from the cold and restless exertion of all their powers in the prison conditions of Swakopmund. Like cattle hundreds were driven to death and like cattle they were buried. This opinion may appear hard or exaggerated, lots changed and became milder during the course of the imprisonment...But the chronicles are not permitted to suppress that such a remorseless rawness [rücksichtslose Roheit], randy sensuality [geile Sinnlichkeit], brutish overlordship [brutales Herrenturm]

was to be found amongst the troops and civilians here that a full description is hardly possible.[97]

The conditions in the concentration camps were so harsh that Colonel F Trench, British Military Attaché in Namibia, wrote as follows to the British Embassy in Berlin on 21 November 1906:

> It is not easy to avoid the impression that the extinction of the tribe would be welcomed by the authorities. The hardness of their fate... excited even the sympathy of two officers who had known them and who reminded me that they [the Witbooi] never murdered or ill treated civilians or prisoners, but waged war without cruelty and proved useful allies against the Hereros... I have observed, however, that a quarter of a century of Colonial Empire has not sufficed to teach the fact that a black man is a human being.[98]

According to the German Imperial Colonial Office's *Report on the Mortality in Prisoner-of-War Camps in German South West Africa*, 7 682 of the 15 000 Herero and the 2 000 Nama died (almost half of them) from October 1904 to March 1907.[99] Major von Estorff reported that since 'September 1906, 1,032 out of 1,795 natives have died on Shark Island. I am not prepared to assume responsibility for the killing nor can I expect my officers to do so...'.[100] Some estimate that only 245 of almost 1 800 prisoners in the Shark Island concentration camp survived.[101] According to Epstein many died because the camps were extremely unsanitary.[102]

The intended meaning of *vernichten*: a political or military strategy or call for genocide?

The consensus amongst scholars is that the *Vernichtungsbefehl* (the extermination order) intended to convey that the Herero must be totally

---

97 Gewald, J-B. & Silvester, J. (2003) *Words cannot be found. German colonial rule in Namibia: An annotated reprint of the 1918 Blue Book*. Leiden: Brill, xx–xxi.
98 Trench, F. (1906). Quoted in Gewald, J-B. & Silvester, J. (2003) *Words cannot be found. German colonial rule in Namibia: An annotated reprint of the 1918 Blue Book*. Leiden: Brill, 171 fn 156.
99 Drechsler, H. (1980) *Let us die fighting: The struggle of the Herero and Nama against the German imperialism (1894–1915)* (Bernd Zöllner, transl). London: Zed Press, 214.
100 *Ibid*, 212.
101 Smith, H.W. (1999) 'The logic of colonial violence: Germany in South West Africa (1904–1907), the United States in the Philippines (1899–1902)'. In Lehmann, H. & Wellenreuther, H. (eds) *German and American nationalism: A comparative perspective*. Oxford/New York: Berg, 205–31, 209.
102 Epstein, K. (1959, October) 'Erzberger and the German colonial scandals, 1905–1910'. 74 (293) *English Historical Review*, 637–63, 648.

annihilated; they agree that Von Trotha meant the word *'vernichten'* to denote annihilation.[103]

On the other hand, some revisionists have argued that the order did not mean that all Herero were to be wiped out.[104] Even some commentators who believe that the events constituted genocide deny that the word was meant literally. Lundtofte argues that *'Vernichten* should rather be understood in connection with the Clausewitz influenced strategy of total war of the period, the implication of the concept being the total destruction of the opponent's military in order to annihilate any further organized resistance'.[105]

Schutztruppe firing a canon at the Waterberg

[103] German author, Wilhelm Kulz, stated in a book published in Berlin in 1909 that 'the Herero people as such were annihilated'. Quoted in Stone, D. (2001) 'White men with low moral standards: German anthropology and the Herero genocide'. 35 (2) *Patterns of Prejudice*, 33, 34.
[104] Nordbruch, C. (2002) *Der Hereroaufstand von 1904*. Stegen am Ammersee: Kurt Vowinckel Verlag.
[105] Lundtofte, H. (2003) 'Radicalization of the German suppression of the Herero rising in 1904'. In Jensen, S.L.B. (ed) *Genocide: Cases, comparisons and contemporary debates*. Copenhagen: Danish Center for Holocaust and Genocide, 15, 30.

It is significant that the extermination order was distributed in Otjiherero so that the Herero would have no doubts about the Germans' intentions.[106] The English translation of this version reads:

> *I am the Great General of the Germans. I am sending a word to you Hereros, you who are Hereros are no longer under the Germans. You have stolen, killed and owe white people. You have cut ears and noses, but now out of cowardice you will not fight. I am saying to you Hereros, you who are great, anyone who catches and brings a chief will be paid 50 pounds, especially chief Samuel Maherero shall get 250 pounds. You Hereros must now leave this land it belongs to the Germans. If you do not do this I shall remove you with the big gun. A person in German land shall be killed by the gun. I shall not catch women and the sick but I will chase them after their chiefs or I will kill them with the gun. These are my words to the Herero nation. The Great General of the Kaiser. Trotha.*[107]

Significantly, Von Trotha emphasised the land in his extermination order: the Otjiherero version ordered all Herero to leave the land, as it thenceforth belonged to the Germans (this will be returned to later).

Von Trotha wrote the proclamation specifically for the Herero, not the German troops. On the same day that the order was pronounced, a number of Herero prisoners were sentenced to death and hung in front of 30 other Herero prisoners; men, women and children.[108] These prisoners were then provided with a copy of the order in Otjiherero and released and were expected to go and inform the other Herero of their fate. Von Trotha's diary entry of 1 October 1904, affirms the targeted audience: 'In the afternoon worked up proclamation *to Herero* with

---

106 The Herero were unambiguous as to the intent of the order and thoroughly experienced its devastating effects. Samuel Kariko, the son of Daniel Kariko, the former Secretary to an Omaruru Chief, stated: 'A new General named von Trotha came and he ordered that all Hereros were to be exterminated, regardless of age or sex. It was then that the wholesale slaughter of our people began. That was towards the end of 1904. Our people had already been defeated in battle and we had no more ammunition...we saw we were beaten and asked for peace, but the Germans refused peace and said all should die. We then fled towards the Sandveld of the Kalahari Desert. Those of our people who escaped the bullets and bayonets died miserably of hunger and thirst in the desert. A few thousand managed to turn back and sneak through the German lines to where there were water and roots and berries to live on.' Gewald, J-B. & Silvester, J. (2003) *Words cannot be found. German colonial rule in Namibia: An annotated reprint of the 1918 Blue Book.* Leiden: Brill, 114.
107 Quoted in Gewald, J-B. & Silvester, J. (2003) *Words cannot be found. German colonial rule in Namibia: An annotated reprint of the 1918 Blue Book.* Leiden: Brill, 108 fn 110.
108 Gewald, J-B. (1994) 'The great general of the Kaiser'. 26 *Botswana Notes and Records,* 67–76, 68.

help from Kean and Philippus'[109] (author's emphasis). This is avowed again in the introductory and closing lines: 'I am the Great General of the Germans. I am sending a word *to you Hereros*...These are my words *to the Herero nation*' (author's emphasis). However, the proclamation was also read to the German soldiers; they were then informed of the contents and given directives for consequent action. The additional section, read to the German soldiers, states:

> This proclamation is to be read to the troops at roll-call, with the addition that the unit that catches a captain will also receive the appropriate reward and that shooting at women and children is to be understood as shooting above their heads, so as to force them to run [away]. I assume absolutely that this proclamation will result in taking no more male prisoners, but will not degenerate into atrocities against women and children. The latter will run away if one shoots at them a couple of times. The troops will remain conscious of the good reputation of the German soldier.[110]

Crucially, as Lundtofte and others have argued, 'Von Trotha's proclamation was carried out to the letter in a war of extermination'.[111] Regarding the warfare, GL Steer rather mordantly wrote in 1939:

> The Hereros went into rebellion, under the Paramount Chief Samuel Maherero. They fought according to a certain savage code, according to which German soldier prisoners were in for a rough time, British and Dutch were treated as old friends and white women and children of all races were not touched. The Germans fought them according to a more civilised code, according to which prisoners were not taken and women and children often raped and bayoneted.[112]

Many eyewitness accounts (recorded in various sources) and many authors have confirmed the Germans' indiscriminate killing of the Herero. Drechsler stated that 'in reality the different treatment of men on the one hand and women and children on the other was not made. All Herero, irrespective of men, women and children, were killed whenever they fell into the hands of

---

[109] Hull, I.V. (2005) *Absolute destruction: Military culture and practices of war in Imperial Germany.* Ithaca: Cornell University Press, 56.

[110] Quoted in Hull, I.V. (2005) *Absolute destruction: Military culture and practices of war in Imperial Germany.* Ithaca: Cornell University Press, 56.

[111] Lundtofte, H. (2003) 'Radicalization of the German suppression of the Herero rising in 1904'. In Jensen, S.L.B. (ed) *Genocide: Cases, comparisons and contemporary debates.* Copenhagen: Danish Center for Holocaust and Genocide, 15.

[112] Steer, G.L. (1939) *Judgement on German Africa.* London: Hodder & Stoughton, 62. Quoted in Stone, D. (2001) 'White men with low moral standards: German anthropology and the Herero genocide'. 35 (2) *Patterns of Prejudice*, 33, 34.

German soldiers'.[113] Similarly, Bedszent affirmed that 'mass shootings of prisoners and decimation of wounded Herero warriors was the order of the day. Even women and children were killed during such battles, sometimes even burned alive'.[114] Thus, the Herero conducted the classical type of war in the sense that they restricted their attacks to German men of military age and excluded women, children, civilians and non-Germans. The Germans did not reciprocate: 'Herero and Nama women and girls were interned in concentration camps and raped by German troops, while the men and boys were tortured and murdered.'[115]

Accordingly, claims that the Kaiser's Hun speech and the language Von Trotha used in the proclamation were mere political rhetoric conflict, both with the manifest intentions and the bulk of the evidence. (The role of the Kaiser and the Hun speech will be dealt with later.)

Numerous pieces of evidence, many predating October 1904, reflect Germany's intention to eradicate or exterminate[116] the Herero. A report from Leutwein to the Colonial Department in February 1904, shortly after the uprising began but months before Von Trotha arrived, shows that the Herero

---

[113] Drechsler, H. (1984) *Aufstände in Südwestafrika*. Berlin, 81. Quoted in Nordbruch, C. (2004) 'Atrocities committed on the Herero people during the suppression of their uprising in German South West Africa 1904–1907? An analysis of the latest accusations against Germany and an investigation on the credibility and justification of the demands for reparation'. Paper delivered to the European American Culture Council, Sacramento, 25 April 2004. Available at: http://www.nordbruch.org/artikel/sacramento.pdf

[114] Bedszent, G. 'Terror und Enteignung'. In *Junge Welt*, 13 March 1998. Quoted in Nordbruch, C. (2004) 'Atrocities committed on the Herero people during the suppression of their uprising in German South West Africa 1904–1907? An analysis of the latest accusations against Germany and an investigation on the credibility and justification of the demands for reparation'. Paper delivered to the European American Culture Council, Sacramento, April 25 2004. Available at: http://www.nordbruch.org/artikel/sacramento.pdf

[115] The African Union Front (www.africanfront.com). Quoted in Nordbruch, C. (2004) 'Atrocities committed on the Herero people during the suppression of their uprising in German South West Africa 1904–1907? An analysis of the latest accusations against Germany and an investigation on the credibility and justification of the demands for reparation'. Paper delivered to the European American Culture Council, Sacramento, 25 April 2004. Available at: http://www.nordbruch.org/artikel/sacramento.pdf

[116] The legal context of the word 'extermination' will be discussed later, but the word was used in a 1956 article describing what was done to the Herero. See Gibson, G.D. (1956, February) 'Double descent and its correlates among the Herero of Ngamiland'. 58 (1) *American Anthropologist* New Series, 109–39, 111. See also (2003, May) 'How the Germans exterminated the Hereros'. *New African*, 62–67.

would be killed regardless of whether they agreed to surrender or not. In the report he wrote:

> The insurgents must know that there is an alternative to death. Otherwise, we will only drive them to despair, bringing on an endless war that will be to our disadvantage. After all, the natives have nothing to lose now but their lives — and they are doomed anyway...[117]

The first sentence indicates that there was talk about killing the Herero and giving no quarter.[118] He confirms that the Herero knew without question that they faced death. This holds true either because they had been told so or because they had already experienced it. Leutwein's report contradicts the argument by Poewe and others that the Germans only aimed to accomplish a military annihilation. Leutwein warns about the problematic consequences of a complete physical extermination and recognises the economic benefit of the Herero as labourers. He previously commented:

> As regards the kind of colonization envisaged, there is in the last analysis only one guide, how to make the desired profits in the surest fashion. Some believe that they can gain this objective by depriving the original population of all rights in favour of the intruder... Others wish to allow the original population to occupy 'their place in the sun'. From the point of view of the expected profits the decision cannot be made according to a single scheme, but must correspond to circumstances.[119]

Obviously, on this occasion, the authorities did not heed his plea, but pursued the policy of extermination. Further, the Governor wrote this to the German Colonial Office and received no counter-order from it or anyone else. It therefore seems that both those in Germany and their regional representatives accepted this 'policy of death' directed at the Herero without discussion or debate. The German government's silence about the pre-1904 atrocities signifies that they condoned them, tacitly approved them or even ordered them.

[117] Drechsler, H. (1980) *Let us die fighting: The struggle of the Herero and Nama against the German imperialism (1894–1915)* (Bernd Zöllner, transl). London: Zed Press, 148.

[118] The Bryce Report, requested by the British Prime Minister to examine the conduct of German soldiers during World War I, notes that there were 'instances in which it is clear that quarter was refused to persons desiring to surrender when it ought to have been given or that persons already so wounded as to be incapable of fighting further were wantonly shot or bayoneted'. *The Bryce Report into German atrocities in Belgium — Report of the Committee on Alleged German Outrages Appointed by His Britannic Majesty's Government and Presided Over by the Right Hon. Viscount Bryce, O.M.*, 12 May 1915.

[119] Gann, L.H. & Duigan, P. (1977) *The rulers of German Africa 1884–1914*. Stanford: Stanford University Press, 75.

When the director of the Colonial Department discovered, in early 1904, that Leutwein intended to negotiate with the Herero, the director ordered him 'to refrain'.[120] Critically, steps were taken to transfer control of the territory from the Colonial Office to the War Office and the General Staff,[121] even though Leutwein[122] argued that the decisions concerning exterminating and banishing the Herero were political and not military and were, therefore, to be left to him as the Governor.[123]

Leutwein clearly saw the possibility of genocide months before it occurred, but Poole argues that the extermination of the locals was considered long before that.[124] In February 1904, missionary Elger wrote to the Rhenish Missionary Society:

> The Germans are consumed with inexpiable hatred and a terrible thirst for revenge, one might even say they are thirsting for the blood of the Herero. All you hear these days is 'make a clean sweep, hang them, shoot them to the last man, give no quarter.' I shudder to think what may happen in the months ahead. The Germans will doubtless exact a grim vengeance.[125]

In March 1904, Socialist deputy August Bebel protested in the *Reichstag* about the 'savage methods' that the German soldiers used. Even Leutwein noted: 'I do not concur with these fanatics who want to see the Herero destroyed altogether.'[126] Leutwein admitted that Bebel 'was thus this time correct in his judgement in many respects', but he added that it was 'only natural, however, that after all that has happened our soldiers do not show excessive leniency'.[127] In May 1904, Leutwein also admitted that only two Herero had been captured: one, having been wounded, had died and the other had been sentenced to death for supposedly attempting to escape. That so few Herero had been captured during such a long period patently points to a policy of taking no prisoners.

---

120 Drechsler, H. (1980) *Let us die fighting: The struggle of the Herero and Nama against the German imperialism (1894–1915)* (Bernd Zöllner, transl). London: Zed Press, 148.

121 Bley, H. (1996) *South-West Africa under German rule 1894–1914*. Evanston, Ill: Northwestern University Press, 159.

122 See Leutwein, T.G. (1906) *Elf Jahre Gouverneur in Deutsch-Südwestafrika*. Berlin: Mittler.

123 Steinmetz, G. (2003, January) 'The devil's handwriting: Precolonial discourse, ethnographic acuity and cross-identification in German colonialism'. 45 (1) *Comparative Studies in Society and History*, 41–95.

124 Poole, G. (1990) *Samuel Maherero*. Windhoek: Gamsberg Macmillan, 313.

125 Drechsler, H. (1980) *Let us die fighting: The struggle of the Herero and Nama against the German imperialism (1894–1915)* (Bernd Zöllner, transl). London: Zed Press, 145.

126 *Ibid*, 148.

127 *Ibid*, 151.

These 'savage methods' occurred even before Von Trotha's arrival and escalated further when he arrived. As Drechsler has noted, under Von Trotha 'it was only a matter of time before the last traces of respect for international law were abandoned in the conduct of the war'.[128]

On 7 October, five days after the official proclamation of the order, Paul Rohrbach, the Settlement Commissioner, wrote: 'It is a veritable misfortune, this extermination policy against the Herero. The Trotha proclamation will harm our reputation in the whole world and will be of no benefit here.'[129] Major von Estorff wrote that it was 'both cruel and stupid policy, to annihilate the Herero people in this fashion'.[130] Von Estorff was no rogue soldier whose views were incongruous or isolated; he was a respected member of the military later promoted to colonel and appointed the *Schutztruppe* commander on 1 April 1909. The commander of the *Grosser Generalstab* also confirmed the policy of extermination and supported Von Trotha. In an official report in November 1904, he wrote that

> *one must agree with General von Trotha's efforts to annihilate the whole Herero nation or to drive them out of the country. After what has occurred, the coexistence of blacks and whites will be extremely difficult, unless the former are kept in a permanent status of forced labour, a kind of slavery. The racial war which has erupted can only be concluded with the annihilation or the total enslavement of the one party.*[131]

Genocidal intent was also evident in German statements and conduct towards the Nama. They too feared the loss of their land. As such, it was not surprising that they rose up in October 1904. Having witnessed the Herero atrocities, their fears of extermination were not unfounded. Von Trotha, in November 1904, wrote about them: 'All the tribes in Africa share the same mentality, in that they only retreat when confronted by violence. My policy was and is, to apply such violence with the utmost degree of terrorism and brutality. I will exterminate the rebellious tribes with rivers of blood.'[132]

---

[128] *Ibid*, 152.
[129] Quoted in Ritter-Petersen, H.G. (1991) *The Herrenvolk mentality in German South West Africa 1884–1914*. DLitt (History). Pretoria: University of South Africa, 209.
[130] *Ibid*.
[131] *Ibid*, 210–11.
[132] Zirkel, K. (1999) 'Military power in German colonial policy: The Schutztruppen and their leaders in the East and South West Africa, 1888–1918'. In Killingray, D. & Omissi, D. (eds) *Guardians of Empire: The armed forces of the colonial powers, 1700–1964*. Manchester: Manchester University Press, 91–113, 101.

Schutztruppe with a Maxim machine gun, first issued around 1904

Although the statement was directed at the Nama, Von Trotha's use of the plural 'tribes' shows that he had his sights trained on more than one group. In fact, the extermination order against the Herero was not the only such order issued by Von Trotha. On 19 May 1905, an order against the Nama stated:

> The great and powerful Emperor of Germany will be lenient with the Namaqua people and has ordered that the lives of those who give themselves up will be spared... [but]... If anyone thinks that after this notice there will be any leniency shown him he had better quit the country, because if he is again seen in German territories he will be shot and thus all rebels will be eliminated.[133]

Ten days later, on 29 May 1905, the final line was amended to read: '...had better quit the country because wherever they are seen in Germany territory they will be shot at until all the outlaws have been exterminated'.[134]

---

[133] Quoted in Gewald, J-B. & Silvester, J. (2003) *Words cannot be found. German colonial rule in Namibia: An annotated reprint of the 1918 Blue Book*. Leiden: Brill, 169.

[134] Governor Sir Hely-Hutchinson to Mr Lyttleton, Telegram, 19 May 1905. Quoted in Gewald, J-B. & Silvester, J. (2003) *Words cannot be found. German colonial rule in Namibia: An annotated reprint of the 1918 Blue Book*. Leiden: Brill, 169 fn 152.

Nama Chief Henrik Witbooi and Nama soldiers

The extermination of about half of the Nama population during this period is proof enough of the intent behind this statement. As mentioned before, the genocidal practices continued after 1904, even after Von Trotha returned to Germany in 1905, and still existed after the end of the war. This is remarkable considering that, by the end of the war, the Herero society had been destroyed. Thus, even after the annihilation of this population, similar intentions and practices persisted right throughout the first decade of the twentieth century. Implementation of the genocide from that point on continued in different ways and with different results. By 1908, the German authorities had removed the chiefs of those few Herero who survived, denied them the right to own land and cattle and prohibited the practise of their own religion.[135]

On 1 December 1905, the new governor, Friedrich von Lindequist, issued a proclamation that read:

Hereros! His Majesty the Emperor of Germany, the High Lord Protector of this Land, has graciously nominated me Governor of this Land a few days after

---

[135] Gewald J-B. (1999) *Herero heroes: A socio-political history of the Herero of Namibia 1890–1923*. Oxford: James Currey, 141.

General von Trotha, who commanded the German troops against you, returned to Germany. His departure means that the war will now cease. Hereros! You know me! Formerly I was for five years in this land as Imperial Judge and as Assessor and councillor, the representative of Governor Leutwein in the days when Manasse of Omaruru and Kambazembi of Waterberg, who were always loyal supporters of mine, still lived. It is my desire that the Rebellion which your Chiefs and Headmen (and the children who followed them) so wickedly began and which has desolated the land should now come to an end, so that Peace and Order may again rule. I therefore call upon the Hereros who still are wandering about the veld and in the mountains and who nourish themselves by eating wild roots and by theft. Come and lay down your arms, Hereros! Thousands of your fellow tribesmen have already surrendered and are being clothed and fed by the Government. I have taken every precaution to ensure that you will be justly treated. That I also personally guarantee to you. Further, it is ordained that from 20th December onwards, that is three weeks from today, no Herero habitations will be searched after and taken, as I wish to give you time to personally to come in peacefully to me and surrender yourselves. Come to Omburo and Otjihaenena! Your Missionaries will be sent there by me. They will also take provisions with them, so that your thirst and great hunger may be appeased. Some small stock will also be left for provisional use of your wives and children in so far as you still possess such for their support. Those who are strong and can work will, when they work with exceptional diligence, receive a small wage. No European soldiers will be stationed at Omburo and Otjihaenena. So that you need have no fear and imagine that further shooting will take place. The sooner you come in and surrender your arms, the sooner can the question of amelioration of the present lot of your captive fellow tribesmen be considered and their freedom later again given to them. If Omburo and Otjihaenena are too far away, anyone may hand in the arms at any Military Post and surrender there. The soldiers at those stations will not shoot either. In addition, the soldiers escorting the transport and travelling through the land will not shoot at you as long as you attempt nothing hostile towards them. Therefore do not be afraid of them. So come quickly in Hereros, before it is too late. In Namaland also there will soon be quiet, as Hendrik Witbooi has been killed by a German bullet and Samuel Isaac has surrendered and is in our hands.[136]

The new governor's declaration again supports the former existence of a shoot-on-sight policy. There would be no need to state that the Herero could surrender without fear of being shot, had this not been the practice. The reassurances contained there imply that the Herero expected to be shot. The announcement led to the surrender of 9 000 Herero.

---

[136] Von Lindequist, quoted in Gewald, J-B. & Silvester, J. (2003) *Words cannot be found. German colonial rule in Namibia: An annotated reprint of the 1918 Blue Book.* Leiden: Brill, 179–80.

The number of Herero killed in the genocide

A major debate in the study of this specific history is that of how many Herero and Nama were killed in the genocide. There seems to be agreement that the Herero losses were comparatively greater than those suffered by the Nama.[137] Critically, the 1904 Nama uprising provided the Germans with the pretext to also occupy and gain possession of Namaland. Yet, while the Herero lost all their land, the Nama did not. Some Namas, whom the Germans considered to have remained supportive of their enterprise, were able to keep their land.[138]

Given the academic disputes, the number of fatalities will be addressed; yet the actual numbers do not invalidate the commission of genocide. Obviously, the greater the number of fatalities, the worse the atrocity committed. Yet many of the dead were not Herero warriors: tens of thousands of those killed were civilians, women and children. Thus, whether 60 000, 80 000 or 100 000 people were killed is immaterial from a legalistic point of view: the intent to commit violations on unarmed men, women and children suffices as evidence of genocide. Similarly, the lack of specific fatality numbers does not negate Germany's liability or influence the claim for reparations. It is useful to note, from a comparative perspective, that while the 'casualty figures are notoriously inaccurate, the total dead was probably greater than in the Boer War, the Crimean War, the Spanish American War, the Seven Weeks War and a dozen or more other conflicts that were fought between 1815 and 1914'.[139]

The dispute about the numbers is often used to deny the impact of the killing spree or even to deny that it happened at all. Genocide denialists exploit the debate by minimising the number of fatalities to deny that genocide had occurred.[140] In addition, many argue that the fatalities resulted from a war the Herero started. The issue of who started the war is contentious (as will be shown). Even if the Herero initiated the war, the Germans drove them to it. Germany knew from previous colonial experiences that the local population was likely to resist. As indicated before, it is likely that the Germans desired and even provoked the war in order to obtain more land. At a minimum, the rebellion was the perfect opportunity for the Germans to punish the Herero, provide a deterrent to others who may have wanted to follow suit and to get

---

[137] Werner, W. (1998) *No-one will become rich: Economy and society in the Herero reserves in Namibia 1913–1946*. Basel: P. Schlettwein, 21.
[138] *Ibid.*
[139] Bridgman, J. (1981) *The revolt of the Hereros*. Los Angeles: University of California Press, 1–2.
[140] Charny, I.W. (2003) 'A classification of denials of the Holocaust and other genocides'. 5 (1) *Journal of Genocide Research*, 11–34, 24.

rid of the Herero through extermination or exile, so that their land and cattle could be taken for settler occupation and farming.

The numbers debate derives, in part, from controversy over how many Herero and Nama existed before the genocide. Brigitte Lau has controversially stated that no 'comprehensive statistics of Herero and Nama population figures or death rates during or after the war exist. To report the contradictory guesswork of the colonizers with confidence is already mystifying'.[141] That there were drastically fewer Herero after the genocide indicates that large numbers either died or went into exile (mainly in Botswana). Even Evans Lewin, who believed that the estimate of 300 000 indigenous people living in GSWA at the time may have been too high, agreed that a dramatic reduction in the population occurred.[142] Thus, part of the dispute is about how many people lived in GSWA at the time of the genocide, how many Herero there were and how many Herero were at the battle of Waterberg.

The following Herero fatality figures and percentages have been cited:

- Helmut Bley: between 75 and 80 percent (60 000 to 80 000);[143]
- Horst Drechsler, relying on a 1911 census, states that there were only 15 130 of the 80 000 Herero left after the genocide — about 65 000 or 81 percent killed;[144]
- Harry Schwirck: 85 percent of the Herero and half of the Nama were exterminated;[145]

---

[141] Lau, B. (1990, June/July) Letter to the editor, *Southern African Review of Books*. Quoted in Berat, L. (1993) 'Genocide: The Namibian case against Germany'. *5 Pace International Law Review*, 165 fn 95. For criticism of the revisionist authors see Dedering, T. (1993, March) 'The German-Herero War of 1904: Revisionism of genocide or imaginary historiography'. 19 (1) *Journal of Southern African Studies*, 80. See also Dedering, T. (1999) 'A certain rigorous treatment of all parts of the nation: The annihilation of the Herero in German South West Africa, 1904'. In Levine, M. & Roberts, P. (eds) *The massacre in history (Vol.1 War and Genocide Series)*. New York/Oxford: Berghahn Books. See the responses to the Lau claims in Melber, H. (1990, August/October) 'Genocide'. *Southern African Review of Books*, 23; Vigne, R. (1990, February/May) 'Diary: Shark Island'. *Southern African Review of Books*, 31; Vigne, R. (1990, August/October) 'Genocide'. *Southern African Review of Books*, 13.
[142] Lewin, E. (1915) *The Germans and Africa. Their aims on the dark continent and how they acquired their African colonies.* London: Cassell, 110.
[143] Bley, H. (1996) *Namibia under German rule*. Hamburg: Lit Verlag, 150.
[144] Drechsler, H. (1980) *Let us die fighting: The struggle of the Herero and Nama against the German imperialism (1894–1915)* (Bernd Zöllner, transl.). London: Zed Press, 214.
[145] Schwirck, H. (2002) 'Law's violence and the boundary between corporal discipline and physical abuse in German South West Africa'. 36 *Akron Law Review*, 81, 89.

- Alison Palmer: Herero numbers were reduced from 80 000 to 16 000 (ie 64 000 killed);[146]
- Dorian Haarhoff: their numbers fell from 90 000 to 16 000 (ie 74 000 killed);[147]
- Peter Fraenkel and Roger Murry assert that 75 000 were killed;[148]
- Raphael Lemkin believed that the number of Herero fell from 90 000 to 15 000 (ie 75 000 killed)[149]
- Governor Leutwein: between 70 000 and 80 000;[150]
- Colonial Director Bernhard Durnburg admitted no less than 75 000 in 1908;[151]
- Isabel Hull: between 60 000 and 80 000;[152]
- Klaus Epstein: 80 000;[153]
- Herero academic and politician Mburumba Kerina found, in 1981, that by 1905, out of a population of 97 000 Herero there were only 20 000 left and by 1913 he suggests 80 000 had died, while out of a population of 130 000 Nama and Damara only 37 743 were alive.[154]
- Lamar Middleton, in 1936: relying on German historians states 100 000;[155]
- Nagan and Rodin: 100 000.[156]

146 Palmer, A. (1998, January) 'Colonial and modern genocide: explanations and categories'. 21(1) *Ethnic and Racial Studies*, 89–115, 90.
147 Haarhoff, D. (1991) *The wild South-West: Frontier myths and metaphors in literature set in Namibia, 1760–1988*. Johannesburg: Witwatersrand University Press, 68.
148 Fraenkel, P. & Murry, R. (1985) *The Namibian Report, No 19*. London: Minority Rights Group International, 6.
149 Lemkin, R. (undated) Manuscript titled 'The Germans in Africa' found at the Jacob Rader Marcus Center of the American Jewish Archives, Cincinnati, the Raphael Lemkin papers, Box 6, Folder 9, 12.
150 Bley, H. (1971) *South-West Africa under German rule 1894–1914*. London: Heinemann, 319.
151 Africanus (1917) *The Prussian lash in Africa*. London: Hodder and Stoughton 36 fn 2. This author suggests that from when the Germans arrived in the 1800s to 1917 the population of GSWA fell from between 750 000 and a million to about 200 000.
152 Hull, I.V. (2005) *Absolute destruction: Military culture and practices of war in Imperial Germany*. Ithaca: Cornell University Press, 7–8.
153 Epstein, K. (1959, October) 'Erzberger and the German colonial scandals, 1905–1910'. 74 (293) *English Historical Review*, 637–63, 639.
154 Kerina , M. (1981) *Namibia: the making of a nation*. New York: Books in Focus, 5.
155 Middleton, L. (1936) *The Rape of Africa*. New York: Harrison Smith and Roman Haas, 276.
156 Nagan, W.P. & Rodin, V. F. (2003–2004) 'Racism, genocide and mass murder: Toward a legal theory about group deprivations'. *National Black Law Journal*, 133, 141.

All these figures suggest that between 60 000 and 100 000 Herero were killed (Wallenkampf differs slightly, saying the estimates vary from 60 000 to 90 000[157]). The only two vastly discrepant figures come from Eveleigh and Calvert. In 1915, Eveleigh suggested that 40 000 Herero were killed.[158] It is likely that he relied on inaccurate estimates by people such as Evans Lewin, who, in 1915, set the total indigenous population of GSWA in 1912 at only 100 000,[159] whereas they really numbered about 300 000. Also in 1915, Calvert noted that only 15 000 to 20 000 Herero were annihilated.[160] His initial figures are questionable, as he suggested that this was about half of the Herero population (who in total numbered more than 100 000).

As mentioned, the discrepancy is partly due to claims that it was not clear how many Herero there were before 1904. Some, such as Werner, state that there were 84 000 Herero in the nineteenth century,[161] while Stoecker notes that there were about 80 000 Herero and about 20 000 Nama in 1890.[162] The claim that 80 000 Herero were at the encampment at the battle of the Waterberg has been disputed by those who argue that there would not have been sufficient food and water for such a large group and their cattle.[163] According to Hull, however, there was plenty of grass and water in 1904, but the Herero had very nearly depleted all of that by the time of the battle.[164]

The other side of the numbers debate concerns the number of Herero alive after 1908. According to some, such as Dawson, there were 15 000, while Cyril Hall has put the number at 20 000.[165] Bridgman and Worley also state that there were 20 000 left in 1906.[166] Peter Carstens has put the number

[157] Wallenkampf, A.V. (1969) *The Herero rebellion in South West Africa: A study in German colonialism*. PhD thesis. Los Angeles: UCLA, 216.
[158] Eveleigh, W. (1915) *South-West Africa*. Cape Town: Maskew Miller, 136.
[159] Lewin, E. (1915) *The Germans and Africa. Their aims on the dark continent and how they acquired their African colonies*. London: Cassell, 110.
[160] Calvert, A.F. (1915) *South West Africa: During the German Occupation 1884–1914*. London: T. Werner Laurie, 24.
[161] Werner, W. (1993, March) 'A brief history of land dispossession in Namibia'. 19(1) *Journal of Southern African Studies*, 29–39, 41.
[162] Stoecker, H. (ed) (1986) *German imperialism in Africa: From the beginnings until the Second World War*. London: C. Hurst & Co, 39–40.
[163] See Sudholt, G. (1975) *Die deutsche Eingeborenenpolitik in Südwestafrika: Von den Anfängen bis 1904*. Hildesheim/New York: Olms, 184.
[164] Hull, I.V. (2005) *Absolute destruction: Military culture and practices of war in Imperial Germany*. Ithaca: Cornell University Press, 34.
[165] Wallenkampf, A.V. (1969) *The Herero rebellion in South West Africa: A study in German colonialism*. PhD thesis. Los Angeles: UCLA, 367.
[166] See Bridgman, J. & Worley, L.J. (1997) 'Genocide of the Herero'. In Totten, S., Parsons, W. & Charney, I. (eds) *Century of genocide*. New York: Garland 3–40, 3.

at 25 000,[167] while Enzo Traverso claims there were only 8 000 left.[168] In 1907 the Rhenish Missionary Society Inspector Johannes Spieker noted in correspondence that 'it is a shame that the number of Herero went down to 10 000. This is due to the inhumane policy of General von Trotha'.[169] A 1928 report by the government of South Africa noted that there were 28 000 Herero.[170] (Of course, the Herero population would have grown in the 20 years after the war, but 28 000 is still dramatically lower than the pre-war figures).

Despite these figures, some have attempted to argue that there were many more Herero survivors than generally accepted. As indicated, Brigitte Lau dismisses the 'contradictory guesswork' and argues that 'the missionaries questioned their predecessors' Herero population estimates of the 1870s (circa eighty thousand) among themselves and, as to survivors, there are contradictory counts by the German General Staff in Windhoek, individual officers, the Colonial Office in Berlin, the Rhenish Mission Society and individual missionaries'.[171]

Although there is also some discrepancy about exactly how many Herero made it through the desert to Botswana, it is generally agreed that those only account for a small proportion of the difference between the pre- and post-genocide numbers. In his thesis, Klaus Lorenz argues that the number of Herero in Botswana in 1930 was much higher (6 000) than previously accepted

---

[167] *Encyclopaedia Americana*, Vol. 14 (1971) New York, 137. Cited in Nordbruch, C. (2004) 'Atrocities committed on the Herero people during the suppression of their uprising in German South West Africa 1904–1907? An analysis of the latest accusations against Germany and an investigation on the credibility and justification of the demands for reparation'. Paper delivered to the European American Culture Council, Sacramento, 25 April 2004. Available at: http://www.nordbruch.org/artikel/sacramento.pdf

[168] See Traverso, E. 'Die Moderne und die Barbarei'. *Sozialistische Zeitung*, 7 December 2000. Quoted in Nordbruch, C. (2004) 'Atrocities committed on the Herero people during the suppression of their uprising in German South West Africa 1904–1907? An analysis of the latest accusations against Germany and an investigation on the credibility and justification of the demands for reparation'. Paper delivered to the European American Culture Council, Sacramento, 25 April 2004. Available at: http://www.nordbruch.org/artikel/sacramento.pdf, 4.

[169] Spieker, quoted in Oermann, N.O. (1999) *Mission, church and state relations in South West Africa under German rule (1884–1915)*. Stuttgart: Franz Steiner Verlag, 100.

[170] Government of South Africa (1928) *The native tribes of South West Africa*. Cape Town: Cape Times Limited, 153.

[171] Lau, B. (1990, June/July) Letter to the editor. *Southern African Review of Books*. Quoted in Berat, L. (1993) 'Genocide: The Namibian case against Germany'. 5 *Pace International Law Review*, fn 95.

and thus more of them must have escaped from GSWA in 1904.[172] However, Jeremy Silvester, Werner Hillebrecht and Casper Erichsen dismissed his argument as fallacious, citing that there were many Herero in Botswana even before 1904.[173] According to them, the genocide would not be disproved even if 6 000 had survived (it also has to be taken into account that by 1930, about 22 years after the war, the population would have recovered to some extent). In this regard, Oermann has suggested that only about 1 000 Herero, including Samuel Maherero, made it to Botswana through the desert,[174] while Hull claims that about 2 000 made it.[175] However, Renee Pennington and Henry Harpending have projected that the number of Herero that fled to Botswana has been significantly underestimated — they believe between 6 000 and 9 000 actually made it there.[176] Nonetheless, the number of Herero in Botswana does not significantly affect the number of genocide survivors. Indisputably, tens of thousands were killed. An admission on the general number killed was given by Leutwein in 1906 when he stated that 'we have expended several hundred million marks and the lives of several thousand German soldiers. As a result we have totally destroyed the pastoral industry of our colony. We have destroyed two-thirds of our native labour. Worse still, we have as yet been unable to respect peace'.[177] Thus he admits that two-thirds of the labour force had been destroyed. He thereby indicates that a sizeable proportion of those who had been fought against had died in the war or through its consequences. By 1907, the Germans themselves reported that of the 15 000 Herero and

---

172 'Researcher into the Waterberg tragedy of 1904 presents a new radical version'. *The Windhoek Observer*, 21 July 2001. See also Bölsche, J. 'Die Peitsche des Bändigers'. *Der Spiegel 3*, 12 January 2004.
173 Silvester, J., Hillebrecht, W. & Erichsen, C. (2001) 'The Herero Holocaust?' *The Namibian Weekender*, 10 August 2001.
174 Oermann, N.O. (1999) *Mission, church and state relations in South West Africa under German rule (1884–1915)*. Stuttgart: Franz Steiner Verlag, 97.
175 Hull, I.V. (2003) 'Military culture and the production of final solutions in the colonies: The example of Wilhelminian Germany'. In Gellately, R. & Kiernan, B. (eds) *The specter of genocide mass murder in historical perspective*. Cambridge: Cambridge University Press, 151.
176 Pennington, R. & Harpending, H. (1993) *The structure of an Africanist pastoral community: Demography, history and ecology of the Ngamiland Herero*. Oxford: Clarendon Press, 109. Pendleton believes that 2 000 Herero fled to South Africa. Pendleton, W.C. (1976) 'Herero reactions: The pre-colonial period, the German period and the South African period'. In Chanaiwa, D. *Profiles of self-determination: African responses to European colonialism in southern Africa*. Present, Northridge: California State University Foundation, 167–94, 178.
177 T. Leutwein, quoted in Gann, L.H. & Duigan, P. (1977) *The rulers of German Africa 1884–1914*. Stanford: Stanford University Press, 75.

2 000 Nama in the concentration camps, more than half died.[178] Additionally, a German journalist, who accompanied Colonial Secretary Dernberg on a visit to GSWA in 1908, noted that 'the Herero as a member of a pastoral people are ideally suited to farming. Unfortunately the Herero people have been largely wiped out by the war'.[179]

In contrast to the tens of thousands of Herero deaths, other than the German soldiers who died during the war or because of illness, only 119 white men, four women and one child were killed.[180]

When did the genocide begin?

A further question academics extensively debate is whether the genocide began before or after the 'order' was given in October 1904. Did the order simply give formal authorisation to an existing process? Hull claims that nothing changed after the October order was proclaimed; the same strategy had been implemented before, albeit not with official endorsement.[181] Yet, she argues that the 2 October extermination order was Von Trotha's response to the Germans' failure to successfully persecute the Herero.[182] When the German troops arrived at the last known water hole on 29 September they found few Herero and were unable to get those remaining to turn and fight. Von Trotha intended to exterminate the Herero because his forces were stretched thin and he was having difficulty getting supplies to them.

---

[178] Packenham, T. (1992) *The scramble for Africa: White man's conquest of the Dark Continent from 1875–1912*. New York: Avon Books, 615.

[179] Cited in Stoecker, H. (ed) (1986) *German imperialism in Africa: From the beginnings until the Second World War*. London: C Hurst & Co, 137.

[180] Pfister, G. (2005) 'Sport, colonialism and the enactment of German identity — *Turnen* in South West Africa', 10. Paper delivered at the 20th International Congress for the Historical Sciences, 3–9 July 2005, Sydney. Available at: www.cishsydney2005.org/images/GertrundPfisterST25.doc

[181] Hull, I.V. (2003) 'Military culture and the production of final solutions in the colonies: The example of Wilhelminian Germany'. In Gellately, R. & Kiernan, B. (eds) *The specter of genocide mass murder in historical perspective*. Cambridge: Cambridge University Press, 156.

[182] The Herero tactic was not to face the Germans, but to flee and then tackle them on their own terms, a kind of guerrilla warfare. Hull, I.V. (2003) 'Military culture and the production of final solutions in the colonies: The example of Wilhelminian Germany'. In Gellately, R. & Kiernan, B. (eds) *The specter of genocide mass murder in historical perspective*. Cambridge: Cambridge University Press, 156.

Troops loading cannons and machine guns on railway cars to transport them from Windhoek

According to Hull, the troops at the Waterberg had recently arrived from Germany and 'were inexperienced, poorly led, tired, frustrated, hungry, but haughty'.[183] Or, Von Trotha might have wished for a single conclusive battle with the Herero and was concerned that if this did not happen a protracted set of smaller battles on their terms would follow, which would be difficult to win and could entail greater German losses. However, neither of these conclusions makes sense, given that the same violations contained in the order had already occurred prior to its proclamation. Bollig and Gewald argue that the introduction of the Metropolitan German Imperial troops, who had no commonality or shared experience with the Herero, facilitated the genocide.[184] However, Tilman Dedering has argued that political reasons drove the extermination of the Herero and that the 'idea was justified in

[183] Hull, I.V. (2005) *Absolute destruction: Military culture and practices of war in Imperial Germany*. Ithaca: Cornell University Press, 51.
[184] Bollig, M. & Gewald, J-B. (2000) 'People, cattle and land — An introduction'. In Bollig, M. & Gewald, J-B. (eds) *People, cattle and land: Transformations of a pastoral society in southwestern Africa*. Köln: Rüdiger Koppe Verlag, 19.

racist terms and came easily to the mind of a battle-hardened warrior, who had been sent to Namibia because he had previously distinguished himself in putting down anti-colonial uprisings in China and East Africa. The "resistance" Von Trotha hoped to uproot once and for all was not military resistance, but a resurgence of the social core of the Herero population, the "old tribal organisations".[185]

While Hull believes that no order to exterminate occurred prior to 2 October she does acknowledge that 'Trotha's open statements approving inhumane warfare and his gaudy trumpeting of the goal of "the destruction of the enemy" created an atmosphere in which soldiers felt that massacre was approved and even expected'.[186] Hence, extermination was already contemplated, implied and at least tacitly endorsed. It is likely that the only difference was that it had not been explicitly verbalised, recorded on paper or publicly revealed before October 1904. Despite this, in all likelihood, Von Trotha ensured that his commanders understood what was required, whether or not this was officially recorded. When Von Trotha commanded the order in written form published in Otjiherero, its existence became unequivocal.

On 16 July 1904, in his diary entry, Von Trotha referred to the Herero as non-humans who need not be dealt with humanely.[187] While Hull rightly argues that this does not amount to a declaration or an order, brutalities were already taking place. Whether this conduct resulted from Von Trotha giving licence to his soldiers to fight within an annihilatory policy is unclear. In August 1904, Von Trotha states that 'forbearance and leniency toward such an enemy is simply a crime committed against one's own soldiers'.[188]

Von Trotha's diary entry of 29 August 1904 reads: 'For the present I will stick with my idea to pursue and fight wherever I can or drive them [through the desert] into English territory and then leave a strong border occupation there so they could not return.'[189] This entry demonstrates his resolve to fight the Herero wherever he found them or drive them across the border. He had already given specific orders on 16 August and 26 August to cordon off the water wells. So even before October he plotted to block the Herero's access

---

[185] Dedering, T. (1993, March) 'The German-Herero War of 1904: Revisionism of genocide or imaginary historiography'. 19 (1) *Journal of Southern African Studies*, 80, 84.
[186] Hull, I.V. (2005) *Absolute destruction: Military culture and practices of war in Imperial Germany*. Ithaca: Cornell University Press, 51.
[187] *Ibid*, 33.
[188] *Ibid*.
[189] *Ibid*, 52–3.

to water and force them into the desert. Although the use of the word 'fight' could be interpreted neutrally, evidence at the time suggests otherwise. 'Fight wherever I can' seemed to mean killing as many as possible, both warriors and civilians.

Various accounts, including Von Trotha's own diary entries, show intent to exterminate even before October. Von Trotha's diary entry of 2 September 1904 reads: 'They have only the hope for a battle that might go better for them or the hopeless escape into the desert.'[190] Although this is not incontrovertible proof and although there were statements about not shooting women and children, his use of the word 'they' does not distinguish between combatants and civilians. The plan was to force all Herero to flee to the desert. If they did not, they would be killed. As for the 2 October order, despite statements that he would not 'catch women and the sick but ... will chase them after their chiefs or ... will kill them with the gun' eyewitness accounts, such as the one by Jan Kubas cited earlier in this chapter, prove that these were empty words.

On 3 September Von Trotha wrote in his diary: 'After them until either they or we can't go on.'[191] Again, he writes 'them' with no differentiation between warriors and civilians. His intention to kill or get rid of all the Herero, even the non-combatants, is evident in his diary entry of 13 September 1904, where he writes: 'Feldherero [those without cattle who got subsistence by hunting and gathering on the veld or plains] women and children come in droves asking for water. I have given renewed orders to drive them all back with force.'[192] Thus, German troops were ordered to refuse water and these Herero, all non-combatants, were treated with force, like combatants. The word 'renewed' is critical because it indicates that this was not the first such order.

In September 1904, Major Ludwig von Estorff confirmed Von Trotha's intent to exterminate the Herero. He wrote:

> *It was a policy which was equally gruesome as senseless, to hammer the people so much, we could have still saved many of them and their rich herds, if we had pardoned and taken them up again, they had been punished enough. I suggested this to von Trotha but he wanted their total extermination.*[193]

---

[190] *Ibid*, 53.
[191] *Ibid*.
[192] *Ibid*.
[193] Von Estorff, L., cited in Gewald, J-B. & Silvester, J. (2003) *Words cannot be found. German colonial rule in Namibia: An annotated reprint of the 1918 Blue Book*. Leiden: Brill, xxi.

Schutztruppe carrying out the shoot-on-sight policy

Von Estorff's words confirm a number of things. They show that German soldiers knew what Von Trotha planned.[194] They also unmistakably confirm Von Trotha's intentions: to punish the Herero, to seek 'total extermination', and not just inflict military defeat. They highlight that even Von Trotha's own people thought his plans were 'gruesome' and 'senseless'. Von Estorff's words also endorse that *vernichten* meant annihilation. If it were mere rhetoric or a military strategy, why would Von Trotha's own officer describe it as 'gruesome' and 'senseless'?

The most incontrovertible evidence of genocidal intent before the October order relates to the killing of a group of 70 Herero prisoners in the first week of September. An African witness, Hendrik Campbell, who commanded the Baster unit, was assisting the Germans. He saw the 70 bodies and was told by his men that they been shot and bayoneted by the German soldiers.

---

[194] Poewe attempts to limit the extent of what occurred at the time, but the accounts of German soldiers recorded in her book belie her efforts to do so. See Poewe, K. (1985) *The Namibian Herero: A history of their psychosocial disintegration and survival.* Lewiston, NY: Edwin Mellen (particularly pages 56–82).

When Von Trotha arrived, there was an argument between Campbell and a German soldier about what had happened and Von Trotha said: 'The entire Herero people must be exterminated.'[195,196] 'Entire Herero people' requires no interpretation. Consequently, all the evidence pieced together — Von Trotha's diary entries, comments by others (including German soldiers), the events on the ground and this statement, a month before the October order — substantiate the intent to commit genocide. The 2 October proclamation was, as Hull claims,[197] *ex post facto* and simply a formally verbalised authorisation of a process that was already underway. The only difference is that it became an official comprehensive policy.

Governor Leutwein realised that genocide was planned and underway. Even before June 1904 he seems to have realised that, when Von Trotha arrived, the Herero were going to be decimated. In the following statement he argues against this objective:

> *I do not concur with those fanatics who want to see the Herero destroyed altogether. Apart from the fact that a people of 60 000 or 70 000 is not so easy to annihilate, I would consider such a move a grave mistake from an economic point of view. We need the Herero as cattle breeders, though on a small scale and especially as labourers. It will be quite sufficient if they are politically dead.*[198]

Accordingly, he urged the Herero to surrender, warning that if they did not, they were going to die. Just a few days before Von Trotha arrived in GSWA, Leutwein sent, by a hundred couriers, a proclamation to the Herero in Otjiherero, which read:

> *Hereros! You well know that after you have risen against you[r?] protector, the German Kaiser, nothing else awaits you but a fight to the death. Until then I cannot stop the war. However, you can stop the war by coming over to me, handing in your guns and ammunition and receiving your expected punishment.*
>
> *However it is well known to me that a lot of you carry no guilt for the many evil affairs that have happened. And these can safely come to me; their lives will be spared. However no mercy will I show to those who have murdered whites and robbed their homes. These will be placed before a court and must receive the value of their guilt. You others however, who have no such guilt upon themselves, be clever*

---

195 Campbell's full testimony about Von Trotha can be found in the Blue Book: Gewald, J-B. & Silvester, J. (2003) *Words cannot be found. German colonial rule in Namibia: An annotated reprint of the 1918 Blue Book*. Leiden: Brill, 117–19.

196 Von Trotha, T., cited in Hull, I.V. (2005) *Absolute destruction: Military culture and practices of war in Imperial Germany*. Ithaca: Cornell University Press, 52.

197 Hull, I.V. (2005) *Absolute destruction: Military culture and practices of war in Imperial Germany*. Ithaca: Cornell University Press, 57 fn 55.

198 T. Leutwein, quoted in Gewald J-B. (1999) *Herero heroes: A socio-political history of the Herero of Namibia 1890–1923*. Oxford: James Currey, 169.

and no longer connect your fate with that of the guilty ones. Leave them and save your life! This I say as representative of your paramount lord, the German Kaiser. Okahandja, 30 May 1904 (Sgd. Leutwein)[199]

Hence, Leutwein suspected or, even knew, what was in store for the Herero even before Von Trotha arrived. Yet, on examination of official German war reports and diaries of German soldiers,[200] Henrik Lundtofte argues that the genocide plan only came to fruition after the battle of Waterberg. He contradicts the view that Von Trotha intended genocide at the Waterberg battle. He maintains that women and children were not meant to be killed and cites the fact that the Germans prepared a camp for about 8 000 Herero captives as proof. Hull also mentions the building of a stockade for 8 000, as well as the ordering of one thousand chains — the number needed for the Herero warriors.[201] and further notes that Von Trotha had ordered that all Herero males be killed even before Waterberg. Why, then, would he want the chains for the warriors? Hull undermines her own argument about the construction of the stockade solely for the 8 000 warriors by stating that the concentration camps were designed to frustrate the Herero's guerrilla warfare tactics. By detaining the civilian population, those engaged in these tactics were prevented from blending into the population. It is debatable whether the stockade was designed to be a concentration camp, but it seems likely that this is the case. After all, internment or concentration camps were already in use for this purpose[202] and had previously been used to the same end by Britain and Spain.[203]

While there was certainly intent to kill all Herero men at Waterberg, the question about the fate of women and children is controversial. Some contend that Von Trotha tried to limit the excesses committed to the men, but it seems that many others were killed as well, even before the order. It would

---

[199] *Ibid.*
[200] The Bryce Report, drawn up to consider and advise on the 'outrages alleged to have been committed by German troops during the present War, cases of alleged maltreatment of civilians in the invaded territories and breaches of the laws and established usages of war' states: 'It appears to be the custom in the German army for soldiers to be encouraged to keep diaries and record in them the chief events of each day.' *The Bryce Report — Report of the Committee on Alleged German Outrages Appointed by His Britannic Majesty's Government and Presided Over by the Right Hon. Viscount Bryce, O.M.*
[201] Hull, I.V. (2003) 'Military culture and the production of final solutions in the colonies: The example of Wilhelminian Germany'. In Gellately, R. & Kiernan, B. (eds) *The specter of genocide mass murder in historical perspective.* Cambridge: Cambridge University Press, 148–9.
[202] *Ibid,* 158.
[203] *Ibid.*

appear that the 'order' to spare women and children occurred only after the Waterberg battle.[204]

The Germans created a stockade to hold only 8 000 at Waterberg, but it is known that there were between 50 000 and 80 000 Herero at the Waterberg. If the space were to accommodate 8 000 prisoners, what was to happen to the rest? The 8 000 places could have been meant for 8 000 warriors, because the Germans were clearly not taking prisoners at the time. Thus, if the stockade was not for combatants, it must have been for other Herero. The policy at that stage was probably not to kill every single Herero individual, as the Germans wanted some prisoners for slave labour.[205] This would account for Krüger's finding that some Herero were taken prisoner at the time.[206] In fact, Gewald has written about the need for labour and claimed that labour recruitment was a possible contributing factor to the outbreak of the war.[207]

A great deal of other evidence reinforces the notion that the intent to exterminate preceded the order, including the fact that German soldiers were often ordered not to take captives. This order was only rescinded at the very end of 1904 by the Kaiser, not because he acted speedily to prevent further mortalities or because of the brutality or illegality of what was happening, but because the policy of killing the Herero was likely to 'damage the regard of other civilized nations for Germany'.[208] The rescission stated that the practise of simply shooting the Herero on sight was no longer acceptable.[209] However, although Germany finally agreed to amend the order, it rejected all attempts to negotiate with the Herero. Because Germany issued the amendment only because the order damaged its prestige and because it amended only the shoot-

---

[204] *Ibid*, 154.
[205] On the labour camps and what labour and for whom the slaves were made to work see Goldblatt, I. (1971) *History of South West Africa: From the beginning of the nineteenth century.* Cape Town: Juta.
[206] Krüger, G. (1999) *Kriegsbewältigung und Geschichtsbewusstsein: Realität, Deutung und Verarbeitung des deutschen Kolonialkrieges in Namibia, 1904 bis 1907.* Göttingen: Vandenhoek & Ruprecht, 118.
[207] Gewald, J-B. (1999) 'The road of the man called Love and the sack of Sero: The Herero-German War and the export of the Herero labour to the South African Rand'. 40 (1) *Journal of African History*, 21–40, 21.
[208] Letter of General von Trotha to the German Governor of German South West Africa, quoted in Drechsler, H. (1980) *Let us die fighting: The struggle of the Herero and Nama against the German imperialism (1894–1915)* (Bernd Zöllner, transl). London: Zed Press, 191.
[209] Drechsler, H. (1980) *Let us die fighting: The struggle of the Herero and Nama against the German imperialism (1894–1915)* (Bernd Zöllner, transl). London: Zed Press, 164.

on-sight-policy, it is questionable whether this amounted to a significant change in intentions.

Was the killing of women and children specifically sought?

Superficially, Von Trotha's orders regarding the treatment of women and children seems to be inconsistent. His 2 October order to the Herero states: 'I shall not catch women and the sick but I will chase them after their chiefs or I will kill them with the gun.' The section addressed to the German troops states that 'shooting at women and children is to be understood as shooting above their heads, so as to force them to run [away]. I assume absolutely that this proclamation...will not degenerate into atrocities against women and children. The latter will run away if one shoots at them a couple of times'. At first glance this might seem like a discrepancy: they will be killed, versus they are merely to be scared off. However, both statements entail shooting at women and children. According to Wallenkampf, the second part of the order (that communicated to the troops) was only issued a day after the first part was announced. He perceives this as possible damage control: the initial order might have drawn criticism, which necessitated an addition to limit negative perceptions.[210]

Lundtofte acknowledges that 'there is no doubt that German forces murdered men, women and children, though Trotha had ostensibly forbidden his soldiers to fire on women and children. While men were liquidated in considerable numbers, it would not appear to have been the intention to systematically murder women and children'.[211] He argues that German soldiers were ordered to shoot into the air when firing on women and children, to drive them into the desert. Yet, whether they were killed by the gun or by deprivation does not change the intent and he undermines his own argument by stating that driving them from the water holes was an effort to exterminate them. He further contradicts himself by adding that 'as was the case at the battle at Waterberg German warfare did not make any distinction between civilians and warriors'.[212]

---

[210] Wallenkampf, A.V. (1969) *The Herero rebellion in South West Africa: A study in German colonialism*. PhD thesis. Los Angeles: UCLA, 354.
[211] Lundtofte, H. (2003) 'Radicalization of the German suppression of the Herero rising in 1904'. In Jensen, S.L.B. (ed) *Genocide: Cases, comparisons and contemporary debates*. Copenhagen: Danish Center for Holocaust and Genocide, 15, 31.
[212] *Ibid*, 15, 35.

Schutztruppe on patrol near the Waterberg in September 1904

Crucially, much of this is based on German reports and German soldiers' diaries. These sources are often contradicted by other sources, such as the statement of a German guide who noted that

> all men, women and children who fell into German hands, wounded or otherwise, were mercilessly put to death. Then the Germans set off in pursuit of the rest and all those found by the wayside and in the Sandveld were shot down or bayoneted to death. The mass of the Herero men were unarmed and thus unable to offer resistance.[213]

Some have also argued that the 'tough words' of the proclamation were designed to impress the Kaiser or the Chief of the General Staff.[214] Hull does not believe that to be likely because, as he argues, the proclamation was for

---

[213] Drechsler, H. (1980) *Let us die fighting: The struggle of the Herero and Nama against the German imperialism (1894–1915)* (Bernd Zöllner, transl). London: Zed Press, 157.

[214] Hull, I.V. (2005) *Absolute destruction: Military culture and practices of war in Imperial Germany*. Ithaca: Cornell University Press, 58.

purely domestic propaganda purposes,[215] but one cannot entirely discount the possibility. It supports the theory that the Kaiser or others wanted and may have ordered decisive action. The genocide was already underway, so the order did not set the process in motion, it merely publicised it into a specific and direct command for the troops.

This does not mean the choice of wording was limited to these reasons. It was also meant to make it clear to the Herero that they were going to be destroyed. The motivation behind the wording was in part to 'persuade' the Herero to flee into the desert, serving the same purpose but 'saving' the German soldiers the effort of actively killing them and perhaps doing less damage to their reputation.

The same applies to the additional section of the order read to the German troops. Although it ostensibly orders the troops to scare the women and children off, the intention was not to protect them but to scare them into the desert to die. In this way the Germans would not appear directly responsible for the ensuing deaths. When Von Trotha instructs the troops to 'remain conscious of the good reputation of the German soldier', it merely implied limiting the active killing of women and children, with the knowledge that the same number would die due to lack of access to food and water. Only if the women and children did not flee as expected were the soldiers to kill them.

Consequently, the additional section of the order read to the troops was not to exercise disciplinary control over the soldiers; they were expected to shoot anyone who did not flee. Expulsion was the primary objective, but killing would suffice. This is clear from Von Trotha's letter to the Chief of the General Staff that he included with a copy of the order on 4 October:

> For me it is merely a question of how to end the war with the Herero. My opinion is completely opposite to that of the Governor and some 'old Africans'. They have waited to negotiate for a long time and describe the Herero nation as a necessary labour force for the future use of the colony. I am of an entirely different opinion. I believe that the nation must be destroyed as such or since this was not possible using tactile blows, it must be expelled from the land operatively and by means of detailed action.[216]

---

[215] Gert Sudholt provides a much narrower and problematic interpretation, ie that the extermination order was simply propaganda. Sudholt, G. (1975) *Die deutsche Eingeborenenpolitik in Südwestafrika: Von den Anfängen bis 1904.* Hildesheim/New York: Olms.

[216] Hull, I.V. (2005) *Absolute destruction: Military culture and practices of war in Imperial Germany.* Ithaca: Cornell University Press, 58–59.

Schutztruppe officers directing the troops as they fire Maxim machine guns and other weapons

Von Trotha was not interested in saving the Herero as a labour force; he wanted to get rid of them. The last line of this extract reveals that until that time, the intention, even before October, had been to destroy the Herero militarily, but this had failed. Von Trotha, thus, explained that the next step was expulsion and that certain actions are to be taken towards that end. He also wrote on 4 October that

> *accepting women and children, who are mostly ill, is an eminent danger to the troops and taking care of them impossible. Therefore, I think it better that the nation perish rather than infect our troops and affect our water and food.*[217]

According to Berat, the soldiers ignored the instruction to fire over the heads of women and children.[218] Instead 'with relentless and systematic energy ... the German soldiery shot and bayoneted thousands of Herero men, women and

---

217 *Ibid*, 59.
218 Berat, L. (1993) 'Genocide: The Namibian case against Germany'. 5 *Pace International Law Review*, fn 75.

children, then clubbed them to death to help them die'.[219] Events on the ground contradict Von Trotha's supposed order that women and children were to be spared; those who were shot or bayoneted were left in their blood.[220] Testimony also reveals that Von Trotha ordered women and children to be killed on occasion, including one specific occasion when he ordered a young Herero woman to be bayoneted.[221]

The multiple killings occurred in 1904 from the time the Germans went on the offensive against the Herero and particularly after the extermination order was issued. However, the killing of women and children did not start in 1904. Even before that time, for example at the Massacre at Hornkrantz a decade earlier, women and children had been killed. At a minimum, the government supported these actions; they may even have ordered them.

Conclusion

The brutality of the German colonisers was not confined to GSWA and predated the Herero-German war. Reports from German East Africa, Samoa and New Guinea testify to widespread corporal punishment, rape and killings. The genocide of the Herero was clearly intended, ordered and committed (through directly killing them and indirectly causing them to starve). Direct evidence — in the form of eyewitness testimonies, statements by opposition politicians in Germany, records of the missionaries, Leutwein, German officers and Von Trotha himself — outweighs the writings and efforts of denialists to minimise the extent of what had happened. Events on the ground and Von Trotha's diaries contradict claims that the use of the word *'vernichten'* was mere political rhetoric or psychological warfare strategy. Equally, there is sufficient evidence to show that the genocidal intent preceded the October order, while Von Trotha was one of the main 'informants'. However one chooses to look at it, numerous records show that between 60 000 and 100 000 Herero died at the hands of the Germans. Similarly, multiple accounts show that no distinction was made between combatants and civilians and that women and children were not shown mercy, despite superficial official attempts at window-dressing.

---

[219] Soggot, D. (1986) *Namibia: The violent heritage*. London: Rex Collings, x.
[220] *Ibid*, 9–10.
[221] Testimony of Manuel Timbu. In Administrator's Office Windhuk [sic] (9ed) (1918) *Report on the natives of South-West Africa and their treatment by Germany*. London: His Majesty's Stationery Office, 56. See also Gewald, J-B. & Silvester, J. (2003) *Words cannot be found. German colonial rule in Namibia: An annotated reprint of the 1918 Blue Book*. Leiden: Brill, 115.

CHAPTER THREE

DID THE KAISER ORDER THE GENOCIDE?

A common goal of all researchers is to piece together who ordered the killings to commence in any given case. If in the twentieth century these mass murders were usually state-sponsored or at least officially sanctioned, who made decisions? What were their motives? These questions are particularly relevant if we want to hold leaders responsible for genocides or other grave human rights abuses before international courts. The problem for historians and jurists is that leaders and their agents try, usually with considerable success, to cover up their crimes and to destroy the evidence. Moreover, some states continue to deny crimes, including cases of mass murder and even genocide, committed by their predecessors. They also limit access to their archives and even persecute or threaten researchers. When scholars are finally granted access to their archives, they often find that evidence has been 'laundered' or destroyed. So reconstructing the decision-making process is often no easy task.[1]

The lowest, most abject outrage ever to be perpetrated by any nation in history, that is what the Germans have done unto themselves. Egged on misled by the tribe of Judah whom they hate, who were guests among them! That was the thanks they got! Let no German ever forget this, nor rest until these parasites have been wiped out from German soil and been exterminated! This poisonous mushroom on the German oak-tree![2]

— Kaiser Wilhelm II, 1919

Introduction

The role of Kaiser Wilhelm II, born Friedrich Wilhelm Viktor Albrecht von Hohenzollern 1859–1941, in the Herero extermination order has been debated over the years. Most people do not believe that the Kaiser gave the order

---

[1] Gellately, R. & Kiernan, B. (2003) 'The study of mass murder and genocide'. In Gellately, R. & Kiernan, B. (eds) *The specter of genocide mass murder in historical perspective.* Cambridge: Cambridge University Press, 10.

[2] Wilhelm II in a letter dated 2 December 1919 to *Generalfeldmarschall* August von Mackensen. Cited in Röhl, J.C.G. (1994) *The Kaiser and his court: Wilhelm II and the government of Germany.* Cambridge: Cambridge University Press, 14.

to General von Trotha.[3] Others, however, have speculated whether the Kaiser was behind the order. Even at the time of the genocide, such conjecture occurred. On 1 December 1906, August Bebel, an opposition Member of Parliament in the *Reichstag*, stated:

> *I don't know whether Herr Von Trotha acted on his own or according to a similar slogan to the one made in 1900: 'Take no quarter, behave so that no Chinese will dare to look askance at a German for a 1 000 years...' Herr Von Trotha must have received secret instructions as to how he was to proceed in South West Africa; I find no other explanation for the fact that he, a general, ordered his men to disregard every principle of military law, civilization and Christianity.*[4]

Bebel was convinced that the Kaiser gave Von Trotha a secret order. Furthermore, Von Trotha's order was very similar to the one the Kaiser gave in relation to China in 1900 (discussed later). At the time, Von Trotha was the commander of the First Asiatic Expeditionary Brigade. In fact, it was in this capacity that he came to the attention of the Kaiser.[5] There is a possibility that, because Von Trotha knew of the Kaiser's order in China, he may have taken it upon himself to carry out similar instructions on his own in GSWA, but in the light of all the evidence marshalled in this chapter this is doubtful.

In addition to Bebel, there were others at the time who also believed the extermination order came from the Kaiser. The diary of Major Stuhlmann of the German forces, who fought at the Waterberg battle, contains the following entry: 'The Herero seems to be gradually seeping back into the country, in spite of the bloody decree of Von Trotha, emanating from Berlin, that all men be shot and all women and children driven from the land.'[6] Stuhlmann clearly believed that the order came from Berlin. In September 1905, the *Cape Argus* newspaper reported that South African transport riders noted, on their return

---

[3]   See for example Gründer, H. (1998) 'Genozid oder Zwangsmodernisierung? Der moderne Kolonialismus in universalgeschichtlicher Perspektive'. In Dabag, M. & Platt, K. (eds) *Genozid und Moderne. Bd 1. Strukturen kollektiver Gewalt im 20. Jahrhundert.* Opladen: Leske & Buderich, 135, 146.
  Hull states that no genocide or even a 'final solution' was ordered from Berlin. Hull, I.V. (2003) 'Military culture and the production of final solutions in the colonies: The example of Wilhelminian Germany'. In Gellately, R. & Kiernan, B. (eds) *The specter of genocide mass murder in historical perspective.* Cambridge: Cambridge University Press, 4.

[4]   Kerina, M. (1981) *Namibia: The making of a nation.* New York: Books in Focus, 53.

[5]   Schrank, G.I. (1974) *German South West Africa: Social and economic aspects of its history 1884–1915.* PhD thesis (History). New York University, 156.

[6]   Quoted in Erichsen, C.W. (2004) *The Angel of Death has descended violently among them: A study of Namibia's concentration camps and prisoners-of-war, 1904–08.* MA thesis (History). Windhoek: University of Namibia, 283.

from GSWA, that German soldiers usually gave the same rationalisation when questioned about the atrocities: 'The Kaiser has ordered us to do this.'[7] This could mean one of two things, either that they believed all orders emanated from the Kaiser or that they knew the Kaiser gave the specific order in this case. Therefore, at the time there was conjecture that Von Trotha did not act alone. Although Bebel surmised that the Kaiser must have given an order similar to the one in his Hun speech, that outburst had served as a lesson at the time, which called for more discretion in order to protect his reputation and that of Germany. For this reason, the role of the Kaiser is under continued debate.

The primary question explored in this chapter is the origin of the infamous order to exterminate the Herero. The evidence will show that the genocide order most likely came from Kaiser Wilhelm II and that it was probably conveyed orally. If it were a written order, the absence of concrete proof should be seen in the context of the vigorous efforts to protect the image of the Kaiser over the years during which he reigned and in the decades thereafter. This chapter will also argue that the people in the highest levels of government and the military knew about the order, but did nothing to stop the carnage until the pressure became too intense to avoid it. International concern was the primary reason for amending the genocide order and evidence will show that Germany's acts were already contrary to international law.

That there is no smoking gun proving that the Kaiser directly and personally ordered the genocide is not surprising, given all that was done to sanitise and edit his words and actions during and after his rule. Thus, a written order would not likely have survived. Röhl illuminates the consequences of this: 'This mentality has, needless to say, gravely affected the availability of evidence down to the present day, not least because, in addition, so much of what was being reserved until after the Kaiser's death was destroyed in the devastation of the Second World War.'[8] Röhl is referring to the destruction of military archives relating to the colonial times[9] by a fire in 1945, before anyone had researched the Herero war.[10] A lack of record-keeping and the sanitising and destruction of documents during World War II all contribute to a dearth of

---

[7] *Cape Argus*, 28 September 1905. Quoted in Erichsen, C.W. (2004) *The Angel of Death has descended violently among them: A study of Namibia's concentration camps and prisoners-of-war, 1904–08*. MA thesis (History). Windhoek: University of Namibia, 43.

[8] Röhl, J.C.G. (1994) *The Kaiser and his court: Wilhelm II and the government of Germany*. Cambridge: Cambridge University Press, 27.

[9] Sole, T.E. (1968, December) 'The Südwestafrika Denkmünze and the South West African campaigns of 1903–1908'. 1(3) *Military History Journal*, 19–23, 20.

[10] Hull, I.V. (2005) *Absolute destruction: Military culture and practices of war in Imperial Germany*. Ithaca: Cornell University Press, 13.

evidence. The original diary of General von Trotha was supposedly lost too, yet as explored below a 1930s typed version survived.

Given these purges, Eric Weitz notes that 'the case, both legal and historical, has to be built from the evidence of actions on the ground and often circumstantial links in the chain of command between those who occupy positions of power and those who carry out the actual killings'.[11] The books and articles that examine the speeches, role and life of the Kaiser pay scant attention to his role in Germany's colonies and even less to his role vis-à-vis the use of German troops in those colonies. Few of these writings examine the Kaiser's interest or actual intervention in Africa and, specifically, in GSWA. Recovering such records in Namibia is also problematic. As Harriet Deacon has found, 'in Namibia, the colonial archive is rather scary'.[12]

Whether Germany takes responsibility, beyond a mere apology, for what occurred more than a century ago seems to depend on the role of the Kaiser and, by extension, that of the German government,[13] specifically whether Von Trotha was ordered to carry out the extermination. However, it is not so simple as Germany is, legally speaking, responsible, regardless of whether Von Trotha received orders to commit the extermination or not. The German state employed Von Trotha and is, thus, liable for his actions.

Regardless of whether there was a direct order from the Kaiser, Germany is complicit in the killing of the Herero because they neglected to act when they found out what was happening. Even after the German government became aware of Von Trotha's actions and the Social Democrats criticised the GSWA events in the *Reichstag*, Von Trotha received their support. This is reflected in the statements of Governor Leutwein who, when raising the issue of the extermination order with the German Foreign Office, 'was answered that von Trotha alone had authority to deal with the natives'.[14] Thus, although Leutwein specifically brought the occurrences in GSWA to their attention, the German Foreign Office told him to leave military matters to Von Trotha. In fact, the words

---

[11] Weitz, E.D. (2003) *A century of genocide: Utopias of race and nation.* Princeton: Princeton University Press, 10.

[12] Deacon, H. (2004) Marion Wallace, health, power and politics in Windhoek, Namibia 1915–1945 (Review)'. 78(4) *Bulletin of the History of Medicine*, 916–17, 916.

[13] In this context, Dan Stone has noted: 'Sometimes it is not clear what role the state, as opposed to, say, the army, has played in the decision to encourage atrocities, as in the case of the Rape of Nanjing (Fogel, 2000) or the genocide of the Hereros in German South-West Africa.' Stone, D. (2004) 'Genocide as transgression'. 7(1) *European Journal of Social Theory*, 45–65, 48.

[14] Bridgman, J. (1981) *The revolt of the Hereros.* Los Angeles: University of California Press, 129.

of the Chief of the Army General Staff demonstrate acceptance of the order. In November 1904, he told the Chancellor: 'His [Von Trotha's] plans to wipe out the entire nation or to drive them out of the country are meeting with our approval.'[15] Some allude to a hands-off approach by the Kaiser, but in fact he was more active in GSWA than elsewhere. According to Jan-Bart Gewald, the 'personal involvement of the German Kaiser Wilhelm II, in deciding how the war was to be fought in German South West Africa, signalled the highest authorisation and endorsement for acts committed in the name of Imperial Germany'.[16]

The debate over who condoned the order is relevant because some argue that the legal question regarding compensation hinges on whether there was an official policy behind the genocide. Yet this is a red herring because Germany is liable for the act of its servants regardless, especially those of the commander of the German forces, who directly or indirectly ordered the slaughter of the Herero. Even if Von Trotha's extermination order of 2 October 1904 was a personal decision, liability flows from the fact that Germany did nothing once it knew about the events. Government silence and inaction amounts to condoning the acts and therefore acted as a ratification of what occurred. In fact, Von Trotha himself stated, *'Qui tacet, consentire videtur* (he who keeps silent seems to consent).'[17] In this regard, command or superior responsibility would apply.[18] In war crime prosecutions, command responsibility is often used to determine liability of superiors for their failure to take steps to stop atrocities or their failure to punish those responsible for their actions when the superiors knew or ought to have known about them. At the minimum, the Kaiser gave Von Trotha extremely wide latitude to act of his own accord. According to Von Trotha's public utterances, the Kaiser told him he must put down the rebellion by any means, fair or foul. This version exhibits more than command responsibility, as the Kaiser instructed Von Trotha to take actions that he understood were foul or illegal. In the context of what German forces did in China during the Boxer Rebellion and in other massacres, the Kaiser could not have been under any illusion about what the German army could

---

[15] Drechsler, H. (1986) *Let us die fighting*. Berlin: Akademie-Verlag, 163.

[16] Gewald, J-B. (2003) 'Imperial Germany and the Herero of Southern Africa: Genocide and the quest for recompense'. In Jones, A. (ed) *Genocide, war crimes and the West: Ending the culture of impunity*. London: Zed Press, 59–77, 60.

[17] From a letter written by General von Trotha, commander of the German Army in GSWA, to German Chancellor Bülow in 1905. Quoted in Chirot, D. 'Are ethnic genocides, cleansings and other such massacres normal?' Available at: http://www.yale.edu/ccr/chirot.doc

[18] Ratner, S. & Abrams, J. (2001) *Accountability for human rights atrocities in international Law: Beyond the Nuremberg legacy* (2ed). Oxford: Oxford University Press, 132–135.

and would do in these circumstances. Evidence shows that the Kaiser was a brutal man who seemed to enjoy inflicting pain on others and who ordered killings at various times, including of his own citizens. As will be shown, he also believed in the extermination of the Jewish people.

The Kaiser specifically knew about Von Trotha's previous conduct, which the selection process that led the Kaiser to appoint him to command the forces in GSWA will demonstrate. Additionally, while the actual events took place, he took his time to intervene. When he did rescind the order, he did so minimally, without taking steps to prevent the other types of abuses that were occurring. Finally, he never took steps to discipline Von Trotha (as will be discussed below), but praised him continually and gave him medals and other awards after the genocide. While it would appear that, although Von Trotha did not reveal all that was going on, except most likely to the Kaiser, the German General Staff knew what he was doing. They might not have been aware of every detail or the full extent to which he was implementing the policy, but they knew a policy existed and supported it explicitly. Rare exceptions to this were motivated by what could practically be achieved in the field. The German staff and the Kaiser met all of Von Trotha needs, supplied large numbers of troops and invested huge amounts of money in the campaign. Hannah Arendt's statement in reference to Adolf Eichmann is equally relevant to Von Trotha and the crimes committed in GSWA: 'Crimes of this kind were and could only be committed under a criminal law and by a criminal state.'[19]

The Kaiser's personality

According to Jonathan Steinberg, the Kaiser's personality was a crucial determinant of what occurred in Germany under his reign.[20] Similarly, his personality was critical to the events in GSWA, especially the way in which Germany waged the campaign against the Herero. General sentiments about the Kaiser are not positive. Thomas A Kohut notes at the beginning of his book that 'Wilhelm II was not a particularly pleasant person who surrounded himself with other not particularly pleasant people. And he was the leader of a nation in which aggressive nationalism, imperialism, racism, social antagonism and sexism were prevalent'.[21] A number of factors linked to his birth and childhood seem to have influenced his personality.

[19] Arendt, H. (1963) *Eichmann in Jerusalem. A report on the banality of evil.* New York: Viking Press, 240. Quoted in Nollkaemper, A. (2003, July) 'Concurrence between individual responsibility and state responsibility in international law'. 52(3) *International and Comparative Law Quarterly*, 615, 621.

[20] Steinberg, J. (1965) *Yesterday's deterrent: Tirpitz and the birth of the German battle fleet.* London: Macmillan, 26.

[21] Kohut, T.A. (1991) *Wilhelm II and the Germans: A study in leadership.* New York: Oxford University Press, vii.

His birth was allegedly complicated and evidence suggests that he sustained a brain injury and damage to his left arm, which was withered and largely unusable. His mother rejected him and he was subjected to a harsh and strictly disciplined upbringing. As a result, he was a 'disturbed, cruel and sometimes even dangerous man'.[22] Many believe the Kaiser had the following characteristics: 'anxiety, inability to work, impulsiveness, self-delusion, ignorance'.[23] Regarding the Kaiser's personality,[24] Whittle wrote, 'By a careful study of the ups and downs in the life of the Kaiser it possible to see that from time to time he experienced a type of climacteric when calm and deliberate proceedings were followed by a short or long period of irritability and instability.'[25] Hull also notes that the Kaiser would impulsively change resolutely laid plans 'almost literally at the last minute and wrench his companions into the helter skelter world of his own whims'.[26] Ludwig has noted that the Kaiser had a 'love of absolutism' and a tendency to conceal his insecurities by adopting 'combative, bellicose postures'.[27] This often affected his judgement and decision-making.

While many regarded him as highly intelligent with an excellent memory,[28] major personality flaws affected his words and actions. Others claim that some of these negative traits resulted from his physically defective arm and the brain injury he supposedly suffered at birth. His mental status in general has been the subject of debate, but the consensus is that he was prone to blunders. This caused a number of political crises, especially in foreign policy. Between 1900 and 1909, Chancellor Bernhard von Bülow often had to smooth the troubled waters caused by the Kaiser, which gave him a certain power over the Kaiser.

In 1894, Professor Ludwig Quidde wrote a book entitled *Caligula: A study in Roman megalomania* in which he publicly accused the Kaiser of being megalomaniacal. Quidde compared the Kaiser to the mad Roman Emperor.[29]

---

[22] Mombauer, A. (1999, March) 'Germany's last Kaiser — Wilhelm II and political decision-making in Imperial Germany'. 4(3) *New Perspective*. Available at: http://www.users.globalnet.co.uk/~semp/wilhelmii.htm

[23] Hull, I.V. (1982) *The entourage of Kaiser Wilhelm II, 1888–1918*. New York: Cambridge University Press, 22.

[24] See also Dorpalen, A. (1952, October) 'Empress Auguste Victoria and the fall of the German monarchy'. 58(1) *American Historical Review*, 17–38.

[25] Whittle, T. (1977) *The last Kaiser: A biography of William II, German Emperor and King of Prussia*. London: Heinemann, 145.

[26] Hull, I.V. (1982) *The entourage of Kaiser Wilhelm II, 1888–1918*. New York: Cambridge University Press, 205.

[27] Ludwig, E. (1970) *Wilhelm Hohenzollern: The last of the Kaisers*. New York: Ames Press, 27.

[28] Hull, I.V. (1982) *The entourage of Kaiser Wilhelm II, 1888–1918*. New York: Cambridge University Press, 15.

[29] Van der Kiste, J. (1999) *Kaiser Wilhelm II: Germany's last Emperor*. Stroud, Gloucestershire: Sutton, 92.

Whether this is accurate or not, many have viewed him as impatient, impetuous, aggressive, blunt, lacking in subtlety, stubborn and prone to terrorising others. During the Chancellorship of Prince von Bülow, Fritz von Holstein,[30] who was the dominant official in Germany's foreign relations for 25 years until 1909, stated that the Kaiser often countermanded his policies. He believed that Wilhelm II was an 'impulsive, sadly completely superficial gentleman, who had not a clue about international law, about political precedent, of diplomatic history or how to handle people'.[31]

The relationship between the Kaiser and the chancellor is a key factor in why the Kaiser might have wanted to keep his order to Von Trotha a secret. In 1900, Chancellor von Bülow stated that if the Kaiser made one more bad move, a coalition of German princes and the *Reichstag* would have him declared unfit to remain in his position.[32] This likely had an enduring effect on their relationship. To some level, the relationship between the Kaiser and the Chancellor was generally close and the latter often stood behind and supported the Kaiser. However, Phillip zu Eulenburg, one of the Kaiser's closest advisors, wrote to Von Bülow in 1903 that the Kaiser had a 'mixture of respect and anxiety' about the Chancellor.[33] On various occasions between 1899 and 1905, words such as 'conceit', 'volubility', 'exaggeration', 'hypersensitivity', 'tactlessness' and 'impulsiveness' were applied to the Kaiser.[34] At the same time, the Kaiser was often irritated with the Chancellor.[35] This may have caused him to keep the order secret, specifically from the Chancellor.

The Herero genocide is also clearly linked to the Kaiser's aggressive behaviour and sadistic streak. On occasion, he would turn the rings on his fingers inwards and squeeze the hand of visiting dignitaries so hard with his unusually strong right hand that it would cause tears in the eyes of the person whom he was greeting.[36] In another incident, he slapped the King of Bulgaria so 'hard on the behind in public' that the king left the country 'white-hot with hatred'.[37] The Kaiser hit Grand Duke Vladimir of Russia with a baton

---

30 See Rich, N. (1965) *Friedrich von Holstein: Politics and diplomacy in the era of Bismarck and Wilhelm II.* Cambridge: Cambridge University Press.
31 Macdonogh, G. (2000) *The Last Kaiser: The life of Wilhelm II.* New York: St Martin's Press, 247.
32 Röhl, J.C.G. (1994) *The Kaiser and his court: Wilhelm II and the government of Germany.* Cambridge: Cambridge University Press, 23.
33 Cecil, L. (1996) *Wilhelm II. Vol II: Emperor and exile, 1900–1941.* Chapel Hill: University of North Carolina Press, 71.
34 *Ibid*, 389 fn 112.
35 *Ibid*, 71.
36 Röhl, J.C.G. (1994) *The Kaiser and his court: Wilhelm II and the government of Germany.* Cambridge: Cambridge University Press, 15.
37 *Ibid.*

and on another occasion, beat up the Duke of Saxe-Coburg-Gotha.[38] He also threatened violence a number of times, including towards his own family. In 1887, he threatened to 'put a bullet through the head' of Prince Alexander of Battenberg and 'club the Battenberger to death'.[39]

The Kaiser ordered brutal and fatal action not only in the colonies but also in Europe and even in Germany. In 1900, he sent a telegraph to the Commanding General to put down a strike of tram workers in Berlin by stating: 'I expect that when the troops move in at least five hundred people should be gunned down.'[40] In fact, this General noted, in 1903, that the Kaiser ordered him on two separate occasions to fire on the citizens.[41] While in this instance he did not follow instructions, the German troops would often carry out the Kaiser's violent orders. One example was in China during the Boxer Rebellion. This rebellion is very relevant to occurrences in GSWA because it demonstrates that the latter was not the only case in which the Kaiser thought that German forces ought to conduct genocide. German soldiers, throughout the Kaiser's rule, committed many atrocities until the end of World War I, when there was an attempt to prosecute the Kaiser for war crimes, especially the treatment of Belgian civilians.[42] Kitchen believes that much of what the Kaiser said was

[38] *Ibid.*
[39] *Ibid.*
[40] *Ibid*, 31.
[41] Kohut, T.A. (1991) *Wilhelm II and the Germans: A study in leadership.* New York: Oxford University Press, 12.
[42] See Willis, J.F. (1982) *Prologue to Nuremberg: The politics and diplomacy of punishing war criminals of the First World War.* Westport, Connecticut: Greenwood Press.

The Bryce Report notes that during World War I 'unarmed civilians were killed in masses' by German troops. If they could commit such atrocities in 1914, there is no reason to doubt that they did so in 1904, ten years before. The Report also notes that there were 'many instances of calculated cruelty, often going the length of murder, towards the women and children of the condemned area... In this tale of horrors hideous forms of mutilation occur with some frequency in the depositions, two of which may be connected in some instances with a perverted form of sexual instinct. A third form of mutilation, the cutting of one or both hands, is frequently said to have taken place... We find many well-established cases of the slaughter (often accompanied by mutilation) of whole families, including not infrequently that of quite small children... These crimes were committed over a period of many weeks and simultaneously in many places and the authorities must have known or ought to have known that cruelties of this character were being perpetrated, nor can anyone doubt that they could have been stopped by swift and decisive action on the part of the heads of the German army... It is proved — (i) That there were in many parts of Belgium deliberate and systematically organised massacres of the civil population, accompanied by many isolated murders and other outrages. (ii) That in the conduct of the war generally innocent civilians, both men and women, were murdered in large numbers, women violated and children murdered... Murder, lust and pillage prevailed over many parts of Belgium on a scale unparalleled in any war between civilised nations during the last three centuries'.

'mere bluff', but he notes that the 'tone which he set had a profound effect on the army'.[43] The German forces often followed the approach he sought and this set the standard for the army.

Public opinion greatly affected the Kaiser, as he craved approval. He frequently responded to the wishes of his subjects.[44] At the same time, he frequently attempted to influence public opinion. Often the Kaiser would commit himself to a particular course of action based on very little information.[45] He repeatedly adopted the views of the last people he spoke to on a particular subject, which may also have affected his views on what to do in GSWA. Thus, he may have reacted to what he read, to what the General Staff and other members of the military told him and, crucially, to what he was told by the GSWA settlers who came to Berlin to lodge complaints before him. One of these visits, in mid-1904, coincided with the time he might have given the genocide order to Von Trotha (as discussed later). Hence, it is possible that the Kaiser, having believed the accounts of the settlers that the Herero were fighting a race war and mutilating the captured Germans, may have given the order.

The Kaiser made many intemperate and violence-seeking statements. He also held racist views and believed in extermination. A number of developments gave impetus to these racist views towards black Africans and other races deemed inferior. Count Joseph Arthur de Gobineau introduced the notion of the superiority of the 'northern races'. His published findings warned of the dangers of race mixing and called for racial purity. Germans generally received his theories well and bought many copies of his books.[46] The purported similarities between Neanderthals and races from Africa (and elsewhere) had gained wide recognition by the end of 1903, at the time of the 'rebellion' in GSWA. Eugen Fischer, president of the International Society for Racial Hygiene in Freiburg, even conducted research in GSWA. He examined the bones of various races and found similarities between Neanderthals and African races. He presented his work at a congress of anthropologists at Worms. For his work, Fischer received the highest award in anthropology,

---

See *The Bryce Report into German atrocities in Belgium — Report of the Committee on Alleged German Outrages Appointed by His Britannic Majesty's Government and Presided Over by the Right Hon. Viscount Bryce, O.M.*, 12 May 1915.

[43] Kitchen, M. (1968) *The German Officer Corps 1890–1914*. Oxford: Clarendon Press, 162.

[44] Kohut, T.A. (1991) *Wilhelm II and the Germans: A study in leadership*. New York: Oxford University Press, 135–36.

[45] *Ibid*, 10.

[46] Schafft, G.E. (2004) *From racism to genocide: Anthropology in the Third Reich*. Urbana: University of Illinois Press, 39.

the Broca-Medallion of the *Ecole d'Anthropologie de Paris*.[47] These 'findings' most certainly influenced the Kaiser's views on race, especially in GSWA, where the possibility of the Herero conducting a race war against his people likely reinforced these beliefs.

In 1899, the Kaiser stated that 'matters will not improve until the troops drag the Social Democrats out of the *Reichstag* and gun them down'.[48] In 1903, he reiterated that he would 'mow down all Social Democrats...but only after they had first plundered the Jews and the rich'.[49] These were not his first recorded anti-Semitic remarks. Over the years, he made many.[50]

Verteidigung von Hohewarte gegen Hereros.

A propaganda postcard showing an alleged German defence against the Herero

[47] *Ibid*, 44.
[48] Röhl, J.C.G. (1994) *The Kaiser and his court: Wilhelm II and the government of Germany*. Cambridge: Cambridge University Press, 14.
[49] *Ibid*.
[50] Cecil, L.(1996) *Wilhelm II. Vol II: Emperor and exile, 1900–1941*. Chapel Hill: University of North Carolina Press, 57.

Count Waldersee recorded one of the earliest in his diary entry of 17 January 1888. He noted that the Kaiser had a great dislike for Jewish people.[51] Waldersee wrote this entry years before his relationship with the Kaiser soured. Already by 1888, the Kaiser exhibited a contemptuous stance towards Jewish people. He did not simply make anti-Semitic remarks; he believed in the full extermination of the Jews. Would it not follow that, if he believed in the inferiority of the Jews and their extermination, he would also have sought the extermination of the Herero?

The Kaiser regularly wrote letters, before and after his abdication, in which he warned of a Jewish world conspiracy. He referred to Jewish people as parasites and called for their annihilation. In 1907, the Kaiser wrote that the Jews need 'stamping out'.[52] On 2 December 1919 he noted in a letter to *Generalfeldmarschall* August von Mackensen:

> The lowest, most abject outrage ever to be perpetrated by any nation in history, that is what the Germans have done unto themselves. Egged on misled by the tribe of Juda whom they hate, who were guests among them! That was the thanks they got! Let no German ever forget this, nor rest until these parasites have been wiped out from German soil and been exterminated! This poisonous mushroom on the German oak-tree![53]

Discovering this statement, Röhl wrote, 'I began to dread, the moment, which seems to be approaching with increasing certainty, when I would discover the unspeakable. And sure enough before long I discovered [it]...in 1919.'[54] Furthermore, the above statement from the Kaiser was no aberration. In 1927, the Kaiser wrote a letter, in English, to an American friend, in which he said (author's emphasis):

> The Hebrew race...are my most inveterate enemies at home and abroad; they remain what they are and always were; the forgers of lies and the masterminds governing unrest, revolution, upheaval by spreading infamy with the help of their poisoned, caustic, satyrical [sic] spirit. If the world wakes up it should mete out to them the punishment in store for them, which they deserve.[55]

---

[51] Kitchen, M. (1968) *The German Officer Corps 1890–1914*. Oxford: Clarendon Press, 80.
[52] Cecil, L. (1996) *Wilhelm II. Vol II: Emperor and exile, 1900–1941*. Chapel Hill: University of North Carolina Press, 57.
[53] Quoted in Röhl, J.C.G. (1994) *The Kaiser and his court: Wilhelm II and the government of Germany*. Cambridge: Cambridge University Press, 14.
[54] Ibid.
[55] Kaiser Wilhelm II to Poultney Bigelow, 14 April 1927. *Bigelow Papers*. New York. Quoted in Röhl, J.C.G. (1994) *The Kaiser and his court: Wilhelm II and the government of Germany*. Cambridge: Cambridge University Press, 210.

The Kaiser's hypersensitivity to criticism[56] and desire for revenge against those who crossed him would lead one to believe that if the Kaiser unequivocally advocated the extermination of the Jews, he likely wished the same fate to befall the Herero. This prickliness was partly because he took things personally. Phillip Eulenburg wrote to the Chancellor in 1903 that the Kaiser had a tendency 'to regard and to evaluate all things and all people solely from a personal point of view...objectivity is lost completely...and subjectivity rides on a biting and stamping charger'.[57] When a 1903 South Pole expedition failed, he regarded the failure as a personal insult because he believed that a successful mission would have enhanced Germany's national pride.[58] Similarly, he perceived the events in GSWA in 1904 as having dented Germany's national pride and prestige, especially when the troops failed in the first six months to quell the 'rebellion' of ill-equipped 'natives'. Thus, as the Kaiser generally responded with 'the darkest pessimism when reports from the front were grim',[59] it is likely that the continual bad news over four or five months regarding the inability of the German troops to overcome the Herero 'rebellion' caused him to respond in the same way.

Numerous occasions speak to the Kaiser's penchant for exacting revenge. Following the murder of two German missionaries in China in 1897, he demanded reprisals.[60] When a German envoy was killed in 1900, he took it as a personal insult and sent a telegram demanding that the 'troops take revenge' and destroy Peking.[61] In 1934, driven by the expectation that he would return to the throne in Germany, he declared, 'Blood must flow, much blood, [the blood] of the officers and civil servants, above all of the nobility, of everyone who has deserted me.'[62] Again, these kinds of pronouncements were not unique but part of a pattern of brutality and violence that the Kaiser supported and ordered, many of which were carried out.

As revenge was a prime motivating factor in the Herero massacre, ordering the genocide of the Herero would have been within his character.

---

56 Hull, I.V. (1982) *The entourage of Kaiser Wilhelm II, 1888–1918*. New York: Cambridge University Press, 17.
57 Kohut, T.A. (1991) *Wilhelm II and the Germans: A study in leadership*. New York: Oxford University Press, 148.
58 *Ibid*.
59 Cecil, L. (1996) *Wilhelm II. Vol II: Emperor and exile, 1900–1941*. Chapel Hill: University of North Carolina Press, 211.
60 Kohut, T.A. (1991) *Wilhelm II and the Germans: A study in leadership*. New York: Oxford University Press, 148.
61 Röhl, J.C.G. (1994) *The Kaiser and his court: Wilhelm II and the government of Germany*. Cambridge: Cambridge University Press, 13.
62 *Ibid*, 15.

[image]

A postcard of Kaiser Wilhelm II with a cannon firing in the background

The debate about the role of the Kaiser: was he the decision-maker or was he a shadow Emperor?

The role of Kaiser Wilhelm II during his years as monarch (1888–1918) has been subject to vigorous debate. On the one hand, some argue that he was merely a silhouette of a ruler who had little real power and whatever public pronouncements he made were likely ignored by those in authority in the civilian government or in the military. John Röhl argued early on that the Kaiser was 'never more than a *Schattenkaiser* — a shadow emperor without say or significance in German affairs'.[63] Yet, in his later work, Röhl notes that the monarchy rose to a central position from the 1870s on and, in many respects, supplanted the position of Chancellor as the dominant exerciser of state control.[64] In 1997, he wrote, 'In the course of the 1890s a new system of power relations was created, a genuinely monarchical regime in which the Kaiser and his court, rather than the Chancellor and "his men", exercised political power and decision-making authority and thus laid down the fundamental guidelines of domestic, foreign and armaments policy.'[65] Others also argue that he had a robust role in the *Kaiserreich*,[66] which afforded him a central position in policy-making and much of what he ordered was done. Even at the time (1900), Friedrich Naumann wrote, 'In present-day Germany there is no stronger force than the Kaiser. The very complaints of the anti-Kaiser democrats about the growth of personal absolutism are the best proof of this fact, for these complaints are not pure invention but are based on the repeated observation that all policy, foreign and internal, stems from the will and word of the Kaiser. No monarch of absolutist times ever had so much real power as the Kaiser has today. He does not achieve everything he wants, but is still more than anybody would have believed possible in the middle of the last century, whose middle years echoed with the dreams of a German republic, ended with more power in the Kaiser's hands than even Barbarossa possessed.'[67]

Rich has also noted that the Kaiser was 'the ultimate authority in the Empire...who insisted on exercising that authority; it was he who dismissed Bismarck, for better or for worse; it was he who demanded simplicity in German foreign policy and who not only countenanced but encouraged the break-up of Bismarck's alliance system; it was he who was primarily responsible for ruining Germany's relations with Britain by his ill-considered statements, by his reckless quest for colonies and by his disastrous fleet programme; it was he, far more than Bismarck, who fostered the quality of grovelling servility in the German administration and who would only tolerate sycophants or

63   Röhl, J.C.G. (1982) 'Introduction'. In Röhl, J.C.G. & Sombart, N. (eds) *Kaiser Wilhelm II: New interpretations. The Corfu Papers*. Cambridge: Cambridge University Press, 7.
64   Röhl, J.C.G. (1994) *The Kaiser and his court: Wilhelm II and the government of Germany*. Cambridge: Cambridge University Press, 4.
65   *Ibid.*
66   *Ibid*, 1.
67   Kohut, T.A. (1991) *Wilhelm II and the Germans: A study in leadership*. New York: Oxford University Press, 167.

mediocrities in his immediate entourage and in the highest positions of the German government — including the German army'.[68]

Critically, the Kaiser had very specific and wide-ranging constitutional powers, which he regularly exercised. As Caldwell has noted, the Kaiser was 'the linchpin of the system in the event of war'.[69] The 1871 German Constitution provided the Kaiser control over foreign policy and the military.[70] This effectively put him in charge, as the General Staff reported directly to him. This was an unusual course of action, as the Chancellor was the chief administrator of the colonies and the governor normally reported to him. It was also common practice for the troops to report to the Chancellor.[71] However, the Kaiser 'repeatedly transgressed the limits laid down for him by the Constitution while exploiting the legally sanctioned prerogative granted to the executive power in a constitutional monarchy'.[72] According to Clark, 'by the time he acceded the throne, Wilhelm had developed an unusually sharp interest in and appetite for power'.[73] Lamar Cecil has stated that the Kaiser was 'tyrannically insistent on having his own way'.[74] After 1890, when Bismarck was forced to resign,[75] the Kaiser dominated the government and there 'was no longer anyone strong enough to check or even guide him'.[76]

The Kaiser sometimes played a lesser role in policy formation, but this was not always the case. In certain areas, he set specific policies and directed the implementation of decisions, such as those relating to the establishment of a fleet.[77] As Jan-Bart Gewald has noted, 'initially Kaiser Wilhelm II began

---

[68] Rich, N. (1965) *Friedrich von Holstein: Politics and diplomacy in the era of Bismarck and Wilhelm II*. Cambridge: Cambridge University Press, 847. Quoted in Röhl, J.C.G. (1982) 'Introduction'. In Röhl, J.C.G. & Sombart, N. (eds) *Kaiser Wilhelm II: New interpretations. The Corfu Papers*. Cambridge: Cambridge University Press, 8.

[69] Caldwell, P. (1994, December) 'National Socialism and constitutional law: Carl Schmitt, Otto Koellreutter and the debate over the nature of the Nazi state, 1933–1937'. 16 *Cardozo Law Review*, 399, 402.

[70] Hull, I.V. (2005) *Absolute destruction: Military culture and practices of war in Imperial Germany*. Ithaca: Cornell University Press, 103.

[71] *Ibid*, 12.

[72] Wehler, H-U. (1985) *The German Empire 1871–1918*. Leamington Spa/Dover, New Hampshire: Berg Publishers, 62.

[73] Clark, C. (2000) *Kaiser Wilhelm II. Profiles in power*. Essex: Pearson Education, 18.

[74] Cecil, L. (1996) *Wilhelm II. Vol II: Emperor and exile, 1900–1941*. Chapel Hill: University of North Carolina Press, ix.

[75] See further Aydelotte, W.O. (1970) *Bismarck and British colonial policy: The problems of South West Africa* (2ed). New York: Russell & Russell.

[76] Aronson. T. (1971) *The Kaisers*. London: Corgi Books, 219.

[77] Balfour, M. (1964) *The Kaiser and his times*. Boston: Houghton Mifflin, 433.

his reign with a strong state filled with checks and balances. A state, which carried the myth of the Kaiser as the supreme determinant in German affairs, whereas in actual fact the Chancellor determined what was to happen. Piece by piece, starting with the deposition of Bismarck, Wilhelm II dismantled the carefully crafted and balanced state erected by Bismarck, until he came to be surrounded by yes men who were prepared to fulfil his whims and dreams as a divinely inspired leader. This transformation of the German state went hand in hand with and did no damage to, what was then the world's most effective bureaucracy'.[78]

Thus, despite checks and balances, the Kaiser slowly assumed greater powers and, on several occasions, his pronouncements were carried out. In part, this was possible because he surrounded himself and appointed people who shared his views and would implement his orders. According to Hull, the Kaiser 'exercised his imperial power more frequently in personnel matters than in other areas and was particularly adamant about choosing the persons with whom he had come into frequent contact'.[79] As will be shown below, it is thus likely that he sent Von Trotha to GSWA because he knew Von Trotha's reputation. It is also likely that the Kaiser met with Von Trotha and could personally have ordered him to carry out the genocide on the Herero.

The Kaiser and the military

The Kaiser held a powerful role within the military. He established his relationship with the armed forces virtually from the moment of his accession; when he took the oath of allegiance before the armed forces and made his first public statement as Kaiser he stated:

> *We belong to each other — I and the army — we were born for each other and will cleave indissolubly to each other, whether it be the will of God to send us calm or storm. You will soon swear fealty and submission to me and I promise ever to bear in mind that from the world above the eyes of my forefathers look down on me and that I shall one day have to stand accountable to them for their glory and honour of the army.*[80]

His own specific and direct interventionist control in the role of the military is evident from early on in his reign, when he established his own Naval Secretariat. Shortly thereafter, he took control away from the War Office and

---

[78] Gewald, J-B. (2003) 'The Herero genocide: German unity, settlers, soldiers and ideas'. In Bechhaus-Gerst, M. & Klein-Arendt, R. (eds) *Die (koloniale) Begegnung: AfrikanerInnen in Deutschland 1880–1945, Deutsche in Afrika 1880–1918*. Frankfurt am Main: Peter Lang, 109–127, 113.

[79] Hull, I.V. (1982) *The entourage of Kaiser Wilhelm II, 1888–1918*. New York: Cambridge University Press, 183.

[80] Balfour, M. (1964) *The Kaiser and his times*. Boston: Houghton Mifflin, 119.

set up an Imperial Naval Office and from then on all commanders reported directly to a State Secretary.[81] He created and implemented some specific policies related to the military.[82] In fact, major tensions existed between the Kaiser, the government and the *Reichstag* about who made decisions regarding the military.[83] Yet only once during the entire reign of the Kaiser did the *Reichstag* assert its right over the military.[84]

Importantly, German generals had relatively easy access to the Kaiser. He had an average of 33 men in his military entourage, although the number increased to over 100 over time.[85] Röhl notes that more than 40 officers had direct access to the Kaiser.[86] These included the chief of the General Staff, the military and naval cabinet chiefs and many other commanders.[87] Yet the number was probably much higher than 40, as Hull points out that at least an additional 62 deputy army commanders also had direct access to the Kaiser, partly as a means to limit civilian oversight.[88] He would get several verbal, military-related reports each week from various military leaders,[89] as well as daily telegrams from across the empire, including from commanders in the field. The General Staff also reported, mostly independently of the War Ministry, directly to the Kaiser.[90] The military cabinet became stronger at the expense of the War Ministry and was frequently in contact with the Kaiser.[91] Consequently, the Kaiser and the generals extensively discussed various matters, most likely including the events in GSWA. According to Wilhelm Dienst, the Kaiser shaped military policy in a number of ways,

---

[81] Ibid, 197.
[82] Howard, M.E. (1967) 'The armed forces'. In *The New Cambridge Modern History XI: Material progress and world wide problems 1870–1898*. Cambridge: Cambridge University Press, 204–42, 221.
[83] Balfour, M. (1964) *The Kaiser and his times*. Boston: Houghton Mifflin, 201.
[84] Kitchen, M. (1968) *The German Officer Corps 1890–1914*. Oxford: Clarendon Press, 31.
[85] Hull, I.V. (1982) *The entourage of Kaiser Wilhelm II, 1888–1918*. New York: Cambridge University Press, 180.
[86] Röhl, J.C.G. (1982) 'Introduction'. In Röhl, J.C.G. & Sombart, N. (eds) *Kaiser Wilhelm II: New interpretations. The Corfu Papers*. Cambridge: Cambridge University Press, 16.
[87] Hull, I.V. (2005) *Absolute destruction: Military culture and practices of war in Imperial Germany*. Ithaca: Cornell University Press, 104.
[88] Ibid, 204.
[89] Hull, I.V. (1982) *The entourage of Kaiser Wilhelm II, 1888–1918*. New York: Cambridge University Press, 31.
[90] Ibid, 176.
[91] Kitchen, M. (1968) *The German Officer Corps 1890–1914*. Oxford: Clarendon Press, 7.

including through his direct contact with the military officers in command.[92] This does not mean that the military always heeded the Kaiser — on many occasions they ignored him. On record is the fact that he kept frequent contact with Von Trotha during the Herero campaign and thereafter. Given Von Trotha's background and his previous missions, it is unlikely that he would have ignored the Kaiser, but rather that he carried out his instructions and did so secretly for the reasons discussed later.

As noted above, the Kaiser maintained a very close relationship with the various branches of the military and met separately with several of them for weekly official reports. In fact, he met military officials more often than civilian officials and was almost always in uniform.[93] The Kaiser kept a huge wardrobe of military uniforms and would change into different uniforms a number of times a day. He also regularly visited the troops and would swear in new recruits, launch ships, award medals and see off troops going to new postings or to fight.

Orders or messages sent to military foes nearly always referred to the Kaiser, indicating the military's deference to him. More often than not, he was intimately involved in the process. His direct involvement in military decision-making, to the exclusion of others in government, is evident in a statement from the Chancellor, who wrote:

> *The whole Chinese business has been organised without my being brought in. I had no advance notice of the military measures, nor of the dispatch of troops nor of Waldersee's appointment. Everything connected with foreign policy is discussed and decided by the Kaiser and Bülow between themselves...All appointments are made without my advice being taken or even asked.*[94]

The Kaiser made it clear that the army was his personal concern and he would not tolerate interference. One could argue that these were mere utterances without effect, but the remarks are stated in a way that indicates that his views were indeed implemented as practice. During discussions regarding the amendment of the process of courts martial, the Kaiser noted:

> *The army and its internal affairs are no concern of the Ministry but are reserved under the constitution to the King as his personal affair. Consequently the Ministry is in no position to assume constitutional responsibility for the army which I command.*[95]

92 Dienst, W. (1982) 'Kaiser Wilhelm II in the context of his military and naval entourage'. In Röhl, J.C.G. & Sombart, N. (eds) *Kaiser Wilhelm II: New interpretations. The Corfu Papers*. Cambridge: Cambridge University Press, 169, 183.
93 Aronson, T. (1971) *The Kaisers*. London: Corgi Books, 197.
94 Quoted in Balfour, M. (1964) *The Kaiser and his times*. Boston: Houghton Mifflin, 228.
95 Balfour, M. (1964) *The Kaiser and his times*. Boston: Houghton Mifflin, 198.

In another letter, written in 1901, he stated to his uncle, King Edward VII, who was on the British throne from 1901 to 1910: 'I am the sole arbiter and master. German Foreign Policy and the Government and Country must follow me, even if I have to face the musik[sic]!'[96] So much opposition mounted to the military in the *Reichstag* that the army attempted to remove matters related to them from this body. They regarded this as an easy accomplishment because they considered the military under the control of the Kaiser, not under the Minister of War.[97]

The Kaiser's role in the military derives from 1867 when the Emperor, as King of Prussia, obtained the position of both commander-in-chief of the army and presidential head. Later, the Emperor became Supreme Commander of 'all the Empire's land forces in peace and war'.[98] Another article in the Constitution permitted him to determine the strength of the army.[99] Despite initial reluctance, the government supported these practices.[100] Röhl points out the Kaiser's most important constitutional right was his right to appoint persons to government, bureaucracy and, crucially, the military.[101] According to Howard, 'officers stood to their sovereign in a special relationship of quasi feudal loyalty very different from the normal obedience and by the citizen to the head of the state. Interference with the internal affairs of the armed forces was thus held to sacrilegious as interference in affairs of the royal household — of which the army was virtually an extension'.[102]

The Kaiser's record of brutality

Generally, academic discourse on the role of Kaiser Wilhelm holds that he merely meddled in military affairs, but did not give clear directives to the experts. However, on many occasions, the Kaiser did in fact give specific orders and expected results. Frequently, he did not hesitate to use ruthless tactics to achieve success. The similarity of strategies used in the colonies

---

96 *Ibid*, 234.
97 Howard, M.E. (1967) 'The armed forces'. In *The New Cambridge Modern History XI: Material progress and world wide problems 1870–1898*. Cambridge: Cambridge University Press, 204–42, 221.
98 German Constitution Art 63 (1)
99 German Constitution Art 63 (4)
100 Wehler, H-U. (1985) *The German Empire 1871–1918*. Leamington Spa/Dover, New Hampshire: Berg Publishers, 147–48.
101 Röhl, J.C.G. (1982) 'Introduction'. In Röhl, J.C.G. & Sombart, N. (eds) *Kaiser Wilhelm II: New interpretations. The Corfu Papers*. Cambridge: Cambridge University Press, 15.
102 Howard, M.E. (1967) 'The armed forces'. In *The New Cambridge Modern History XI: Material progress and world wide problems 1870–1898*. Cambridge: Cambridge University Press, 204–42, 221.

indicates that brutality was not an aberration, nor the policy of a lone and wayward military leader, but a systematic government policy directed at the indigenous population in all these areas. Yet, to this day in Germany, many see the Herero war as an aberration. It has been stated: 'Does Germany, as it clearly did with the Berlin exhibition, choose to see the Namibian war as a colonial aberration or as an integral part of twentieth century German history?'[103]

The Kaiser's directives are clearly evident in a number of events. His notorious Hun speech, addressing the German soldiers on their way to China in 1900, provides an example of his gory statements. In this speech, he said (author's emphasis):

> *The tasks which the newly established German Empire has to undertake overseas are more onerous indeed than many of my countrymen have expected. The German Empire has a natural duty to protect its citizens in so far as they get into difficulties abroad... Its means of doing this is our army... Your comrades in the navy have already stood the test; they have demonstrated to you that our training is based on sound foundations... A great task awaits you. You have to remedy the serious wrong which has been done. There has been no precedent in world history for the presumptuous action of the Chinese in disregarding international rights of a thousand years standing and showing their contempt in such a shocking way for the sanctity of the envoy and the rights of the guest. It is all the more disgraceful that the offence should have been committed by a nation which prides itself upon its ancient culture. This shows you, however, what comes of cultures which are not founded on Christianity. All heathen cultures, no matter how attractive and excellent they may be, collapse at the first catastrophe. Live up to Prussia's traditional steadfastness! Show yourselves Christians, happily enduring in the face of heathens! May honour and fame attend your colours and arms! Give the world an example of virility and discipline! You are well aware that you have to face a brave and well-armed and savage foe. [When you make contact with him, you know that] no pardon will be given and prisoners will not be made. Anyone who falls into your hands falls to your sword! Just as the Huns under their King Etzel created for themselves a thousand years ago a name which men still respect, you should give the name of Germans such cause to be remembered in China for a thousand years that no Chinaman, no matter whether his eyes be slit or not, will dare to look a German in the face. Carry yourselves like men and may the blessing of God go with you; each one of you bears with him the prayers of an entire people and my good wishes. Open the road for culture once and for all.*[104]

---

[103] Gewald, J-B. and Silvester, J. (2003) *Words cannot be found. German colonial rule in Namibia: An annotated reprint of the 1918 Blue Book.* Leiden: Brill xxxvi–xxxvii.

[104] Quoted in Balfour, M. (1964) *The Kaiser and his times.* Boston: Houghton Mifflin, 226–27.

His political advisors were outraged and concerned by this statement as they knew that such careless comments could do great damage to the German prestige abroad. Hence, they attempted to limit the damage his speech could cause by editing it and removed most of the problematic parts. However, when the full text emerged it caused a predictable public outcry.

Thus, the Kaiser's need for revenge against the murder of Germans is not only apparent in GSWA, when he reacted to the death of about 150 Germans at the hands of the Herero in 1904. He took all rebellions and killings of Germans personally, as the case of China demonstrates.

Although the Kaiser was 'surrounded by yes men who were prepared to fulfil his whims and dreams as a divinely inspired leader',[105] his advisors attempts to tone down his words show that, even then, they knew that most other countries accepted norms outlawing such immoral conduct. The Kaiser, on the other hand, did not regard this type of warfare as problematic. He saw nothing wrong with what he said and dismissed all the commotion about it. Upon seeing the censored version of his speech in the press, he complained that the best parts of his address had been omitted.[106] Thus, if at that time he did not believe his words were inappropriate or his requests illegal, it is unlikely he would have had qualms giving a comparable order a few years later.

On 2 July 1900, about a month before the infamous Hun speech, the Kaiser made a similar speech to another group of departing soldiers. On that occasion he demonstrated more control, but still clearly formulated a desire for retribution — to punish the rebels with ferocity. In this speech he stated (the emphasised section was deleted from the official version):

> *Into the midst of the deepest peace — alas, not surprising to me — the torch of war has been hurled. A crime unprecedented in its brazenness, horrifying in its cruelty, has struck my trusted representative and carried him off. The ambassadors of the other powers are in danger of their lives and along with them your comrades who were dispatched for their protection. Perhaps, they have today fought their last battle. The German flag has been insulted and the German Empire held up to scorn. This demands an exemplary punishment and revenge.* I hope...to take revenge such as the world has never before witnessed.[107]

---

[105] Gewald, J-B. (2003) 'The Herero genocide: German unity, settlers, soldiers and ideas'. In Bechhaus-Gerst, M. & Klein-Arendt, R. (eds) *Die (koloniale) Begegnung: AfrikanerInnen in Deutschland 1880–1945, Deutsche in Afrika 1880–1918*. Frankfurt am Main: Peter Lang, 109–127, 113.

[106] O'Connor, R. (1973) *The Boxer Rebellion*. London: Robert Hale, 182.

[107] Johann, E. (ed) (1966) *Reden des Kaisers: Ansprachen, Predigten und Trinksprüche Wilhelms II*. Munich, 86–88. Translated by R.S. Levy. Available at: http://www.assumption.edu/users/McClymer/hi119net/KaiserWilhelmIIBoxers.html

Captured Herero with German troops

He demonstrated clear intentions to take revenge on and punish those behind the conduct. Similarly, he would 'discipline' the Herero for rising up and killing Germans in January 1904. The treatment the Herero received in the concentration camps also evidences this desire to punish them, at the request of Von Trotha.[108] The Germans discriminated against Herero prisoners in the provision of limited food rations, blankets and clothing and denying altogether milk, a staple for the Herero.[109] It was only after Von Trotha left that the rations were marginally increased.[110]

The Kaiser's other acts of indiscretion include the decision to occupy Kiaochow in 1897.[111] His instruction to the German navy was to achieve their

---

[108] Hull, I.V. (2003) 'Military culture and the production of final solutions in the colonies: The example of Wilhelminian Germany'. In Gellately, R. & Kiernan, B. (eds) *The specter of genocide mass murder in historical perspective.* Cambridge: Cambridge University Press, 158.
[109] *Ibid.*
[110] *Ibid*, 159.
[111] Blue, G. (1999) 'Gobineau on China; Race theory, the "Yellow Peril" and the critique of modernity'. 10(1) *Journal of World History*, 93–139, 123.

goals 'if necessary, with the most brutal ruthlessness' and that they ought not spare the 'mailed fist'.[112] Whittle notes that by 1900 'four bulky volumes of Imperial speeches had already been printed, many of them harmful to the Kaiser and Germany'.[113] In one such speech, the Kaiser stated, 'You have sworn loyalty to me. You have only one enemy and that is my enemy. In the present social confusion it may come about that I order you to shoot down your relations, brothers or parents, but even then you must follow my orders without a murmur.'[114]

The Kaiser did far more than simply give volatile speeches. He was responsible for many senior appointments, including personally appointing Count Waldersee without consulting the Chancellor. Additionally, it seems as if the Kaiser and Von Bülow were in control of the German forces during the Boxer Rebellion. The Chancellor at the time, Hohenlohe, was so upset about this that he resigned from office, at which time Von Bülow replaced him.[115] At that stage, the Kaiser's relationship with Von Bülow was positive, but it later soured significantly. In his memoirs, the Kaiser admitted that he gave up his personal relationship with the Chancellor in 1908.[116] (He does not reveal the extent to which it was strained on other occasions.) Accordingly, this may have led the Kaiser to ask Von Trotha to keep the details of his involvement in GSWA secret. He would not have wanted the Chancellor to know, as the constitutionality of whose domain — the Kaiser's or the Chancellor's — events in GSWA were under, was questionable. The Kaiser might have thought that the Chancellor would have objected upon realising the extent of his involvement. In fact, the Chancellor did object to the tactics employed and pressed the Kaiser to rescind the extermination order, which he eventually did, some months later.

During World War I, some ten years after the genocide in GSWA, the Kaiser continued to order that German forces take no prisoners.[117] An example of his willingness to direct brutality indiscriminately, including against women and

---

[112] Ibid, 93–139, 124.
[113] Whittle, T. (1977) *The last Kaiser: A biography of William II, German Emperor and King of Prussia*. London: Heinemann, 189.
[114] Ibid, 145.
[115] Blue, G. (1999) 'Gobineau on China; Race theory, the "Yellow Peril" and the critique of modernity'. 10(1) *Journal of World History*, 93–139, fn 107 & fn 110.
[116] Wilhelm II (1922) *The Kaiser's memoirs* (English translation T.R.Y. Barra). New York: Harper & Brothers, 120.
[117] Röhl, J.C.G. (1982) 'Introduction'. In Röhl, J.C.G. & Sombart, N. (eds) *Kaiser Wilhelm II: New interpretations. The Corfu Papers*. Cambridge: Cambridge University Press, 31. See also Horne, J. & Kramer, A. (2001) *German atrocities 1914: A history of denial*. New Haven: Yale University Press.

children, is evident early on in the war when he wrote to Austrian Kaiser Franz Joseph that

> *everything must be put to fire and sword: men, women and children and old men must be slaughtered and not a tree or house left standing... [these] methods of terrorism [will terminate the war in two months, while] considerations of humanity [will unnecessarily prolong the struggle].*[118]

If he had no qualms ordering such actions against white Europeans, he certainly is likely to have taken the same steps ten years earlier against black Africans. Furthermore, the Kaiser replicated the starving of the Herero in September 1914, when he wanted to starve 90 000 Russian prisoners of war to death.[119] On that occasion, ten years after Von Trotha drove the Herero into the waterless, foodless desert, the Kaiser was again willing to let Russian prisoners of war die in similar fashion by driving them onto a barren piece of land.[120] During World War II, the Kaiser congratulated Hitler when he defeated France in 1940, a clear indication of where his support lay.[121]

While some have posited that the Kaiser's outbursts were ignored and that he did not control the German forces, the troops did indeed frequently heed his call. The following extract from a German soldier's report from China belies the argument that the Kaiser's orders were ignored:

> *I tell you only this, you can not imagine what happens over here. You should have seen how we entered the city after victorious struggle. Everyone we met was cut down, men, women, children. Oh, how the women screamed. But the Kaiser's order was pardon will not be given. We have sworn faithfulness and obedience and we have to keep our oath.*[122]

These demonstrations of allegiance to the Kaiser were commonplace. Even the Supreme Commander for the Allied forces, Count Waldersee, was anxious

---

[118] Adams, W. (1923) 'The American Peace Commission and the punishment of crimes committed during war'. 39 *Law Quarterly Review*, 245, 248, quoting the Kaiser's letter to Austrian Kaiser Franz Joseph. Cited in Lippman, M. (2002, Fall) 'Aerial attacks on civilians and the humanitarian law of war: Technology and terror from World War I to Afghanistan'. *California Western International Law Journal*, 1, 2.

[119] Röhl, J.C.G. (1982) 'Introduction'. In Röhl, J.C.G. & Sombart, N. (eds) *Kaiser Wilhelm II: New interpretations. The Corfu Papers.* Cambridge: Cambridge University Press, 31. See also Horne, J. & Kramer, A. (2001) *German atrocities 1914: A history of denial.* New Haven: Yale University Press.

[120] Masson, J. (2001) *Jakob Marengo: An early resistance hero of Namibia.* Windhoek: Out of Africa, 1.

[121] *Ibid.*

[122] Schöng, H. (1959) *Der Imperialismus und Chinas Politik.* Berlin (DDR) S. 144. Available at: http://www.zum.de/psm/imperialismus/rums24/rums24_62e.php3

to satisfy the German Kaiser and thus carried out a series of 'ruthless punitive expeditions' against those sympathetic to the rebellion in China in the area around Beijing.[123] In fact, Waldersee and the German troops implemented the orders of the Kaiser studiously and killed large numbers of Chinese, an occurrence that the troops from other countries despised.[124] Despite this evidence, some have argued that the Kaiser's statements should be read not as explicit military orders, but rather as expressions of the militaristic and nationalist exuberance that he represented. Yet, some of the atrocities attributed to the Kaiser were so extreme that many called for his prosecution after World War I, as the Peace Treaty contained provisions to this effect.[125] Legally, there appeared to be no problem in prosecuting and convicting him for many crimes; crimes recognised internationally today. Professor Quincy Wright, of Harvard University, wrote an article, in 1919, on the legal liability of the Kaiser under both international and domestic law. He concluded by recommending prosecution before an international tribunal under international law.[126] However, the Netherlands, where the Kaiser was in exile, refused to be party to such events and no trial occurred. The Australian Prime Minister, William Morris (Billy) Hughes, also commented on the prospect of prosecuting Kaiser Wilhelm II, saying it 'would be a very serious thing if this man was brought up for trial and not convicted'.[127] Bass also notes that any investigation into Germany's aggression would undoubtedly raise questions about Russia's complicity. He notes that an 'aggression charge' would invite 'infinite disputation', an unwelcome 'meticulous examination of the history of European politics for the past 20 years that would sprawl to questions like Russia's strategic railways'.[128] So questions relating to the crime of aggression were under consideration. The international community recognised at the time what was illegal, even if not all states practised what they preached. This failing continues even today. States claim not to tolerate such practices as torture, but in reality they often do.

---

[123] Sharf, F.A. & Harrington, P. (2000) *China 1900: The eyewitnesses speak. The experience of Westerners in China during the Boxer Rebellion, as described by participants in letters, diaries and photographs*. Mechanicsburg, Pennsylvania: Stackpole, 211.

[124] Blue, G. (1999) 'Gobineau on China; Race theory, the "Yellow Peril" and the critique of modernity'. 10(1) *Journal of World History*, 93–139, 124–25.

[125] See Horne, J. & Kramer, A. (2001) *German atrocities 1914: A history of denial*. New Haven: Yale University Press.

[126] Wright, Q. (1919, February) 'The legal liability of the Kaiser'. 13(1) *American Political Science Review*, 120–28, 128.

[127] Bass, G.J. (2000) *Stay the hand of vengeance*. Princeton: Princeton University Press, 68.

[128] *Ibid*, 71–2.

In 1918, Admiral Hohman noted the following:

What sins Germany has committed in the last three decades it must now pay for. It was politically paralysed through its blind faith in, [and] its slavish devotion to the will of a puffed-up, vainglorious and self over-estimating fool.[129]

Thus, according to this admiral, Germany had committed various crimes over 30 years, most of them linked to Wilhelm II. He is an example of those who do not subscribe to the position that the Kaiser never gave direct orders or that, when he did, they were ignored. It is interesting that even in 1918 a senior military leader from Germany deemed accountability for these crimes possible.

In summary, the Kaiser's specific role in the massacres that took place during his reign is not entirely clear. Yet he operated within a climate of colonial oppression and, as the person who took the lead in many of the colonies, it is not beyond the realm of possibility that he played a significant part. As shown, there are clear precedents demonstrating that the Kaiser did give orders similar to the one in GSWA and that these orders were frequently implemented. Hence is not impossible, but rather likely, that he would have given such orders again.

The role of the Kaiser in the colonies

The Kaiser's role in the colonies, and especially GSWA, was not as limited as many have suggested. He took a key interest in the colonies and played a pre-eminent role. Upon ascending the throne, he prioritised strategies for increasing the international prestige of his country and saw the possession of colonies as one way to achieve a higher status. He also recognised that Germany's limited overseas holdings affected *Weltpolitik* (world policy) and Germany's 'place in the sun'.[130] He expressed his belief in the importance of developing German colonies as such:

I have nearly seventy millions of people...and we shall have to find room for them somewhere. When we became an empire, England had her hands on nearly everything. Now we must fight to get ours. That is why I am developing our world markets...[131]

---

[129] Röhl, J.C.G. (1994) *The Kaiser and his court: Wilhelm II and the government of Germany.* Cambridge: Cambridge University Press, 27.

[130] Schrank, G.I. (1974) *German South West Africa: Social and economic aspects of its history, 1884–1915.* PhD (History). New York University, 73.

[131] Davis, A.N. (1918) *The Kaiser as I know him.* New York: Harper & Brothers, 133.

The Kaiser, in fact, had more power to direct policy and military activity in the colonies than he did at home. According to Hull, he had the constitutional right to replace civilian control with that of the military in the provinces (colonies).[132] He also developed a particular interest in the military activities in the colonies, a pattern that emerged early on in his reign.

When the Kaiser replaced Chancellor Bismarck with Graf von Caprivi in 1890,[133] the first task he gave the new Chancellor was to establish a new department (*Kolonial-Abterleng*) to manage colonial affairs. This department would be answerable to the Chancellor, except on matters regarding foreign relations. That same year, the Colonial Council (*Kolonialrat*) was established and the Kaiser nominated all its members.[134] The Colonial Office received guidance from the Colonial Council. The Kaiser even played a significant role in governing GSWA. There was in an Advisory Council of 40 people — 20 elected and 20 nominated by the governor — and, crucially, the Kaiser appointed the governor.[135] During the 30 years of German rule, East Africa and Togo had eight governors, Cameroon seven and GSWA six.[136]

The Kaiser also involved himself in putting down rebellions in the colonies. In Cameroon, in 1895, the Kaiser sent troops to deal with an insurrection.[137] When there was no result in dealing with the rebellion in East Africa, the Kaiser sent two cruisers and 150 marines.[138] The manner in which the rebellious police officers, employed by the Germans, were dealt with — summary execution — formed part of a general pattern of dealing with resistance in most German colonies.

---

[132] Hull, I.V. (2003) 'Military culture and the production of final solutions in the colonies: The example of Wilhelminian Germany'. In Gellately, R. & Kiernan, B. (eds) *The specter of genocide mass murder in historical perspective*. Cambridge: Cambridge University Press, 145.

[133] Georg Leo Graf von Caprivi de Caprara de Montecuccoli. Esterhuyse, J.H. (1968) *South West Africa: The establishment of German authority in South West Africa*. Cape Town: C. Struik, 167.

[134] Epstein, K. (1959, October) 'Erzberger and the German colonial scandals, 1905–1910'. 74(293) *English Historical Review*, 637–63, 639.

[135] Eveleigh, W. (1915) *South-West Africa*. Cape Town: Maskew Miller, 146.

[136] Gann, L.H. and Duigan, P. (1977) *The rulers of German Africa 1884–1914*. Stanford: Stanford University Press, 68.

[137] Stoecker, H. (ed) (1986) *German imperialism in Africa: From the beginnings until the Second World War*. London: C Hurst & Co, 65.

[138] Hull, I.V. (2003) 'Military culture and the production of final solutions in the colonies: The example of Wilhelminian Germany'. In Gellately, R. & Kiernan, B. (eds) *The specter of genocide mass murder in historical perspective*. Cambridge: Cambridge University Press, 138.

The Kaiser and German South West Africa

Even before the events of 1904, the Kaiser was directly involved in determining governance in GSWA. In January 1889, he sent 21 soldiers, disguised as explorers, under Captain Kurt von Francois to GSWA to ensure a military presence.[139] In 1890, he addressed a contingent of soldiers leaving Germany to go to GSWA.[140] In 1893, he ordered the manufacture of a copy of a cross that the Portuguese navigator, Diogo Cão, had placed north of Swakopmund in 1484 and sent it to GSWA.[141] In 1894, Governor Leutwein, in a letter to Henrik Witbooi, stated:

> *My own presence here proves it: Major von François was recalled to Germany and in his place His Majesty the German Kaiser has sent me with specific orders to carry on the war to your destruction, unless you surrender. I do not know you and I have no personal enmity against you at all, but shall of course carry out my orders and fight you to the death.*[142]

Leutwein made it clear that he had direct orders from the Kaiser. This could, of course, be an isolated example. Or it could be merely a way of enhancing the official nature of the directive by invoking the name of Kaiser. Yet, as shown, the Kaiser gave a similar order to quell the Boxer Rebellion in China. Witbooi, too, accepted that the order came from the Kaiser. In a later letter to Leutwein, Witbooi stated, 'Now Your Honour is the second to arrive from the Kaiser with orders against me, also with peace and treaty offers.'[143] According to Lundtofte, 'considerable prestige was invested in the outcome of the conflict due to the unprecedented extent of the intervention of the General Staff and the Kaiser'.[144] This certainly speaks to the direct involvement of the Kaiser

---

[139] Schrank, G.I. (1974) *German South West Africa: Social and economic aspects of its history, 1884–1915*. PhD (History). New York University, 73.

[140] Diary of soldier Henker — in Gewald, J-B. (2003) 'The Herero genocide: German unity, settlers, soldiers and ideas'. In Bechhaus-Gerst, M. & Klein-Arendt, R. (eds) *Die (koloniale) Begegnung: AfrikanerInnen in Deutschland 1880–1945, Deutsche in Afrika 1880–1918*. Frankfurt am Main: Peter Lang, 109–27, 122.

[141] Vogt, A. (1995) *National monuments in Namibia*. MA thesis. University of Stellenbosch, xxiv.

[142] Leutwein to Witbooi, Keetmanshoop, 9 April 1894. Reproduced in Heywood, A. & Maasdorp, E. (transl) (1989) *The Hendrik Witbooi papers*. Windhoek: National Archives of Namibia, 148.

[143] Witbooi to Leutwein, Naukluft, 6 May 1894. Reproduced in Heywood, A. & Maasdorp, E. (transl) (1989) *The Hendrik Witbooi papers*. Windhoek: National Archives of Namibia, 153.

[144] Lundtofte, H. (2003) 'Radicalization of the German suppression of the Herero rising in 1904'. In Jensen, S.L.B. (ed) *Genocide: Cases, comparisons and contemporary debates*. Copenhagen: Danish Center for Holocaust and Genocide Studies, 15, 44.

and, hence, the Kaiser likely was involved in the extermination order. In addition, the Kaiser's signature on a peace treaty created by Leutwein and the Nama is further evidence of his involvement in GSWA, even though he postponed signing it for about a year. Already, the settler community thought the terms of the peace agreement too lenient and objected vociferously to its provisions.[145] As noted earlier, the settler community played a significant role in the war and the extermination.

As mentioned above, the Kaiser took a keen interest in rebellions in all German territories, but especially in GSWA. Prior to the Herero rebellion, when the Bondelswartz rose up in 1903, the Kaiser's reaction was 'loud and violent'.[146] Furthermore, the Kaiser, as a result of settler complaints, perceived Governor Leutwein's attitude towards the locals, although not always as benevolent as sometimes portrayed, as too lenient. The settler community pressured Leutwein to take extreme measures; they published articles and wrote to the Government in Berlin demanding stern steps, including the total extermination of some groups.

Some have argued that the Kaiser was not the sole mastermind of the military campaigns in GSWA, but that several German departments were involved in planning the colonial war.[147] Yet he ordered Count Georg von Stillfried und Rattonitz to draw up a secret report on GSWA and the Herero question. Drechsler notes that 'it provides evidence that the Kaiser, circumventing all his ministries, was obtaining direct information about the situation in South West Africa from someone else of noble rank'.[148] The secrecy of the report speaks volumes about the handling of the issue and the likelihood that any subsequent orders might also have remained secret. According to Erichsen, the Kaiser took this report 'to heart, in as much as the report was a virtual blue print of events that took place during and following the Herero war'.[149] Despite the secrecy of the report, Von Trotha, when he arrived in GSWA, implemented the specific suggestions made in the report, including summary executions, deportations, slave labour, the wearing of identification tags and the creation of concentration camps. The only logical conclusion is that the Kaiser must have passed the recommendations of the report on to him. Thus,

---

[145] Swan, J. (1991) 'The Final Solution in South West Africa'. 3(4) *Military History Quarterly*, 36–55, 38.

[146] Cocker, M. (1998) *Rivers of blood, rivers of gold: Europe's conflict with tribal peoples*. London: Jonathan Cape, 271.

[147] Dr Tilman Dedering, e-mail exchange. January 2005.

[148] Drechsler, H. (1986) *Let us die fighting*. Berlin: Akademie-Verlag, 145.

[149] Erichsen, C.W. (2004) *The Angel of Death has descended violently among them: A study of Namibia's concentration camps and prisoners-of-war, 1904–08*. MA thesis (History). University of Namibia, 271.

the position of Drechsler and others who attribute the extermination order solely to Von Trotha is questionable. Drechsler does recognise the complicity of the German government to some extent by noting that they were fully aware of what Von Trotha was doing during this campaign against the Herero.[150]

The German Colonial Society and other similar groups, such as the Colonial Federation and the National Colonial Association, played a critical role in the response of the German government and, particularly, the view the Kaiser took of the developments in GSWA from January 1904. While the Colonial Federation and the National Colonial Association were deemed extremist organisations and the Colonial Society more moderate, the latter nevertheless adopted a harsh response to the developments in GSWA. At its General Assembly meeting on 27 May 1904 the Society recommended that German forces put down the uprising with severity, confiscate the land of the indigenous population and give compensation to the settlers for their loss by way of government funds and confiscated land. The numerical strength of the Society — 31 390 members in mid-1904 — must have added clout to its voice. The majority of its members were military officers, government officials and businessmen,[151] which would have given them greater access to the Kaiser and senior officials in the military. It is not likely a coincidence that a delegation of GSWA settlers arrived in Germany and met with the Kaiser at the same time that General von Trotha arrived in GSWA and received his orders. The German Colonial Society financed the settlers' trip and facilitated their meeting with the Kaiser.[152]

The Kaiser was committed to the settlement of GSWA by German settlers and went out of his way to promote this venture. Erichsen notes: 'Indeed on the exact day of the attack on the Waterberg, Kaiser Wilhelm II launched a new programme that sought to attract settlers to the colony by providing funds for land and livestock.'[153] Erichsen also lists this development in the introduction to his thesis, in which he gives a chronology of events. While he cites GSWA Deputy Governor Oskar Hintrager's 1955 book as the reference for this

---

150 Drechsler, H. (1980) *Let us die fighting: The struggle of the Herero and Nama against the German imperialism (1894–1915)* (Bernd Zöllner transl). London: Zed Press, 156–68.
151 Swan, J. (1991) 'The Final Solution in South West Africa'. 3(4) *Military History Quarterly*, 36–55, 40.
152 Pierard R.V. (1964) *The German colonial society 1882–1914*. PhD thesis (Modern History). State University of Iowa, 288–93.
153 Erichsen, C.W. (2004) *The Angel of Death has descended violently among them: A study of Namibia's concentration camps and prisoners-of-war, 1904–08*. MA thesis (History). University of Namibia, 300.

event, there is no mention of it in Hintrager's book.[154] Nonetheless, the Kaiser frequently met with settler groups and received regular reports from them, as well as newspaper reports, about the situation in GSWA, even before January 1904. Prior to the war, he supported the views of the settlers by expressing extremist opinions regarding potential action in GSWA. In a note on the margin of a report he received from Chancellor von Bülow in November 1903, he stated that the General Staff of the army ought to have complete freedom to conduct military operations and should be unrestrained by political concerns contemplated by the Foreign Office or the Chancellor.[155] The Kaiser noted:

> *We must strengthen and increase in number our entire battalion, otherwise we run the danger of losing our entire colonial position...Civilisti taceunt in militaribus!*[156]

Column of *Schutztruppe* going to battle on horseback

[154] Hintrager, O. (1955) *Suedwestafrika in der deutschen Zeit.* Munchen: Kommissionsverlag, 232.
[155] Schrank, G.I. (1974) *German South West Africa: Social and economic aspects of its history, 1884–1915.* PhD (History). New York University, 144.
[156] Ibid.

After the start of the war, he received information about the colony, including the uncompromising views of the settlers, with increased regularity. According to Helmut Bley and others, 'it may be argued quite categorically that neither the German authorities in South West Africa nor the settlers had intended to wage such a total war'.[157] Yet, although some people may not have supported a 'total war', it is clear that, even before the war, some settlers and officials in Berlin desired a military solution. This desire only intensified as the war began, developing into a comprehensive propaganda campaign by the settlers and the German authorities, who claimed that the Herero were fighting a race war and were mutilating the corpses of dead Germans. While Hull notes that the settlers' inflammatory rhetoric at the start of the revolt certainly contributed to an atmosphere conducive to the annihilation,[158] the settler community demanded severe and brutal action long before the 'revolt' began. The settlers may have changed their position when they realised the negative consequences of Herero extermination for them, but they continued to support other actions taken by the authorities to repress and fragment the Herero as a nation. As noted earlier, it is more than probable that these views influenced the Kaiser and that he therefore may have been disposed to order the genocide.

Immediately after the uprising occurred in January 1904, the Kaiser, in the absence of Governor Leutwein, who was putting down another rebellion elsewhere, used his authority to order reinforcements to the colony. He followed events with 'passionate interest and growing impatience [and] could not restrain his glee at the reports of victory'.[159] He went so far as to send a message of congratulations to the Section Head, Major Estorff, in February 1904.[160] He proclaimed 'war', an 'emergency' that needed 'large-scale reinforcements'.[161] According to Cocker, the Kaiser was intimately involved and complained about the lack of information on 'developments,

---

[157] Bley, H. (1967) 'German South West Africa after the conquest 1904–1914'. In Segal, R. & First, R. (eds) *South West Africa: Travesty of trust*. London: Andre Deutsch, 35–53, 37.

[158] Hull, I.V. (2003) 'Military culture and the production of final solutions in the colonies: The example of Wilhelminian Germany'. In Gellately, R. & Kiernan, B. (eds) *The specter of genocide mass murder in historical perspective*. Cambridge: Cambridge University Press, 145.

[159] Bridgman, J. (1981) *The revolt of the Hereros*. Los Angeles: University of California Press, 96.

[160] *Ibid*, 96–7.

[161] Cocker, M. (1998) *Rivers of blood, rivers of gold: Europe's conflict with tribal peoples*. London: Jonathan Cape, 271.

dispositions, terrain etc. and about the interference in what he believed was purely a military matter'.[162]

Soon after the war broke out, Berlin, rather than Windhoek, directed operations.[163] The Kaiser took charge and directed the War Office, the Naval Office and the General Staff in the conduct of the war.[164] He ordered that the ship *Habicht* land at Swakopmund and its commander take charge until the governor returned.[165] This was no disinterested, powerless Kaiser with little authority or power.

Governor Leutwein's position was in further jeopardy when he signed a treaty, the Peace of Kalkfontein, with the Bondelswartz on 27 January 1904. It is not clear whether he acted on his own or was pressurised by Berlin, but he was consequently subjected to a volley of abuse from the white settlers, who were in a veritable 'pogrom mood'.[166] Because of the regular (sometimes daily) communications by telegram between GSWA and Berlin, the Kaiser knew of these objections. According to Bley, the information provided by the settlers and their complaints about Leutwein influenced the Kaiser to order Leutwein not to negotiate any peace agreement with the Herero.[167]

On 8 February 1904, three days before Leutwein returned to Windhoek, the Kaiser ordered that henceforth the General Staff and General Alfred von Schlieffen would control the troops and the conduct of the war.[168] The Colonial Department attempted, unsuccessfully, to have the War Ministry control the war.[169] Placing the conduct of the war under the General Staff ensured that the Kaiser controlled the methodology, the policies employed and the decisions about which units to deploy.[170] The state of emergency, which

---

[162] *Ibid.*
[163] Ngavirue, Z. (1972) *Political parties and interest groups in South West Africa: A study of a plural society.* PhD thesis. Oxford University, 144.
[164] *Ibid.*
[165] Hull, I.V. (2005) *Absolute destruction: Military culture and practices of war in Imperial Germany.* Ithaca: Cornell University Press, 8.
[166] Schrank, G.I. (1974) *German South West Africa: Social and economic aspects of its history, 1884–1915.* PhD (History). New York University, 145 citing to Drechsler, H. (1986) *Let us die fighting.* Berlin: Akademie-Verlag, 137.
[167] Bley, H. (1967) 'German South West Africa after the conquest 1904–1914'. In Segal, R. & First, R. *South West Africa: Travesty of trust.* London: Andre Deutsch, 35–53, 40.
[168] Hull, I.V. (2005) *Absolute destruction: Military culture and practices of war in Imperial Germany.* Ithaca: Cornell University Press, 12.
[169] Bley, H. (1971) *South West Africa under German rule 1894–1914.* London: Heinemann, 155.
[170] Hull, I.V. (2005) *Absolute destruction: Military culture and practices of war in Imperial Germany.* Ithaca: Cornell University Press, 12.

Von Trotha instituted even before he got to GSWA,[171] may also have been a directive from the Kaiser. Without a state of emergency, the colony would have remained under the control of the Chancellor and the oversight of the *Reichstag*. However, in a state of emergency, GSWA fell under the military (the General Staff) and, thus, the Kaiser. While Leutwein was still the governor, the Kaiser convinced the Colonial Department to forbid Leutwein from entering into negotiations,[172] which would suggest that he had already made the decision to get rid of the Herero. He also rejected a request for senior civil servants to conduct an investigation to determine the cause of the Herero war.[173] On 1 December 1905, Governor Lindequist proclaimed that he had cancelled concessions given to the Witbooi on orders he received from the Kaiser.[174] Hence, the Kaiser played an integral role in all of the events surrounding the Herero War.

The Kaiser's specific position on taking Herero land is evidenced by his signing of the confiscation order in 1905, which stated that Germany would confiscate all Herero land and cattle.[175] He extended this confiscation order to the Nama in 1907.[176] Those ordinances even extended to land in Herero reserves and to all Herero, even those groups who had not gone to war. In the case of non-combatants, German forces could not use the war as an excuse for confiscating their land, which demonstrates that war was a mere pretext to gain more land. Thus, the Herero were not paranoid to assume they were at risk of losing their land, as many argued.

GSWA was so important to Germany that, when the opposition in the *Reichstag* managed to block the budgeting of resources for the construction of another railway line in the territory in 1906, Germany called for elections. These elections became known as the 'Hottentot's election'. This was not the first time the *Reichstag* blocked the allocation of resources. Before April 1897, when Admiral Alfred von Tirpitz became Naval Secretary, the *Reichstag* more than once refused to support the Kaiser's plan for naval expansion.[177] Crucially, the *Reichstag* continued to approve significant finances for the

---

[171] *Ibid*, 63.
[172] *Ibid*, 12.
[173] Bley, H. (1971) *South West Africa under German rule 1894–1914*. London: Heinemann, 158.
[174] Drechsler, H. (1980) *Let us die fighting: The struggle of the Herero and Nama against the German imperialism (1894–1915)* (Bernd Zöllner transl). London: Zed Press, 191.
[175] Ritter-Petersen, H.G. (1991) *The Herrenvolk mentality in German South West Africa 1884–1914*. DLitt (History). Pretoria: University of South Africa, 241.
[176] *Ibid*.
[177] Balfour, M. (1964) *The Kaiser and his times*. Boston: Houghton Mifflin, 205.

territory during the war and long after, in the hope of securing greater German settlement. In 1910, expenses reached 32 million marks, while income was only 13 million marks.[178] Thus, the *Reichstag* played a determining role in decision-making for GSWA. Therefore, the genocide and the subsequent events cannot be simply the result of a military culture. While the *Reichstag* did not always determine policy, it continually granted increased resources, especially during the war.

Even before the 1907 elections, which addressed the policies in the colonies, the *Reichstag* debates preceding those elections (28 November to 4 December 1906) centred on the budget for GSWA, part of which would go to the military campaign (75%) and the rest on the railways (25%). The opposition parties attacked the military policy and questioned the associated expenditure. The Government and other political parties saw this attack as an interference with the powers of the Kaiser and argued that it was not the role of the *Reichstag* to determine the course of the war or the manner in which it was fought.[179] Thus, the majority in the *Reichstag* supported the budgetary allocations and German actions in the colony and therefore did not attempt to change the provisions that allowed the Kaiser and the military power and latitude in conducting their campaign. In the end, the Herero war was the most expensive war undertaken by Germany before World War I. The *Reichstag* sanctioned the cost, as well as the reparations paid to the German settlers who suffered losses during the war.

Did the Kaiser appoint General von Trotha?

Many have argued that the Head of the War Cabinet, Graf Hülsen-Haeseler, with the support of the Kaiser, insisted on appointing Von Trotha to quell the Herero uprising. This view relies on a report at the time in a German newspaper, *Der Reichsbote*.[180] Yet, it seems that the Kaiser played a more direct role than simply supporting the nomination. According to Bley, the Kaiser decided on Von Trotha.[181] Likewise, Silvester and Gewald maintain

---

[178] Prein, P. (1994) 'Guns and top hats: African resistance in German South West Africa 1907–1915'. 20(1) *Journal of African Studies*, 99–121, 102, fn 18.

[179] Crothers, G.D. (1968) *The German elections of 1907*. New York: Columbia University Press, 75.

[180] Erichsen, C.W. (2004) *The Angel of Death has descended violently among them: A study of Namibia's concentration camps and prisoners-of-war, 1904–08*. MA thesis (History). Windhoek: University of Namibia, 37, relying on Poole, G. (1990) *Samuel Maherero*. Windhoek: Gamsberg MacMillan, 245.

[181] Bley, H. (1971) *South West Africa under German rule 1894–1914*. London: Heinemann, 159.

that the Kaiser personally selected Von Trotha for the GSWA assignment.[182] Berat concurs, noting that the Kaiser independently and specifically chose Von Trotha to end the Herero uprising,[183] with full knowledge of his military record.[184] Clark notes that Wilhelm overruled Von Bülow, the Chief of the General Staff, the Minister of War and the Director of the Colonial Office on the appointment.[185] In a telegram the Kaiser sent to Von Trotha after he received accolades for his duties in GSWA, the Kaiser acknowledged that he had appointed Von Trotha (although one could argue that this is merely official protocol and does not necessarily suggest a personal involvement in the appointment).[186]

However, whether the Kaiser personally chose Von Trotha or merely supported his appointment, it is not surprising that he picked Von Trotha over Leutwein. According to Röhl, the Kaiser 'never wavered in his preference for the military over mere civilians'.[187] Appointing Von Trotha gave him further control and the possibility to exterminate the Herero. Accordingly, he prohibited negotiations with the Herero without his consent.[188] That the Kaiser overruled Von Bülow in the appointment of Von Trotha may be part of the reason why the latter kept the Kaiser's order secret (as will be discussed). It may also have been due to the ongoing tension over the constitutional domain of the Kaiser. Clark notes, 'Whereas the Centre demanded the immediate reduction of the military contingent in South-West Africa and insisted upon the observance of budgetary probity, defenders of the monarchical prerogative rejected all such claims on the grounds that it was the Emperor who had the exclusive right of decision in matters pertaining to the defence of the Reich

---

[182] Gewald, J-B. and Silvester, J. (2003) *Words cannot be found. German colonial rule in Namibia: An annotated reprint of the 1918 Blue Book.* Leiden: Brill, 106 fn 107.

[183] Berat, L. (1990) *Walvis Bay: The last frontier.* New Haven: Yale University Press, 179.

[184] Bensman, T. *Forgotten victims: African tribe wants apology.* Available at: http://www.pewfellowships.org/stories/namibia/forgotten-victims.html

[185] Clark, C. (2000) *Kaiser Wilhelm II. Profiles in power.* Essex: Pearson Education, 103.

[186] Ritter-Petersen, H.G. (1991) *The Herrenvolk mentality in German South West Africa 1884–1914.* DLitt (History). Pretoria: University of South Africa, 211.

[187] Röhl, J.C.G. (1982) 'Introduction'. In Röhl, J.C.G. & Sombart, N. (eds) *Kaiser Wilhelm II: New interpretations. The Corfu Papers.* Cambridge: Cambridge University Press, 16.

[188] Hull, I.V. (2003) 'Military culture and the production of final solutions in the colonies: The example of Wilhelminian Germany'. In Gellately, R. & Kiernan, B. (eds) *The specter of genocide mass murder in historical perspective.* Cambridge: Cambridge University Press, 150 fn 29.

territories.'[189] Again, this demonstrates how the Kaiser demanded and achieved control in certain areas. According to Hull, a 'tactic that Wilhelm used in his conspiracy against self-understanding was to choose entourage members whose personalities tended to confirm his own, rather than to challenge it'.[190] This is further support for the Kaiser's selection of Von Trotha to command the genocide.

Why the Kaiser chose Von Trotha

The Kaiser and others were aware of Von Trotha's credentials for brutality and ruthlessness and these fit their objectives in GSWA. In fact, Von Trotha's cruel tactics appear in many accounts. For example, John Wellington notes that Von Trotha had 'much military experience in the wars of 1866 and 1870 to 18711. As the leader of the China expedition in 1900 and the Commander in German East Africa during the years 1894 to 1897 he had won a great reputation for his utterly ruthless methods with rebels'.[191] Henrik Lundtofte notes that 'Trotha in the years 1894–97 as commander-in-chief of German forces in German East Africa won distinction for his brutal defeat of the so-called Wahehe Rising'.[192] Von Trotha himself said of the warfare in East Africa:

> This method of conducting war, through burning, was hardly congenial to me at the beginning. But then and now I cannot help but conclude from later conflicts that any kindness in this regard is interpreted by the natives as weakness.[193]

In 1895, when the local community in East Africa would not relinquish some rebel leaders, Von Trotha wanted to hang a prisoner every month until they did. In this regard, he declared: 'Terrorism can only help.'[194] Bebel quotes letters from German troops serving in China that allege extreme cruelty towards the Chinese, as well as looting and murder. According to him, the actions of the German troops in China (just a few years prior to the events in GSWA) constituted

---

[189] Clark, C. (2000) *Kaiser Wilhelm II. Profiles in power.* Essex: Pearson Education, 103.

[190] Hull, I.V. (1982) *The entourage of Kaiser Wilhelm II, 1888–1918.* New York: Cambridge University Press, 22.

[191] Wellington, J.H. (1967) *South West Africa and its human issues.* Oxford: Clarendon Press, 207.

[192] Lundtofte, H. (2003) 'Radicalization of the German suppression of the Herero rising in 1904'. In Jensen, S.L.B. (ed) *Genocide: Cases, comparisons and contemporary debates.* Copenhagen: Danish Center for Holocaust and Genocide Studies, 45.

[193] Hull, I.V. (2005) *Absolute destruction: Military culture and practices of war in Imperial Germany.* Ithaca: Cornell University Press, 26.

[194] *Ibid*, 27.

a commonplace war of conquest and a war of revenge and nothing more...a war of revenge so barbarous that it has found no equal during the last centuries and not often in a history at large...[195]

The events in China and GSWA exhibit parallels in motive and intent. The Germans also employed similar strategies in different parts of Africa. German forces massacred thousands of people in order to put down the rebellions in East Africa and they received orders to starve the population into submission.[196] Many of the soldiers deployed to deal with these rebellions arrived with Von Trotha and he was told to end the rebellion by any means necessary. As Mamdani has noted:

Lest the reader be tempted to dismiss General Lothar von Trotha as an improbable character come to life from the lunatic fringe of the German officer corps, one given a free hand in a distant and unimportant colony, I hasten to point out that the general had a distinguished record in the annals of colonial conquest, indeed the most likely reason he was chosen to squash a protracted rebellion. Renowned for his brutal involvement in the suppression of the Chinese Boxer Rebellion in 1900 and a veteran of bloody suppression of African resistance to German occupation in Rwanda, Burundi and Tanzania, General Trotha often enthused about his own methods of colonial warfare: 'The exercise of violence with crass terrorism and even with gruesomeness was and is my policy. I destroy the African tribes with streams of blood and streams of money. Only following this cleansing can something new emerge, which will remain.'[197]

Mamdani agrees with the point made earlier — that Von Trotha was not a rogue commander, but that this conduct was common, condoned and accepted throughout German colonial history. In this regard, Bebel noted as early as 1889:

Fundamentally, colonialism entails the maximum exploitation of a foreign population...Whenever we turn to the history of colonialism during the last three centuries, we always encounter deeds of violence and oppression against colonial peoples, abuses that not uncommonly end with their complete extermination. The impelling motive is always gold, gold and more gold.[198]

[195] Stoecker, H. & Sebald, P. (1987) 'Enemies of the colonial idea'. In Knoll, A.J. & Gann, L.H. (eds) *Germans in the tropics: Essays in German colonial history* (2ed). New York/London: Greenwood Press, 59–72, 61.
[196] See Blackshire-Belay, C.A. (1992, December) 'German imperialism in Africa: The distorted images of Cameroon, Namibia, Tanzania and Togo'. 23(2) *Journal of Black Studies*, 235–46, 242.
[197] Mamdani, M. (2001) *When victims become killers: Colonialism, nativism and the genocide in Rwanda*. Princeton: Princeton University Press, 7. (Footnotes omitted.)
[198] Bebel, A. Quoted in Stoecker, H. & Sebald, P. (1987) 'Enemies of the colonial idea'. In Knoll, A.J. & Gann, L.H. (eds) *Germans in the tropics: Essays in German colonial history* (2ed). New York/London: Greenwood Press, 59–72, 60.

Von Trotha had been part of the German armed forces that mercilessly quelled the Boxer Rebellion; he knew the Kaiser ordered that no one be spared and understood what was expected of him in GSWA, even if he was not specifically told (which I contest). He was chosen above a number of other officers to end the rebellion because those who chose him were aware of his record and probably wanted it replicated. Schrank suggests that it was Von Trotha's command of the first Asiatic Expeditionary Brigade in China in 1900 that caught the attention of the Kaiser.[199]

Whereas in all other German colonies the governor or the civilian authority maintained control, in GSWA Germany stripped Leutwein of control in 1904 and vested it only in Von Trotha, indicating the importance accorded to his appointment. Consequently, the direct line of authority from the Kaiser became paramount and Leutwein was sidelined. As Steinmetz notes, 'Theodor Leutwein's situation in 1904 represents the most extreme limitation of autonomy. But Von Trotha was remarkably autonomous from the General Staff, just as Leutwein had been from the Colonial Department until 1904.'[200]

Thus, the situation in GSWA went from one extreme to the other overnight. While Leutwein nominally remained the governor, in reality Von Trotha took over his position. Leutwein returned to Germany and later, in August 1905, resigned his governorship.[201] In contrast, the general's superiors afforded him substantial autonomy. It can be presumed that Von Trotha's autonomy was not as measureless as has been suggested, but that he was in fact given very direct orders, orders that were not made public and which he would obey until directly countermanded by the Kaiser himself. Thus, the power accorded to Von Trotha must be seen in the context of the order given by the Kaiser.

The Kaiser was not interested in reaching a settlement with the Herero. He (and others) wanted a military resolution. Appointing Von Trotha, rendering Leutwein impotent and forbidding negotiation clearly show a premeditated plan to deal with the Herero without compunction.

---

[199] Schrank, G.I. (1974) *German South West Africa: Social and economic aspects of its history, 1884–1915.* PhD (History). New York University, 156.
[200] Steinmetz, G. (2005) 'From "Native Policy" to exterminationism: German Southwest Africa, 1904'. In *Comparative Perspective, Theory and Research in Comparative Social Analysis, Paper 30.* Los Angeles: Department of Sociology, UCLA, fn 66. Available at: http://repositories.cdlib.org/cgi/viewcontent.cgi?article=1036&context=uclasoc
[201] *Encyclopaedia Britannica Volume VII* (1911), 804.

Did the Kaiser give Von Trotha a specific genocide order?

Regarding the Kaiser's involvement and the directive he may have given Von Trotha, the latter himself claimed the following:

> *I did not receive any instructions or directives on being appointed Commander-in-Chief in South West Africa. His Majesty the Emperor only said that he expected me to crush rebellion by fair means or foul and to inform him later of the causes that provoked the uprising.*[202]

Von Trotha admits that, at minimum, he had liberal licence and virtually unqualified authority to commit illicit and possibly illegal acts. At the time, Bebel stated in the *Reichstag* that the Kaiser's 1900 Hun speech probably inspired Von Trotha's conduct.[203] However, Zirkel notes, 'Wilhelm II gave Trotha de facto absolute power',[204] while Bridgman writes that the 'Emperor was careful not to limit his freedom of action by specific instruction or directives'.[205] Bridgman's recognition that Von Trotha was not restricted in deciding what action to take is an implicit admission that even illegal methods would be permitted. Von Trotha's own acknowledgment that 'foul' methods could be used echoes this. However, Hull argues that the use of words 'by all means' was common language in the context of the colonies.[206] If this is true, however, it only confirms that the authorities condoned such ruthless methods, if not expected them.

It also would appear that the Kaiser told Von Trotha to be ruthless, as on 4 October 1904, some two days after the extermination order, he wrote to the Chief of the Army General Staff:

> *Since I neither can nor will come to terms with these people without express orders from His Majesty the Emperor and King, it is essential that all sections of the nation be subjected to rather stern treatment. I have begun to administer such treatment on*

---

[202] Drechsler, H. (1980) *Let us die fighting: The struggle of the Herero and Nama against the German imperialism (1894–1915)* (Bernd Zöllner transl). London: Zed Press, 153–54.

[203] Stoecker, H. & Sebald, P. (1987) 'Enemies of the colonial idea'. In Knoll, A.J. & Gann, L.H. (eds) *Germans in the tropics: Essays in German colonial history* (2ed). New York/London: Greenwood Press, 59–72, 64.

[204] Zirkel, K. (1999) 'Military power in German colonial policy: The Schutztruppen and their leaders in the East and South West Africa, 1888–1918'. In Killingray, D. & Omissi, D. (eds) *Guardians of Empire: The armed forces of the colonial powers, 1700–1964*. Manchester: Manchester University Press, 91–113, 100.

[205] Bridgman, J. (1981) *The revolt of the Hereros*. Los Angeles: University of California Press, 180.

[206] Hull, I.V. (2005) *Absolute destruction: Military culture and practices of war in Imperial Germany*. Ithaca: Cornell University Press, 28.

my own initiative and, barring orders to the contrary, will continue to do so as long as I am in command here...[207]

Von Trotha said that he 'can [-not]' and 'will [not]' negotiate with the Herero. If he had not been able to negotiate because the Herero were not amenable, he presumably would have said so. However, he adds that he would not do so without the express orders of the Emperor. It is therefore likely that he could not negotiate because the Kaiser ordered him not to and he was not able to go against those orders unless the Kaiser amended them.

Von Trotha's claim that the Kaiser did not give him directives but merely told him that he needed to crush the uprising in GSWA clearly seeks to protect the Kaiser. There is no other reason for such an explicit explanation for something that supposedly never occurred. In addition, why would he have met with the Kaiser in the first place if the orders were simply to put down the rebellion and report back?

German *Schutztruppe* on patrol

[207] Drechsler, H. (1980) *Let us die fighting: The struggle of the Herero and Nama against the German imperialism (1894–1915)* (Bernd Zöllner transl). London: Zed Press, 161.

While the Kaiser did meet frequently with the chiefs of the various branches of the armed forces, there was no specific reason to meet with Von Trotha, apart from the need to discuss a course of action in GSWA. Hence, it is likely that the Kaiser's contact with Von Trotha was instrumental in achieving his goal in GSWA. Evidence shows that he regularly communicated directly with Von Trotha. He sent various messages to Von Trotha, at least one of which arrived shortly before the extermination order. The Kaiser sent this message after the Waterberg battle of August 1904 in response to Von Trotha's report about the battle. The Kaiser wrote:

> *With thanks to God and with great joy I have received your report from Hamakari concerning the successful attack of August 11 against the main force of the Hereros. Though the heavy losses suffered because of the stiff resistance of the enemy are to be regretted yet the bravery which the troops displayed under the greatest tension and deprivation...fill me with pride and may I give to you, to your officers and men my imperial thanks and fullest recognition of what you have done. William.*[208]

Critically, when Von Trotha discussed these orders, he did not refer to his superiors in the military or in the government. Neither did he refer to the *Reichstag*. He only discussed what the Kaiser said to him (that he had a free hand) and that he must await alternative commands from the Kaiser in order to change his tactics. This would suggest that originally the Kaiser gave him direct orders. It is even implicit in his earlier statement that the Kaiser expected him to crush the rebellion by any means, fair or foul. One can further deduce that, before Von Trotha arrived in the region in mid-1904, he met with the Kaiser, as the following suggests: 'His Majesty the Emperor only said that he expected me to crush the rebellion.' The word choice exhibited here suggests that the Kaiser made the statement directly to him. Yet, it is likely as well that the Kaiser did in fact expound upon his expectations concerning the Herero.

Von Trotha's assertion that he would not change course until the Kaiser ordered him to do so belies the Kaiser's alleged passivity. A statement by Colonel Berthold Karl Adolf von Deimling in 1906 uses similar language, highlighting the importance of the Kaiser's consent before undertaking a change in the course of action. When discussing the number of troops in GSWA in the *Reichstag* on 28 May 1906, Von Deimling stated that he would not withdraw a single soldier from the territory 'unless my Emperor issues a command to that effect'.[209] In addition, the fact that the Kaiser did not act swiftly following appeals from the

---

[208] Bridgman, J. (1981) *The revolt of the Hereros*. Los Angeles: University of California Press, 126.

[209] Lewin, E. (1915) *The Germans and Africa. Their aims on the dark continent and how they acquired their African colonies*. London: Cassell, 123.

Chancellor and others to rescind the extermination order is proof of his pivotal role. They implored him at the end of 1904 to rescind it, but he only responded some weeks later. This alone shows that he was in charge and that the Chancellor required his consent in order to have the order amended.

While Goldblatt, in his 1971 book,[210] wrote that the response to the extermination order was instantaneous and that the Kaiser repudiated the order, he did not do so immediately. After he was officially told, it took some weeks of persuading to force him to act. In fact, Chancellor von Bülow had trouble convincing the Kaiser, who was enthusiastic about the way Von Trotha was waging war.[211] Zirkel also notes that the Kaiser's eventual decree lifting the extermination order was intentionally so vague that the general could actually continue what he was doing 'almost without interference'.[212] The genocidal intent continued for at least a year,[213] as is proven by the continued presence of the cordon forcing the Herero into the desert and preventing access to the water wells until the end of 1905.[214] Thus, while the Kaiser lifted the specific extermination order in word, the deeds continued and the intent to achieve the same result persisted *de facto*.

Would Von Trotha have kept the genocide order secret?

As indicated thus far, it is likely that the specific extermination instruction came from the Kaiser and that he and Von Trotha wanted to keep this fact secret. The attempt to suppress the Kaiser's outburst on the docks in Bremen as the troops were leaving for China is not an isolated example — as shown before, there were many occasions on which statements or orders by the Kaiser were edited or censored.[215] The German government acknowledged that the Kaiser's utterings required refinement to make them more palatable. Before 1918, 'the entire machinery of state was employed to suppress unpalatable truths…'[216] This statement from 1902 evidences this practice:

210 Goldblatt, I. (1971) *History of South West Africa, from the beginning of the nineteenth century*. Cape Town: Juta, 132.
211 Helbig, H. (1983) *Mythos Deutsch-Südwest*. Weinheim, Basel: Beltz, 158.
212 Zirkel, K. (1999) 'Military power in German colonial policy: The Schutztruppen and their leaders in the East and South West Africa, 1888–1918'. In Killingray, D. & Omissi, D. (eds) *Guardians of Empire: The armed forces of the colonial powers, 1700–1964*. Manchester: Manchester University Press, 91–113, 100.
213 Drechsler, H. (1986) *Let us die fighting*. Berlin: Akademie-Verlag, 156.
214 Palmer, A. (1998, January) 'Colonial and modern genocide: Explanations and categories'. 21(1) *Ethnic and Racial Studies*, 89–115, 94.
215 Röhl, J.C.G. (1982) 'Introduction'. In Röhl, J.C.G. & Sombart, N. (eds) *Kaiser Wilhelm II: New interpretations. The Corfu Papers*. Cambridge: Cambridge University Press, 26.
216 *Ibid*.

When...I made [the] communication to the Kaiser... His Majesty replied in such a way that I was constrained to ask him whether he wished me to convey such a message to His Majesty's Government. 'No,' said His Majesty. 'You surely know me well enough to translate what I say into diplomatic language.' 'In that case,' I said, 'I propose to report that Your Majesty has received the communication with satisfaction.' 'Yes,' replied His Majesty, 'you may say, with great interest and great satisfaction', a meaning which even those intimately acquainted with His Majesty might easily have failed to gather from his original remark, which was; 'The noodles seem to have had a lucid interval.'[217]

Thus, it was evidently common knowledge that the Kaiser expected others to be diplomatic when reporting what he said or did. Even without a specific directive from the Kaiser or his advisors, Von Trotha, having served in China, would have known that the full instruction was not to be made public; otherwise criticism would follow as it had after the Hun speech. According to Röhl, 'No matter how concerned the Kaiser's entourage and statesmen grew over the Kaiser's personality, however, no matter how rebellious they became as a result of personal insult or policy difference, they all stopped short of divulging their misgivings to the general public...'[218]

While criticism of the Kaiser abounded throughout his reign, it certainly did not come from those around him. Even in 1923, when the Kaiser was in exile and one of his appointees, Count Zedlitz-Trutzschler, published a book that was critical of him, these revelations were met with immense criticism.[219] Röhl argues that this indicates '[t]he extent of the pressure to prevent unflattering revelations about Wilhelm II's true nature' becoming public.[220]

Since many records, publications and diaries were sanitised to remove comments that would reflect negatively on the Kaiser,[221] it is likely that Von Trotha's diary, which was likely to contain sensitive information about the Kaiser's role in the events of GWSA, would also have been edited. It seems as though his original handwritten diary was lost, but a typed transcript from 1930 made by his second wife, Lucy, as well as another version of the diary (a

---

[217] Balfour, M. (1964) *The Kaiser and his times*. Boston: Houghton Mifflin, 241.
[218] Röhl, J.C.G. (1982) 'Introduction'. In Röhl, J.C.G. & Sombart, N. (eds) *Kaiser Wilhelm II: New interpretations. The Corfu Papers.* Cambridge: Cambridge University Press, 27.
[219] Zedlitz-Trutzschler, R. (1951) *Twelve years at the imperial German court*. London: Nisbet & Co.
[220] Röhl, J.C.G. (1982) 'Introduction'. In Röhl, J.C.G. & Sombart, N. (eds) *Kaiser Wilhelm II: New Interpretations. The Corfu Papers.* Cambridge: Cambridge University Press, 25.
[221] *Ibid*, 24–25.

bound typescript version made later) exist.[222] According to Hull, a professional secretary appears to have typed the 1930 version, as the keystrokes indicate that someone well versed with a typewriter did the typing.[223] Hull believes that little was omitted in the process of typing the transcript, because even minute geographical details were retained. Yet, it is also possible that the *raison d'etre* for the typed version(s) was to exclude sensitive details the general recorded in the original. While Hull's argument seems plausible, it does not necessarily indicate that there was no intentional exclusion of particulars that might have been problematic in the 1930s. Hull does note that she used the 1930 version and that the 'ms. was reread several times, each reading leaving a trace in colored crayon or pencil of passages the reader(s) apparently wished to omit from a possible published version'.[224] This does not, of course, address which details failed to make it from the original written version into the typed document. The fact that two typed versions of the original existed should raise questions, specifically: why, if the original document was important enough to give rise to two typed versions, it was supposedly lost? One would have thought that great care would go into protecting such a valuable document, such as placing it in an archive or a museum. Hence, the possibility exists that the 1930 version may have been edited to omit details that Von Trotha's family deemed unfavourable to him or the Kaiser.

[222] Von Trotha was born on 3 July 1948 and died on 31 March 1920. His first wife, Bertha Neumann (born 1850), died on 9 October 1905 in Berlin while Von Trotha was waging the genocide campaign against the Herero. The Kaiser agreed to relieve him of his command in GSWA on 2 November 1905. Von Trotha left GSWA about month after her death, on 17 November 1905. Thus, his leaving GSWA at that time may have been connected to her fate. His second wife, Lucy Goldstein Brinkmann, whom he married in 1912, survived him and passed away seemingly only in 1958. She probably played a key role in sanitising his diary and military record. So may his two sons from his first marriage. His two sons had no children, but his extended family takes an interest in his activities and has visited Namibia as a 'gesture of reconciliation'. At an event there on 15 November 2004 one of the members of the family gave a speech in which he stated: 'We do not intend to play those events down or try to put them into perspective by saying that other European colonial powers had proceeded in the same or a similar way. No, in view of the facts, we would like to say the following to the Herero people and to you, one of their highest representatives: we, members of the Trotha family are ashamed of the terrible events that took place a hundred years ago. We deeply regret what happened to your people and children to the so Nama: the cruel and unjustified death of tens of thousands of men, women and children.'
See the Von Trotha family website. Available at: http://www.trotha.de/
[223] Hull, I.V. (2005) *Absolute destruction: Military culture and practices of war in Imperial Germany.* Ithaca: Cornell University Press, 30 fn 110.
[224] Ibid.

Second from left, Lehrk, owner of Hotel Stadt Windhoek, on his left Governor Leutwein, *Oberleutenant* von Trotha and General von Trotha. The younger Von Trotha was General von Trotha's nephew

Interestingly, the press reported that the Von Trotha family, who have the diary today, have claimed that it does not deal with the order. The family believes that the General acted on behalf of the German government. They state that his diaries do not mention his role in the killings in the Herero war and that they 'do not tell us anything about that tragedy and his warfare. They talk more about his leisure, sports and hunting hobby'.[225] Interestingly, the

---

[225] Hamta, M. (2004) 'Von Trotha family backs Herero compensation'. *Africa News Service*, 13 September 2004.

family believes that the Herero, Nama and Damaras require special assistance from Germany to help rebuild their ancestral heritage.[226]

What is unquestionably clear is that assertions unflattering to the Kaiser had been edited out of other records after his reign. This was common practice specifically around this time, but continued at least into the 1960s and possibly beyond. If the sanitising of his accounts continued after the Kaiser no longer held office, why would it not have happened on this occasion, when he was still in office? In fact, such omissions are far more likely to have taken place when the Kaiser was alive and specifically while he continued to reign. Given this context, was Von Trotha likely to reveal what the Kaiser had ordered? Was he not more likely to have done as others did and sanitise the reports to protect the Kaiser? If he was concerned about whose hands his diary might fall into someday, he might even have taken care not to include sensitive information. Von Trotha had a track record of limiting the flow of information, as is evident in the General Staff report of 1906, which states that Von Trotha did not provide all the details about the events. It is also relevant that in Von Trotha's orders to his soldiers and others there is no information about the Herero war. This control of information was so fiercely enforced that a civilian engineer, Richard Denker, was prosecuted and sentenced to five years in prison for writing an article about the atrocities committed by German soldiers (discussed later). In one of his unpublished manuscripts, Raphael Lemkin notes that 'every effort was made by German officials to keep details of the scandalous conditions in the colonies from the ears of the world'.[227] Nowhere was this more so than in GSWA during the Herero genocide, when German officials made supreme efforts to keep much of the

---

[226] Ibid.

Seemingly, General von Trotha's family have some responsibility regarding the events in GSWA. The role of the Von Trotha family in the Herero genocide goes beyond that of the General. One account names his nephew, Thilo von Trotha, in the carrying out of killings. Quoted in Gewald, J-B. and Silvester, J. (2003) *Words cannot be found. German colonial rule in Namibia: An annotated reprint of the 1918 Blue Book*. Leiden: Brill, 172.

It is reported that the issues of the Herero war and its links to the Von Trotha family 'haunts his German descendants'. Hamta, M. 'Von Trotha family backs Herero compensation'. *Africa News Service*, 13 September 2004. See earlier.

Ritter-Petersen, H.G. (1991) *The Herrenvolk mentality in German South West Africa 1884–1914*. DLitt (History). Pretoria: University of South Africa, 242.

The family meets twice yearly to discuss these issues. Von Trotha's great-grandnephew has offered his 'deepest regrets' over what occurred. It is further reported that the Von Trotha family supports a discussion regarding reparations between the German government and the Herero.

[227] Lemkin, R. Undated and unpublished manuscript: 'The Germans in Africa'. Jacob Rader Marcus Center of the American Jewish Archives, Cincinnati; the Raphael Lemkin papers, Box 6, Folder 9, 3.

information out of the news. During this period, even the opposition parties in the *Reichstag* continually claimed that they were not fully informed and that many of the brutalities occurring were not reported to them. In this context, it is not surprising that, if the Kaiser had given the order, he would not have allowed its release for public consumption.

The role of German law in keeping the genocide order secret

It is also possible that Von Trotha did not reveal the Kaiser's order because he feared being subject to criminal prosecution or imprisonment. Disclosing such information might have caused him to lose his position in the military, as well as his pension. He could have feared being liable under the German Criminal Code,[228] of which numerous provisions may have been applicable at the time. One article, 'diplomatic treason', was directly applicable. Article 92 of the Criminal Code of the German Empire provided that 'anyone who intentionally...knowing that it is essential for the welfare of the German Empire or a Federal State that such be kept secret from another government, communicates to such other government or makes publicly known any State secret or plan of a fortress or any instrument, document or intelligence...shall be liable to Penal Internment of not less than two years'.

Thus, Von Trotha may have been liable or may have believed that he could be liable under this provision. Section 95 of the Code might have also applied. This article provided that 'anyone who insults the Kaiser...shall be liable to Confinement of not less than two months or to Military Detention of from two months to five years'. Only in 1908 was this article amended to incorporate the provision that it applied to insults committed maliciously, deliberately and with intent to dishonour. Thus, before 1908, the offence was widely constituted and these limitations did not apply. Clearly, these provisions could have applied had Von Trotha publicly stated that the Kaiser was behind the order. Section 186 of the Criminal Code may also have been applicable. It provided for the crime of defamation for 'anyone who asserts or publishes in regard to another a fact which he is unable to prove likely to make such other person despicable or disgrace him in public opinion, shall be guilty of Insult and liable to a Fine not exceeding six hundred marks or Detention or Confinement not exceeding one year. If the Insult is offered in public or is circulated by means of any writing, picture or representation, the punishment shall be a Fine not exceeding one thousand five hundred marks or confinement not exceeding two years'.

---

[228] Gage, R.H. & Waters, A.J. (transl) (1917) *Imperial German Criminal Code*. Johannesburg: W.E. Horton & Co.

If the Kaiser denied giving the order, Von Trotha may have been liable under Section 187, which made it an offence to assert or publish 'an untrue fact'. Section 187 makes the offences covered by Sections 186 and 187 more severe if the 'prosperity' of the person insulted is affected. Von Trotha may also have been concerned about Section 112, which provided that 'anyone who incites or induces a member of the Imperial Army or Navy to disobey an order of his superior…shall be liable to Confinement not exceeding two years'.

Furthermore, Section 31 might also have applied in this case, as it provides that 'anyone who publicly affirms or disseminates fictitious or misrepresented facts, knowing that they are fictitious or misrepresented, in order thereby to bring state measures or orders of the authorities into contempt, shall be liable to a Fine not exceeding six hundred marks or to a Confinement not exceeding two years'. Section 31 may have been of further concern to Von Trotha as it provided that 'anyone sentenced to Penal Internment is thereby permanently incapacitated by law for service in the German Army or Navy and for appointment to any public office'. All these provisions specifically applied to the military: Section 10 provided that the 'Criminal Code of the German Empire applies generally to German Military persons in so far as military laws do not otherwise provide'. Von Trotha may have been especially concerned as, in addition to the penal provisions, Section 95 also provided that a person convicted of this offence could lose his public office.

Of relevance is that these laws were regularly enforced. One example, which demonstrates the application of these laws specifically in the context of the events in GSWA, concerns a 1906 interview with engineer Richard Denker. The *South African News* published an article using comments Denker made about the German troops and the atrocities they committed in GSWA. The German consulate at the Cape contacted the authorities in GSWA about the article, who then arrested Denker in GSWA, charged him with making insulting comments and sentenced him to five years' imprisonment. One of the components of his sentence was that he had to pay for the publication of notices in newspapers such as the *Windhuker Nachrichten*, the *Deutsch-Suedwestafrikanischen Zeitung* and the *South African News* that detailed his sentence and the reason for it. Thus, the law clearly outlined severe penal sanctions for making insulting or damaging comments about a range of actors. The posting of relevant notices regarding such offenses in newspapers shows the government's sincerity in taking such crimes seriously.[229]

---

[229] Erichsen, C.W. (2004) *The Angel of Death has descended violently among them: A study of Namibia's concentration camps and prisoners-of-war, 1904–08*. MA thesis (History). Windhoek: University of Namibia, 5–7.

Denker was a civilian, so one can deduce that if he received such punishment; military personnel would be even more likely to simply follow orders and not publicly voice complaints about these orders. In this context, it is virtually inconceivable that Von Trotha would have thought it safe to make any statements about the Kaiser, the military or anything else that might be construed negatively or affect the image of Germany or the German military.

In general, the Kaiser had a strong aversion to the reporting of military affairs in the press. He tried to prevent such publications unless they were positive towards him or to the issues in which he believed. He attempted to stop military officers from publishing in journals whose political stance he did not support.[230] Furthermore, the military stifled the expression of officers, even retired ones. The Kaiser threatened them with courts martial and the courts of honour.[231]

It is likely that Von Trotha would not have revealed the order even after retirement, as the consequences of German officers expressing their opinions were prominent in the news at the time. One German officer, Oberstleutnant von Wartenburg, had his title and uniform removed.[232] Another former military officer, Colonel AD Gädke, wrote an article suggesting there could be a conflict between the duty an officer owed to his country and the duty owed to the Kaiser. The War Ministry brought him before a court of honour. In February 1904, the court decided that Gädke should be deprived of his title and uniform. Gädke refused to accept the decision, arguing that these courts had no jurisdiction over retired officers.[233] All of these events were featured in the news at the time Von Trotha was about to leave for GSWA. While he was in GSWA, the Gädke case further unfolded. The military wanted to prosecute Gädke for wearing a uniform he was not entitled to wear and public debate over his guilt flourished. While a jury-court acquitted Gädke in 1906, its decision was appealed. A compromise surfaced in October 1906 that accepted that no one told Gädke upon his retirement that he fell under the jurisdiction of the honour courts, thus permitting the charge to be dropped. The army was, however, not satisfied with the result of the case and, in regulations of December 1906, some of the rules regarding the jurisdiction of the honour

---

[230] Kitchen, M. (1968) *The German Officer Corps 1890–1914*. Oxford: Clarendon Press, 58.
[231] Ritter, G. (1970) *The problem of militarism in Germany*, Vol. II (transl H. Norden). Coral Gables, Florida: University of Miami Press, 105.
[232] Kitchen, M. (1968) *The German Officer Corps 1890–1914*. Oxford: Clarendon Press, 59.
[233] Ibid, 59–60.

courts were amended. On 12 February 1907, Gädke again wrote an article in the *Berliner Tageblatt* arguing that these amended orders were unconstitutional. He was again tried in September 1907 and this time convicted. The courts dismissed his appeal in February 1908.[234] The press reported these events and Von Trotha must have resolved that he would not be safe, even upon retirement, to reveal the orders given by the Kaiser.

Gädke was not the only military official under review for such offenses. In 1907 and 1908, *Reichstag* MP Hans Paasche, an army major, merely criticised the situation in the officers' messes in Berlin. His case was referred to the courts of honour and he had to withdraw his comments.[235] Kitchen notes that 'these cases... were examples of the way in which the army used all the power at its command to force officers, even when they had left the regular army, to keep to the path of political orthodoxy, resorting, where necessary, to methods which were constitutionally highly dubious'.[236] Gädke wrote an article in 1911 asserting that these processes amounted to 'an act of force, a strong moral pressure, which is used to bind the individual officer to a particular political line and to make him submit to an utterly one-sided view of the state'.[237] All these cases and pronouncements must have cautioned Von Trotha to be circumspect in what he said and did during and after his career.

Furthermore, Von Trotha personally took part in sanitising accounts of events in GSWA. In August 1905, he prohibited German forces from giving statements to the *Windhuker Nachrichten*, as that newspaper had criticised the way the war had been conducted.[238] Other measures included taking steps to limit what the troops themselves revealed about the war. He specifically ordered German soldiers returning home not to talk to the press. The military command also prohibited them from publishing their letters or diaries. Von Trotha not only restricted the information flow by the soldiers under his command, he also occasionally inhibited the information he provided to the General Staff in Berlin. A 1906 report of the General Staff in Berlin noted in reference to the cordoning off of the Sandveld:

---

[234] *Ibid*, 62.
[235] *Ibid*, 63.
[236] *Ibid*.
[237] *Ibid*.
[238] Drechsler, H. (1980) *Let us die fighting: The struggle of the Herero and Nama against the German imperialism (1894–1915)* (Bernd Zöllner transl). London: Zed Press, 188.

General von Trotha's reports did not contain sensational news during this time. The drama happened at the dark stages of the Sandveld. When the rainy season came, the scene received light and our patrols could reach to the borders of Bechuanaland; the horrifying picture of armies who died of thirst was revealed to their eyes.[239]

Von Trotha kept everyone in the dark about his actions and the consequences of his order, including the General Staff and the Kaiser. Yet, this seems out of character with his general conduct and prior behaviour, when he reported fully on his operations. It also seems unwarranted, as the Kaiser later praised and rewarded him for his achievements in GSWA. Surely the Kaiser would not have done so if Von Trotha had not followed orders or if he was unhappy about his conduct after the extermination order was countermanded at the end of 1904?

Hull argues that if the Kaiser had given Von Trotha such an order, even orally, Von Trotha would have acknowledged it when he defended his conduct in private correspondence to his superiors, Chief of Staff Alfred von Schlieffen, Chancellor von Bülow and Governor Leutwein.[240] Von Trotha knew the order would be 'controversial' (as even Hull admits).[241] Given their history of disagreement, it is improbable that he would have trusted Leutwein and given him ammunition to attempt to reverse the course of action. If he had been told not to reveal the order to anyone, why would he then have told these individuals, realising the possible consequences for himself and the Kaiser? Even if he had taken them into his confidence, would he have done so in full view others? It is also highly unlikely that he would have trusted non-military personnel with the information. While he may have told his superiors, he would not have done so in such a way that the communication could have been compromised, either then or in the future. The outcry over the Kaiser's Hun speech and the events of Boxer Rebellion, with which he was intimately involved, would have forced him to think twice. It may simply have been that Von Trotha did not trust the means of communication or that these individuals would read such correspondence. He probably did not trust

---

[239] Großer Generalstab (1906) (ed) *Die Kämpfe der deutschen Truppen in Südwestafrika. Auf Grund amtlichen Materials bearbeitet von der Kriegsgeschichtlichen, Abteilung I des Großen Generalstabes. Band I. Der Feldzug gegen die Hereros*. Berlin: Ernst Siegfried Mittler & Sohn, 214. Cited in Hinz, M.O. (2003) 'One hundred years later: Germany on trial in the USA — The Herero reparations claim for genocide'. 1(1) *Namibian Human Rights Online Journal*, 4. Available at: http://www.hrdc.unam.na/journal/V1_N1_Dec2003/Docs/Herero_case.doc

[240] Hull, I.V. (2003) 'Military culture and the production of final solutions in the colonies: The example of Wilhelminian Germany'. In Gellately, R. & Kiernan, B. (eds) *The specter of genocide mass murder in historical perspective*. Cambridge: Cambridge University Press, 145.

[241] *Ibid*, 156.

that private correspondence would actually remain private. Hull's argument does not consider the fact that the Kaiser and/or others may have instructed Von Trotha not to reveal the direct order. We know from a letter Von Trotha wrote on 7 December 1904, that the Kaiser told him not to have anything to do with the Chancellor.[242] This letter highlights a few points and is yet another example of the communication between Von Trotha and the Kaiser. It also underscores that the Kaiser wanted the GSWA campaign to remain under his authority and it suggests tensions between the Kaiser and the Chancellor. This letter may therefore partly explain why Von Trotha would never have revealed that the Kaiser gave the extermination order. At the same time, it confirms that the Kaiser was in specific command over military activities in GSWA during the war.

It is also important to link the Kaiser's barring of a relationship between Von Trotha and the Chancellor with the consequences of the Hun speech. Major Stuhlmann, in his diary, published later, noted that 'it was announced to us today that our relatives are forbidden to publish our diaries or else we will be punished. I am of the opinion that, however justifiable the measures are, they are [to be seen] in light of the vastly exaggerated *Hunnenbriefe*...'[243] As noted earlier, that speech caused Bülow to threaten to bar the Kaiser from speaking at events in general, at least not without an approved speech. It also resulted in the Kaiser's brother seeing the troops off from Kiel.[244] One of the best ways for the Kaiser to limit interference from the Chancellor, especially in GSWA, would have been to keep information from him. This would have been especially important if the orders were similar to those in the Hun speech, ie to take no quarter. It would also explain the Kaiser's instruction to Von Trotha not to discuss his activities with the Chancellor. Had the Chancellor got wind of the Kaiser's intentions, he might have tried to alter the course of events.

The Kaiser gave a speech on the Herero rebellion on 20 January 1904, but it was short and simply called for the restoration of law and order.[245] It was probably a scripted speech and this time the Kaiser was presumably coached and implored not to deviate from the text.

It is possible that others knew of the order given to Von Trotha. One person who might have known was the Kaiser's chief of the *Militaire Maison General*,

---

242 Hull, I.V. (2005) *Absolute destruction: Military culture and practices of war in Imperial Germany*. Ithaca: Cornell University Press, 63.
243 Quoted in Erichsen, C.W. (2004) *The Angel of Death has descended violently among them: A study of Namibia's concentration camps and prisoners-of-war, 1904–08*. MA thesis (History). Windhoek: University of Namibia, 8 fn 6.
244 Hull, I.V. (2005) *Absolute destruction: Military culture and practices of war in Imperial Germany*. Ithaca: Cornell University Press, 136 & 136 fn 20.
245 Ibid.

Hans von Plessen. He told Von Trotha before he left for GSWA: 'Just don't lose your nerve.'[246] It could have been a reference to the tough conditions that Von Trotha was about to face, although Von Trotha had ample experience in such settings — that was one of the reasons why the Kaiser had chosen him for the task. For what other reason would he lose his nerve regarding the warfare he was to conduct? General von Plessen's words of caution probably had a dual intention: had he been aware of the extermination order, he might have wanted to implore Von Trotha not to 'go soft'. In addition, he could also have been forewarning Von Trotha about the severe criticism that he would face, ie the diplomatic and international 'fall-out' following the extermination of the Herero.

Some argue that if the Kaiser had given the extermination order, Von Trotha would have mentioned it in his defence when he and the Chancellor quarrelled about the subject. Further, he would likely have recorded it in his diary. Even when criticised for his conduct, Von Trotha never blamed anyone else for what occurred.[247] However, as shown, there are many reasons why Von Trotha would not have revealed the Kaiser's involvement. He was the Kaiser's general and proud of it. He signed his orders 'the Great General of the Mighty Kaiser, von Trotha'. He would have done nothing to undermine the Kaiser. Von Trotha knew that Leutwein, Bülow and various political parties in the *Reichstag* opposed the conduct and that if the truth emerged, even more criticism of the Kaiser would follow. Even Hull, who does not believe that the Kaiser gave the order, states: 'A loyal self-sacrificing soldier might have hidden such an order from the public...'[248]

Von Trotha may have wanted the Kaiser to publicly endorse his conduct. He told the Chancellor, in January 1905, that he had asked the Chief of the General Staff 'whether His Majesty agreed with his harsh stance'.[249] It seems as if Von Trotha suggested that the Chancellor should check with the Kaiser regarding whether he supported what he was doing. It is even possible that Von Trotha had told the Chancellor that this is what the Kaiser wanted and that the Chancellor should check that with the Kaiser. Von Trotha told the Chancellor, 'I never received an answer. *Qui facet, consentire videtur*. I had to assume that my position was approved at the highest level.'[250]

On 9 March 1909, Von Trotha reiterated that the absence of a veto implied that he had the necessary support. He wrote a letter to the *Berliner Neuste*

---

246 *Ibid*, 30.
247 *Ibid*, 28.
248 *Ibid*.
249 *Ibid*, 29.
250 *Ibid*.

Nachrichten in which he stated: 'Already in September 1904 I had made no bones about how I intended to end the uprising and numerous times I offered my resignation if this policy was rejected.'[251] He thus made it clear that he continually sought approval and that the Kaiser did not countermand him until the Kaiser supposedly and reluctantly modified the order late in 1904.

Undoubtedly, the Kaiser and others knew what was happening; they received regular reports from Von Trotha, Governor Leutwein and others. Various members of the *Reichstag* raised objections in the House and many individuals wrote to the Kaiser, telling him directly what was occurring. One soldier even wrote to the Kaiser recommending that German forces poison the wells. There is no proof that he received that letter, but that German forces implemented the recommendation is solid evidence.[252] Von Trotha therefore had no reason to doubt that the Kaiser approved of his conduct. He regularly requested confirmation of what he was doing. He wanted to ensure, on an ongoing basis, that the Kaiser approved of his methods, as he knew there was controversy in Germany about how German forces were quelling the rebellion. Because he obviously received no censure or counter-orders, he proceeded with the approach and strategies familiar to him. While this may be military routine, it also corresponded with what the government wanted; it conformed to state culture.

Even in 1905, the Kaiser was supportive of Von Trotha. On 19 January 1905 he wrote to Von Trotha: 'You have entirely fulfilled my expectations when I named you to Commander of the *Schutztruppe* and it is a pleasure to express to you again my complete recognition for your accomplishments so far.'[253] The Kaiser says he is thanking Von Trotha again, indicating a regular correspondence in which he had previously expressed his appreciation. In addition, the Kaiser expresses his 'complete recognition' of and support for Von Trotha's actions, a few weeks after he ostensibly rescinded the extermination order. There is nothing negative in the letter; on the contrary, the words and tone exhibit enormous gratitude. The phrase 'entirely fulfilled my expectations' is significant, as it shows that Von Trotha did exactly what the Kaiser expected of him. 'Entirely' could be a reference to the comprehensive defeat of the Herero, but it most probably refers to the extent of the annihilation achieved by then.

---

[251] *Ibid.*

[252] Madley, B. (2004, June) 'Patterns of frontier genocide 1803–1910: The aboriginal Tasmanians, the Yuki of California and the Herero of Namibia'. 6(2) *Journal of Genocide Research*, 167–192, 186.

[253] Hull, I.V. (2005) *Absolute destruction: Military culture and practices of war in Imperial Germany*. Ithaca: Cornell University Press, 30.

In contradiction, Bridgman and Worley have stated that the '[d]estruction was not the deliberate policy of the German Government in Berlin, but rather the decision of the local commander'.[254] However, this does not align with a later statement in the same article, which said that 'this was Genocide because it was an attempt by representatives of the German Government to destroy a whole people with the knowledge and the tacit approval of the Kaiser and the General Staff...'[255] This second statement implicitly acknowledges that it was deliberate policy, as the lack of action from those in the know (in this case the highest authorities) makes them legally responsible and liable for the actions of their employees.

While Lundtofte argues that 'Trotha was given free hands by the Kaiser to pacify the rebels',[256] the German Government and the Kaiser knew what was happening. An abundance of evidence shows that the Kaiser was not only well aware of the ongoing actions of his representatives in German South West Africa, but that he supported them actively.[257] Lundtofte actually undermines his own argument by noting, 'Trotha's carte blanche existed on paper only'.[258] At a minimum, the Kaiser and the Government had direct knowledge from reports they received, but even without these, the facts were clearly in the public domain in Germany at the time, because the genocide provoked vociferous protests. In addition, Von Trotha wrote to the Chief of the Army on 4 October 1904 and specifically informed him of developments. It has been suggested that the intent to commit genocide was apparent this letter. Yet no one told Von Trotha to stop what he was doing. Berlin was certainly aware of what was happening.[259] On 5 December 1904, Chancellor von Bülow stated in the *Reichstag*, 'we are not so cruel and we are not so stupid as to think that

---

[254] Bridgman, J. & Worley, L.J. (1997) 'Genocide of the Herero'. In Totten, S., Parsons, W. & Charney, I. (eds) *Century of genocide*. New York: Garland 3–40, 3. This was also the view of Germany's development aid minister, Heidemarie Wieczorek-Zeul, who delivered an apology to the Herero at Waterberg on 14 August 2004.

[255] *Ibid.*

[256] Lundtofte, H. (2003) 'Radicalization of the German suppression of the Herero rising in 1904'. In Jensen, S.L.B. (ed) *Genocide: Cases, comparisons and contemporary debates*. Copenhagen: Danish Center for Holocaust and Genocide Studies, 15, 30.

[257] Drechsler, H. (1980) *Let us die fighting: The struggle of the Herero and Nama against the German imperialism (1894–1915)* (Bernd Zöllner transl). London: Zed Press, 195.

[258] Lundtofte, H. (2003) 'Radicalization of the German suppression of the Herero rising in 1904'. In Jensen, S.L.B. (ed) *Genocide: Cases, comparisons and contemporary debates*. Copenhagen: Danish Center for Holocaust and Genocide Studies, 15, 44.

[259] Letter in Drechsler, H. (1980) *Let us die fighting: The struggle of the Herero and Nama against the German imperialism (1894–1915)* (Bernd Zöllner transl). London: Zed Press, 189.

the only means of restoring orderly conditions is to be found in shooting down those half-starved Herero bands, dying of thirst, who are streaming out of the desert. Of this there can be no question'.[260] His speech recognises their conduct and the criticism thereof. In fact, the Chancellor was the one who persuaded the Kaiser to change the extermination order, indicating that the order was common knowledge. Furthermore, the order was acknowledged in the official German General Staff Report, which noted that the 'sealing off of the Sandveld executed with iron discipline over months completed the work of extermination'.[261]

While the German government amended the direct order in late 1904, nothing much changed regarding the way they conducted the war in the colony and the cordon remained into the middle of 1905.[262]

Although Bridgman, Worley and others have argued that the evidence does not attribute the directives to the German state, but to a rogue commander, this does not hold water. Von Trotha's conduct was not eccentric or unique; German forces subsequently employed similar tactics in other parts of the world. As Madley comments: 'The genocide of the Herero advanced along lines similar to the Tasmanian and Yuki cases, with variations.'[263] At minimum, the German state knew of and supported Von Trotha's ruthless conduct; but most likely, the Kaiser specifically ordered his actions, which the General Staff supported.

Military culture

Some have argued that the genocide in GSWA was not the result of a specific order, but simply an extension of the military culture observed by the German armed forces. Packenham notes that this was the Kaiser's first war and the

---

260 Quoted in Goldblatt, I. (1971) *History of South West Africa, from the beginning of the nineteenth century*. Cape Town: Juta, 132.
261 Großer Generalstab (ed) (1906) *Die Kämpfe der deutschen Truppen in Südwestafrika. Auf Grund amtlichen Materials bearbeitet von der Kriegsgeschichtlichen, Abteilung I des Großen Generalstabes. Band I. Der Feldzug gegen die Hereros*. Berlin: Ernst Siegfried Mittler & Sohn, 214. Cited in Hinz, M.O. (2003) 'One hundred years later: Germany on trial in the USA — The Herero reparations claim for genocide'. 1(1) *Namibian Human Rights Online Journal*, 4. Available at: http://www.hrdc.unam.na/journal/V1_N1_Dec2003/Docs/Herero_case.doc
Also cited in various other sources.
262 Stoecker, H. (ed) (1986) *German imperialism in Africa: From the beginnings until the Second World War*. London: C Hurst & Co, 58.
263 Madley, B. (2004, June) 'Patterns of frontier genocide 1803–1910: The aboriginal Tasmanians, the Yuki of California and the Herero of Namibia'. 6 (2) *Journal of Genocide Research*, 167–192, 181.

opportunity for Germany to show the might of its huge standing army.[264] He also argues that, besides its role in the Boxer Rebellion, the German army had 'earned no battle honours for a generation. Small wonder that thousands of soldiers now volunteered for the front as if some great Power threatened the Fatherland'.[265] However, according to Trutz von Trotha, 'Imperial Germany alone waged thirteen wars between 1884 and 1908 simply to subdue its African colonies and keep them under control. This figure includes only the more important confrontations. The more or less comprehensive "punitive expeditions" amount to hundreds.'[266] In fact, in GSWA alone, between 1891 and 1897, there were more than 60 large-scale 'punitive expeditions'.[267] Therefore, the Herero war was not the Kaiser's first opportunity to demonstrate the strength of the German troops. He did, however, conclude that it was his first war fought in the limelight and thus a decisive victory was not only important for Germany's image at home but also for its international status. Packenham underscores the importance of this war for the Kaiser and Germany by devoting an entire chapter in his book, *The scramble for Africa*, to the Herero War, entitling it 'The Kaiser's First War'.[268] Yet, as noted above, although there is some debate over whether smaller skirmishes or less important conflicts constituted war, technically, this was not his first war.

Hull argues that the events in GSWA were not a result of ideology, but merely military practice. She points out that the same practices occurred in East Africa, when the quelling of the Maji-Maji rebellion resulted in the death of between two and three hundred thousand people and continued during World War I. According to Hull, these two events signify that the military preferred solving political problems by 'total unlimited force'[269] and that the brutal methods employed cannot be attributed to the orders given, but to the way the soldiers conducted the campaigns. Yet in GSWA the bulk of the forces

---

264 Packenham, T. (1992) *The scramble for Africa: White man's conquest of the Dark Continent from 1875–1912*. New York: Avon Books, 609.
265 Ibid.
266 Von Trotha, T. (1999) 'The fellows can just starve. On wars of pacification in African colonies of Imperial Germany and concept of total war'. In Boemeke, M.E., Chickering, R. & Förster, S. (eds) *Anticipating Total War: The German and American Experience 1871–1914*. Cambridge: Cambridge University Press, 415–35.
267 Ibid.
268 Packenham, T. (1992) *The scramble for Africa: White man's conquest of the Dark Continent from 1875–1912*. New York: Avon Books, 602–655.
269 Hull, I.V. (2005) *Absolute destruction: Military culture and practices of war in Imperial Germany*. Ithaca: Cornell University Press, 161.

were volunteers and settlers,[270] who had not served in the other places where the military culture that Hull addresses held sway. Granted, some of the soldiers in leadership positions were previously stationed elsewhere. However, these were not the foot soldiers; they were military personnel in the position to give the commands. Hence, it is extremely likely that the troops simply carried out an order (or orders). To some extent, the volunteers and settlers may have wanted to impress their leaders and those in command in Berlin, but there is enough evidence to suggest that Von Trotha and/or the Kaiser ordered the military to do the things they did. Most of the soldiers would, no doubt, have presumed that the Kaiser had given the order.

Gewald disagrees with this analysis and argues that 'German soldiers and settlers were never directly ordered to commit the atrocities committed. Instead a social space was created in central and southern Namibia of 1904 to 1908 in which the atrocities committed were deemed acceptable'.[271] This, however, does not accord with the extermination order and other evidence about commands given to the soldiers by their superiors on the battlefield. The soldiers did not set up and run the concentration camps, nor did they perpetrate the other atrocities off the battlefield. Consequently, I cannot support Gewald and Hull's views that the carnage was merely due to a pervasive military culture and a confluence of social and political circumstances. Rather, the military was supporting and carrying out policies of the state and the society at large. It is clear, in this regard, that there was a '[s]pread of military values into the German Society'.[272]

The Kaiser saw the military as his personal fiefdom in which he would not permit interference. He regarded the military as the key to building a Germany that could serve as an example to other countries. Hull notes that

> his basic political desires are not difficult to discern. They were: 1) to uphold the dignity, power and repute of the Prusso-German monarchy and 2) to make Germany the most powerful, most respected nation in the world. The first desire had several corollaries: the sanctity and isolation of the army had to be safeguarded and the chief force which threatened the monarchical status quo, namely social democracy, had to be suppressed...[273]

---

[270] Gewald, J-B. (2003) 'The Herero genocide: German unity, settlers, soldiers and ideas'. In Bechhaus-Gerst, M. & Klein-Arendt, R. (eds) *Die (koloniale) Begegnung: AfrikanerInnen in Deutschland 1880–1945, Deutsche in Afrika 1880–1918*. Frankfurt am Main: Peter Lang, 109–127, 122.

[271] *Ibid*, 109–127, 124.

[272] Wehler, H-U. (1985) *The German Empire 1871–1918*. Leamington Spa/Dover, New Hampshire: Berg Publishers, 156.

[273] Hull, I.V. (2005) *Absolute destruction: Military culture and practices of war in Imperial Germany*. Ithaca: Cornell University Press, 230.

Thus, the Kaiser supported — and mostly directed — the conduct of the military and the military did not go to war without authorisation. At a minimum, the Kaiser condoned and often ratified the practices of the military through praise, medals, etc. While Hull impugns the military for what occurred and argues that they were able to determine military policy and practices, it was not a military dictatorship. Germany had a civilian government that had at least some authority over the military. The Kaiser was the head of the executive and his actions represented the German state. Thus, the German state is responsible for them.

Fundamentally, the legislature determined military expropriation. While there were attempts to limit the *Reichstag*'s supervisory role over the military by getting a seven-year and later a five-year budget approved, the *Reichstag* did raise and debate military matters whenever the public considered them important. Critically, the *Reichstag* continually showed its approval by granting more funds and increasing the size of the military. The figures evidence this support:[274]

Date	Monetary amounts	Approximate number of troops
1870	40.9 million marks	400 000
1880	45.1 million marks	434 000
1890	45.1 million marks	509 000
1900	56.1 million marks	629 000
1913	67 million marks	864 000

The monetary and personnel allocations to the military and their growth in peacetime prove that the government and *Reichstag* endorsed military conduct. Furthermore, as military expenditure increased, the German government, despite financial pressures, publicly proclaimed in 1899 that they approved of the increased military budget.[275] They added that the people of Germany were happy to pay the additional costs of this. This certainly suggests neither a lack of support for the military allocations, nor a denunciation of what the military were doing. It is also in stark contrast with the *Reichstag*'s attitude to the general financial allocations for the colonies, about which they were extremely concerned. Often the *Reichstag* enforced limitations on the colonial budgets.[276]

[274] Wehler, H-U. (1985) *The German Empire 1871–1918*. Leamington Spa/Dover, New Hampshire: Berg Publishers, 148.

[275] Best, G. (1991) 'The restraint of war in historical and philosophical perspectives'. In Delissen, A. & Tanja, G. (eds) *Humanitarian law of armed conflict: Challenges ahead*. Dordrecht/Boston/London: Martinus Nijhoff, 11.

[276] Dale, R. (1976) 'Colonial rulers and ruled in South West Africa and the Bechuanaland Protectorate 1884–1966'. *Journal of Southern African Affairs*, 95–110, 109 fn 45.

At times when the Kaiser ordered acts he received expropriations as a result, but typically it was only the minority parties who complained about the conduct of the military. Individuals in the *Reichstag* who warned that the German forces usually put down these revolts in very brutal ways were scorned and ignored. Even after the *Reichstag* received and publicised reports in which information about German forces shooting captured prisoners was contained, it did nothing to stop these executions. The Kaiser, General Staff, government or legislature gave adequate notice if they wanted to limit or stop such practices. The government rarely called the military to account for their conduct and placed no limits on military expropriation if they were not complying with the wishes of the *Reichstag* or government. If the civilian government had not wanted the huge number of deaths they would quickly have put a stop to it, but they did not. In fact, they allowed these practices to occur over extended periods, all the way through the colonial period and into World War I. Hull's argument would be similar to claiming that the SS in Nazi Germany deserved blame for the atrocities committed on Jews, gays, gypsies and others and not the German government who supported their activities.

That claims for retribution against the Herero came from all quarters shows that the atrocities in GSWA were not simply a by-product of a military culture. A novel called *Peter Moor's Journey to South West*, published in 1906, sold 100 000 copies, in that year alone, in Germany. It was also a set-work book in German schools from 1908.[277] Clearly, the public was aware of events in GSWA and widely supported the call for tough action.[278] According to Gambari, the German populace generally tacitly approved the actions taken.[279] The *Berliner Zeitung* noted: 'We must make a repeat of the uprising impossible under all circumstances by sharp and ruthless punishment.'[280] The settlers in GSWA also wanted 'vindictive' action taken against the Herero.[281] This belies the view

---

[277] Pakendorf, G. (1987) 'The literature of expropriation: "Peter Moor's journey to South-West" and the conquest of Namibia'. In Totemeyer, G., Kandetu, V. & Werner, W. (eds) *Namibia in perspective*. Windhoek: Namibian Council of Churches, 172–183, 176.

[278] Hull, I.V. (2005) *Absolute destruction: Military culture and practices of war in Imperial Germany*. Ithaca: Cornell University Press, 18.

[279] Gambari, I.A. (1971, October). 'Review of H Bley "South West Africa under German Rule, 1894–1914"; South-West Africa (Namibia): Proposals for Action'. 9(3) *Journal of Modern African Studies*, 484–86, 484.

[280] *Berliner Zeitung*, 4 February 1904. Quoted in Hull, I.V. (2005) *Absolute destruction: Military culture and practices of war in Imperial Germany*. Ithaca: Cornell University Press, 18.

[281] Hull, I.V. (2005) *Absolute destruction: Military culture and practices of war in Imperial Germany*. Ithaca: Cornell University Press, 21.

of some authors, such as Helmut Walser Smith, who claim that the German constitution limited public or political debate about the violence perpetrated.[282]

While many authors downplay the role of the *Reichstag* in colonial and military matters, the facts and events suggest otherwise. Less than a week after the rebellion began on 12 January 1904 the *Reichstag* debated the matter.[283] The *Reichstag's* support for the military was such that, by 19 January 1904, it approved the extra resources necessary to the military campaign in GSWA.[284] At the time, they granted an additional 2.8 million marks for the troops to suppress the rebellion, without any opposition — not even from individuals such as August Bebel.[285] The military alone did not take the decision to rush troops to GSWA; the Chancellor, the Colonial Office, the Kaiser and others also supported it.[286] In addition, there were public debates and the German public and the settlers in GSWA supported the actions. Furthermore, until June 1904, the troops in GSWA were under the civilian governor, not the military in Berlin. At the time, Governor Leutwein admitted that excesses occurred and again no one did anything to discipline him or the troops involved. A no-quarter policy was evidently already in place, as German forces took no prisoners.

Regarding the question of oversight and accountability, Smith cites Gordon Craig, who notes *apropos* the events in the Shark Island concentration camp that 'the specific tradition of German Militarism in which the army constituted an intrusion into which no one may dare peer with critical eyes limited the extent to which responsible ministers were forced to react to parliamentary criticism'.[287]

---

[282] Smith, H.W. (1999) 'The logic of colonial violence: Germany in South West Africa (1904–1907), the United States in the Philippines (1899–1902)'. In Lehmann, H. & Wellenreuther, H. (eds) *German and American nationalism: A comparative perspective*. Oxford/New York: Berg, 205–31, 209.

[283] Packenham, T. (1992) *The scramble for Africa: White man's conquest of the Dark Continent from 1875–1912*. New York: Avon Books, 604.

[284] Wallenkampf, A.V. (1969) *The Herero rebellion in South West Africa: A study in German colonialism*. PhD thesis. Los Angeles: UCLA, 1.

[285] Packenham, T. (1992) *The scramble for Africa: White man's conquest of the Dark Continent from 1875–1912*. New York: Avon Books, 604.

[286] *Ibid*.

[287] Smith, H.W. (1999) 'The logic of colonial violence: Germany in South West Africa (1904–1907), the United States in the Philippines (1899–1902)'. In Lehmann, H. & Wellenreuther, H. (eds) *German and American nationalism: A comparative perspective*. Oxford/New York: Berg, 205–31, 209; also quoting Craig, G. (1955) *The Politics of the Prussian army 1640–1945*. London: Oxford University Press, 247.

Herero prisoners in the port of Lüderitz on their way to Shark Island

Smith uses the example of Bernhard Durnburg, the Colonial Secretary who, in 1907, argued that as a civilian minister he could not interfere in the brutality of the Shark Island concentration camp, as this fell under the context of war. While this is probably true in terms of the division of authority in the colonies during times of war, this was not the case during times of peace when responsibility for the colonies rested with civilian control, not the military. During war, the military maintained control and had to report to the Kaiser, not to the civilian rulers. Thus the military was not without oversight and accountability: it was accountable to the Kaiser and, thus, to the government. However, Durnburg stated that if he had pressed the officer in command, the latter would have told him that the circumstances demanded such action. Thus Durnburg claimed he could not offer any difference of opinion or direction to the officer[288] and hence abdicated his responsibility in this regard. Yet, one could ask whether

---

[288] Smith, H.W. (1999) 'The logic of colonial violence: Germany in South West Africa (1904–1907), the United States in the Philippines (1899–1902)'. In Lehmann, H. & Wellenreuther, H. (eds) *German and American nationalism: A comparative perspective.* Oxford/New York: Berg, 205–31, 209.

Durnberg essentially supported the action and was therefore not inclined to argue with or counter-direct the officer. While Durnburg avowed regretting the brutality, it is probable that he did not, because he could have asked the Kaiser to intervene had he wanted the conduct to stop. Therefore, the question is whether he was truly unable to act or whether he was rather unwilling to do so. Wehler has noted:

> *The German Empire retained the old Prussian distinction between the monarch's right of command and the authority of the military administration, by way of which the Prussian Minister of War passed on information to the Reichstag. From the time of the Constitutional Conflict onwards the issue at stake was whether the monarch's right of command, kept free of any representative control, could be maintained or even extended, in the face of parliamentary demands for a say in this sphere. In fact, it was decided that on the question of the right of command, the Emperor's orders were exempt from ministerial endorsement, although both the Imperial Constitution and the Prussian Constitution made the validity of royal decrees formally dependent on this. The sovereign's right of command survived as an essential element of late absolutist rule and, consequently, could scarcely be given a defined place in liberal constitutional law. It represented a stubbornly preserved relic of the old feudal order, with the King as the charismatic leader of a warrior host by virtue of his royal blood, to whom the latter was bound by a bond of personal loyalty. Throughout the nineteenth and twentieth centuries this notion persisted in the ideal of the Prussian ruler as a Supreme War-lord, a title which Richter aptly described as a constitutional-cum-mystical concept. This warrior chieftain figure-head stood above a network of institutions, of which three were particularly important: the Military Cabinet, the General Staff and the Ministry of War.*[289]

While military matters were outside the domain of the civilian structures because the Imperial Constitution (in Articles 60 to 62) deferred the size of financial allocations to the military,[290] the *Reichstag* could and did debate military conduct. Although their role in terms of military policy or legislation was limited, the Chancellor and Minister of War were not accountable to the Kaiser only. The *Reichstag* continuously accepted its limited role and often ratified military expenditure after the fact. Thus, the legislature accepted its role and supported the military in most cases, which amounts to condoning its activities. As Smith notes, the culture was such that there was deference to the military on military matters.[291] Yet, deference is a choice, indicating

---

[289] Wehler, H-U. (1985) *The German Empire 1871–1918*. Leamington Spa/Dover, New Hampshire: Berg Publishers, 148–49.
[290] *Ibid*, 146.
[291] Smith, H.W. (1999) 'The logic of colonial violence: Germany in South West Africa (1904–1907), the United States in the Philippines (1899–1902)'. In Lehmann, H. & Wellenreuther, H. (eds) *German and American nationalism: A comparative perspective*. Oxford/New York: Berg, 205–31, 210.

acceptance of the wishes and views of others. The military was ultimately under the control of government and obeyed the orders of the Kaiser. Also, military officers, who acted as his advisors, surrounded the Kaiser.

Despite this ostensibly limited role of the civilian government, the events in GSWA entered debates in the *Reichstag* and elsewhere, as has been noted earlier in this chapter. For the most part, the *Reichstag* supported the activities of the troops in GSWA; only the opposition parties raised objections. Thus the government, and the state as a whole, was responsible for the brutality because it passively condoned the actions and allowed the events to continue. As Naimark has stated, 'Political elites do not act alone in pursuing the goals of ethnic cleansing, however. They are backed up by state and party apparatuses, police forces, militaries and paramilitaries'.[292] Furthermore, in GSWA, it was not the military that wanted the Herero off their land. Nor did the military want German settlers to move onto the land and take over Herero cattle and other herds. The government desired these things. While punishing the Herero provided motivation for what the military did, it was not the only reason for the genocide.

At times, civilian leaders implored the military to take no prisoners and to deal harshly with the indigenous peoples. The Hun speech is a perfect example. Unquestionably, these practices became part of the military culture and certainly the military deserves some blame for the excesses, but this fundamentally ignores the fact that the Kaiser and others actually ordered the acts. As shown, no one ordered the military to stop these practices. The *Reichstag* did nothing to stop the killing of captured prisoners. It took no steps to discipline the actors who were violating state policies. All of this is proof that the incidents were not merely military practice, but were rooted in state practice and ideology. So important was crushing the rebellion that 6000 troops[293] arrived in GSWA by July 1904, of whom 1500 fought at Waterberg.[294] The genocide sought to demonstrate to other European states the power of the military and the 'intolerance of threats to the German nation'.[295] Thus, Palmer asserts,

---

[292] Naimark, N.M. (2001) *Fires of hatred: Ethnic cleansing in the twentieth century Europe*. Cambridge: Harvard University Press, 4.

[293] Altogether 19 000 troops went to GSWA, although only 3 000 fought. Of these 676 were killed and 76 went missing, while 689 died of disease. Hull, I.V. (2005) *Absolute destruction: Military culture and practices of war in Imperial Germany*. Ithaca: Cornell University Press, 88.

[294] *Ibid*, 21 fn 71.

[295] Palmer, A. (1998, January) 'Colonial and modern genocide: Explanations and categories'. *21(1) Ethnic and Racial Studies*, 89–115, 101.

it is possible that the military crushing of the Herero in 1904–1905 had instrumental value to demonstrate to other colonial powers, particularly Britain, that Germany possessed both the power and ability to deal effectively with any threats to its nation and to protect its own interest.[296]

Quelling the rebellion by the Herero and the Nama so completely may also have helped the Kaiser acquire more resources for the military so that it could grow. At the time, the Kaiser 'fumed' that the 'Foreign Office and the Colonial Office had the temerity to propose a reduction of our colonial forces to save money! Instead they must be brought to battalion strength lest we lose all our colonial possessions'.[297]

In spite of the number of troops sent to GSWA by June 1904, before Von Trotha arrived German forces had made little headway against the Herero. Because most of the German troops at the time were naval troops, they were not good marksmen, nor were they good on horseback, while Herero warriors were skilled.[298] The German troops had some successes, including at Otjihinamaparero (25 February 1904), Onganjira (9 April 1904) and Oviumbo (13 April 1904).[299] Critically, the General Staff perceived Leutwein's victory at Oviumbo to be a defeat, because Leutwein made a strategic retreat for a military advantage.[300] According to the General Staff, any retreat was 'unbearable and unthinkable'.[301] Directly thereafter, the Kaiser rode roughshod over objections to the appointment of Von Trotha.[302] As Oviumbo was not the only defeat — German forces also suffered a defeat on 13 March 1904, when the Herero killed 25 soldiers[303]— this must have been the last straw for the Kaiser. He wanted a tough, brutal general to deal once and for all with the Herero. German pride was suffering, especially because those in Germany knew that the Herero were not as well equipped as the Germans and yet, until Von Trotha

---

[296] *Ibid.*
[297] Cocker, M. (1998) *Rivers of blood, rivers of gold: Europe's conflict with tribal peoples.* London: Jonathan Cape, 271.
[298] Hull, I.V. (2005) *Absolute destruction: Military culture and practices of war in Imperial Germany.* Ithaca: Cornell University Press, 21.
[299] *Ibid*, 22.
[300] Hull, I.V. (2003) 'Military culture and the production of final solutions in the colonies: The example of Wilhelminian Germany'. In Gellately, R. & Kiernan, B. (eds) *The specter of genocide mass murder in historical perspective.* Cambridge: Cambridge University Press, 146.
[301] *Ibid.*
[302] Hull, I.V. (2005) *Absolute destruction: Military culture and practices of war in Imperial Germany.* Ithaca: Cornell University Press, 25.
[303] *Ibid*, 21–22.

arrived, they were often able to beat the Germans in battle.[304] As Hull argues, the fact that the 'superior' Germans could not defeat the 'inferior' Africans must have been very humiliating.[305] More prestige was lost when the Herero were able to capture many of the settlers' cattle. The considerable loss of troops and the fact that the Germans were still not able to score many victories even after reinforcements arrived (due to the nature of the terrain, the climate and the Herero guerrilla tactics), all affected German psyche.[306] That the Herero also killed 158 white settlers must have fuelled the need to deal harshly with them and to ensure that they would not be able to repeat such acts. On 4 March 1904, the director of the Colonial Office, Dr Oscar W Stuebel, stated in the *Reichstag*: 'Germany's honour demands the repression of the uprising by all means.'[307]

Not only did the Herero kill many German soldiers but many also died from disease. Altogether about 1 500 soldiers died either at the hands of the Herero or from sickness. From April 1904 to June 1905, alone, 321 German troops died of illness. This increased the urgency to neutralise the Herero quickly and efficiently. When Von Trotha arrived to put down the rebellion, he had relatively few troops. That, along with the fact that the Herero waged their campaign effectively, meant that the Germans had to deal with them in a single battle, with only the resources at Von Trotha's disposal. Without a major success then, the Herero would have been able to regroup, making it very difficult for the German troops who had long supply lines and would have to wait for reinforcements. In fact, in March 1904, three months after the rebellion supposedly began, only 1 567 new troops had arrived and by August there were still only 4 000 German soldiers.[308] The German troops' inability to defeat the Herero and the threat that they might not be able to do so in the future also intensified the pressure to find a new approach. At least one German soldier communicated this to the Kaiser, suggesting in a letter to

---

[304] Stoecker, H. (ed) (1986) *German imperialism in Africa: From the beginnings until the Second World War*. London: C Hurst & Co, 55.

[305] Hull, I.V. (2003) 'Military culture and the production of final solutions in the colonies: The example of Wilhelminian Germany'. In Gellately, R. & Kiernan, B. (eds) *The specter of genocide mass murder in historical perspective*. Cambridge: Cambridge University Press, 146.

[306] Stoecker, H. (ed) (1986) *German imperialism in Africa: From the beginnings until the Second World War*. London: C Hurst & Co, 56.

[307] Hull, I.V. (2003) 'Military culture and the production of final solutions in the colonies: The example of Wilhelminian Germany'. In Gellately, R. & Kiernan, B. (eds) *The specter of genocide mass murder in historical perspective*. Cambridge: Cambridge University Press, 146.

[308] Madley, B. (2004, June) 'Patterns of frontier genocide 1803–1910: The aboriginal Tasmanians, the Yuki of California and the Herero of Namibia'. 6 (2) *Journal of Genocide Research*, 167–192, 185.

him that it was necessary to resort 'to some new stratagem', such as poisoning the water wells. The soldier justified this plan by saying, 'After all, we are not fighting against an enemy respecting the rules of fairness, but savages.'[309] Although the German Criminal Code prohibited the administering of poison in Section 229, the army took up this suggestion.[310]

The desire to achieve a peaceful environment in GSWA, attractive to German settlers, with access to good, arable land and without competition from the indigenous people, also shaped the German response to the rebellion. However, their reaction also stemmed from their wish to punish the Herero while deterring other groups from rising up in the future. The punitive motivation behind the Herero genocide is borne out by the following statement in an official German military report:

> The shutting off of the Sandveld, which was carried on for months with iron firmness, completed the work of destruction... The death rattle of the dying and the shrieks of the maddened people — these echoed through the solemn silence of eternity. The court had now concluded its work of punishment.[311]

Germany intended for this forceful punishment to deter not only other groups in GSWA, such as the Nama, from resisting the colonial enterprises, but also other groups elsewhere in the Empire, such as those in East Africa. The strategy was not particularly successful: even after the Herero killings, indigenous populations in German territories all over Africa rose up, including the Nama, who joined the Herero uprising.

As argued before, those at the highest level knew about and allowed these atrocities to occur, indicating some level of approval. That Von Trotha replaced Leutwein as governor in November 1904, some time after the extermination order surfaced, publicly indicates that those in authority condoned the order. If the military was not happy with Von Trotha, it would either have left the status quo in place or replaced him. Finally, Von Trotha's

---

[309] Drechsler, H. (1980) *Let us die fighting: The struggle of the Herero and Nama against the German imperialism (1894–1915)* (Bernd Zöllner transl) London: Zed Press, 147. Quoted in Madley, B. (2004, June) 'Patterns of frontier genocide 1803–1910: The aboriginal Tasmanians, the Yuki of California and the Herero of Namibia'. 6 (2) *Journal of Genocide Research*, 167–192, 186.

[310] Gage, R.H. & Waters, A.J. (translators) (1917) *Imperial German Criminal Code*. Johannesburg: W.E. Horton & Co.

[311] Madley, B. (2004, June) 'Patterns of frontier genocide 1803–1910: The aboriginal Tasmanians, the Yuki of California and the Herero of Namibia'. 6 (2) *Journal of Genocide Research*, 167–192, 188. This translation differs somewhat from the one previously cited.

appointment, a promotion for him, further demonstrated Germany's support for his style and methods.

Praise and support

Despite his knowledge of the brutality in GSWA, Kaiser Wilhelm II 'seemed reluctant to depart from Von Trotha's policy of extermination'.[312] This reluctance demonstrates, at the minimum, his support for the policy, but might also indicate that he initiated the order. As noted above, he did, some days later, order an amendment to the policy, by raising the price on the heads of the Herero *kapteins* and asking that mercy be shown to those Herero willing to surrender.[313] Yet this only happened after the Chancellor explicitly urged the Kaiser to consider saving the lives of the Herero, which the Kaiser only conceded to eight days later.[314] For some years, however, many violations of international law continued.

There is debate about whether pressure on the German government (in part by the Social Democratic Party)[315] caused it to recall Von Trotha or if he asked to be relieved of his command. The Kaiser, the Colonial Office and the military evidently supported his methods and would not have recalled him without adequate pressure. Officials in the Colonial Office saw Von Trotha's 1904 extermination policy as a 'sensible solution' and they filed reports of misconduct without recourse.[316] Even when the information leaked, the primary concern was not the information itself, but who had released it. The treatment of the Herero and other groups in the concentration camps and the mortality figures of those in captivity provide further evidence of the Kaiser et al's support of these policies. A German missionary noted that in 1905 the conditions under which the Germans kept the Herero resulted in more than 30 deaths each day.[317] The missionary referred to an article by Von Trotha in the *Swakopmunder Zeitung* in which he wrote about the treatment of Herero prisoners.

---

[312] Drechsler, H. (1986) *Let us die fighting*. Berlin: Akademie-Verlag, 164.
[313] Ibid.
[314] Ibid.
[315] Stoecker, H. & Sebald, P. (1987) 'Enemies of the colonial idea'. In Knoll, A.J. & Gann, L.H. (eds) *Germans in the tropics: Essays in German colonial history* (2ed). New York/London: Greenwood Press, 59–72, 64.
[316] Bridgman, J. & Worley, L.J. (1997) 'Genocide of the Herero'. In Totten, S., Parsons, W. & Charney, I. (eds) *Century of genocide*. New York: Garland 3–40, 21.
[317] Goldblatt, I. (1971) *History of South West Africa, from the beginning of the nineteenth century*. Cape Town: Juta, 146.

Herero prisoners in chains

Von Trotha acknowledged that 'the destruction of the all rebellious Native tribes is the aim of our efforts'.[318] Even after the Kaiser rescinded the extermination order at the end of 1904, efforts to decimate the Herero continued. As noted before, the lifting of the order did not effect much change and the cordon forcing the Herero into the desert remained until the middle of 1905.[319]

That Von Trotha publicly wrote about his intent in the local newspaper hardly shows any diffidence about these efforts. The same obvious intent to exterminate is present even in 1905. In fact, the Kaiser adhered to a policy of extermination and taking no prisoners until 1907, when, to deal with the rebelling Nama, he ordered that 'a price of 20 000 Marks [be put] on Morenga's head and to wipe out the whole bunch without mercy'.[320] These orders hardly suggest passivity! In addition, the manner in which German forces pursued and killed Jakob Morenga and the rewards and medals the

---

[318] Quoted in Goldblatt, I. (1971) *History of South West Africa, from the beginning of the nineteenth century.* Cape Town: Juta, 146.
[319] Stoecker, H. (ed) (1986) *German imperialism in Africa: From the beginnings until the Second World War.* London: C Hurst & Co, 58.
[320] Drechsler, H. (1986) *Let us die fighting.* Berlin: Akademie-Verlag, 201.

military gave to those responsible shows the zeal of the Germans to deal severely with Morenga and the Bondelswartz. This ardour is probably because the Bondelswartz dared to rebel again; Leutwein was in fact addressing this rebellion when the Herero rebelled in January 1904. This time around, the Germans likely wanted to ensure that the locals learned their lesson and that others contemplating insubordination were deterred.

The period from 1890 to 1906 contained several colonial scandals.[321] A number of senior officials, such as Karl Peters in East Africa; Governor Leist, Judge Wehlan and Governor von Puttkamer in Cameroon; and Governor von Horn in Togo were convicted and dismissed for cruelty and maladministration. At the same time, Germany allowed Von Trotha to continue with his campaign.[322] According to Epstein, when *Reichstag* deputy Matthias Erzberger's continual attack on the events in the colonies eventually caused the dissolution of the *Reichstag* in 1907, all those involved were vehemently criticised. Despite Erzberger's criticism of the way the populations in the colonies had been treated and his general opposition to what Von Trotha had done, he 'diverged from his general line to defend Trotha personally'.[323]

After Von Trotha's return to Germany, the Imperial Chancellor in the *Reichstag* vigorously defended him on 8 December 1905.[324] So appreciative of Von Trotha was the German state that it awarded him Germany's highest decoration, the *Pour Le Mérite*.[325] When the Kaiser gave this decoration to Von Trotha, he sent a telegram that was read out in the *Reichstag*. It stated:

I gladly express to you that you have to the fullest extent justified my faith in your knowledge and military experience, which moved me to appoint you as the

---

[321] Epstein notes that 'Erzberger became aroused by the inefficiency of Germany's colonial system, the brutality of incompetent colonial administrators, the privileges granted to colonial companies, the extermination of native populations and the arrogance shown by the officials of the Berlin colonial department towards the constitutional rights to the *Reichstag*...it must be noted that each of his criticisms was combined with constructive proposals for ending the evils that he denounced: lack of system, brutality and incompetence of officials, privileged commercial companies and an un-Christian attitude to native peoples'. Epstein, K. (1959, October) 'Erzberger and the German colonial scandals, 1905–1910'. 74(293) *English Historical Review*, 637–63, 639.

[322] Bullock, A.L.C. (1939) *German's colonial demands*. London: Oxford University Press, 91.

[323] Epstein, K. (1959, October). 'Erzberger and the German colonial scandals, 1905–1910'. 74(293) *English Historical Review*, 637–63, 648.

[324] Lewin, E. (1915) *The Germans and Africa. Their aims on the dark continent and how they acquired their African colonies.* London: Cassell, 121.

[325] Du Preez, P. (1994) *Genocide the psychology of mass murder.* London: Boyars/Bowerdean, 20; Bley, H. (1971) *South West Africa under German rule 1894–1914*. London: Heinemann, 165.

commander of the Schutztruppe in South West Africa in difficult times. I wish to express my Imperial gratitude and my warm acknowledgement of your excellent accomplishment by conferring on you the award, Pour le Mérite....[326]

This telegram attests that Von Trotha acted in accordance with the Kaiser's orders. Von Trotha also received four other 'prestigious medals from other German states and a full pension'.[327] That the cabinet itself discussed Von Trotha's pension again reflects the involvement, oversight and responsibility of the German government for the military.

According to Drechsler, Von Trotha's decorations and the Chancellor's public praise of him were attempts to hide the failure of his campaign.[328] However, that is highly unlikely. Such public praise and the number medals awarded to him reflects the support for his work. The Kaiser made extensive statements about the positive role played by those involved. In a speech in the *Reichstag* on 28 November 1905, he stated:

The development of our protectorates has suffered considerably due to the revolt in Southwest Africa and the East African rebellions; the fatherland had to pay a high price in form of monetary costs and in the sacrifice of human blood. I know that I express the sentiment of the nation when I heartily thank officers and men who answered my call and heroically defended our possession, risking their own lives. Their great sacrifices have not been in vain. Recent dispatches regarding the submission of the Witbooi give us reason to hope that law and order soon will be restored in the protectorate which has undergone such a trial.[329]

On 19 March 1907 the Kaiser also authorised and awarded medals in two classes for service rendered in the South West campaign.[330] Even those involved

---

[326] Ritter-Petersen, H.G. (1991) *The Herrenvolk mentality in German South West Africa 1884–1914*. DLitt (History). Pretoria: University of South Africa, 211.
[327] Hull, I.V. (2005) *Absolute destruction: Military culture and practices of war in Imperial Germany*. Ithaca: Cornell University Press, 69.
[328] Drechsler, H. (1986) *Let us die fighting*. Berlin: Akademie-Verlag, 223 fn 73.
[329] Speech held by Kaiser Wilhelm II on the Occasion of the Opening of a Legislative Period in the *Reichstag*, 28 November 1905. In Penzler, J. (ed) *Die Reden Kaiser Wilhelms II*. Vol. 3: 1901–1905. Leipzig, 289. Available at: http://www.zum.de/psm/imperialismus/wilhelm1905.php
[330] For an event which has been described as 'over-kill...the manner of the killing must certainly have satisfied Kaiser Wilhelm's primitive instincts to wipe out the whole bunch without mercy'. One hundred and five German South West Africa Commemoration medals were awarded to the British Cape Mounted Police, who were accompanied by a German officer, for their role in the killing and capture of a group of Nama, including Jacob Marengo, on 20 September 1907, some 85 kilometres in the then Cape Colony. The British commanding officer, Major Elliott, was awarded the DSO and the Royal Prussian Order of the Crown, Second Class and the German government awarded 90 clasps that were endorsed

in the extermination atrocities of 1904 and other conflicts received awards and recognition.[331] Combatants and those who tended the sick and wounded received a bronze version and those individuals who assisted in moving the troops and supplies, including the crews of German shipping companies chartered to ferry troops and supplies, received a steel version.[332] That the Kaiser personally designed the medals, that they were bestowed three years after the campaign began and that they included services rendered during the specific extermination period point to obvious support for the campaign, not to any attempt to hide a failure. These factors, especially his involvement in the design of the medals, indicate the Kaiser's affinity for the campaign. The Chief-die-sinker at the Royal Prussian Mint in Berlin, Otto Schultz,[333] cut the dies, which further underscores the official nature and importance placed on these medals. A certificate accompanying the bronze medals read, 'By order of His Majesty the King and Emperor, this commemorative medal in bronze given by the same all highest — is awarded to...in recognition of his

---

'Kalahari 1907'. Masson, J.R. (1995, June) 'A fragment of colonial history: The killing of Jakob Marengo'. 21(2) *Journal of South African Studies*, 247–256. See also Alexander, N.E. (1981, June). 'Jakob Marengo and Namibian History'. 7(1) *Social Dynamics*, 1–8.

It must be noted that at least 200 battles took place between the Nama and the Germans, of which at least 30 were with Marengo. Masson, J. (2001) *Jakob Marengo: An early resistance hero of Namibia*. Windhoek: Out of Africa, 17.

[331] Sixteen additional bars were added to the medals awarded for the specific campaigns during which gross atrocities were committed. The first six were for:
1. Herero-land: 17 January 1904–15 August 1906;
2. Omaruru: 17 January 1904–12 May 1905;
3. Onganjira: 9 April 1904;
4. Waterberg: 24 May 1904–15 August 1906;
5. Omaheke: September 1904 — June 1905;
6. Gross-Namaland: 27 October 1904–25 May 1906; 18 December–26 December 1908.

How many medals or how many people were awarded bars is unknown as these records were destroyed during the World War II bombing. Sole, T.E. (1968, December) 'The Südwestafrika Denkmunze and the South West African campaigns of 1903–1908'. 1(3) *Military History Journal*, 19–23.

The issue of medals was controversial, as many German soldiers and officials perceived them to have been handed out in an unfair manner. The medals handed out for the killings of Jacob Marengo was seen to be given to those who had only devoted a few hours to his capture, while those who had been involved in trying to apprehend him for years were overlooked. Calvert, A.F. (1915). *South West Africa: During the German Occupation 1884–1914*. London: London: T. Werner Laurie, 32.

[332] Sole, T.E. (1968, December) 'The Südwestafrika Denkmunze and the South West African campaigns of 1903–1908'. 1(3) *Military History Journal*, 19–23.

[333] *Ibid.*

faithful participation in the campaign against the rebellious natives in South West Africa'.[334] The government gave as many as 16 bars with the bronze medal for specifically named campaigns, even some of the most problematic campaigns where genocide and other atrocities had occurred. That it publicly endorsed these specific events and campaigns indicates the State's support of these actions. Again, the Kaiser's public personal and endorsement of the medal supports the evidence of his link to Von Trotha's campaign.

As noted above, Von Trotha even declared his specific designs on the Herero in a newspaper article. The silence of the German authorities in response was tantamount to approval.[335] While the genocide order from the German government may well not have been explicit, it was implicit in the instructions Von Trotha received: that he was to put down the rebellion by any means 'fair or foul'. Hence, Von Trotha's policy may well have been a calculated official instruction that the government simply decided not to publicly issue or endorse.

Even a German government report drawn up in 1908 did not rebuke Von Trotha for his conduct in the war. Although the interim report included a section entitled 'Conduct of the war', that section was absent in the final report.[336] It did not refer to *Vernichtungspolitik*.[337] The Kaiser's directive to amend the extermination order was the only countermanding of the orders extolling the use of brutality and ruthlessness by the military toward those in GSWA. Even then, Germany did not retract the order immediately or willingly. When it was withdrawn, it was not because of the brutality employed, but because the Kaiser was under pressure to do so. This pressure was the result of several factors, including that it was impractical to assume Germany could kill all the Herero as they needed the population's labour and the brutality was negatively affecting Germany's reputation. Thus, the conduct was clearly both military and state practice. Whatever military culture existed did not evolve in isolation; it developed in the context of a state that accepted and sanctioned such practices, a state that explicitly or implicitly expected such conduct.

---

[334] *Ibid.*
[335] According to Bantekas states usually take four different types of acts towards troops who commit offences: no action, administrative action, non-judicial punishment and court martial. Bantekas, I. (2003) *Principles of direct and superior responsibility in international humanitarian law*. Manchester: Manchester University Press, 115. That none was taken against Von Trotha and that he was in fact rewarded, is revealing.
[336] Hull, I.V. (2005) *Absolute destruction: Military culture and practices of war in Imperial Germany*. Ithaca: Cornell University Press, 195.
[337] *Ibid.*

Crucially, the Kaiser continued to oversee events in GSWA even after 1904. On 1 December 1905, when Lindequist, the new governor, announced the cancellation of any concessions for the Witbooi, he was acting in line with orders from the Kaiser.[338] Thus, at that point the Kaiser was still directing the campaign in GSWA. It is therefore plausible that he had been doing so in 1904 when General von Trotha was in command. The Kaiser invested himself so much in GSWA that when opposition to additional budgetary allocations for the colony increased in the *Reichstag*, Chancellor Von Bülow read a prepared letter from the Kaiser that dissolved parliament.[339] Such an extreme measure underscored the significance the Kaiser and Bülow accorded to GSWA.

Conclusion

The Kaiser's role in the Herero genocide would appear to have been far more significant than existing literature has acknowledged. It is important to contextualise his role in the events in terms of the German politics at the time, which incorporated the need for *lebensraum*, the quest for an African colony where German emigrants could settle, where land was plentiful, cheap and arable. GSWA met these goals. These factors, combined with the Kaiser's appetite for exacting revenge, shaped his specific involvement in the genocide. His appetite for revenge was addressed above; it was lucidly demonstrated following the murder of German envoy Clemens von Ketteler in China. Annika Mombauer remarked 'it is not surprising in the light of what is known of Wilhelm II's character that his reaction to these events was one of outrage and indignation and that he was spoiling for a fight. His initial response was characteristically out of proportion. Bernhard von Bülow, then Foreign Secretary, later recorded in his memoirs that he had "never seen Kaiser Wilhelm...in such excitement as during the first phase of the Chinese confusion".'[340]

On another occasion, the Kaiser sent the German fleet to China to avenge the murder of two Catholic missionaries in Shandong (although, some have argued that the Kaiser intended to acquire Kiaochow before the deaths of

---

[338] Drechsler, H. (1980) *Let us die fighting: The struggle of the Herero and Nama against the German imperialism (1894–1915)*. (Bernd Zöllner transl). London: Zed Press, 191.

[339] Erichsen, C.W. (2004) *The Angel of Death has descended violently among them: A study of Namibia's concentration camps and prisoners-of-war, 1904–08*. MA thesis (History). Windhoek: University of Namibia, 252.

[340] Mombauer, A. (2003) 'Wilhelm Waldersee and the Boxer Rebellion'. In Mombauer, A. & Deist, W. (eds) *The Kaiser: New Research on Wilhelm II's role in Imperial Germany*. Cambridge: Cambridge University Press, 91–118, 94–95.

the missionaries).[341] Consequently, his need to restore Germany's wounded reputation when its troops failed to defeat the Herero in combat prior to mid-1904 and his desire to avenge the deaths of the German settlers must have motivated his exceedingly ruthless approach in dealing with the Herero.

The fact that no specific proof of the Kaiser's role has emerged is most likely due to the common practice of editing his frequently embarrassing and problematic speeches and correspondence. Von Trotha's diary might have contained evidence of a specific order, but, as discussed, the original version inexplicably disappeared. Thus, it is unclear whether the Kaiser explicitly ordered genocide, but the evidence outlined here suggest it is likely he did, even if he expressed this wish in the vague terms Von Trotha used when he reported what the Kaiser had told him to do.

While Hull and others believe that the 'final solution' in GSWA developed from Germany's military culture,[342] there is sufficient evidence to question this. One must question why the military supplanted civilian control in the colony. In other colonies where rebellions occurred, Germany did not replace the Governor's rule with military control. Why did it do so in GSWA? It must have been because the Kaiser planned to implement a new/different policy soon thereafter and, for this plan to succeed, the military had to have more control, specifically under the leadership of Von Trotha — a man with a reputation for being merciless.

In the nineteenth century, after the departure of Chancellor Bismarck, significant constitutional power lay in the hands of the Chancellor. The new Kaiser, Wilhelm II, changed this without opposition from the German state and the *Reichstag*. Thus, the state and *Reichstag* permitted the changes and allowed the Kaiser to play a greater role than before. When the war occurred in GSWA, the *Reichstag* — despite knowing what was happening — did little to rein in the activities of their troops stationed there. This, therefore, establishes its responsibility for what took place.

The current perception amongst the Herero is that the order did not emanate from Von Trotha, but that the genocide was authorised at the highest levels of the German government. Various statements by Herero leaders demonstrate this belief. Paramount Chief Riruako gave one such speech at a press conference on 19 August 2004. He stated that the atrocities 'resulted in the decimation of

---

[341] Blue, G. (1999) 'Gobineau on China; Race theory, the "Yellow Peril" and the critique of modernity'. 10(1) *Journal of World History*, 93–139, fn 106.

[342] Hull, I.V. (2003) 'Military culture and the production of final solutions in the colonies: The example of Wilhelminian Germany'. In Gellately, R. & Kiernan, B. (eds) *The specter of genocide mass murder in historical perspective.* Cambridge: Cambridge University Press, 145.

our population, their disenfranchisement and the dissolution of our wealth, in land, material and livestock, ruthlessly executed by the German Colonial forces under direct instruction from the German Government of that time.'[343] The Herero clearly blame the German government. In 2004, when the Paramount Chief of the Herero challenged the adequacy of a mere apology, he stated: 'Today, Germany is the heir to the spoils of this ill-conceived expansionist campaign, executed by the Government of Kaiser Wilhelm II...[thus a] Marshall plan and program should be presented to the Herero people.'[344]

---

[343] Paramount Chief Riruako, responding to the official apology of the Federal Republic of Germany given on August 14.
[344] *Ibid.*

Conclusion

Introduction

It is nearly unanimously agreed today that between 1904 and 1907 to 1908 Germany conducted genocide, as legally defined, of the Herero of then German South West Africa (GSWA), today Namibia. The Herero genocide is unique in that the order to annihilate the Herero was publicly proclaimed and specifically made known to the target group in their own language. The official proclamation initially sought the extermination specifically of the Herero. However, other groups, especially the Nama, were later targeted because of their rich land holdings and their intransigence against the Germans. The severe treatment meted out to the Nama and the major reduction in their population numbers may also fit the definition of genocide.

German settlers in the territory who wanted the land and cattle of the indigenous Herero and the public in Germany, incited by propaganda that the Herero were conducting a race war, bayed for Herero blood.

Propaganda postcard of Herero revolt

German troops, many of whom had previously exercised brutal treatment on indigenous populations in different parts of the world, killed men, women and children without distinction. Many other atrocities were committed, including the rape of Herero women. These events initially occurred under the command of General Adrian Dietrich Lothar von Trotha, most likely at the instruction of Kaiser Wilhelm II — both had a history of ordering and conducting brutal extermination-type practices. Von Trotha embarked on a planned, announced, systematic and indiscriminate extermination of the Herero community.

The order to wipe out the Herero community became the first genocide of the twentieth century.[1] Between 60 000 and 100 000 people; almost all civilians and non-combatants, many of them women and children, were executed by German troops in various ways or were forced into the desert to die of starvation and thirst or by drinking water at water wells poisoned by German troops. Maybe 20 000 of the original Herero population of about 100 000 were left in the end. The extermination order (*Vernichtungsbefehl*) was issued on 2 October 1904. Due to pressure on him, Kaiser Wilhelm reluctantly and after a long delay rescinded the order in December 1904. But the genocide not only took place in those few months from October 1904 to December 1904, when the official extermination order was operative. A policy of taking no Herero prisoners was in force before the official order was proclaimed and the genocide began at least as early as August 1904. Furthermore, the eradication of the Herero continued after the genocide order was lifted.

Initially, the genocide of the Herero was achieved by means of German bullets and clubs, by hanging, by burning the huts where they lived or by forcing them into the desert to die.[2] When the order was amended, the extermination continued in a less overt manner. A few thousand Herero were captured and placed in concentration camps, where thousands died due to ill treatment, disease and starvation. Different and smaller diet rations were given to Herero prisoners than to prisoners from other communities. In addition, they were used as slave labour for both public and private enterprise. Some of the concentration camps were run by the colonial authorities, whereas others

---

[1] Zimmerman has called the events in GSWA 'perhaps the first explicitly genocidal policy ever'. Zimmerman, A. (2003) 'Adventures in the skin trade: German anthropology and colonial corporeality'. In Penny, H.G. & Bunzl, M. (eds) *Worldly provincialism: German anthropology in the Age of Empire*. Ann Arbour: University of Michigan Press, 157.

[2] Fraenkel, P. & Murry, R. (1985) *The Namibian Report, No 19*. London: Minority Rights Group International, 6.

were run by private companies, such as Woermann shipping lines and Arthur Koppel Company (companies now being sued by the Herero).[3] The latter ran their own concentration camps and paid a rental fee to the German authorities for the right to use Herero slave labour in their own enterprise.

Thus Germany's genocide against the Herero ranks among the most egregious human right catastrophes of the twentieth century. Remarkably, despite the advancements in international criminal, humanitarian and human rights law, it also remains one of the least understood, acknowledged or redressed. This book has outlined the major events in Germany and then-GSWA in the early 1900s in an attempt to shed light on the genocide as an intentional campaign by the German state to exterminate the Herero. Evidence presented here indicates that Germany's extermination of the Herero embodied a concerted effort to claim the tribe's territory as a means to expand the German colonial empire.

In the course of this examination, the following themes have emerged:

- the Herero genocide was motivated by German colonial policy at the time;
- the unique importance that GSWA held for Germany at the turn of the twentieth century fuelled the genocide;
- the Herero genocide was undertaken in response not only to domestic policy pressures but international ones as well;
- the two goals of the Herero genocide were land acquisition and German pride, though racism ran as a strong undercurrent throughout the campaign;
- the Herero genocide was an explicit state action ordered by the Kaiser; and
- the Herero genocide served as a training exercise — perhaps unconsciously — for the Holocaust.

German colonial policies

While Germany's actions against the Herero were certainly unmatched in scale and brutality by their actions elsewhere in the world, they were not completely out of character. On the contrary, German officials at home and abroad were notoriously ruthless in their subjugation of colonial subjects.

---

3   Woermann lines was involved even earlier: in early 1904, Herero working in Swakopmund were interned on two Woermann line ships anchored off the coast of the town for use as labour. See Erichsen, C.W. (2004) *The Angel of Death has descended violently among them: A study of Namibia's concentration camps and prisoners-of-war, 1904–08*. MA thesis (History). University of Namibia, ch 2, 57. Arthur Koppel Company was involved in railway construction and used Herero slave labour for that purpose. (This will be dealt with further when the Herero court cases are examined.)

Admittedly, the same state of affairs held true for other European colonies in Africa. Germany was hardly alone in subjugating indigenous peoples throughout its colonies or brutally quelling rebellion. As mentioned in Chapter Two, the British brutalised the people of present-day Kenya. Neither was Germany's abuse confined to GSWA or the Herero alone. German colonial administrators conducted a murderous campaign against modern-day Tanzanians around the same time as the Herero genocide and routinely employed corporal punishment against the indigenous people of Cameroon and East Africa. Within GSWA, colonial administrators had previously abused non-Herero peoples, most notably the Nama.

However, the Herero's possession of valuable land and cattle, in addition to their unrelenting resistance to German domination, marked them specifically for extinction by their colonial oppressors. Germany's prolonged subjugation of the tribe is evidence of its disgust with the Herero's resistance. Even after the cessation of active hostilities between the Herero and GSWA settlers in 1907, Germany maintained a ban on Herero ownership of cattle, replaced traditional leaders with colonial administrators and indirectly compelled the Herero to join the formal labour market. All of this occurred despite General von Trotha's departure from GSWA and the arrival of a new governor, Von Lindequist. The persistence of murder, dispossession and oppression even after these fundamental personnel changes in the territory indicates that the lingering intent to quash entirely what little remained of Herero identity — ostensibly to prevent further rebellion and cement Germany's domination of the territory — represented more than a few personalities in GSWA; it extended to Berlin.

In addition to murdering, raping and enslaving the Herero, German colonial officials responded to Herero insolence by creating reserves to accommodate the tribe once settlers had acquired their land. The Rhenish missionaries, who disapproved, leaked this plan to the Herero. The reservist strategy provided yet another impetus for the Herero to revolt in 1904. Indeed, as shown in Chapter One, disagreement between the Herero and GSWA administrators over the reserves' borders preceded the revolt.

While, prior to 1904, German forces targeted the Herero with corporal punishment and sexual violence, it was not until the issuance of Von Trotha's extermination order, or *vernichtungsbefehl*, that their subjugation became systematised and unprecedented in intensity. As recounted in Chapter Two, the proclamation did not mince words about German intent to end Herero existence in GSWA: they were to be shot on sight. In practice, the Germans even exterminated women and children. As argued in Chapter Two, persistent refutation of the order's existence only fuels German denialist claims;

claims that are less plausible given the discovery of the Blue Book, a British documentation of the genocide. This study confirms Germany's intent to annihilate the Herero completely through starvation, dislocated and outright murder.

In these respects, the experience of the Herero — while consistent with European and German colonial policy at the time — is among the most devastating endured by an indigenous people in Africa at the turn of the twentieth century.

German South West Africa's unique status among Germany's colonies

As this book has shown, GSWA was more than a distant acquisition to the German state. Rather, Germany considered it a second Fatherland, an emigration destination for German settlers in search of more farmland and a *tabula rasa* upon which to impose German culture. This single-minded focus — among German colonial administrators and the German people at home and abroad — accounts for Germany's ruthless grip on the territory, regardless of the costs.

As Chapter One illustrated, Berlin's investment in the territory, as well as that of German corporations at the time, demonstrate GSWA's vaulted status within Germany. As early as 1898, German capital dominated the GSWA economy, necessitating the protection of the German government. Germany responded to the call by investing 278 million marks in GSWA between 1884 and 1914, more than its expenditures in Cameroon, Togo and German East Africa combined. The years preceding and following the Herero rebellion witnessed the most intense spending.

In addition, Germany deployed a disproportionate amount of troops to GSWA in comparison to its other colonies. Moreover, African conscripts were not permitted to serve in GSWA, unlike in Germany's other colonies, because of the sensitivity of the settler population. Also, military forces were not the only people recruited to live in GSWA: from 1878, German colonial planners actively recruited German women to relocate to the province as an incentive to draw German men, but, more importantly, to end the proliferation of interracial relationships that had begun from the moment the first Germans' arrived. Relations between German settlers and local women threatened, through the creation of a mixed race, to dilute the Reich's authority in the colony and the very 'Germanness' of the new state. Germany promptly passed edicts outlawing interracial marriages.

It was Governor Leutwein's and the Herero's resistance to Germany's plan to create a German state in Southern Africa that ignited the desire for outright extermination of the tribe. Correspondence from the settlers to Berlin in the years leading up to the genocide indicated the emigrants' increasing fatigue with the Governor' lax policies toward the Herero, including restrictions on the acquisition of Herero land. The settlers saw such policies as a direct threat to their economic and cultural livelihoods in this 'new Germany' and threatened to take matters into their own hands should Berlin remain idle.

German and international politics at the turn of the twentieth century

The political landscape in the international arena, as well as in the German state, also drove Germany's aggressive behaviour in its colonies. In the early 1900s, colonies were a means by which Western states achieved stature on the international stage. This fuelled Germany's race to acquire and retain as much land as possible outside of Europe. Germany built its colonies upon two distinct models: those for trade and those for settlement. As illustrated in this book, GSWA fell into the latter category and thus merited the harsh rule that Germany imposed upon indigenous people who threatened its aims. However, Germany's barbaric treatment of its settlement holdings led to it being the first state to lose its possessions after World War I.

Moreover, Germany was not in the same league as other Western powers, such as Great Britain and France, when it came to the race to colonise the New World. As a result of Germany's late entry into the colonial race, it engaged in particularly brutal methods to acquire sufficient territory — in size and prestige — in order to place it on par with its European brethren. This inferiority complex is partly to blame for Germany's atrocious treatment of its colonies, as it sought to acquire trade routes, emigration space and new cultural outposts. Thus, when the Herero dared to rise up against German oppression in 1904, colonial soldiers, administrators and settlers responded swiftly and brutally, calling for their outright extermination in the wake of the slaughter of less than 200 settlers. This disproportionate response was due in part to Germany's desire for land, cattle and security, but it was also about avenging Germany's honour on the international stage. The difficulty that Germans faced in quelling Herero discontent created further embarrassment for the country at a time when national prestige was measured in part by colonial conquest. A decisive victory over and strong message to the Herero was thus essential as a matter of German pride and stature.

Thus GSWA was not just any colony. Germany hoped it would become a 'new Germany', a place that could accommodate the thousands of émigrés that Germany had been losing to the United States and other countries because the Fatherland's territory and markets had become too small for its booming population. However, to entice Germans to move to Southern Africa as early as 1882, the country's leadership had to promise them land, security and the opportunity to live as Germans lived in a place distant from Europe. Media reports and correspondence that characterised GSWA as Germany's last hope for settlement, highlighted in chapter one, created a greater need for these policies. To the extent that the Herero interfered with Germany's pursuit of its goal for a new cultural outpost in Africa — through resistance or sovereignty over valuable land, German forces and settlers felt they had to extinguish these people.

The aims of the Herero genocide

As this book has shown, the authoritarian nature of the German state did not drive Germany's genocide against the Herero. While it is true that, at the time, Germany fostered a militarised culture that facilitated the execution of the genocide, historical events indicate that this culture was not the driving force behind the state's policy to exterminate the Herero. Rather, the 1904 genocide bore the twin aims — one philosophical and one practical — of preserving German pride and acquiring land from the Herero. As indicated above, the genocide had the philosophical goal of raising Germany's profile within its own state and Europe. The violent means by which German authorities snuffed out the Herero rebellion not only intended to demonstrate its force to the Herero, but to other nations and the German people themselves. The military response was yet another method by which Germany could demonstrate its unwillingness to yield colonial ground — politically or territorially.

Evidence presented in chapter one of General von Trotha's statements reveals that he consciously viewed Herero massacres as a means by which to crush the tribe. While public executions of Herero had begun well before 1904, the genocide order systematised the practice and clearly linked it to Germany's land and power grab in the colony. The General's outrage at Herero resistance further inspired him to teach the rebellious tribe a lesson and secure Germany's authority as a colonial power in the eyes of its European neighbours.

Secondly, as Germany's targeting of the Herero made clear, the extermination, expulsion and enslavement of the tribe was a practical attempt to acquire land to appease the demands of the growing German settler population in GSWA. In an otherwise inhospitable terrain plagued by drought and mountains, the Herero nation possessed much of what little arable land was available in GSWA at the time. Moreover, as evidenced in chapter one, limited land allocation by the German government to former soldiers did not satisfy settlers' demands. The clamouring of German settlers — who, beginning in 1903, were lured to GSWA with the promise of land and opportunity — for Herero land, at any cost fuelled the colonial and national administrations' violent anti-Herero campaigns.

As illustrated in Chapter One, the Herero were singled out for extermination by Germany because they inhabited the lion's share of arable land — to say nothing of cattle — from among Namibia's many ethnic groups. However, German officials did not resort to violence immediately. They began with campaigns of trickery or deceit. For example, they changed the unit of measure agreed up with their Herero trading partners or plied Herero chiefs with alcohol to secure land transfers. However, the Germans failed to grasp the indigenous concept of land tenure, which revolved around collective usufruct rather than individual title. Thus, despite the contracts that Germans thought they had concluded with the Herero, the tribe never seriously entertained the idea that it had completely surrendered its sovereign territorial rights to the settlers. As a result, Germany employed more forceful means of land acquisition, such as military and bureaucratic control, followed by outright force between 1894 and 1915.

Unfortunately, nature intervened in the Herero's quest to retain their land and between 1896 and 1899 the tribe was beset with an ecological blow that compelled it to cede some of its land rights. A rinderpest epidemic decimated much of the Herero's livestock, while having less impact upon the settlers' inoculated stocks. With the Herero in a weak economic position, German settlers instituted several legislative ploys to divest the tribe of its remaining assets. The colonists enacted draconian trespass and credit laws that the Herero could only repay in cattle for lack of currency. Not only did this dispossession leave the Herero economically depressed, but the absence of meat and milk compromised their diet and the loss of stock injured their sense of ethnic pride given that cattle were integral to Herero culture. As a result of these handicaps, the Herero were forced into the labour market and remained justifiably bitter against the Germans.

Thus, it was little surprise when the Herero rose up against the settlers in GSWA in 1904. Contrary to the wisdom of the time, the rebellion did not take Germany by surprise. Indeed, it had arguably designed the policies presaging the conflict to provoke precisely such a response. As a result, the revolt presented the Kaiser with the opportunity — in the guise of admittedly brutal, though smaller-scale massacres of settlers by Herero rebels — to unveil his new settlement policy, which required the commission of genocide. The speed with which the Germans disposed the Herero — in less than a year — indicates that Germany had planned this policy extensively. It was not simply a response to a surprise Herero attack.

A third latent motivation behind the Herero genocide was Germany's racist ideology that placed the Aryan race above all others, a belief that would reappear decades later as a motivation behind the Holocaust. German propaganda at the time cast the Herero as an inferior race and at the same time characterised the tribe as launching a racist offensive against settlers via mutilation and indiscriminate murder. This dualistic public relations campaign enabled the German state to muster support at home for its suppression of any Herero autonomy in GSWA. While evidence suggests that the previously mentioned practical and philosophical concerns motivated the genocide, Germany's racist ideology certainly facilitated the execution of the order.

This ideology can be found in several of Von Trotha's statements, as recounted in chapter two, evincing his hatred for the Herero people and his belief that they 'only respond' (ie vacate their land) to brute force. Such statements serve as further evidence that Germany's actions at the turn of the twentieth century did not merely aim to quell a spontaneous indigenous insurgency but rather represented a premeditated, intentional extermination of the entire Herero tribe in the names of nationalism, land and racism. Not even the isolated incidents of German humanity toward the Herero can blunt the historical record — in the form of newspaper accounts and government statements at the time — evidencing genocide. Even Germany's Western counterparts — the very nations to whom Germany sought to demonstrate its strength — expressed their disapproval of the events unfolding in GSWA in 1905.

German state action

This book has argued that, contrary to conventional wisdom, the Herero genocide was not the by-product of a rogue German general whose behaviour his Berlin superiors left unchecked in GSWA. On the contrary, in waging a campaign of murder, dispossession and enslavement against the Herero, Von Trotha was carrying out the express orders of the Kaiser himself. This is a clarification of great import as the Kaiser's control over the genocide order would result in the responsibility of the German state for the Herero genocide and forms the basis for criminal liability and reparations from Germany to the Herero.

Evidence presented in chapter two — including Von Trotha's statements of obedience to the Kaiser — demonstrates that the spirit of the extermination order originated in Berlin and was not the diabolical rampage of a single deluded officer in the field. Furthermore, on a purely circumstantial basis, the Kaiser's aggressive rhetoric against the Chinese during the Boxer Rebellion, as well as that pertaining to the Herero in general, illustrates that the genocide order was in keeping with the Kaiser's character. History has shown the Kaiser to be anything other than a magnanimous keeper of the colonies. On the contrary, he viewed Germany's territories as subhuman and beyond the scope of any legal protection. Accordingly, he subjected peoples under German colonial control to brutal treatment; the Herero were his — and by extension, the German state's — greatest victims by the end of 1905.

In addition, chapter three presented, in great detail, evidence that the genocide order originated with the Kaiser and that he expressed it orally to Von Trotha. Admittedly, there is no 'smoking gun' in the form of a written order from the leader to his general. However, this book presents an analysis of the Kaiser's personality, leadership ethos, military background and pattern of brutality in GSWA and beyond that paints a picture of a man capable of, and indeed likely to have ordered, the annihilation of a tribe who stood in the way of his colonial vision and national pride. Moreover, an examination of the Kaiser's conduct at the turn of the twentieth century, including the appointment of Von Trotha after the extermination policy had been announced — a man the Kaiser knew had a violent background in Germany's other African colonies — reveals that the Kaiser carefully orchestrated the Herero genocide in the years preceding the tribe's rebellion.

Even Von Trotha's own denials do not negate the probability that he received his extermination orders from the Kaiser. First, at a minimum, the volatile Von Trotha admitted to having free reign to quell the Herero rebellion by any means necessary. Second, the general's loyalty to the Kaiser is in perfect concert with a subordinate's desire to protect his leader. In addition, it appears to have been German policy to redact any criticism of the Kaiser from the private papers of government and military officials at the time. Finally, Von Trotha certainly would have faced serious negative consequences — including imprisonment — for divulging the Kaiser's role in the genocide. Yet Von Trotha's denials cannot obdurate the communications detailed in chapter three that show that he was in frequent and direct contact with the Kaiser regarding progress in GSWA and that the Kaiser approved of Von Trotha's results and, by extension, his tactics.

However, it was not merely the General who protected the truth emerging about the role of the Kaiser. As suggested above, Von Trotha would have been subject to criminal prosecution for revealing the source of his orders. This was the case under German criminal law, which made the revelation of state secrets or criticism of the Kaiser punishable by imprisonment and loss of pension. State practice in Germany in the early 1900s indicates that the authorities made good on these provisions and indeed jailed at least one German critic of the government's actions in GSWA.

Despite this evidence against the Kaiser, as chapter three indicates, he still has his defenders, including those who argue that rather than an intentional campaign to exterminate the Herero out of desire for land and racial superiority, the genocide instead was the by-product of a violent German military culture. Yet, despite the truth that Germany's military was habitually cruel and that the German state itself was highly militarised, several facts render this theory less plausible.

First, as evidenced in chapters one and two, it was the German settlers, not the troops stationed in GSWA, who cried for Herero blood. Second, the military did not assume troop control in GSWA until June 1904, long after a habit of abuse had formed and indications of a planned annihilation had surfaced under civilian control. Third, German politicians in Berlin appear to have known and debated the actions in GSWA at the onset of the twentieth century. Finally, the Kaiser maintained a tight grip on the military, seeing it as his instrument of expansion; it is highly unlikely that it could have run amok without his approval or, at the very least, his notice.

The liability of the German state however, does not obscure the very active role of corporations and private individuals in perpetrating the genocide. Indeed, as argued in chapter one, it was the settlers' call for Herero land and subjugation that ultimately compelled German authorities to plan and execute the genocide. Newspaper accounts and correspondence between the settlers and Berlin in 1902 and 1903 reveal an emigrant population tired of the perceived preferential treatment of the Herero and intent on their subordination and outright extermination. Governor Leutwein's proclamation, which prohibited the repayment of Herero debt in land, particularly angered the settlers because it deprived them of yet one more means by which to deceive the tribe from surrendering their territory. In addition, not only did settler complaints and media stories alert Germany to settler discontent, but they also notified the Herero about the possibility of reprisals from Germany or the settlers. This provided further fuel for the Herero uprising of 1904, as well as Germany's brutal response.

In addition, the historical evidence presented in chapter one reveals that German settlers themselves took up arms against the Herero in an effort to subdue and enslave — if not murder — them. Accordingly, like the German state, these entities and individuals (through their descendants) would be criminally and civilly liable for actions undertaken in 1904.

Yet the truth remains, despite government denial and academic revisionism, that the Kaiser was the chief architect of the extermination of the Herero in GSWA and, as a result, the German state bears responsibility for indigenous losses and injury during the genocidal campaign of 1904. As argued in chapter three, it is for the Kaiser's actions — or at the very least, Germany's tacit consent to his conduct — that present-day Germany must apologise and make amends to the Herero.

The Herero genocide as a precursor to the Holocaust

Though many have disputed the connection, this book has argued that the events in GSWA in 1904 served as a kind of training ground for the German state's conduct in Western Europe from 1938 to 1945. While this volume concedes that colonialism, rather than fascism, propelled the Herero genocide, the similarity of methods employed against the groups targeted for extermination suggest that GSWA was a laboratory of sorts for the Holocaust.

For example, in 1904 GSWA witnessed the classification of the Herero, like the Jews of 1940s Germany, as an inferior race. This categorisation was a means by which German officials justified their ethnic-cleansing campaigns against the two groups at home and abroad. German policymakers polished their racist discourse in GSWA against the Herero in such a way that allowed them to deploy it again in Europe against the Jews decades later. Not only did racism against the Herero and the Jews aid in eliciting support for genocide from the German people, but it conveniently allowed the German state to cast the two ethnic groups as beyond the reach of international humanitarian law protection based on the assertion that those peoples were somehow less than human.

Similarly, German colonial authorities during the early 1900s banned interracial marriage, encouraged genetic experimentation on the Herero, enforced the wearing of ethnic identity symbols, herded Herero into concentration camps, exterminated Herero and mutilated their body parts, just as Nazi officers did during the Holocaust. Thus, while German officials may not have envisioned the future link between the two genocides in 1904, the extermination of the Herero at the turn of the twentieth century undoubtedly provided the German state with part of the experience it required to carry out the Holocaust 30 years later.

Conclusion

This book has argued, on the basis of historical evidence, that Germany's extermination of the Herero in 1904 was a calculated campaign designed to rid GSWA of a formidable and land-rich people in order to cement Germany's status on the colonial stage and provide the German state with a cultural outpost to accommodate its growing population. This intentional policy was nothing short of genocide.

In the course of this argument, several themes have emerged that warrant review: (1) German colonial policy at the turn of the twentieth century laid the foundation for the Herero genocide; (2) GSWA's status as 'new Germany' precluded the option of military, economic or social failure in the colony; (3) international and domestic political pressures fuelled the Herero genocide; (4) Germany conducted the Herero genocide in order to acquire Herero land, rebuild German pride and fulfil Germany's racist ideology; (5) the Kaiser ordered the genocide; and (6) Germany's actions in GSWA in 1904 provided it with relevant experience to the orchestration of the Holocaust decades later.

While, as chapter two acknowledged, controversy surrounds the precise number of Herero killed and driven into exile, as well as the actual date of the start of the genocide, such details do not obscure the near annihilation of the Herero or the intent with which Germany committed it. This book has made clear that Germany intentionally dispossessed, raped, enslaved and murdered the Herero for the express purposes of proving itself on the world stage, acquiring land for a new cultural outpost in Africa and for fulfilling its own racist beliefs. It is for these state actions that present day Germany must now remedy.

Germany's colonial occupation of GSWA has had, and continues to have, profound effects on the identity and memory of the Herero and their relations with other groups in modern-day Namibia. German customs have influenced the tribe's dress and religious practices, a vivid reminder of their past. The decimation of a large proportion of the tribe's population has reduced the Herero to a mere minority in independent Namibia. The dispossession of land and cattle amongst the Herero left them economically disabled, even to this day.

BIBLIOGRAPHY

Adalian, R.P. (1997) 'The Armenian genocide'. In Totten, S., Parsons, W.S. & Charny, I.W. (eds) *Century of genocide: Eyewitness accounts and critical views.* New York/London: Garland.

Adams, F., Werner, W. & Vale, P. (1990) *The land issue in Namibia: An inquiry.* Windhoek: Namibian Institute for Social and Economic Research, University of Namibia.

Administrator's Office Windhuk [sic] (ed) (1918) *Report on the natives of South-West Africa and their treatment by Germany.* London: His Majesty's Stationery Office.

Afreds, J. (2000) 'History and nation-building. The political uses of history in post-colonial Namibia'. *MFS-Reports:* 2. Uppsala: Department of Economic History.

Africa Watch (1992) *Accountability in Namibia: Human rights and transition to democracy.* New York: Human Rights Watch.

Alexander, N. (1983) *The Namibian war of anti-colonial resistance 1904–1907.* Windhoek: Namibian Review Publications.

Alexander, N.E. (1981, June) 'Jakob Marengo and Namibian History'. 7(1) *Social Dynamics, 1–8.*

Alexandrowicz, C.H. (1973) *The European-African confrontation.* Leiden: Sijtoff.

Alnaes, K. (1989) 'History of trauma'. 30 (1) *Journal of African History,* 179.

Alvarez, A. (2001) *Governments, citizens and genocide: A comparative and interdisciplinary approach.* Bloomington: Indiana University Press.

Amupadhi, T. (2003) 'German Scouts cancel Herero War remembrance following Nujoma's threat'. *Africa News Service,* 11 August.

Anderson, R. (2005, July) 'Redressing colonial genocide under international law: The Hereros' cause of action against Germany'. *California Law Review,* 1155.

Ankomah, B. (1999, October) 'The butcher of Congo'. 387 *New African,* 14–18.

Appulus, E. (1997) 'Hendrik Witbooi: SWAPO's phoney Hero'. *Windhoek Observer,* 20 December.

Arendt, H. (1951) *The origins of totalitarianism.* New York: Harcourt Brace & Jovanovitch.

Arendt, H. (1963) *Eichmann in Jerusalem. A report on the banality of evil.* New York: Viking Press.

Aronson. T. (1971) *The Kaisers.* London: Corgi Books.

Aydelotte, W.O. (1970) *Bismarck and British colonial policy: The problems of South West Africa 1883–1885* (2ed). New York: Russell & Russell.

Baehr, P. (ed) (2003) *The portable Hannah Arendt.* New York: Penguin.
Balabkins, N. (1993) *West German reparations to Israel.* Piscataway, NJ: Rutgers University Press.
Balfour, M. (1964) *The Kaiser and his times.* Boston: Houghton Mifflin.
Barkan, E. (2000) *The guilt of nations: Restitution and negotiating historical injustices.* Baltimore: Johns Hopkins University Press.
Bauer, G. (1999) 'Challenges to democratic consolidation in Namibia'. In Joseph, R. (ed) *State conflict and democracy in Africa.* Boulder: Lynne Rienner.
Bauer, G. (2000) 'Namibia in the first decade of independence: How democratic?' 27 *Journal of Southern African Studies*, 33–55.
Bauman, Z. (1989) *Modernity and the holocaust.* Cambridge: Polity.
Baumgart, W. (1987) 'German imperialism in historical perspective'. In Knoll, A.J. & Gann, L.H. (eds) *Germans in the tropics: Essays in German colonial history.* New York/London: Greenwood Press.
Beckett, E.W. (1980, August) 'England and Germany in Africa'. XLVIII *Fortnightly Review* XLVIII, 128–43.
Becker, H. (1989) 'Namibia und die Deutschen'. 156 (8) *Blätter des iz3w.*
Bedoukian, K. (1978) *Some of us survived: The story of an Armenian Boy.* New York: Farrar, Straus & Giroux.
Bedszent, G. 'Terror und Enteignung'. In *Junge Welt*, 13 March 1998.
Bensman, T. 'Tribe demands Holocaust reparations: Germany's genocidal war against Namibia's Herero was rehearsal for World War II atrocities'. *The Salt Lake Tribune*, 18 March 1999.
Berat. L. (1990) *Walvis Bay: The last frontier.* New Haven: Yale University Press.
Berat, L. (1990) 'Namibia: The road to independence and the problem of succession of states'. 18 *Journal of Political Science*, 33.
Berat, L. (1993) 'Genocide: The Namibian case against Germany'. 5 *Pace International Law Review*, 165.
Beris, A.P.J. (1996) *From mission to local church: One hundred years of mission by the Catholic Church in Namibia.* Windhoek: Roman Catholic Church.
Blackshire-Belay, C.A. (1992, December). 'German imperialism in Africa: The distorted images of Cameroon, Namibia, Tanzania and Togo'. 23 (2) *Journal of Black Studies*, 235–46.
Bley, H. (1968) *Kolonialherrschaft und Sozialstruktur in Deutsch-Südwestafrika 1894–1914.* Hamburg, Leibniz.
Bley, H. (1967) 'Social discord in South West Africa 1894–1904'. In Gifford, P. & Louis, W.M.R. (eds) *Britain and Germany in Africa: Imperial rivalry and colonial rule.* New Haven: Yale University.

Bley, H. (1967) 'German South West Africa after the conquest 1904–1914'. In Segal, R. & First, R. *South West Africa: Travesty of trust.* London: Andre Deutsch, 35–53.

Bley, H. (1971) *South West Africa under German rule 1894–1914.* London: Heinemann.

Blue, G. (1999) 'Gobineau on China; Race theory, the "Yellow Peril" and the critique of modernity'. 10(1) *Journal of World History*, 93–139.

Boahen, A. (1989) *African perspectives on colonialism.* Baltimore: Johns Hopkins University Press.

Boesche, R. (1995) *Theories of tyranny from Plato to Arendt.* University Park, PA: Pennsylvania State University Press.

Boehmer, E. (1995) *Colonial and postcolonial literature: Migrant metaphors.* Oxford: Oxford University Press.

Böhlke-Itzen, J. (2004) *Kolonialschuld und Entschädigung: Der deutsche Völkermord an den Herero (1904–1907).* Frankfurt am Main: Brandes & Apsel.

Bollig, M. & Gewald, J-B. (2000) 'People, cattle and land — An introduction'. In Bollig, M. & Gewald, J-B. (eds) *People, cattle and land: Transformations of a pastoral society in South Western Africa.* Köln: Rudiger Koppe Verlag.

Bollig, M. & Gewald, J-B. (eds) (2000) *People, cattle and land: Transformations of a pastoral society in South Western Africa.* Köln: Rudiger Koppe Verlag.

Bölsche, J. 'Die Peitsche des Bändigers'. *Der Spiegel* 3, 12 January 2004.

Bravenboer, B. & Rusch, W. (1997) *The first 100 years of state railways in Namibia.* Windhoek: Trans-Namibian Museum.

Breitman, R. (1991) *The architect of genocide: Himmler and the Final Solution.* New York: Alfred Knopf.

Bridgland, F. 'Germany's genocide rehearsal'. *The Scotsman*, 26 September 2001.

Bridgman, J. (1981) *The revolt of the Hereros.* Los Angeles: University of California Press.

The Bryce Report into German atrocities in Belgium — Report of the Committee on Alleged German Outrages Appointed by His Britannic Majesty's Government and Presided Over by the Right Hon. Viscount Bryce, O.M., 12 May 1915.

Bullock, A.L.C. (1939) *German's colonial demands.* London: Oxford University Press.

Cameron, V.L. (1890, August). 'England and Germany in Africa: III'. XLVIII *Fortnightly Review*, 144–63.

Calvert, A.F. (1969) *South-West Africa during the German occupation 1884–1914.* New York: Negro University Press.

Calvert, A.F. (1915) *South West Africa: During the German occupation 1884–1914.* London: T. Werner Laurie.

Carstens, P., Klinghardt, G., & West, M. (1987) (eds) *Trails in the thirstland: The anthropological field diaries of Winifred Hoernle*. Cape Town: Centre For African Studies, University of Cape Town.

Cecil, L. (1996) *Wilhelm II. Vol II: Emperor and exile, 1900–1941*. Chapel Hill: University of North Carolina Press.

Cesaire, A. (1996) *Discourse on colonialism*. New York: New York University Press.

Clark, C. (2000) *Kaiser Wilhelm II. Profiles in power*. Essex: Pearson Education.

Clemente, S. E. (1992) *For King and Kaiser: The making of the Prussian army officer, 1860–1914*. New York: Greenwood Press.

Cocker, M. (1998) *Rivers of blood, rivers of gold: Europe's conflict with tribal peoples*. London: Jonathan Cape.

Cohrssen, F.K. (1994) *A critical evaluation of the juridical status of Walvis Bay in colonial and post-colonial international law and practice, 1868–1993*. PhD, University of Natal.

Colijn, G.J. (2003) 'Carnage before our time: Nineteenth century colonial genocide'. 5 (4) *Journal of Genocide Research*, 617–625.

Cook, S. & Borah, W. (1971) *Essays in population history: Mexico and the Caribbean*. Berkeley, CA: University of California Press.

Cooper, A.D. (2001) *Ovambo politics in the twentieth century*. Lanham: University Press of America.

Cornevin, R. (1969) 'The Germans in Africa before 1918'. In Gann, L.H. & Duigan, P. *Colonialism in Africa 1870–1960*. Cambridge: Cambridge University Press, 223.

Craig, G. (1955) *The Politics of the Prussian army 1640–1945*. London: Oxford University Press.

Crothers, G.D. (1968) *The German elections of 1907*. New York: Columbia University Press.

Culver, J. (Jr) 'Berlin Anti-Colonial Conference: 120 Years of African resistance'. 116 *The Black Commentator*, 2 December 2004. Available at: http://www.blackcommentator.com/116/116_berlin_conference.html

Dale, R. (1976) 'Colonial rulers and ruled in South West Africa and the Bechuanaland Protectorate 1884–1966: A framework for comparative study'. 1 *Journal of Southern African Affairs*, 95–110.

Davis, A.N. (1918) *The Kaiser as I know him*. New York: Harper & Brothers.

Deacon, H. (2004) Marion Wallace, health, power and politics in Windhoek, Namibia 1915–1945 (Review)'. 78(4) *Bulletin of the History of Medicine*, 916–17.

Deckert, M. E. (1966) 'The causes of the Herero uprising of 1904–1906 in South West Africa'. In Cordier, A.W. (ed) *Columbia Essays in International Affairs*. New York: Columbia University Press 255.

Dedering, T. (1999) 'A certain rigorous treatment of all parts of the nation: The annihilation of the Herero in German South West Africa, 1904'. In Levine, M. and Roberts, P. (eds) *The massacre in history.* New York: Oxford: Berghahn Books.

Dedering, T. (1999) 'The prophet's "War against Whites": Shepherd Stuurman in Namibia and South Africa 1904–1907'. 40 (1) *Journal of African History,* 1–19.

Dedering, T. (1993, March) 'The German-Herero War of 1904: Revisionism of genocide or imaginary historiography'. 19 (1) *Journal of Southern African Studies,* 80.

Diamond, J. (1997) *Guns, Germs and Steel: The Fates of Human Societies.* New York: W. W. Norton Publishers.

Diebold, E., Engelhardt, S. & Iskenius, D. (2004) 'Facing the past to liberate the future: Colonial Africa in the German mind'. 6 *Humanity in Action. Reports of the 2004 Fellows in Denmark, Germany and the Netherlands.* New York.

Dienst, W. (1982) 'Kaiser Wilhelm II in the context of his military and naval entourage'. In Röhl, J.C.G. & Sombart, N. (eds) *Kaiser Wilhelm II: New interpretations. The Corfu Papers.* Cambridge: Cambridge University Press, 169.

Dorpalen, A. (1952, October) 'Empress Auguste Victoria and the fall of the German monarchy'. 58(1) *American Historical Review,* 17–38.

Drechsler, H. (1980) *Let us die fighting: The struggle of the Herero and Nama against the German imperialism (1894–1915)* (Bernd Zöllner transl). London: Zed Press.

Drechsler, H. (1986) *Let us die fighting.* Berlin: Akademie-Verlag.

Drechsler, H. (1966) *Südwestafrika unter deutscher Kolonialherrschaft — Der Kampf der Herero und Nama gegen den deutschen Imperialismus (1884–1915).* Berlin: Akademie-Verlag.

Dreyer, R.F. (1987) *The mind of official imperialism: British and Cape government perceptions of German rule in Namibia from the Heligoland-Zanzibar Treaty to the Kruger telegram, 1890–1896.* Essen: Reimar Hobbing.

Du Pisani, A. (1987) 'Namibia: The historical legacy'. In Totemeyer, G., Kandetu, V. & Werner, W. (eds) *Namibia in perspective.* Windhoek: Council of Churches.

Du Pisani, A. (1986) *SWA/Namibia: The politics of continuity and change.* Johannesburg: Jonathan Ball.

Eckert, A. (1997) 'Theories of colonial rule'. 38 (2) *Journal of African History,* 325.

Eltzbacher, O. (1905, October) 'The German danger to South Africa'. 58 *The nineteenth century and after,* 524–38.

Epstein, K. (1959) 'Erzberger and the German colonial scandals, 1905–1910'. 74 (293) *English Historical Review*, 637–63.
Erichsen, C.W. (2003 August/September) 'Namibia's island of death'. *New African*, 46.
Erichsen, C.W. (2004) *The Angel of Death has descended violently among them: A study of Namibia's concentration camps and prisoners-of-war, 1904–08*. MA thesis (History). University of Namibia.
Erichsen, C. (2008) *'What the Elders Used to Say' Namibian Perspectives on the Last Decade of German Colonial Rule*. Windhoek: Namibia Institute for Democracy and the Namibian-German Foundation.
Esterhuyse, J.H. (1968) *South West Africa: The establishment of German authority in South West Africa*. Cape Town: C. Struik.
Eveleigh, W. (1915) *South-West Africa*. Cape Town: Maskew Miller.
Finzsch, N. (2008) '"[..] Extirpate or remove that vermine": Genocide, biological warfare, and settler imperialism in the eighteenth and early nineteenth century' 10(2) *Journal of Genocide Research*, 215-232.
First, R. (1967) *South West Africa*. Baltimore: Penguin Books.
Flint, J. (ed) (1976) *The Cambridge history of Africa, Volume 5*. Cambridge: Cambridge University Press.
Fröschle, H. 'Ein normaler Kolonialkrieg, kein Genozid'. 262 *FAZ*, 11 November 2002.
Gage, R.H. & Waters, A.J. (1971) *Imperial German Criminal Code* (English translation). Johannesburg: W E Horton & Co.
Gann, L.H. (1973) 'South West Africa under German rule, 1894–1914'. 6 (1) *The International Journal of African Historical Studies*, 121–126.
Gann, L.H. (1987) 'Marginal colonialism: The German case'. 1–17. In Knoll, A.J. & Gann, L.H. (eds) *Germans in the tropics: Essays in German colonial history*. New York/London: Greenwood Press.
Gann, L.H. & Duigan, P. (1977) *The rulers of German Africa 1884–1914*. Stanford: Stanford University Press.
Gewald, J-B. (1994) 'The great general of the Kaiser'. 26 *Botswana Notes and Records*, 67–76.
Gewald, J-B. (1996) *Towards redemption: A socio-political history of the Herero of Namibia between 1890 and 1923*. Leiden: CNWS Publications.
Gewald, J-B. (1999) *Herero heroes: A socio-political history of the Herero of Namibia 1890–1923*. Oxford: James Currey.
Gewald, J-B. (1999) 'The road of the man called Love and the sack of Sero: The Herero-German War and the export of the Herero labour to the South African Rand'. 40 (1) *Journal of African History*, 21–40.
Gewald, J-B. (2000) 'Colonization, genocide and resurgence: The Herero of Namibia, 1890–1933'. In Bollig, M. & Gewald, J-B. (eds) *People, cattle and*

land: Transformations of a pastoral society in South Western Africa. Köln: Rudiger Koppe Verlag.

Gewald, J-B. (2002) 'Missionaries, Hereros and motorcars: Mobility and the impact of motor vehicles in Namibia before 1940'. 35 (2–3) *International Journal of African Historical Studies*, 257–85.

Gewald, J-B. (2002) 'Flags, funerals and fanfares: Herero and missionary contestations of the acceptable, 1900–1940'. 15 (1) *Journal of African Cultural Studies*, 105.

Gewald, J-B. (2003) 'Herero genocide in the twentieth century: Politics and memory'. In Abbink, J., De Bruijn, M. & Van Walraven, K. (eds) *Rethinking resistance: Revolt and violence in African history*. Leiden: Brill.

Gewald, J-B. (2003) 'Imperial Germany and the Herero of Southern Africa: Genocide and the quest for recompense'. In Jones, A. (ed) *Genocide, war crimes and the West: Ending the culture of impunity*. London: Zed Press, 59–77.

Gewald, J-B. (2003) 'The Herero genocide: German unity, settlers, soldiers and ideas'. In Bechhaus-Gerst, M. & Klein-Arendt, R. (eds) *Die (koloniale) Begegnung: AfrikanerInnen in Deutschland 1880–1945, Deutsche in Afrika 1880–1918*. Frankfurt am Main: Peter Lang, 109–127.

Gewald, J-B. and Silvester, J. (2003) *Words cannot be found. German colonial rule in Namibia: An annotated reprint of the 1918 Blue Book*. Leiden: Brill.

Gibson, G.D. (1956, February). 'Double descent and its correlates among the Herero of Ngamiland'. 58 (1) *American Anthropologist* New Series, 109–39.

Goldhagen, D. (1996) *Hitler's willing executioners: Ordinary Germans and the Holocaust*. New York. Vintage Books.

Goldblatt, I. (1971) *History of South West Africa, from the beginning of the nineteenth century*. Cape Town: Juta & Co.

Goldstone, R.J. (2004) 'International human rights and criminal justice in the first decade of the 21st century'. 11 *Human Rights Brief* 3.

Government of South Africa (1928) *The native tribes of South West Africa*. Cape Town: Cape Times Limited.

Great General Staff of the Imperial Germany (1915) *The war book of the German General Staff* (J.H. Morgan transl). New York: McBride, Nast & Co.

Großer Generalstab (ed) (1906) *Die Kämpfe der deutschen Truppen in Südwestafrika. Auf Grund amtlichen Materials bearbeitet von der Kriegsgeschichtlichen, Abteilung I des Großen Generalstabes. Band I. Der Feldzug gegen die Hereros*. Berlin: Ernst Siegfried Mittler & Sohn.

Gründer, H. (1998) 'Genozid oder Zwangsmodernisierung? Der moderne Kolonialismus in universalgeschichtlicher Perspektive'. In Dabag, M. &

Platt, K. (eds) *Genozid und Moderne. Bd 1. Strukturen kollektiver Gewalt im 20. Jahrhundert.* Opladen: Leske & Buderich, 135.

Gründer, H. (2004) *Geschichte der deutschen Kolonien.* Paderborn: Ferdinand Schöningh Verlag.

Haarhoff, D. (1991) *The wild South-West: Frontier myths and metaphors in literature set in Namibia, 1760–1988.* Johannesburg: Witwatersrand University Press.

Hakata, M. (2001, January) 'Hereros sue Germany for reparations'. *New African,* 12–14.

Hamta, M. (2004) 'Von Trotha family backs Herero compensation'. *Africa News Service,* September 13.

Hayes, P., Silvester, J., Wallace, M. & Hartman, W. (1998) *Namibia under South African rule: Mobility and containment 1915–1946.* Oxford: James Currey.

Helbig, H. & L. (1983) *Mythos-Deutsch-Südwest: Namibia und die Deutschen.* Weinheim/Basel: Beltz Verlag.

Helbig, H. (1983) *Mythos-Deutsch-Südwest: Namibia und die Deutschen.* Weinheim/Basel: Beltz Verlag.

Hellberg, C-J. (1997) *Mission, colonialism and liberation: The Lutheran Church in Namibia 1840–1966.* Windhoek: New Namibia Books.

Hempenstall, P.J. (1978) *Pacific islanders under German rule. A study in the meaning of colonial resistance.* Canberra: Australian National University Press.

Hempenstall, P. (1987) 'The neglected empire: The superstructure of the colonial state in the German Melanesia'. In Knoll, A.J. & Gann, L.H. (eds) *Germans in the tropics: Essays in German colonial history* (2ed). New York/London: Greenwood Press, 93.

Hendersen, W.O. (1938) 'Germany's trade with her colonies, 1884–1914'. 9 (1) *Economic History Review,* 1–19, 2.

Hendrickson, H. (1994) 'The long dress and the construction of Herero identities in southern Africa'. 53 (2) *African Studies,* 25–54.

Heywood, A., Lau, B. & Ohly R. (eds) (1992) *Warriors, leaders, sages and outcasts in the Namibian past.* Windhoek: Michael Scott Oral Records Project.

Heywood, A. & Maasdorp, E. (transl) (1989) *The Hendrik Witbooi papers.* Windhoek: National Archives of Namibia.

Heywood, A. & Maasdorp, E. (transl) (1995) *The Hendrik Witbooi papers* (2ed). Windhoek: National Archives of Namibia.

Hintrager, O. (1955) *Suedwestafrika in der deutschen Zeit.* Munchen: Kommissionsverlag.

Hishongwa, N. (1997) *The contract labour system and its effects on family and social life in Namibia: A historical perspective.* Windhoek: Gamsberg MacMillan.

Hochschild, A. (1999) *King Leopold's ghost — A story of greed, terror and heroism in colonial Africa.* New York: Houghton Mifflin.

Horne, J. & Kramer, A. (2001) *German atrocities 1914: A history of denial*. New Haven: Yale University Press.
Howard, M.E. (1967) 'The armed forces'. In Hinsley, F. (ed) *The new Cambridge modern history XI: Material*.
Howard, R.E. (1986) *Human rights in Commonwealth Africa*. Totowa, New Jersey: Rowman & Littlefield.
Hull, I.V. (1982) *The entourage of Kaiser Wilhelm II, 1888–1918*. New York: Cambridge University Press.
Hull, I.V. (2003) 'Military culture and the production of final solutions in the colonies: The example of Wilhelminian Germany'. In Gellately, R. & Kiernan, B. (eds) *The specter of genocide mass murder in historical perspective*. Cambridge: Cambridge University Press.
Hull, I.V. (2005) *Absolute destruction: Military culture and practices of war in Imperial Germany*. Ithaca: Cornell University Press.
Illife, J. (1969) *Tanganyika under German rule, 1905–1912*. Cambridge: Cambridge University Press.
Ipsen, K.(1999) *Völkerrecht: Ein Studienbuch* (4ed). München: C.H. Becksche Verlag.
JanMohamed, A.R. (1986) 'The economy of Manichean allegory: The function of racial difference in colonialist literature'. In Gates, H.L. (ed) *Race, Writing and Difference*. Chicago: University of Illinois Press.
Jaspers, K. (2001) *The question of German guilt*. New York: Fordham University Press
Jere-malanda, R. (2000, June) 'Massacre in the desert'. *You*, 34–40.
Johann, E. (ed) *Reden des Kaisers: Ansprachen, Predigten und Trinksprüche Wilhelms II* (Munich, 1966) Translated by R.S. Levy. 86–88. Available at: http://www.assumption.edu/users/McClymer/hi119net/KaiserWilhelmIIBoxers.html
Kandetu, V. (2005, January) 'Namibia: Cold discourse upon chronic pain'. 436 *New African*, 64–6.
Katjavivi, P. (1989) *A History of Resistance in Namibia*. Paris, London & Addis Ababa: UNESCO.
Kaulich, U. (2003) *Die Geschichte der ehemaligen Kolonie Deutsch-Südwestafrika (1884–1914) Eine Gesamtdarstellung* (2ed). Frankfurt am Main: Peter Lang.
Kennedy, P. (1982) 'The Kaiser and German *Weltpolitik*: Reflections on Wilhelm II's place in the making of German foreign policy'. In Röhl, J.C.G. & Sombart, N. (eds) *Kaiser Wilhelm II, new interpretations: The Corfu papers*. Cambridge/New York: Cambridge University Press.
Kerina, M. (1981) *Namibia: the making of a nation*. New York: Books in Focus.
Kesting, R.W. (1998) 'Blacks under the swastika: A research note'. 83 (1) *The Journal of Negro History*, 84–99.

Kindt, L. (1905, December 12) 'Vom Aufstand in Ostafrika'. XI (25) *Koloniale Zeitschrift*, 435-37.
Kitchen, M. (1968) *The German Officer Corps 1890–1914*. Oxford: Clarendon Press.
Knoll, A.J. (1939) *Togo under imperial Germany 1884–1914*. Stanford: Hoover Institution Press.
Knoll, A.J. & Gann, L.H. (eds) (1987) *Germans in the tropics: Essays in German colonial history*. New York/London: Greenwood Press.
Kohut, T.A. (1991) *Wilhelm II and the Germans: A study in leadership*. New York: Oxford University Press.
Kössler, R. (2007) 'Facing a fragmented past: Memory, culture and politics in Namibia', 33(2) *Journal of Southern African Studies*, 361-82.
Krautwurst, U.R. (1997) *Tales of the 'land of stories': Settlers and anti-modernity in German colonial discourses on German South West Africa, 1884–1914*. Phd (History). Connecticut: University of Connecticut.
Krüger, G. (1999) *Kriegsbewältigung und Geschichtsbewusstsein: Realität, Deutung und Verarbeitung des deutschen Kolonialkrieges in Namibia, 1904 bis 1907*. Göttingen: Vandenhoek & Ruprecht.
Lau, B. (1989) 'Uncertain certainties: The Herero-German war of 1904'. *Mibagus*, 2.
Lau, B. (1990, June/July) Letter to the editor, *Southern African Review of Books*.
Lau, B. & Renier, P. (1993) *100 years of agricultural development in colonial Namibia: A historical overview of visions and experimenting*. Windhoek: The National Archive of Namibia.
Lemkin, R. (1944) *Axis rule in occupied Europe: Laws of occupation — analysis of government — proposals for redress*. Washington DC: Carnegie Endowment for International Peace.
Lemkin, R. (1945) 'Genocide — A modern crime'. *Free World*, April 4, 39.
Lemkin, R. (undated) Untitled and unpublished manuscript dealing with the Herero, Jacob Rader Marcus Center of the American Jewish archives Cincinnati; the Raphael Lemkin Papers, Box 6, Folder 12.
Lemkin, R. (undated) Unpublished manuscript: *The Germans in Africa*. Jacob Rader Marcus Center of the American Jewish Archives, Cincinnati; the Raphael Lemkin papers, Box 6, Folder 9.
Leutwein, T.G. (1906) *Elf Jahre Gouverneur in Deutsch-Südwestafrika*. Berlin: Mittler.
Lewin, E. (1915) *The Germans and Africa. Their Aims on the Dark Continent and how they acquired their African Colonies*. London: Cassell.

Louis, W.M.R (1967) 'Great Britain and German expansion in Africa 1884–1919'. In Gifford, P. & Louis, W.M.R. (eds) *Britain and Germany in Africa: Imperial rivalry and colonial rule.* New Haven: Yale University.

Louis, W.R. (1967) *Britain and Germany's lost colonies 1914–1919.* Oxford: Clarendon Press.

Lovejoy, P. (2000) *Transformation in slavery: A history of slavery in Africa* (2ed). Cambridge: Cambridge University Press.

Lugard, F.D. (1922) *Dual mandate in British tropical Africa.* London/Edinburgh: William Blackwood & sons.

Lundtofte, H. (2003) 'Radicalization of the German suppression of the Herero rising in 1904'. In Jensen, S.L.B. *Genocide: Cases, comparisons and contemporary debates.* Copenhagen: Danish Center for Holocaust and Genocide Studies 27.

Luttig, H.G. (1933) *The religious system and social organization of the Herero: A study in Bantu culture.* Utrecht: Kemink & Zoon.

Macdonogh, G. (2000) *The Last Kaiser: The life of Wilhelm II.* New York: St Martin's Press

Mackenzie, K. (1974, March) 'Some British reactions to German colonial methods 1885–1907'. 17(1) *The Historical Journal,* 165–75.

Madley, B. (2004) 'Patterns of frontier genocide 1803–1910: The aboriginal Tasmanians, the Yuki of California and the Herero of Namibia'. 6 (2) *Journal of Genocide Research,* 167–192.

Maier, C.S. (1988) *The unmasterable past: History, Holocaust and German national identity.* Cambridge, Massachusetts: Harvard University Press.

Malan, J.S. (1995) *Peoples of Namibia.* Pretoria: Rhino Publishers.

Masson, J. (2001) *Jakob Marengo: An early resistance hero of Namibia.* Windhoek: Out of Africa.

Masson, J.R. (1995) 'A fragment of colonial history: The killing of Jakob Marengo'. 21 (2) *Journal of South African Studies,* 247–256, 255.

Masson, J.R. (1995, June) 'A fragment of colonial history: The killing of Jakob Marengo'. 21(2) *Journal of South African Studies,* 247–256.

Melber, H. (1985) 'Namibia: The German roots of Apartheid'. 27 (1) *Race and Class,* 63–77, 73.

Mokopakgosi, B. (1988, July). 'Review: *The Namibian Herero: A history of their psychological disintegration and survival'.* 87 (348) *African Affairs,* 480–81.

Mombauer, A. (1999, March) 'Germany's last Kaiser — Wilhelm II and political decision-making in Imperial Germany'. 4(3) *New Perspective* Available at: http://www.users.globalnet.co.uk/~semp/wilhelmii.htm

Mombauer, A. (2003) 'Wilhelm Waldersee and the Boxer Rebellion'. In Mombauer, A. & Deist, W. (eds) *The Kaiser: New Research on Wilhelm II's*

role in Imperial Germany. Cambridge: Cambridge University Press, 91–118.
Morgenthau, H. (1918) Ambassador Morgenthau's story. New York: Double Day.
Muir, R. (1917) The expansion of Europe: The culmination of modern history (2ed). Boston/ New York: Houghton Mifflin.
New York Times current history: The European war. Vol xxvii. New York: New York Times, 1920, 322.
Ngavirue, Z. (1972) Political parties and interest groups in South West Africa: A study of a plural society. PhD thesis. Oxford University.
Niekerk, C. (2003) 'Rethinking a problematic constellation: Postcolonialism and its Germanic contexts'. 23 (1&2) Comparative Studies of South Asia, Africa and the Middle East, 58.
Nordbruch, C. (2002) Der Hereroaufstand von 1904. Stegen am Ammersee: Kurt Vowinckel Verlag.
Nordbruch, C. (2004) Völkermord an den Herero in Deutsch-Südwestafrika? Widerlegung einer Lüge. Tübingen: Grabert Verlag.
Nuhn, W. (2000) Feind überall: Der große Nama-Aufstand (Hottentottenaufstand) 1904–1908 in Deutsch-Südwestafrika (Namibia). Bonn: Bernard & Graefe.
Nujoma, S. (1986) 'Preface'. In Dreschler, H. Let us die fighting. Berlin: Akademie-Verlag.
Nujoma, S. (2001) Where others wavered: The autobiography of Sam Nujoma. London: Panaf Books.
O'Donnell, K. (1999) 'Poisonous women: Sexual danger, illicit violence and domestic work in German Southern Africa 1904–1915'. 11 (3) Journal of Woman's History, 32–54.
Oermann, N.O. (1999) Mission, church and state relations in South West Africa under German rule (1884–1915). Stuttgart: Franz Steiner Verlag.
Oermann, N.O. (2003) 'The law and the colonial state: Legal codification versus practise in a German colony'. In Eley, G. & Retallack, J. (eds) Wilhelminism and its legacies: German modernities, imperialism and the meanings of reform, 1890–1930. New York: Berghahn.
Ofcansky, T.P (1981) 'The 1889–97 rinderpest epidemic and the rise of British and German colonialism in Eastern and Southern Africa'. 8 (1) Journal of African Studies, 31–38.
Olusoga, O. & Erichsen, C.W. (2010) The Kaiser's Holocaust: Germany's forgotten genocide and the colonial roots of Nazism. London: Faber and Faber.
Osterhammel, J. (1997) Colonialism: A theoretical overview. Princeton, N.J: Markus Weiner.
Otavi Mines Minerals 100th anniversary commemorative publication (1900–2000).
Packenham, T. (1992) The scramble for Africa: White man's conquest of the Dark Continent from 1875–1912. New York: Avon Books.

Paech, N. (2004) 'Der juristische Weg der Wiedergutmachung: Schadenersatz für Völkermord?' In Böhlke-Itzen, J. (ed) *Kolonialschuld und Entschädigung: der deutsche Völkermord an den Herero (1904–1907)*. Frankfurt am Main: Brandes & Apsel.

Pakendorf, G. (1987) 'The literature of expropriation: Peter Moor's journey to South-West and the conquest of Namibia'. In Totemeyer, G., Kandetu, V. & Werner, W. (eds) *Namibia in perspective*. Windhoek: Council of Churches in Namibia.

Pankhurst, D. (1995) 'Towards reconciliation of the land issue in Namibia: Identifying the possible, assessing the probable'. 26 *Development and Change*, 551–585.

Pendleton, W.C. (1976) 'Herero reactions: The pre-colonial period, the German period and the South African period'. In Chanaiwa, D. *Profiles of self-determination: African responses to European colonialism in southern Africa*. Present, Northridge: California State University Foundation.

Pennington, R. & Harpending, H. (1993) *The structure of an Africanist pastoral community: Demography, history and ecology of the Ngamiland Herero*. Oxford: Clarendon Press.

Penny, H.G. & Bunzl, M. (eds) *Worldly provincialism: German anthropology in the Age of Empire*. Ann Arbour: University of Michigan Press.

Penzler, J. (ed) *Die Reden Kaiser Wilhelms II. Vol. 3: 1901–1905*. Leipzig. Available at: http://www.zum.de/psm/imperialismus/wilhelm1905.php

Pfister, G. (2005) 'Sport, colonialism and the enactment of German identity — *Turnen* in South West Africa'. 24. Paper delivered at the 20th International Congress for the Historical Sciences 3–9 July 2005, Sydney. Available at: www.cishsydney2005.org/images/GertrundPfisterST25.doc

Pierard, R. (1971) 'The transportation of white women to German South West Africa, 1898–1914'. 12(3) *Race* 317– 322.

Pierard, R.V. (1964) *The German colonial society 1882–1914*. PhD thesis (Modern History). State University of Iowa.

Pitswane, J. (1992) 'Namibia: Challenges of the first decade'. In Benjamin, L. & Gregory, C. (eds) *Southern Africa at the crossroads?* Rivonia: Justified Press.

Poewe, K. (1985) *The Namibian Herero: A history of their psychosocial disintegration and survival*. Lewiston, NY: Edwin Mellen.

Poole, G. (1991) *Samuel Maherero*. Windhoek: Gamsberg MacMillan.

Prein, P. (1994) 'Guns and top hats: African resistance in German South West Africa 1907–1915'. 20 (1) *Journal of African Studies*, 99–121.

Procter, R. (1988) *Racial hygiene medicine under the Nazis*. Cambridge, Massachusetts: Harvard University Press.

Rahn, W. (1997) 'Sanitätsdienst der Schutztruppe für Südwestafrika während der Aufstände 1904–1907 und der Kalahari-Expedition 1908'. Beiträge zur eutschen Kolonialgesichte.

Read, J.S. (1969) 'Kenya, Tanzania and Uganda'. In Milner, A. (ed) *African penal systems*. London: Routledge & Kegan Paul, 91–164.

Rees, W.L. (1888, November). 'German conduct in Samoa'. XXIV *Nineteenth Century*, 734–52.

Report of the British Consul, Roger Casement, on the Administration of the Congo Free State — British Parliamentary Papers, 1904, LXII, Cd. 1933.

Report of the International Commission to Inquire into the Causes and Conduct of the Balkan Wars, Washington 1914.

Rich, N. (1965) *Friedrich von Holstein: Politics and diplomacy in the era of Bismarck and Wilhelm II*. Cambridge: Cambridge University Press.

Richardson, H.J. (1984) 'Constitutive questions in the negotiations for Namibian independence'. 78 *American Journal of International Law*, 76.

Ritter-Petersen, H.G. (1991) *The Herrenvolk mentality in German South West Africa 1884–1914*. DLitt (History). Pretoria: University of South Africa.

Robinson, R. (1986) 'The eccentric idea of imperialism, with or without Empire'. In Mommsen, W.J. & Osterhammel, J. (eds) *Imperialism and after: Continuities and discontinuities*. London: Allen & Unwin.

Röhl, J.C.G. (1982) 'Introduction'. In Röhl, J.C.G. & Sombart, N. (eds) *Kaiser Wilhelm II: New interpretations. The Corfu Papers*. Cambridge: Cambridge University Press.

Röhl, J.C.G. (1994) *The Kaiser and his court: Wilhelm II and the government of Germany*. Cambridge: Cambridge University Press.

Röhl, J.C.G. (2001) *Wilhelm II. Der Aufbau der persönlichen Monarchie 1888–1900*. München: CH Beck Verlag.

Röhl, J.C.G. & Sombart, N. (eds) *Kaiser Wilhelm II: New interpretations. The Corfu Papers*. Cambridge: Cambridge University Press.

Rohrbach, P. (1907) *Deutsche Kolonialwirtschaft, vol. I: Südwestafrika*. Berlin/Schoneberg: Buchverlag der Hilfe.

Roosevelt, T. (1904) State of the Union Addess, 6 December 1904. Available at: http://www.infoplease.com/t/hist/state-of-the-union/116.html

Sarkin, J. (1999) 'The necessity and challenges of establishing a truth and reconciliation commission in Rwanda'. 21 *Human Rights Quarterly*, 767.

Sarkin, J. (2002) 'Finding a solution for the problems created by the politics of identity in the Democratic Republic of the Congo (DRC): Designing a constitutional framework for peaceful co-Operation'. In Konrad Adenauer Foundation (eds) *The Politics of Identity*. Pretoria: Konrad Adenauer Foundation.

Sarkin, J. (2004) 'The coming of age of claims for reparations for human rights abuses committed in the South'. 1 *Sur International Human Rights Journal*, 67–125.

Sarkin, J. (2007) 'The Historical origins, convergence and interrelationship of international human rights law, international humanitarian law, international criminal law and international law: Their application from at least the nineteenth century'. 1(1) *Human Rights and International Legal Discourse*, 125–172.

Sarkin, J. (with C Fowler) (2008) 'Reparations for historical human rights violations: The international and historical dimensions of the alien torts claims act genocide case of the Herero of Namibia' *Human Rights Review* (September 2008), 331–360.

Sarkin, J. (2009) *Colonial Genocide and Reparations Claims in the 21st Century: The Socio-Legal Context of Claims under International Law by the Herero against Germany for Genocide in Namibia, 1904–1908*. Westport: Praeger Security International.

Sarkin, J. (2009) 'The origins of international criminal law: Its connection to and convergence with other branches of international law'. 4(1) *Hague Justice Journal* 5–41.

Sarkin, J. & Binchy, W. (eds) (2001) *Human rights, the citizen and the state*. Dublin: Round Hall, Sweet & Maxwell.

Sarkin, J., Van de Lanotte, J. & Haeck, Y. (eds) (2001) *Resolving the tensions between crime and human rights: European and South African perspectives*. Antwerpen: Maklu.

Saunders, C. (2003) 'Liberation and democracy: A critical reading of Sam Nujoma's "autobiography"'. In Melber, H. (ed) *Re-examining liberation in Namibia: Political cultures since independence*. Uppsala: Nordic Africa Institute 87.

Schaller, D.J. (2005) 'Raphael Lemkin's view of European colonial rule in Africa: Between condemnation and admiration'. 7(4) *Journal of Genocide Research*, 531–38.

Schaller, D.J. (December 2008) 'Colonialism and genocide – Raphael Lemkin's concept of genocide and its application to European rule in Africa', 50 *Development Dialogue*, 75–84.

Schaller, D.J. & Zimmerer, J. (eds) (2008) *The Origins of Genocide: Raphael Lemkin as a Historian of Mass Violence*, London: Routledge.

Schmokel, W.W. (1985) 'The myth of the white farmer: Commercial agriculture in Namibia 1900–1983'. 18 (1) *International Journal of African Historical Studies*, 93–108.

Schnee, H. (1926) *German colonization past and future: The truth about the German colonies*. London: George Allen & Unwin.

Schnieder, T. (1967) 'Political and social development in Europe'. In *The new Cambridge modern history, XI: Material progress and worldwide problems, 1870–1898*. Cambridge: Cambridge University Press.

Schneider-Waterberg, H.R. (2003) 'Konzentrationslager als Einrichtungen kolonialer Kriegsführung in Südlichen Afrika. Zum Bedeutungswandel eines Begriffes'. *6 Befunde und Berichte zur Deutschen kolonialgeschichte*, 11–19.

Schöng, H. (1959) *Der Imperialismus und Chinas Politik*. Berlin (DDR) S. 144. Available at: http://www.zum.de/psm/imperialismus/rums24/rums24_62e.php3

Schrank, G.I. (1974) *German South West Africa: Social and economic aspects of its history 1884–1915*. PhD thesis (History). New York University.

Schwabe, K. (1904) *Mit Schwert und Pflug in Deutsch-südwestafrika: Vier Kriegs- und Wanderjahre*. Berlin.

Schwirck, H. (2002) 'Law's violence and the boundary between corporal discipline and physical abuse in German South West Africa'. *36 Akron Law Review*, 81.

Schwerin, K. (1972) 'German compensation for victims of Nazi persecution'. *67 Northwestern University Law Review*, 479.

Schwerin, K. (1995) 'German compensation for victims of Nazi persecution'. In Kritz, N. (ed) *Transitional Justice, Vol. II*. Washington, DC: United States Institute for Peace, 51.

Shandley, R.R. (ed) (1998) *Unwilling Germans? The Goldhagen debate*. Minneapolis: University of Minnesota Press.

Sharf, F.A. & Harrington, P. (2000) 'China 1900: The eyewitnesses speak. The experience of Westerners in China during the Boxer Rebellion, as described by participants in letters, diaries and photographs'. Mechanicsburg, Pennsylvania: Stackpole.

Silvester, J. (1998) 'Beasts, boundaries and buildings: The survival and creation of pastoral economics in Southern Namibia 1915–35'. In Hayes, P., Silvester, J., Wallace, M. & Hartman, W. *Namibia under South African rule: Mobility and containment 1915–1946*. 95–116. Oxford: James Currey.

Silvester, J., Hillebrecht, W. & Erichsen, C. (2001) 'The Herero Holocaust?' *The Namibian Weekender*, 10 August 2001.

Smith, H.W. (1999) 'The logic of colonial violence: Germany in South West Africa (1904–1907), the United States in the Philippines (1899–1902)'. In Lehmann, H. & Wellenreuther, H. (eds) *German and African nationalism: A comparative perspective*. Oxford: Berg.

Smith, H.W. (1998) 'The talk of genocide, the rhetoric of miscegenation: Notes on the debates in the German *Reichstag* concerning Southwest Africa, 1904–14'. In Friedrichsmeyer, S., Lennox, S. & Zantop, S. (eds)

The imperialist imagination: German colonialism and its legacy. Ann Arbor: University of Michigan Press.

Soggot, D. (1986) *Namibia: The violent heritage.* London: Rex Collings.

Sole, T.E. (1968) 'The Sudwestafrika Denkmunze and the South West African campaigns of 1903–1908'. 1(3)

Spraul, G. (1988) 'Der "Völkermord" an den Herero: Untersuchungen zu einer neuen Kontinuitätsthese'. 12 *Geschichte in Wissenschaft und Unterricht,* 713–39.

Stals, E.L.P. (1984) *Duits-Suidwes-Afrika na die groot opstande.* Pretoria: Staatsdrukker.

Steer, G.L. (1939) *Judgement on German Africa.* London: Hodder & Stoughton.

Steinberg, J. (1965) *Yesterday's deterrent: Tirpitz and the birth of the German battle fleet.* London: Macmillan.

Steinmetz, G. (2003, January) 'The implications of colonial and postcolonial studies for the study of Europe'. 32 (3/4) *European Studies Newsletter (Council for European Studies),* 1–3.

Steinmetz, G. (2003, January). 'The devil's handwriting: Precolonial discourse, ethnographic acuity and cross-identification in German colonialism'. 45 (1) *Comparative Studies in Society and History,* 41–95.

Steinmetz, G. (2005) 'From "Native Policy" to exterminationism: German Southwest Africa, 1904'. In *Comparative Perspective, Theory and Research in Comparative Social Analysis, Paper 30,* 4–5. Los Angeles: Department of Sociology, UCLA, 1. Available at: http://repositories.cdlib.org/cgi/viewcontent.cgi?article=1036&context=uclasoc

Steinmetz, G. (2007) *The Devil's Handwriting: Precoloniality and the German Colonial State in Qingdao, Samoa, and Southwest Africa.* Chicago: The University of Chicago Press.

Stoecker, H. & Sebald, P. (1987) 'Enemies of the colonial idea'. In Knoll, A.J. & Gann, L.H. (eds) *Germans in the tropics: Essays in German colonial history* (2ed). New York/London: Greenwood Press.

Stoecker, H. (ed) (1986) *German imperialism in Africa: From the beginnings until the Second World War.* London: C. Hurst & Co.

Stoecker, H. (1987) 'The position of Africans in the German colonies'. In Knoll, A.J. & Gann, L.H. (eds) *Germans in the tropics: Essays in German colonial history* (2ed). New York/London: Greenwood Press, 119–29.

Stone, D. (2001) 'White men with low moral standards: German anthropology and the Herero genocide'. 35 (2) *Patterns of Prejudice,* 33.

Stratton, J. (2003) 'It almost needn't have been the Germans: The state, colonial violence and the Holocaust'. 6 (4) *European Journal of Cultural Studies,* 507–527.

Sudholt, G. (1975) *Die deutsche Eingeborenenpolitik in Südwestafrika: Von den Anfängen bis 1904.* Hildesheim/New York: Olms.

Swan, J. (1991) 'The Final Solution in South West Africa'. 3(4) *Military History Quarterly*, 36–55.

Tan, C.C. (1967) *The Boxer Catastrophe*. New York: Octagon Books.

Thompson, L. (ed) (1969) *African societies in Southern Africa*. London: Heinemann.

Troup, F. (1950) *In face of fear: Michael Scott's challenge to South Africa*. London: Faber & Faber.

Uzoigwe, G.N. (1976) 'Spheres of influence and the doctrine of the hinterland in the partition of Africa.' 3 *Journal of African Studies*, 183–203.

Van der Kiste, J. (1999) *Kaiser Wilhelm II: Germany's last Emperor*. Stroud, Gloucestershire: Sutton.

Van Onselen, C. (1973) 'Reaction to rinderpest in Southern Africa 1896–97'. 13 (3) *Journal of African History*.

Vedder, H. (1966) *South West Africa in early times*. New York: Barnes & Noble.

Vidal-Naquet, P. (1992) *Assassins of Memory: Essays on the Denial of the Holocaust*. New York: Columbia University Press.

Vigne, R. (1990, February/May) 'Diary: Shark Island'. *Southern African Review of Books*, 31.

Vigne, R. (1990, August/October) 'Genocide'. *Southern African Review of Books*, 13.

Voeltz, R.A. (1988) *German colonialism and the South West Africa Company, 1884–1914; Allies in Apartheid — Western capitalism in occupied Namibia*. (Monographs in International Studies, Africa Series No. 50) Athens, Ohio: Ohio University Center for International Studies.

Voeltz, R.A. (2000) 'Review of mission, church and state relations in South West Africa under German rule (1884–1915)'. 33 (1) *The International Journal of African Historical Studies*, 153.

Vogt, A. (1995) *National monuments in Namibia*. MA. University of Stellenbosch.

Von Falkenhausen, H. (1906) *Ansiedlerschicksale: Elf Jahre in Deutsch-Südwestafrika 1894–1904*. Berlin: Reimer

Von Francois, C. (1899) *Deutsch-Südwest-Afrika*. Berlin: Dietrich Reimer, 133. Quoted in Kienetz, A. (1975, December) *Nineteenth-century South West Africa as a German settlement colony*. PhD thesis. University of Minnesota.

Von Trotha, T. (1994) *Koloniale Herrschaft: Zur soziologischen Theorie der Staatsentstehung am Beispiel des 'Schutzgebietes Togo'*. Tübingen: J.C.B. Mohr.

Von Trotha, T. (1999) 'The fellows can just starve. On wars of pacification in African colonies of Imperial Germany and concept of total war'. In Boemeke, M.E., Chickering, R. & Förster, S. (eds) *Anticipating Total War: The German and American Experience 1871–1914*. Cambridge: Cambridge University Press, 415–35.

Wallenkampf, A.V. (1969) *The Herero rebellion in South West Africa: A study in German colonialism*. PhD thesis. Los Angeles: UCLA.

Walther, D.J. (2002) *Creating Germans abroad: Cultural policies and national indemnity in Namibia*. Athens, Ohio: Ohio University Press.

Watts, N.H.Z. (1983) 'The roots of controversy'. In Rotberg, R.I. (ed) *Namibia: Political and economic prospects*. Cape Town: David Philip.

Wehler, H-U. (1985) *The German Empire 1871–1918*. Leamington Spa/Dover, New Hampshire: Berg Publishers.

Weigend, G.G. (1985, April) 'German settlement patterns in Namibia'. 75(2) *Geographical Review*, 156–69.

Weindling, P. (2002) *Epidemics and genocide in Eastern Europe, 1890–1945*. Oxford/New York: Oxford University Press.

Wellington, J.H. (1967) *South West Africa and its human issues*. Oxford: Clarendon Press.

Werner, W. (1993) 'A brief history of land dispossession in Namibia'. 19 (1) *Journal of Southern African Studies*, 29–39.

Werner, W. (1997) 'From colonial pastures to enclosures: The development of land tenure in Herero reserves'. Windhoek: *NEPRU Working Paper no. 60*.

Werner, W. (1997) *Land reform in Namibia: The first seven years*. Windhoek: Namibian Economic Policy Research Unit.

Werner, W. (1998) *No-one will become rich: Economy and society in the Herero reserves in Namibia 1913–1946*. Basel: P. Schlettwein.

Whittle, T. (1977) *The last Kaiser: A biography of William II, German Emperor and King of Prussia*. London: Heinemann.

Wilcox, S.S. (2004) 'The South West Africa People's Organisation 1961–1991: A guide to archival resources and special collections in the Western Cape, South Africa'. 1 *Occasional e-publications series*. Cape Town: University of Cape Town.

Wildenthal, L. (2001) *German woman for Empire, 1885–1945*. London: Duke University Press.

Wildenthal, L (1996) 'She is the victor: Bourgeois women, nationalist identities and the ideal of the independent women farmers in German South West Africa'. In Eley, G. (ed) *Society, culture and the state in Germany 1870–1930*. Ann Arbour: University of Michigan.

Wilhelm II (1922) *The Kaiser's memoirs* (English translation T.R.Y. Barra). New York: Harper & Brothers.

Wood, B. (ed) (1988) *Namibia 1884–1984: Readings on Namibia's history and society*. London: Namibia Support Committee.

Woolsey, T. S. (1891) *Introduction to the study of international law* (6ed). New York: Charles Scribner's sons.

Wright, Q. (1919, February) 'The legal liability of the Kaiser'. 13(1) *American Political Science Review*, 120–28.
Zedlitz-Trutzler, R. (1951) *Twelve years at the imperial German court*. London: Nisbet & Co.
Zimmerer, J. (2008) 'Colonialism and the holocaust: Towards an archeology of genocide' 50 *Development Dialogue*, 95-123.
Zimmerer, J. (2008) 'Colonial Genocide: The Herero and War (1904-1908) in German South West Africa and its Significance'. In Stone, D. (ed) *The Historiography of Genocide*. London: Palgrave, 323-343.
Zimmerer, J. (2008) 'War, concentration camps and genocide in South-West Africa. The first German genocide'. In Zimmerer, Jürgen and Zeller, Joachim (eds) *Genocide in German South-West Africa. The Colonial War of 1904-1908 and its Aftermath*. Monmouth: Merlin Press.
Zimmerer, J. and Zeller, J. (2003) *Völkermord in Südwestafrika. Der Kolonialkrieg (1904–1908) und seine Folgen*. Berlin: Christoph Links Verlag.
Zimmerer, J. and Zeller, J. (2008) *Genocide in German South-West Africa: The Colonial War of 1904–1908 and its aftermath*. Monmouth: Merlin Press
Zimmerman, A. (2003) 'Adventures in the skin trade: German anthropology and colonial corporeality'. In Penny, H.G. & Bunzl, M. (eds) *Worldly provincialism: German anthropology in the Age of Empire*. Ann Arbour: University of Michigan Press.
Zimmerman, A. (2001) *Anthropology and antihumanism in imperial Germany*. Chicago: University of Chicago Press.
Zirkel, K. (1999) 'Military power in German colonial policy: The Schutztruppen and their leaders in the East and South West Africa, 1888–1918'. In Killingray, D. & Omissi, D. (eds) *Guardians of Empire: The armed forces of the colonial powers, 1700–1964*. Manchester: Manchester University Press, 91–113.
Zweig, R.W. (1987) *German reparations and the Jewish world: A history of the claims conference*. Boulder, Colorado: Westview Press.
Zweig, R. (2001) *German reparations and the Jewish world*. London: Frank Cass.

INDEX

Entries are listed in letter-by-letter alphabetical order. Page references in *italic* indicate where a photograph or table relating to the index entry term can be found.

A

alcohol use 93
Alexander, Neville 36, 81
Alexander, Prince of Battenberg 163
Allgemeine Zeitung 46
Alte Feste 3, 10*n*32, 38*n*16
America *see* United States of America
anthropologists 23-26, 164-165
apology to Hereros (2004) 211*n*254, 232 *see also* reconciliation
Arenberg, Prince Franz von 61
Arendt, Hannah 1, 21, 160
Arthur Koppel Company 2*n*7, 235, 235*n*3
assaults on native people 106-107
atrocities
    by German troops 10-12, 154, 163*n*42, 234-236
    by Hereros 10

B

Bass, G.J. 180
Bastards of Rehoboth and the Problem of Miscegenation in Man, The 25
Baster people 33, 37, 65
battle of Waterberg 18, *19*, 76, *126*, 143, 148-149, 150, 197
Bebel, August 11, 32, 83, 131, 156-157, 192-193, 195, 217
Bedszent, G. 129
Belgium 163*n*42
Berat, L. 111, 153, 191
Bergdamara people 87, 117

Berlin Conference (1884–1885) 4
Berliner Neuste Nachrichten 209-210
Berliner Tageblatt 206
Berliner Zeitung 216
Berlin Geographische Nachrichten 53-54
Berseba Hottentot people 65
Bethanie tribe 37, 65
Bismarck, Chancellor Otto von 3*n*10, 55, 62, 169, 170, 171, 182
Bismarck Archipelago 5
bison 115
Bley, H. 24, 29, 81, 122, 137, 187, 188, 190
Blockmann, Clara 60
Blue Book 13, 30-31, 111-112, 122, 237
Boehmer, Elleke 98-99
Bollig, M. 143
Bondelswartz tribe 35, 37, 41, 44-46, 55, 65, 80-81, 99, 184, 188, 226
Bonn, Prof. Moritz 60
borders in Africa 4
Botha, C. 88
Botswana, migration of Hereros into 18, 137, 140-141
Botswana National Archives 111
Boxer Rebellion 17-18, 159, 163, 178, 183, 193, 194, 241 *see also* China; Hun speech
Bridgman, J. 82-83, 84, 96, 117, 139, 195, 211

Brinkmann, Lucy Goldstein 199, 200*n222*.
Britain 11, 98-99, 103, 108, 120, 236
British Cape Mounted Police 227*n330*-228*n330*
British War Blue Book *see* Blue Book
Bryce Report, The 130*n118*, 148*n200*, 163*n42*-164*n42*
Bulgaria, King of 162
Bülow, Chancellor Bernhard von *see* Von Bülow, Chancellor Bernhard

C

Caldwell, P. 170
Caligula: A study in Roman megalomania 161
Calvert, A.F. 139
Cameroon 5, 58, 62, 105, 106, 123, 182, 226, 236
Campbell, Hendrik 146-147
Cão, Diogo 183
Cape Argus 118-120, 156-157
Cape colonialists 62, 120
Cape Times 119
Caprivi, Georg Leo, Graf von 55-56, 182
Caprivians 33
Caroline Islands 5
Carstens, Peter 139-140
Catholic Mission 89
cattle of Hereros 69-74, 70, 77, 86, 88-89
Cecil, Lamar 170
Charite University, Berlin 22*n80*
children
    mixed-race 13, 91-92
    as slave labour 2*n7*
    treatment of Herero children 1-2, 128-129, 145, 148-149, 150-154, 163*n42*

China 5, 156, 159, 179-180, 192-193, 230-231 *see also* Boxer Rebellion; Hun speech; Kiaochow, China
church, role of 16 *see also* Rhenish missionaries
civilian deaths, German 10*n32*, 38*n16*
Clark, C. 170, 191-192
Cleverly, John J. 43
Cocker, M. 187-188
Colonial Council 182
Colonial Federation 185
Colonial Genocide and Reparations Claims in the 21st Century 6
Colonial Office, Germany 53, 85, 131, 182, 191, 217, 222, 224
Colonial Society *see* German Colonial Society (DKG)
colonisation by Germany
    GSWA's importance 51-59, 237-239
    policies for colonies 235-237
    reasons for 5-6, 51-53, 238-239
    role of Kaiser Wilhelm II 181-182
Coloured people 33
comfort women 1
concentration camps
    Alte Feste 3
    of British 27*n105*
    closure of 38, 86
    conditions in 97, 122-125, 177, 224, 234-235
    mortality rate in 2, 125, 142, 224
    Shark Island concentration camp 97, 125, 217-218, *218*
    at Waterberg 148
Cooper, A.D. 103
Cornevin, R. 29

corporal punishment 105-106
Craig, Gordon 217
Credit Ordinance (1903) 83
criticism of Herero genocide 31-32

D

DKG *see* German Colonial Society (DKG)
Damara people 4, 33, 35, 138, 202
Dar es Salaam 106
Deacon, Harriet 158
Dedering, Tilman 143-144
Deimling, Col. Berthold Karl Adolf von 197
denialist efforts, Herero genocide 111-113, 136
Denker, Richard 202, 204-205
Denkschrift 86
Durnburg, Colonial Director Bernhard 89, 93, 138, 218-219
Der Reichsbote 190
Deutsche Bank 56, 82n243
Deutsche Kolonialgesellschaft *see* German Colonial Society (DKG)
Deutsche Kolonialgesellschaft 45
Deutsche Kolonialzeitung 56, 57
Deutsche Südwestafrikanische Zeitung 47
Deutsche Zeitung 13
Deutsch Süd-Afrika in 25 Jahre 101
Deutsch Südwestafrikanische Zeitung 57
diamond mining 49
Dienst, Wilhelm 172-173
Disconto-Gesellschaft 57, 82n243
diseases, in GSWA 53, 122, 222
Drechsler, Horst 95, 128-129, 132, 137, 184-185, 227
Dreyer, Ronald 120
Drumbl, Mark 15
Duigan, P. 26-27, 53, 73-74, 87

Du Pisani, A. 36-37

E

East Africa *see* German East Africa
Eckert, Andreas 94
Edward VII, King of Britain 174
Eichmann, Adolf 160
Elf Jahre 82
Elger, Missionary August 47-48, 123, 131
Eliot, Sir Charles 120
Elliott, Major 227n330
Eltzbacher, O. 31-32
Epstein, K. 87, 125, 138
Erichsen, C. 28, 141
Erichsen, C.W. 184, 185-186
Erzberger, Matthias 226
Estorff, Major Ludwig von *see* Von Estorff, Major Ludwig
ethnic groups in Namibia 33-35
Eulenburg, Phillip 162, 167
Eveleigh, W. 139
executions
  in GSWA 110
  Herero Chief Kambahahiza Nikodemus Kavikunua 40
  of Hereros 40, 47, 86, 127, 146-147
  Nama soldiers 66
experimentation on humans 25, 27n106, 244
extermination order
  english translation of 102, 102n2, 110, 127-128
  evidence of 157-158, 233, 236-237, 242
  German law and 203-212
  meaning of *vernichten* 125-135, 146, 154
  rescission of 96, 117-118, 149-150, 198, 224-225, 229

secretiveness of 198-212
Von Trotha and 198-203
Wilhelm II and 155-157, 159, 195-198
wording of 151-152

F

First, Ruth 35
First Asiatic Expeditionary Brigade 156
Fischer, Eugen 25-26, 164-165
flogging *see* corporal punishment
forced labour *see* slave labour
forced removals 8 *see also* land ownership
Foster, Don 14
Fraenkel, Peter 138
Francke, Hauptman 10
Franz Joseph, Kaiser of Austria 179
Franzmann tribe 35, 37, 55
Fraser, Hendrik 123
'functionalist' approach 16

G

GSWA *see* German South West Africa
GSWA Company 54-56
Gädke, Col. A.D. 205-206
Gambari, I.A. 216
Gann, L.H. 26-27, 53, 73-74, 87
geneticists 2 *see also* anthropologists
Genocide Convention 11
German armed forces *see* German troops
German Colonial Society (DKG) 54, 58n120, 61, 64, 185
German East Africa 5, 28, 53, 58, 62, 103, 105-106, 154, 182, 192-193, 213, 236
German-Herero war *see* Herero-German war

German law 107, 203-212, 242
German New Guinea 5, 103, 154
German settlers *see* settlers, German
German Social Democrats *see* Social Democrats, Germany
German South West Africa
attracting German settlers to 60-64
capital invested by Germany 56, 57-58, 237
German troops in *see* German troops
German women in 60-61
importance to Germany 51-59, 237-238
Kaiser Wilhelm II and 183-190
land ownership by indigenous peoples (1903) 65
negative perceptions of 55
peace, need for 59-60
reasons for establishment of 51-57
German South West Africa Company 54-56
German troops
with captured Hereros *121, 177*
fatality figures 38n16, 142, 222
on horseback *186, 196*
loading cannons and machine guns *143*
marching from Windhoek Railway Station *39*
numbers of 58-59, 215, 220, 222, 237
on patrol *151, 196*
as settlers in GSWA 62-63
at war in GSWA 76, 114, 115, *126, 133, 146, 153, 165*

Gewald, J-B. 38, 42, 49, 71, 81, 82, 94-95, 96, 143, 149, 159, 170-171, 190-191, 214
Gilroy, Paul 26
Gobineau, Count Joseph Arthur de 164
Goldblatt, I. 12, 44, 74, 198
Goldhagen, Daniel 28
Göring, Heinrich Ernst 54, 91
Griffiths, Percival 118-119
Grosser Generalstab 45, 132
guilt 14-15

H

Haarhoff, Dorian 138
Hague Convention (1899) 1n3, 84n258
Hall, Cyril 139
Harpending, Henry 141
Harrland, Paul 116-117
Herero genocide
    background 1-4, 110-125
    reasons for 7-14, 41-51, 85-86, 93-101, 104, 223, 239-241, 244-245
    responsibility of 216-217
    time frame of 67-68, 142-150
Herero-German war
    brutalities before 1904 103-110
    financial cost of 94, 190
    genocidal intent of 88
    praise and support for 224-230, 241-243
    reasons for 75, 80-83
Herero people
    atrocities by 10
    atrocities on 14-16, 106-107, 118-122, 131-132, 134, 146, 177
    clothing of 34-35
    fatality figures 136-142, 154
    history of 33-34
    as labour 87, 152-153
    land ownership of 65
    leaders of 43, 45n46
    negotiations with 131, 195-196
    postcards of 9, 23, 95
    prisoners of war 121, 177, 225
    rebellion of 7-8, 14, 36-42, 226, 233, 236
    relationship with Witboois 59
    reserves for 14, 77-80, 236
    slogans of women 72
    treatment of children 1-2, 128-129, 145, 148-149, 150-154, 163n42
    treatment of women 1-2, 2n6, 30, 107, 128-129, 145, 148-154, 163n42
    Waterberg battle 148-149
Herz, Richard 116
Hillebrecht, Werner 141
Hintrager, Deputy Governor Oskar 38, 185-186
Hitler, Adolf 23, 179
Hohenlohe, Chancellor 178
Hohenzollern, Friedrich Wilhelm Viktor Albrecht von *see* Wilhelm II, Kaiser of Germany
Hohman, Admiral 181
Holocaust 20-28, 29, 244
Holstein, Fritz von 162
Hornkrantz Massacre 154
'Hottentot's election' 189
Howard, M.E. 174
Howard, R.E. 103
Howard-Hassmann, Rhoda 111
Hughes, William Morris (Billy) 180
Hull, I.V.
    extermination order 16, 147, 151-152, 156n3, 195, 207-208, 209, 213-215

fatality figures 138, 139, 141
military culture of Germany 26, 187
Von Trotha' diary 200
Waterberg battle 142-144, 148
Wilhelm II, Kaiser of Germany 161, 172, 182, 192
Hülsen-Haeseler, Graf 190
human experimentation 25, 27n106, 244
human skulls 2, 22, 22n80, 24
Hun speech 19, 129, 157, 175-176, 195, 208, 220 *see also* Boxer Rebellion; China

I

identification passes of Hereros 84, 86-87
Iliffe, John 106
image of Germany *see* pride of Germany
Indian Mutiny (1857) 99
'intentionalist' perspective 16
'interactive' approach 16
international politics at turn of 20th century 238-239
International Society for Racial Hygiene, Freiburg 164
interracialism 13, 21n74, 89-93, 90, 237
Irle, Reverend 73

J

Jameson Raid 56
Jaspers, Karl 14
Jewish people 166
Jonassohn, K. 24, 25
Journal of the African Society 114
justice system, bias of 107

K

Kaiser Wilhelm II *see* Wilhelm II, Kaiser of Germany
Kaiser Wilhelm Institute of Anthropology, Berlin-Dahlem 24, 25
Kariko, Under-Chief Daniel 106
Kavango people 33
Kavikunua, Chief Kambahahiza Nikodemus 40
Kenya 103, 236
Kerina, M. 42, 138
Kesting, R.W. 25, 103
Ketteler, Clemens von 230
Khoi people 55
Kiaochow, China 5, 58n121, 177-178, 230 *see also* China
Kienetz, A. 54
Kitchen, M. 163-164, 206
Kluz, Dr W. 101
Kohut, Thomas A. 160
Kooper, Simon 38
Krüger, G. 149
Kubas, Jan 122
Kuhlman, August 10, 82, 120
Kültz, Mr 92
Kulz, Wilhelm 64
Kutako, Samuel 68, 72

L

land ownership
    acquisition of land by German settlers 63, 67-69
    acquisition of land by Germany 13-14
    confiscation order (1905) 189
    Germany's need for 54, 62-63
    Herero-German war as means to gain 8-9, 49, 74-77, 80-83, 84-89, 239-240

indigenous concept of land tenure 240
   by indigenous peoples 65, 136
   land-control system 74-75
   natural disasters and 69-71
   reasons for targeting Herero and Nama land 64-66
   reserves for Hereros 77-80
   strategies to obtain 66-83
Langenburg, Hohenlohe 85
Lau, Brigitte 111, 137, 140
laws in Germany, role of 203-212, 242
Leist, Governor 226
Lemkin, Raphael 11, 118, 138, 202
Leutwein, Governor Theodor von
   Bondelswartz rebellion 80-81
   Elf Jahre 82
   extermination order 147-148, 158-159
   Herero fatality figures 138, 141
   interracialism 91
   land sale restrictions 71
   letter to Henrik Witbooi 183
   military success of 221
   negotiations with native people 96, 131, 188
   Peace of Kalkfontein 188
   photographs of 9, *43*, *78*, *201*
   policies of 8-9
   reserves for Hereros 78-79
   role of 41-50, 60, 72-73, 75-76, 86, 106-107, 129-130, 194
Leutwein, Paul 46-47
Lewin, Evans 137, 139
Liebknecht, Wilhelm 32
Lindequist, Governor Friedrich 64, 134-135, 189, 230
livestock of Hereros *see* cattle of Hereros

Lorenz, Klaus 140-141
Lüderitz, Adolf 53
Lüderitz railway line 123, *124*
Ludwig, E. 161
Lundtofte, H. 38-41, 75-76, 104, 109, 126, 128, 148, 150, 183, 192, 211

M

Mackensen, August von 166
Mackenzie, Kenneth 31
Madley, B. 8, 73, 109
Maherero, Chief Samuel 45-46, 49, 67-68, 71, 79, 81, 106, 108-109, 127, 128, 141
   photographs of *48*, *78*
Maji-Maji rebellion 104, 213
Mamdani, M. 27, 193
Marengo, Jacob *see* Morenga, Jakob
Marrana Islands 5
Marshall Islands 5
Massacre at Hornkrantz 154
Masson, J. 37, 77
Mbanderu people 34-35, 75, 94
medals awarded for Herero-German war 227-229
Melber, H. 36, 38
methodology 28-35
Metropolitan German Imperial troops 143
Middleton, Lamar 138
military culture of Germany 212-224, 243
missionaries, role of 16 *see also* Rhenish missionaries
mixed marriages 21n74, 91-92 *see also* interracialism
Mombauer, Annika 230
Morenga, Jakob 37, *100*, 225-226, 227n330-228n330, 228n331
Murry, Roger 138

N

Nagan, W.P. 138
Naimark, N.M. 220
Nama people 33, 35
   Chief Henrik Witbooi 78, *134*
   execution of 66
   fatality figures 136-142
   genocidal intent towards 132-134, 233
   land ownership 64-66
   peace treaty with 184
   postcards of 23, 78
   rebellion of 37
Namib, meaning of 33*n130*
Namibia, history of name 33 *see also* German South West Africa
National Colonial Association 185
natural disasters 69-71, 78, 240
Naumann, Friedrich 169
negotiations with Hereros 131, 195-196
Netherlands 180
Neumann, Bertha 200-*n222*
New Guinea 5, 103, 154
Nordbruch, Claus 112-113, 116-117

O

Oermann, N.O. 95, 141
opposition to Herero genocide 31-32
order for extermination *see* extermination order
Otavi Mine Company 2*n7*, 74, 82*n243*
Otavi railroad 82-83, 99
Oviumbo battle (1904) 18, 221
Owambo people 33, 64-65
Owl, The 100

P

Paasche, Hans 206

Packenham, T. 212-213
Palmer, A. 85-86, 138, 220-221
Palva Islands 5
passes Hereros had to carry 84, 86-87
Pathological Institute, Berlin 22
Peace of Kalkfontein 188
Pennington, Renee 141
peoples of Namibia 33-35
Peter Moor's Journey to South West 216
Peters, Karl 226
Pfister, G. 89
Plessen, Hans von 209
Poewe, K. 121, 130
poisoning of water wells 1, 1*n3*, 114-116, 210, 223 *see also* water wells
Police Zone 87*n273*, 88-89
politics at turn of 20th century 238-239
Poole, G. 131
postcard industry 22
pride of Germany 14, 93-101, 167, 221-222, 238
prisoners of war 218 *see also* concentration camps
   policy regarding 120-122
   Russian 179
Pritchard, Stanley Archibold Markham 114
propaganda campaign in Germany 13, *114*
punitive motivation of Herero genocide 177, 223
Puttkamer, Governor von 226

Q

Quidde, Prof. Ludwig 161

R

racist ideology of Germany 10, 24-25, 27, 240-241, 244
railway lines
   Lüderitz railway line 123, *124*
   Otavi railroad 82-83, 99
Ratzell, Friedrich 57
rebellion of Herero (1904) 7-8, 14, 36-42, 226, *233*, 236
reconciliation, 2005 announcement by Germany 38 *see also* apology to Hereros
Red Line 87*n*273
Red Nation tribe 35, 37, 65
Rehoboth Baster people 33, 37, 65
Reichsbote, Der 190
Reichstag 7, 189-190, 215-217, 219-220, 226
reputation of Germany *see* pride of Germany
reserves for Hereros 14, 77-80, 236
Rhenish missionaries 91, 236
Rhenish Missionary Society 62, 78, 89, 96, 131, 140
Rhodes, Cecil John 56
Rich, N. 169-170
rinderpest epidemic 13, 69-71, 87*n*273, 240
Riruako, Paramount Chief Kuaima 231-232
Rodin, V.F. 138
Röhl, J.C.G. 157, 166, 168-169, 172, 174, 191, 199
Rohrbach, Paul 12, 25, 61, 66-67, 71-72, 81, 90, 102, 132
Rooinasie tribe *see* Red Nation tribe
Rosebery, Lord 120
Russian prisoners of war 179

S

Samoa 5, 58*n121*, 103, 154
San people 33
Saxe-Coburg-Gotha, Duke of 163
Scales-Trent, Judy 23
Schlieffen, Alfred, Graf von 11, 17, 77, 188
Schrank, G.I. 15, 194
Schultz, Otto 228
Schutztruppe see German troops
Schwirck, H. 107-108, 137
scorched earth policy 104
Scramble for Africa, The 213
settlers, German, role of 9-10, 15-16, 47-51, 59-64, 84-85, 99, 184, 187, 238, 243
Shark Island concentration camp 97, 125, 217-218, *218 see also* concentration camps
Silvester, J. 141, 190-191
Simmons, D. 98
Simon Kooper tribe 65
skulls of Hereros 2, 22, 22*n80*, 24
slave labour, Hereros as 2*n*7, 15, 30, 122-123, *124*, 130, 234-235
Smith, H.W. 217-218, 219
Social Democrats, Germany 32, 83, 158, 165
Soggot, D. 20-21, 28, 85
Solomon Islands 5
South African News 204
Spieker, Johannes 140
state of emergency in GSWA 188-189
Steer, G.L. 128
Steinberg, Jonathan 160
Steinmetz, G. 194
Stillfried und Rattonitz, Count Georg von 184
Stoecker, H. 61-62, 87, 105, 139

INDEX

Stratton, J. 21, 103
strike by tram workers, Berlin 163
Stubel, Colonial Director 32
Stuebel, Dr Oscar W. 85, 222
Stuhlmann, Major 156, 208
Stuhlmar (German soldier) 117
Superior Genetic Health Court 25
Swakopmunder Zeitung 224
Swan, J. 15

T

Tabula rasa 8, 237
Tanzania 104, 236
Tattenbach, Minister von 75
Tecklenburg, Hans 37n5, 94
terminology 33
Timbu, Manuel 122
Tirpitz, Admiral Alfred von 189
Togo 5, 58, 62, 103, 105, 182, 226
trade in GSWA 5, 71-72
Traverso, Enzo 140
Treaty of Versailles 3n11, 6
Trench, Col. F. 125
tribes of Namibia 33-35
Trotha, von *see* Von Trotha
Tswana people 33

U

United States of America 8, 115, 238
University of Freiburg 22n80

V

Van Onselen, Charles 73
Vedder, Dr Heinrich 124-125
Veldschoendragers 37, 55, 65
Vernichtungsbefehl see extermination order
Versailles Treaty 3n11, 6
Vladimir, Grand Duke of Russia 162-163
Voeltz, Richard 76

Von Bülow, Chancellor Bernhard 11-12, 32, 50, 161, 162, 178, 191, 198, 208-209, 211-212, 230
Von Deimling, Col. Berthold Karl Adolf 197
Von Estorff, Major Ludwig 125, 132, 145-146, 187
Von Francois, C. 57, 63, 69, 121-122, 183
Von Holstein, Fritz 162
Von Horn, Governor 226
Von Ketteler, Clemens 230
Von Leutwein, Governor Theodor *see* Leutwein, Governor Theodor von
Von Lindequist, Friedrich *see* Lindequist, Governor Friedrich
Von Mackensen, August 166
Von Plessen, Hans 209
Von Puttkamer, Governor 226
Von Schlieffen, Alfred *see* Schlieffen, Alfred, Graf von
Von Stillfried und Rattonitz, Count Georg 184
Von Tattenbach, Minister 75
Von Trotha, General Lothar
   arrival in GSWA 39, 49
   control of information flow 202, 205-208
   diary of 127-128, 144-145, 158, 199-201
   extermination order 85, 102, 110-115, 117-118, 127-128, 142-145, 198-203, 209-210, 242
   family of 200n222, 201-202, 202n226
   land ownership 77
   military experience of 192-194
   Nama people 132-133
   photographs of *17, 201*

praise for 226-227, 229
recall of 224
relationship with Kaiser
  Wilhelm II 18-20, 156, 171,
  173, 178, 190-198
role of 12-13, 25, 44, 59, 87, 122,
  132-133, 144-147
treatment of women and
  children 150-153
Von Trotha, *Oberleutenant* 201
Von Trotha, Thilo 202*n*226
Von Trotha, Trutz 94, 213
Von Wartenburg, Oberstleutnant
  205
Von Weber, Ernst 54

W

Wahehe Rising 192
Waldersee, Count 166, 179-180
Wallenkampf, A.V. 139, 150
Walther, D.J. 52
War Office 131, 171-172, 188
Wartenburg, Oberstleutnant von
  205
Waterberg battle 18, *19*, 76, *126*,
  143, 148-149, 150, 197
water wells 1, 1*n*3, *12*, 13, 114-116,
  115, 144-145, 210, 223
Weber, Ernst von 54
Wehlan, Judge 226
Wehler, H-U. 219
Weitz, Eric 158
Wellington, J.H. 12, 192
Wepener, F. 119-120
Werner, W. 71, 139
Whittle, T. 161, 178
Wilhelm II, Kaiser of Germany
  brutality of 174-181

criticism of 199
GSWA and 183-190
military power of 171-174, 214-
  215
personality of 160-167
postcard of *168*
quoted 155
relationship with Chancellor
  208
relationship with Von Trotha
  18-20, 160, 190-198, 209-211,
  226-227
role of 16-20, 49-50, 159-160,
  168-171, 181-182, 230
speeches of 19, 129, 157, 175-
  178, 195, 198-202, 208, 220,
  227
Windhuker Nachrichten 206
Witbooi, Chief Henrik 78, 106, 108-
  109, *134*, 135, 183
Witbooi tribe 55, 59, 65, 122, 189,
  230
Woermann Line 2*n*7, 235
women
  German women in GSWA 89,
    92-93, 237
  treatment of Herero women 1-2,
    2*n*6, *30*, 107, 128-129, 145,
    148-154, 163*n*42
Worley, L.J. 139, 211
Wright, Prof. Quincy 180

Z

Zedlitz-Trutzschler, Count 199
Zimmerman, A. 23-24
Zirkel, K. 27-28, 60, 195, 198
Zürn, Lt Ralf 22, 38, 81, 95
Zwartboois 65